VALUING HEALTH FOR POLICY

Valuing
Health
for
Policy

An Economic Approach

EDITED BY
George Tolley, Donald Kenkel,
and Robert Fabian

THE UNIVERSITY OF CHICAGO PRESS
Chicago and London

George Tolley is professor of economics at the University of
Chicago. Donald Kenkel is assistant professor of economics
at Pennsylvania State University. Robert Fabian is research
associate at the University of Illinois at Chicago.

The University of Chicago Press, Chicago 60637
The University of Chicago Press, Ltd., London
© 1994 by The University of Chicago
All rights reserved. Published 1994
Printed in the United States of America
03 02 01 00 99 98 97 96 95 94   1 2 3 4 5

ISBN: 0-226-80713-4   (cloth)

Library of Congress Cataloging-in-Publication Data

Valuing health for policy : an economic approach / edited by
  George Tolley, Donald Kenkel, and Robert Fabian.
        p.   cm.
    Includes bibliographical references and index.
      1. Medical care—Cost effectiveness—Econometric
    models.   2. Diseases—Economic aspects—Mathematical
    models.   I. Tolley, George S., 1925–   . II. Kenkel,
    Donald Scott, 1959–   .   III. Fabian, Robert G.
    RA410.5.V35   1994
    338.4'33621—dc20   94-9537
                                                 CIP

For Alice and Catherine Tolley
For Delia, William, Daniel and Jennifer Kenkel
For Laura Shaeffer

Contents

Preface

This book is devoted to advancing the theory and measurement of health values and to contributing to their use in policy. Several different approaches to valuing health outcomes have been used in the past. We are concerned with the methodological grounding of the approaches and their usability. We argue strongly for a willingness to pay approach grounded in individual preferences, but we point out that, properly synthesized, other approaches also throw light on health values.

In prior studies, more attention has been given to mortality than morbidity. We present empirical results from our own research applying the willingness to pay approach to morbidity, considering both light and heavy symptoms. We also bring together other values on mortality and morbidity drawn from the literature of economics and public health.

We demonstrate how health values can be used in helping to answer a wide range of policy questions. How stringent should environmental and occupational safety regulations be? How far should the treatment provided by Medicaid go? Is the sacrifice in health care from cost-cutting measures of health maintenance organizations warranted? Should funding for research on Alzheimer's disease be increased? Should more money be spent on programs to discourage smoking? What are appropriate bases for awarding damages in wrongful injury and death suits? Should health values be used to help guide clinical decisions?

This volume is the culmination of several years of work which began as a study of the health effects of environmental pollution sponsored by the U.S. Environmental Protection Agency (EPA) and continued, with a wider focus, centered at the University of Chicago. George Tolley of the University of Chicago and Lyndon Babcock of the University of Illinois at Chicago were codirectors of the project during the EPA phase. Glenn Blomquist and Gideon Fishelson spent nearly a year in residence at the University of Chicago during this formative period. Alan Carlin of the EPA was an important and valuable influence on the early work.

We gratefully acknowledge help received at various stages from Gary Albrecht, Janet Anderson, Kevin Croke, Maureen Cropper, Edna Loehman,

Edward Mensah, Paul Portney, Mordechai Schechter, William Schulze, V. Kerry Smith, and W. Kip Viscusi. Sandy Jones and Alyce Monroe tirelessly typed the drafts of this manuscript. Karen Peterson rendered important editorial service, improving the quality of the finished work.

1

Overview

George Tolley, Donald Kenkel, and Robert Fabian

1.1. Purpose

This book is offered as a contribution to deciding how much to spend on health. Because health is a basic human concern, some of the most vital issues facing individuals and society pertain to protecting and improving health. Important as health is, as a society we do not impoverish ourselves by forgoing all other worldly goods and services for the sake of health. Nor do we go to the other extreme of completely ignoring health consequences. Somehow, choices are made to pursue various health-affecting activities. The costs of these choices take the form of observable health care payments, as well as costs that are more difficult to measure, such as using costly manufacturing procedures to enhance worker safety or eating less fatty foods.

An implication in much of the public health literature is that the priceless nature of human life makes it inappropriate to discuss health in monetary terms. However, avoiding the question of how to achieve the proper balance in various health-affecting activities based on their worth or value can lead to gross anomalies. Health may then be determined by irrelevant or happenstance events. The arousal of public opinion about particular diseases often leads to the neglect of other diseases that cause greater suffering. Objective criteria are needed to replace judgments about need that are too frequently made hastily and casually.

The problem of valuing health arises in a great many situations. In the provision of medical services and other health care, concern for cost containment conflicts with the desire to provide the best care possible. For instance, hospital expenditures can be lowered by reducing the average length of stay, but at the expense of an increased number of complications. In the control of occupational and product safety, regulations create costs for employers, producers, and ultimately consumers but yield returns in the form of reduced risks of accidents and illness. Public health measures, such as educating people for better lifestyles, and disease-reducing environmental policies affecting air, water, and hazardous wastes require incurring costs in order to improve health. Activity of the courts in medical and health

1

matters, which has been increasing, inevitably requires mortality and morbidity valuation as part of damage awards.

In all of these policy areas, consideration needs to be given to how far to go in bearing costs to achieve better health. Attention is inescapably drawn to the worth placed on health. The question of how much cost to bear to reduce the risk of mortality has in fact received a good deal of attention. The more complex and perhaps more important question of the worth of reducing various types of morbidity has in comparison been very neglected. Distinctions are needed between light and heavy symptom illnesses, where valuation is even more difficult. Beyond this, the relation between mortality and morbidity values needs to be investigated.

Progress in valuing health has been hindered by the lack of an adequate framework, data shortcomings, and econometric estimation problems. There remains an unmet need for state-of-the-art estimates based on what we know now, along with a continuing need for more data and improvement in the methodological basis of estimates.

This book contains a broad assessment and reconciliation of approaches to valuing morbidity and mortality, followed by new efforts to estimate the benefits of reducing health risks. The results fill major gaps in existing estimates of health values, and they make a number of methodological contributions important to future work.

As an overview, this chapter discusses in general terms what we call the economic approach to valuing health. A principle aim is to illustrate the contribution the economic approach can make to a variety of policy areas.

1.2. Organization of the Remainder of This Book

Part 1 is a comparative analysis of approaches that have been used to value health. Studies using a variety of approaches have yielded empirical estimates of the value of different health conditions. Many of the estimates are incomplete, however, since important components of the value of health such as pain and suffering are left out. Other differences, such as the reliability of the estimates or whether they are on an aggregate or individual basis, raise further problems in comparability. The goal of Part 1 is to synthesize the existing fragmentary evidence to obtain systematic, useful information on the value of health.

Part 2 turns to frontier problems in valuing widespread light symptom illnesses and includes an original study of the value of symptoms, including coughs, headaches, and a more serious condition, angina pectoris (chest pain). Common symptoms have received almost no attention, partly because they do not involve dramatic consequences such as mortality or large amounts of medical expenses or lost earnings. However, policies that provide relief from such symptoms for many people may be quite valuable. The contingent valuation approach is promising in this situation because it yields estimates with conceptually desirable qualities. In the contingent valuation study described here, surveys have been conducted that attempt to elicit from respondents their willingness to pay for a nonmarket good, hypothetically assuming, or contingent upon, a market for the good. Given the refinements in methodology and the scope of the study presented in Part 2, we believe the results provide extremely useful information about the value of the health conditions considered.

Part 3 is concerned with the development of approaches for valuing life-threatening illnesses. Earlier studies of the value of mortality risks due to occupational or traffic accidents relate primarily to unforeseen, instant death. The problem of valuing a serious life-threatening illness is much more complicated. The condition may eventually be fatal, but an important part of the value of avoiding such a condition is the avoidance of the lengthy period of illness preceding death. For many serious conditions there is a long latency period, so the most severe consequences are only realized in middle or old age. Finally, the uncertainty of the course and outcome of the illness is an inherent part of the problem. Part 3 of this book develops a comprehensive approach to overcome the formidable obstacles to the empirical estimation of the value of serious life-threatening illnesses. Directions for future work are also discussed.

Part 4 summarizes the findings of the book and demonstrates how the findings can be applied to policy problems. A set of state-of-the-art health values is developed. The use of these values is illustrated by returning to examples of each of the policy areas discussed below in this chapter.

We believe the economic approach to valuing health described in this book will be extremely useful for a wide range of policies. Below in Section 1.5 we provide a series of examples of the types of policy questions that can be addressed. In keeping with this perspective, most of this book is written to be accessible to readers with a range of backgrounds. We hope in particular that policy makers and researchers interested in medical cost containment and public health issues will find this book useful. At a few points, rigorous analysis requires the use of the calculus-based formal models of economics. Readers unfamiliar with these models should still be able to get a great deal out of the introductions and conclusions to these chapters. Some readers may want to focus mainly on the book's last section on policy applications. Others interested in methodology as well as applications should of course turn to the earlier sections.

1.3. The Economic Approach to Valuing Health

At a fundamental level, this book is about the choices people make concerning matters affecting their life and health, as consumers of these goods. The choice of this orientation was made in order to maximize the usefulness of the study for policy purposes. The economic approach to the study of consumer behavior is centered around the concept of individual choice, where items are consciously bought and sold. The same concept can be applied to health, even though many of the choices that people make concerning their health involve commitments of time and effort, choices of lifestyle, and so on, rather than explicit purchases of goods.

Just as for any other consumer good, the benefit of an improvement in health is the amount society is willing to pay for that improvement. Although seemingly noncontroversial, this suggests that the earlier methodology of valuing health according to medical expenditures and earnings forgone due to illness or death is fundamentally in error. In studies using this methodology, medical expenditures and forgone earnings are known as the "economic costs of illness." The economics profession has moved far beyond these so-called economic costs, however. The concept of willingness to pay is much broader and will be influenced by the pain and suffering illness causes as well as other factors. As reviewed in Part 1, studies that estimate willingness to pay for health have taken different empirical approaches but share a common conceptual framework.

The economic approach to valuing health based on how much society is willing to pay is usually traced back to a 1968 article by Schelling (1984) and to Mishan (1971). It is almost surprising how widely accepted the approach has become in the years following these essays. The approach was well-received by economists because it was the natural extension of the methodology of applied welfare economics to the area of health. The willingness to pay approach is increasingly gaining acceptance in policy circles. In fact, in at least some cases the main reason the willingness to pay approach is not used is the lack of reliable estimates of the value of the relevant health effects.

At other times, the economic approach is still misunderstood. When values are placed on morbidity and mortality risks, it is not meant to imply that society would willingly sacrifice the health or life of identified individuals for certain sums of money. Instead, there is an important distinction between improving the health or saving the life of an identified individual versus changing the probabilities of illness or death for some group. Schelling (1984, p. 115) argues that lives of identifiable individuals "are part of ourselves, not [necessarily] a priceless part but a private part that we value in a different way, not just quantitatively but qualitatively, from the way we measure the incidence of death among a mass of unknown human beings, whether that population includes ourselves or not." Thus an individual will make decisions differently about his own death when he does not expect to die except eventually. Similarly, social choices about medical intensive care units will be seen in a different light when only anonymous beneficiaries are involved. Anonymity is a way of rendering life-and-death decisions a matter of consumer choice.

People frequently say that death and life are sacred and that attempting to put a price tag on them goes contrary to their priceless nature. They are indeed priceless to all of us, and there are times when their sanctity must be placed ahead of other considerations. Nevertheless, patients and their loved ones, as well as doctors and nurses, must make health care choices. The role of policy makers is to establish frameworks that permit rational choices to be made that best contribute to decisions made in times of stress and crisis. People make life-affecting and health-affecting decisions all the time. The question is how to make these decisions better, rather than randomly or irrationally, as often happens.

1.4. The Distribution of Income and Access to Health

Many people feel that income constraints should not limit access to the health care system. Recognizing the importance of lifestyle decisions and other factors outside of the health care system, a more comprehensive proposition is that constraints should not limit individuals' access to health. For instance, the dramatic effects of the antismoking campaign have been unevenly distributed across society: smoking prevalence has declined five times faster among the more educated compared with the less educated (Pierce et al. 1989). Some high-prevalence groups have been selected by cigarette companies for special marketing efforts. Should public health policy makers also target these groups for special antismoking campaigns?

Returning to the concept of consumer choice, if smoking is more prevalent among some groups because they lack sufficient information about health hazards to make informed choices, active public policy might be appropriate. (In fact, Chap. 16 uses this as an example to illustrate the use of the health values and concludes that expanding school-based health education about smoking is probably appropriate.) However, given their preferences and constraints, some people will still make informed consumer choices that are destructive of their own health. In dealing with these individuals at the level of social policy, it is important to have a picture of the world as it is, not merely a picture that emerges from inquiries that begin by assuming all people are alike and constraints are nonexistent. The deficiency in this latter view is that it does not recognize people as individuals who are distributed diversely in society both with respect to preferences and to constraints.

Because of the differences in the constraints they face, people with different incomes will make different choices about health. This being the case, for many analysts the unequal distribution of income in our nation raises fundamental concerns about the applicability of the concept of consumer choice to health problems. The idea that low-income consumers use less medical care because they choose to, given their constraints, seems almost beside the point to observers concerned with the low health status of the economically deprived. Fuchs (1983, pp. 148–49) argues that, while the problems created by income inequality are not unique to the health care sector, more equal access to health may be desirable on practical grounds: "While elementary justice seems to require greater equality in the distribution of medical care, the question is complicated by the fact that the poor suffer deprivation in many directions. Economic theory suggests it might be better to redistribute income and allow the poor to decide which additional goods and services they want to buy. As a practical matter, however, it may be easier to achieve greater equality through a redistribution of services (such as medical care) than through a redistribution of money income."

Instead of merely making access more equal, should health be treated as a preeminent good, and should all persons be regarded as equally deserving to receive that good? Some work in the public health literature seems to suggest this approach, but it is contrary to the economic point of view. As Fuchs (1983, p. 143) observes, "for most Americans, better health is not the only, or even the most important goal." Forcing Americans of any economic status to behave as if health were the most important goal is contrary to their voluntary choices and should not be the goal of public policy.

While there are sometimes sharp differences of opinion as to the validity and relevance of the economic point of view in the analysis of health problems, it is easy to overstate them. Some public health professionals tend to reject the economic approach on egalitarian grounds. However, it is an empirical question whether the distribution of income is an important determinant of willingness to pay for health. In the study reported in Chapter 8, income is not systematically related to people's willingness to pay to avoid the health problems considered. In this case, to follow consumers' choices the economic approach need make no distinctions across the income distribution.

More generally, the approach of this book and other studies using the economic approach is to focus on the willingness to pay of an average person in the population at risk for a health problem. In many cases the population at risk includes people at different income levels, so the use of this average tends to put the analysis on a fairly egalitarian basis. In other cases the population at risk may be disproportionately drawn from one extreme or the other of the income distribution: for instance, the risks of lead exposure are particularly high for inner-city children in poverty. In these cases it is important to examine conclusions drawn from the willingness to pay framework in light of problems raised by the unequal distribution of income.

1.5. Major Policy Areas to Which This Book Is Relevant

Although it is difficult to make a comprehensive list, six policy areas for which health value estimates are particularly important are discussed below. The first area, health and safety regulation, is notable because of the substantial role health value estimates already play in the policy process. This is in sharp contrast to the other policy areas, where the economic approach to valuing health is less advanced but shows great potential for improving policy. For example, health value estimates could make an important contribution to the difficult process of setting priorities to achieve rational medical cost containment. This is the second policy area discussed below. The determination of medical research priorities is the third policy area. It is closely related to the cost containment area, which is forcing more and more difficult choices on the health care industry. This area is doubly important, however, because medical research is the source of the great gains in medical productivity that our society enjoys.

A fourth policy area is public health policy concerned with influencing personal habits and lifestyles important to health, such as smoking, drinking, diet, and exercise. The fifth area concerns the courts, where valuing health is an essential part of awarding damages in personal injury and wrongful death lawsuits. The sixth area is use of health values in clinical practice. Each area will be considered in turn.

HEALTH AND SAFETY REGULATION. Regulation of economic activity has long played a role in American life. In recent years the reach of regulation has extended to a wide variety of matters affecting the health of American citizens. Workplace conditions are regulated by the Occupational Safety and Health Administration (OSHA). Environmental matters are regulated by the Environmental Protection Agency (EPA). All levels of government— federal, state, and local—have become involved. Regulation is costly; some regulations add billions of dollars in cost to the American economy each year.

At least at the federal level, economic estimates of the value of health play an important role in the formation of health and safety regulations. In particular, a 1981 executive order (no. 12291) requires that any new major regulation be subject to a benefit-cost analysis. (The order notes that Congress can enact statutes that prohibit benefit-cost analysis of regulations, however.) Since health improvements are major components of the benefits of potential regulations for many federal government agencies, this created a large demand for estimates of the value of health. For one example, the papers in Smith (1984) provide a detailed assessment of the impact of the executive order on EPA policies.

The economic approach to valuing health, and particularly estimates of willingness to pay for mortality risk reductions, were rapidly incorporated into policy making. Viscusi (1986) points out that, when considering an OSHA industry standard in 1984, the debate was not over the appropriateness of the economic approach but over the relative merits of the different estimates. The value of a small reduction in mortality risks is often summarized by the value of a statistical life, which shows the willingness to pay by a group of people to reduce mortality risks enough so that one life is expected to be saved, in a statistical sense. OSHA valued a statistical life at $3.5 million, the Office of Management and the Budget urged use of a $1 million value, and one congressman suggested a $7 million value. Disagreements over estimates continue: *Newsweek* (1988) describes current practice as "a bizarre bazaar of prices," with OSHA, the Consumer Product Safety Commission, the EPA, and the Federal Aviation Administration adopting different values for statistical lives. It is worth reiterating that in this instance all agencies agreed upon the validity of the economic approach. Apparently, the economic approach to valuing health is given formal status only in the U.S. (via Executive Order 12291) but is used in an ad hoc way in some other Organization for Economic Cooperation and Development countries, though not at all in others (Pearce and Markandya 1989).

In a number of instances, however, the use of economic health values in the U.S. federal regulatory process has been resisted and blocked. Viscusi (1992, chap. 14) provides a comprehensive assessment of the performance of major federal regulations in the 1980s. For 33 health, safety, and environmental regulations, he compares the average regulatory cost per life saved to estimates of the value of a statistical life. He concludes that 13 regulations pass the benefit-cost test—that is, the benefits of the reduced mortality risks exceed the regulatory costs—while the remaining 20 fail the test. Eight of the 20 regulations that failed the benefit-cost test were ultimately rejected by the agencies, but Viscusi notes that several regulations with very low efficacy were enacted. Lutter and Morrall (1993) point out that all but one of the enacted regulations that failed the benefit-cost test fall under statutes that arguably do not permit benefit-cost analysis.

Even agencies that in principle advocate the willingness to pay approach have at times been unable to implement it fully. Fisher's (1984) description of the guidelines for performing regulatory impact analyses, official EPA policy as of 1983, provides an interesting example. As a result of data limitations, morbidity effects of pollutants are valued according to the costs of the relevant illnesses, where the costs include medical expenditures and forgone earnings. As noted in the EPA guidelines, and as is discussed in more detail in chapter 3, the amount an individual is willing to pay for a reduction in morbidity can be quite different from the costs of illness. The estimates of the value of morbidity in this book together with ongoing research should rapidly make the cost of illness approach obsolete.

The federal health and safety regulatory process demonstrates that the economic approach to valuing health has advanced sufficiently to be a practical part of policy formation. The need for more widespread acceptance of benefit-cost analysis and of further advances should not be downplayed, however. Advances in morbidity valuation are particularly needed, as attention turns from dramatic policies that can save lives to the less dramatic but probably more common policies that have day-to-day effect on health and comfort. It is also vital that the economic approach be adopted by policy makers at the state and local level, where many of these policy decisions will be made.

COST CONTAINMENT. Much has been said about the festering problems of health care utilization and costs and the problem of introducing proper incentives for cost containment. Our objective is to complement this discussion with the demand-side analysis needed to guide resources in the most useful directions. Without information on the value of health, it is impossible to make rational judgments whether too much or too little is being spent either on general health care or on specific medical interventions.

It has been widely noted that we devote a large and growing share of our national resources to health care. Employers' health care costs per worker have been rising rapidly and are also expected to grow further. Medicare payments to the elderly promise to become the largest single component of the federal budget in the not-too-distant future. Doctors, health care professionals, and other concerned with health policies are increasingly aware of the fact that resources available for health care are finite and that one of the most pressing overall problems is how to put the resources to their best use and how to draw the line between spending on health and other things.

Two important public policy studies directed at cost containment, which recognize the importance of the composition of public demand for medical services, illustrate the research needs this book is intended to meet. The first is the widely discussed medical priority-setting project presented to the Oregon legislature in 1989. The second is the LORAN Commission (1988) study done for the Harvard Community Health Plan.

Introducing cost into considerations of the delivery of medical services has always been painful, largely because of the special place health has in our values as citizens. Oregon faced the necessity of confronting resource limitations in establishing eligibility requirements for Medicaid assistance. As an example of the stark choices they faced, Welch and Larson (1988, p. 171) stated, "Medicaid could either extend its funding for basic health care to include about 1500 persons not covered previously, or continue to fund a program of organ-transplantation (bone marrow, heart, liver and pancreas) for a projected 34 patients." There was no avoiding the choice of treating some patients to the exclusion of others. That necessity led the state to attempt an evaluation of the benefits that patients would receive from the medical services they provided. Priorities were forced upon the state because of scarcity; program benefits were recognized as the key to establishing rational priorities.

The task of estimating benefits was given to a panel of experts. Four groups were formed, composed of physicians, nurses, social workers, and health and social program administrators. Each group specialized on a particular phase of the life cycle, from prenatal to geriatric. Their task was to develop lists of care categories and rank order the lists in terms of importance. An executive group, drawn from the individual groups, consolidated the work, defined broad areas of health services to be offered through Medicaid, and developed management guidelines.

The Oregon program explicitly recognizes the scarcity of medical resources and the importance of knowing the benefits of different medical programs in intelligently allocating public funds to them. This is a valuable first step in the direction of effective public policy. We believe the approach could be greatly improved using willingness to pay, placing more weight on the relation of population preferences to expert preferences, and using more logical ranking procedures taking account of costs.

The Harvard Community Health Plan (HCHP), founded in 1969 and enrolling more than 360,000 members, came to recognize the impossibility of providing its membership with the benefits of the virtually boundless expansion of medical technology. In 1985 they established the LORAN Commission "to develop guidelines for evaluating and approving new medical technologies that might benefit HCHP's membership" (LORAN Commission 1988, p. 10). The work of the commission was conducted with nationwide objectives in mind—"in response to a call to confront issues of national significance" (p. 10). The commission was composed of distinguished citizens from a wide cross section of society. The commission's deliberations were deep reaching and complex and continued during 3 years of meetings.

During the course of the commission's deliberations, questions of relative values and individual worth came to the surface, posing problems similar to those faced in Oregon. The dramatic case of Baby L led the commission to the consensus that choices must be made that preclude the universal provision of available technologies and interventions. Baby L had suffered profound brain damage, with no prospect for recovery. Baby L received care which in two years had "cost well over $1 million; her home nursing care cost $7000 a month" (p. 17). Some commission members had believed in the adage "everything medically possible must always be provided" (p. 15). The case of Baby L convinced them to abandon that belief. Choices among competing technologies and interventions have to be made in order to avoid serious misdirection of medical resources.

How to determine the values on which to make choices was a difficult task. One witness suggested a solution: "Assign a value to the intervention and compare it with values assigned other interventions. . . . The Commission's members embraced his concept, but could not accede to a mathematical formula, concluding that simple formulas for comparing the values cannot be found" (p. 20). The solution the commission recommended was to establish a number of years' worth of earnings that should be devoted to extending a member's life for 1 year (p. 39). Recalling the Baby L tragedy, they say, "As more and more years of earnings of others are devoted to extending a life for a short time, it becomes clear that choices must be made between competing goods. A rational analysis of this kind can offer guidance" (p. 39).

While the LORAN Commission recognized the inevitability of choices and is highly commendable in this regard, to us the use of the number of years worth of earnings to be devoted to extending a life for 1 year as a criterion is a non sequitur. It has nothing to say about the quality of the life extended, much less the vast number of medical procedures that do not affect longevity but are nonetheless valuable to patients. The multiple dimensions of health are reflected in the willingness to pay concepts that are the basis for the economic approach to valuing health. Using willingness to pay results, the ranking criterion suggested above for the Oregon program would be used as an aid to decisions.

These two major examples of public policy analysis, the Oregon plan and the LORAN Commission report, exemplify the role applied welfare economics could play in medical decision making. This book attempts to supply usable values of the type for which the Oregon and LORAN studies were groping.

MEDICAL RESEARCH PRIORITIES. The rationale for government participation in medical research is well established. Government research has the broad-based support of the taxpayer, who is the beneficiary when highly uncertain lines of investigation bear fruit. Those who bear the cost of government-sponsored research receive full benefit. The successful research efforts of private business firms, in contrast, while profitable, generally provide benefits beyond those that are paid for by the firms' customers. Business firms are unable to internalize all of the benefits they create. The well-known result is that the private sector by itself would produce too little medical research.

Medical research spending from all sources has grown impressively since 1960. Measured in 1988 constant dollars, spending on research and development increased from $3.5 billion in 1960 to $18.7 billion in 1988. In 1988, federal spending was $8.454 billion, or 45% of the total. Industry spending was about the same—$8.22 billion. State and local spending

TABLE 1.1.   Federal Spending and Deaths, by Disease

Condition	Federal Spending for Research, Education, and Prevention, 1989 (in Million $)	Gross Numbers of Deaths, 1989 (Estimated)
Cancer	1,449	494,422
AIDS and HIV	1,306	34,388
Heart disease	1,008	777,626
Diabetes	267	. . .
Stroke and hypertension*	182	138,169
Alzheimer's	127	. . .

SOURCE.—Winkenwerder, Kessler, and Stolec (1989), tables 4 and 5.
   *Federal spending is for stroke and hypertension; numbers of deaths refers to those caused by cerebrovascular disease. See Winkenwerder, Kessler, and Stolec (1989) for details.

($1.272 billion) and private nonprofit organizations ($0.744 billion) made up the remainder.

The distribution of these research expenditures among major diseases is suggested by the first column of Table 1.1, which gives total federal spending on research, education, and prevention for cancer, AIDS and HIV, heart disease, diabetes, stroke and hypertension, and Alzheimer's disease. The second column shows the number of deaths due to each condition, with the exception of diabetes and Alzheimer's. The estimates are from a study by Winkenwerder, Kessler, and Stolec (1989).

One contribution of the study by Winkenwerder et al. is that it highlights the opportunity cost of federal AIDS spending. Advocates of higher federal outlays for AIDS, such as the General Accounting Office (1988) and the presidential AIDS commission (Report of the Presidential Commission on the Human Immunodeficiency Virus Epidemic 1988), should recognize that to spend more money on AIDS means either spending less on other diseases or spending a greater total on medical research and less on other goods and services. As a first impression, it seems hard to justify spending less on other diseases, and in fact the pattern of spending seems confused. While a number of other factors are clearly relevant, a limited measure of the importance of a disease is the number of deaths it causes. Heart disease causes the most deaths, but federal spending is higher for both cancer and AIDS/HIV. In fact, spending on AIDS/HIV is almost as high as spending on cancer, although cancer causes more than 10 times the number of deaths. Heart disease accounts for more than 20 times the number of deaths estimated for AIDS/HIV in 1989. Even though AIDS deaths are estimated to increase rapidly, the ratio of heart disease deaths to AIDS deaths remains over 10 for 1992, which is far as Winkenwerder, Kessler, and Stolec (1989) make their extrapolations.

The estimates presented in Table 1.1 draw attention to important questions about medical research spending: Should we spend more or less money on medical research? In what proportions among the diseases should that money be spent? Knowing the number of deaths caused by each disease is not enough to answer these questions, however. In addition to knowing the value placed on averting a death, we need to know the value of other aspects of these diseases. For instance, diabetes and Alzheimer's disease often are not direct causes of death, but they cause a great deal of suffering. The value of reducing the suffering of the 5.8 million persons known to have diabetes in 1984 or the millions of Alzheimer's patients are important benefits of medical research.

Moreover, to properly utilize knowledge of the benefits and costs of medical research, one needs to think in terms of marginal amounts rather than totals. After making the distinction between marginal and total amounts, the pattern of federal research spending presented in Table 1.1 seems more appropriate than at first appearance. The choice between spending more money on AIDS/HIV research or spending more money on research into heart disease should be made by comparing at the margin the benefits of an extra dollar's worth of research into either disease. The marginal benefits of AIDS/HIV research may be much higher than for many other types of research because AIDS/HIV is a relatively new and poorly understood problem. This book is concerned with how better to estimate marginal benefits of improved health that could then be compared with marginal costs as an aid to improving decisions for medical research.

ENCOURAGING BETTER LIFESTYLES. The American public in recent years has revealed a substantially increased interest in personal health. This interest has been accompanied by a recognition that personal habits and lifestyle are more important than any other determinant of health over which the individual has control. Lifestyles have changed accordingly, most notably through increased exercise and reduced consumption of tobacco, alcohol, and fatty foods. Illicit drug use is an unfortunate but major countertendency.

The discovery of this knowledge through medical research has been essential to the observed changes in behavior. For example, even a few years ago many people did not recognize the importance of controlling cholesterol. The expansion of the number and types of public health professionals, devoted to the study of health behavior and the development of policies aimed at improving health behavior, has complemented medical research in a way that has transformed the medical care product. The rising level of prosperity in our society has also contributed to the change in the nation's health habits. Education appears to be the chief correlate of the change because educated people are best able to assimilate the new knowledge. A willingness to take longer views is also an important health characteristic of better-off people, enabling them to remember their goals and accept delayed, long-term results.

A challenge to public policy is to extend the benefits of improved self-management to less well-off members of society. Public health research is heavily committed to this. The present volume is relevant to the issue of self-management because individual and household preferences are the basis of behavior. The importance of the values of people as we find them is central to this approach. Its importance is not yet adequately understood or appreciated in much of the current public health literature.

The Public Health Service publishes a "Prevention Profile" (National Center for Health Statistics 1990) that describes at 3-year intervals the nation's progress toward 1990 goals established by the Surgeon General's 1979 report (U.S. Public Health Service 1979). The goals concern "major health problems still confronting Americans [that] are rooted in lifestyle or environmental factors that are amenable to change" (p. 9). Five health goals, related to the complete life cycle, and 15 broad priority areas are identified where progress can be achieved through public, private, and individual efforts. We will focus on four of these areas to indicate how the methods and results of this book apply to public health policy making where individual choice is an important factor. The areas are smoking, drinking, diet, and exercise.

We begin by briefly describing the goals set forth in the 1979 Surgeon General's report. Among the main objectives related to smoking are to reduce the prevalence of smoking among people over 18 years of age to below 25% and to reduce smoking prevalence to below 6% for the population aged 12–18. As an additional objective, smoking prevalence among pregnant women should be no more than half the prevalence of all women smokers. At least 35% of all workers should be offered cessation programs at the work site or in the community. Other goals relate to awareness, no-smoking laws, surveillance, and average tar yield of cigarettes.

Alcohol-related deaths from motor-vehicle accidents should be reduced to 9.5 per 100,000 population by 1990, as compared to 11.5 deaths in 1977, according to the Surgeon General's goals. The cirrhosis death rate should be reduced to 12 per 100,000 population in 1990, from 13.5 in 1975. Other goals include non-motor-vehicle accident deaths, incidence of infants born with fetal alcohol syndrome, and various alcohol consumption goals.

Examples of nutritional goals pertain to obesity and cholesterol. The report recommends that no more than 10% of men and 17% of women should be overweight by 1990—down from 23.7% and 26% in 1971–74, respectively. The mean serum cholesterol level in the adult population should be at or below 200 milligrams per deciliter by 1990, compared to 214 for men and 217 for women in 1971–74.

A major exercise goal in the Surgeon General's report is to have at least 60% of the population aged 18–64 getting vigorous physical exercise, compared to 35% in 1974–75. For the 10–17 age group, the goal is over 90%. For the over 65 population, 50% should engage in appropriate physical activity, compared to 36% in 1975.

These, briefly, are some of the public health goals that grew out of the 1979 Surgeon General's report. Let us note some aspects of these goals that make this book relevant to their formulation. First of all, a good deal of judgment has been used in establishing priorities in the amount of progress that is to be achieved among the various goals. For example, the alcohol consumption goal seems conservative: "By 1990, per capita consumption of alcohol should not exceed current levels" (p. 72). A major smoking goal, by contrast, is much more ambitious: the proportion of adult smokers is to be reduced by one-fourth (from 34% to 25%). Second, the goals are partial and are stretched out over an 11-year period—1979–90. In no case is the goal complete elimination of the problem, and the goals recognize that progress takes time—more for some objectives than for others. If goals were costless to achieve, problems would be completely eliminated immediately.

These characteristics reflect the realization that the Surgeon General's goals benefit citizens to different degrees and that achieving these goals is costly. Ideally, the goal priorities and the timetable would be established by balancing the benefits of health gains against the costs of achieving them so that the overall extent of gains would be maximized within the resources available to the public health sector.

The measures of health values in this book provide part of the quantitative foundation needed to establish national priorities. The profile of benefits measured in Chapter 15 is not complete for every public health policy requirement, but the methods needed to obtain those values on an ongoing basis are spelled out.

Program cost measurement is not the subject of this book. Yet careful measurement of costs, carried out elsewhere, complement health values. The usefulness of program cost estimates is greatly enhanced by the availability of health value estimates because together they provide a powerful tool for public health policy analysis.

HEALTH VALUES AND THE LEGAL SYSTEM. Lawsuits have become a prominent part of people's quest for good health. Wrongful death, wrongful injury, and environmental cases are flourishing, in contrast to a simpler era when people more passively accepted misfortune as part of life. Economies of scale in the practice of health law have been achieved by the widening application of class action suits.

The environment has been a particularly important area where law has become a major force in shaping the public health climate. Environmental audits have become an important part of building ownership. They are frequently required by the buyer when a building is sold. Elimination of environmental hazards is typically a condition of sale in these cases and can consume a substantial part of the building's value. Federal and state legislation, mandatory environmental audits, and hazard abatement could reduce the market value of the nation's building stock by billions of dollars and have serious repercussions on the quality and size of that stock. Of course, the benefits of all of these actions are once again in the form of health improvements.

Business firms and government itself feel the effects of tort law liability. The Johns-Manville case, which produced billions of dollars in liabilities through class action lawsuits by workers exposed to asbestos particles, is perhaps the most famous. The presence of dioxin in the defoliant Agent Orange gave rise to class action suits seeking compensation for exposure that had uncertain health effects.

Wrongful death and wrongful injury suits have become an important force in our economy, as people seek redress for damages that may or may not entail responsibility on the part of the accused. The difficult issue of pain and suffering is often involved in these cases. Judgments involving pain and suffering sometimes seems arbitrary and are often thought to be excessive. Courts have traditionally preferred to use forgone earnings and medical treatment costs as measures of damage. They dislike pain and suffering because of incentives for victims to overstate subjective losses. The situation may be improving somewhat as it becomes more widely appreciated that earnings losses and medical expenses understate losses. Nevertheless, progress needs to be made in both legal and economic thinking before a solid foundation for determining values can be put in place.

There is a need in all of these areas involving court decisions for quantitative knowledge of the damages done to injured parties. Effects of court decisions can be far ranging, affecting many related markets. Quantitative knowledge as to whether damages are commensurate with costs of avoiding them is an indispensable input into evaluation of the legal system. One of the major purposes of this book is to develop more adequate measures of life and limb. The precise role these measures should play in the legal system depends on whether the objective of the courts is to compensate victims, to provide proper incentives to deter harmful behaviors, or some combination of these and other goals.

Our major policy recommendations in this area are that nonpecuniary damages should be correctly incorporated into damage assessments and that the marginal gains of increased caretaking should be balanced against the costs. Compensation of victims is a different matter, involving equity among victims of natural and man-made mishaps, as well as incentives for potential victims to take care. We will return to these matters in Chapter 16.

HEALTH VALUES IN CLINICAL PRACTICE. Health values can make a contribution to allocative decisions that must be made at the clinical level, either by individual doctors in the course of their day-to-day practice or by decision-making groups at the hospital level. Clinical decisions are shaped by policies directed at more remote levels of the health care delivery system. Cost containment and research priority policies are examples of forces that shape clinical decisions by establishing the supply of resources available for clinical practice. Important allocative decisions must still be made at the clinical level, however. Health values, by providing background information about the general population, can assist the practitioner in making these decisions in individual cases and can also be of help in a third-party payer context. Provision of health values for the supplementary and interpretative roles they can play in assisting clinical decisions is the sixth policy area considered in this book.

PART ONE

Health Values
A Comparative Analysis

Overview of Part One

A wide variety of approaches to valuing the benefits of health improvements have been used. While the special case of valuing mortality has received much attention, the problems of valuing morbidity risks alone, or of valuing the more general case of a combination of morbidity and mortality risks, have received less attention. The goal of Part 1 is to provide a comparative review of approaches to valuing changes in health and a synthesis of the empirical results of the various approaches.

In Chapter 2 a model of health investment is developed that yields a general expression for the value of changes in risks to human health. Chapter 2 provides a conceptual framework for the remainder of the volume. The proposition that costs of illness and preventive expenditures are lower bounds to the preference-based willingness to pay measure is carefully examined. In addition, the relationship between the value of a certain change in health and the value of a change in health risks is explored.

In the remaining chapters of Part 1, measures of health values from many previous studies are compared and evaluated. Chapter 3 reviews the cost of illness approach. Estimates from existing aggregate cost of illness studies are put on a per-case-of-illness or per-day-of-illness basis, to be comparable to what an individual would be willing to pay. In this way, estimates of the values of a range of health effects are developed that can be used to evaluate policy changes. A careful review of the conceptual and empirical background of the cost of illness approach is also undertaken.

Chapter 4 examines the results of the limited number of studies that apply the contingent valuation method to valuing morbidity. This chapter includes the new results from the contingent valuation experiments discussed in detail in Part 2. Consideration is given to the accuracy of contingent valuation estimates and to how results from the different studies compare.

Chapter 4 also reviews the available evidence on comparisons of the cost of illness and contingent valuation approaches. The most conclusive evidence on this question is from the data collected in the contingent valuation experiments of Part 2. These data are used to test the hypothesis that a cost

21

of illness measure is a lower bound to willingness to pay as revealed by contingent valuation.

Chapter 5 draws implications for the value of health from studies of the household production of health. While relevant work is limited, several studies are reviewed that yield illustrative empirical estimates of the value of acute morbidity.

Chapter 6 discusses an approach widely used by health professionals: the quality-adjusted life year, or *qualy*, approach. The chapter describes the qualy approach and compares it to the economic approach used in this book. A major goal of the chapter is to incorporate useful results from qualy analysis into the framework of this book, enlarging available estimates of health values.

2
Framework for Valuing Health Risks

Mark Berger, Glenn Blomquist, Donald Kenkel, and George Tolley

2.1. Introduction

In this chapter we develop a model of health investment that yields a general expression for the value of changes in risk to human health. The preference-based values of morbidity risks and mortality risks are ex ante dollar equivalents of changes in expected utility associated with risk changes. The values of changes in morbidity risks and mortality risks are related to two alternative measures, costs of illness and preventive expenditures, which are thought to be lower bounds on the value of risk reductions. We demonstrate that these alternative measures are not even special cases of the more general measure and that the size relationships among the three measures are complex. Also, we derive the relationship between willingness to pay for risk changes and the consumer surpluses associated with health changes that occur with certainty.

This chapter begins with a review of several approaches to valuing changes in risks that are currently in use. The model of health risk behavior is developed, and implications for benefit estimation from the model are discussed.

2.2. Approaches to Valuing Health Risks

Cost of Illness

The traditional approach to measuring the benefits of improved health is based on avoidance of disease damages. The damage avoidance approach, which is the form used by health professionals and some health economists, is also referred to as the *cost of illness approach* or sometimes the *earnings expenditure approach*. The cost of illness approach relies heavily on the idea that people are producers, that is, human machines. Outlays for health services are seen as investments that improve people as productive agents and

This material was originally published in M. C. Berger, G. C. Blomquist, D. Kenkel, and G. S. Tolley, "Valuing Changes in Health Risks: A Comparison of Alternative Measures," *Southern Economic Journal* 53 (April 1987): 967–84. Reprinted with permission.

yield a continuing return in the future. The yield for improvements in health is the labor product created plus any savings in health care expenditures due to any reduction in disease (see Mushkin 1962, pp. 130 and 136). The costs of health degradation are the damages caused by the disease (or accident). The health expenditures made, the value of the resources used in supplying health care, are referred to as the *direct cost of illness*. The loss of labor earnings due to sickness and premature death, the value of the lost product of labor, is referred to as the *indirect cost of illness*. The value of health improvements is the sum of the reductions in direct and indirect costs of illness, that is, the damages that will be avoided. Studies employing the cost of illness approach include Weisbrod (1971), Cooper and Rice (1976), and Mushkin (1979).

Several deficiencies in the cost of illness approach are recognized: (1) the indirect costs are zero for retirees, full-time homemakers, and other people who do not work in the market; (2) an arbitrary decision must be made about forgone consumption expenditures, that is, gross or net labor earnings; (3) individuals are viewed as having no control over their health or health care expenditures; and (4) there is little basis in economic theory for the use of the costs of illness in benefit-cost analysis. An attempt has been made by Landefeld and Seskin (1982) to reformulate costs of illness values to more closely approximate a theoretically correct measure, but their study primarily focuses on externalities, and an approach more closely tied to individual optimization seems more appropriate. Chapter 3 examines in much greater detail the cost of illness approach as a possible source of estimates of the benefits of health risk reduction.

Willingness to Pay in Contingent Markets

The absence of a market for health as such has prompted consideration of direct questioning techniques to elicit willingness to pay for changes in health risks. Through a survey interview or laboratory experiment a hypothetical market is established, and individuals are asked to purchase changes in health directly contingent upon the existence of the market. Contingent valuation of mortality risks was pioneered by Acton (1973) in his study of heart attack treatment and has been used by Loehman et al. (1979) to value morbidity related to air pollution. Currently, there is renewed interest in direct questioning because it yields conceptually correct values of health risk that are difficult to estimate using other techniques.

Contingent valuation is considered in detail in Part 2. Empirical results applied to the value of morbidity are reviewed in Chapter 4.

Household Production of Health and Preventive Expenditures

While the cost of illness approach concentrates on damages or costs following the onset of illness, individuals can and do incur costs in efforts to prevent illness from ever occurring. In Grossman's (1972) model of consumption and production of the commodity "good health," individuals combine purchased goods such as medical care and their own time to produce health capital. Willingness to pay is the value of healthy time and is the sum of two terms: (1) the increment in labor earnings that is possible, and (2) the monetary value of the gain in utility associated with better health. Thus, the household production model gives a conceptual foundation for the relevance of labor earnings (indirect costs) for morbidity, but it also implies that a preference-based value will depend on the costs of producing health (preventive expenditures) and a utility, or consumption, value. An example of the household production approach is Cropper's (1981) micro study of the effect of air pollution on days lost from work due to illness. To value the health changes, she multiplies the wage rate by a factor derived from a specific production function.[1] This and other studies using the household production approach are discussed in Chapter 5.

The recognition that health is partly endogenous has also spawned the idea that health improvements permit a reduction in preventive expenditures and that the savings of preventive expenditures is the value of the health improvement. This general approach has been suggested as a way to measure the benefits of reducing pollution where the expenditures prevent not only damages to human health but also damages to property and so forth. Courant and Porter (1981) characterize the literature as having reached a limited consensus that such expenditures represent a lower bound to the total costs of pollution, a conclusion they dispute.

Smith and Desvousges (1985) find that households make adjustments to reduce the risk of exposure to hazardous wastes through drinking water. In their sample of households in suburban Boston, nearly 30% purchased bottled water regularly to avoid hazardous wastes, while smaller fractions installed water filters and attended public meetings as ways to reduce the risks. This study provides important evidence that averting or preventive behavior in response to pollution risks can be significant. However, the relation between preventive expenditures and the benefits of improved health has received too little attention. We explore this relationship.

Willingness to Pay in Implicit Markets

One implication of household production models of health is that individuals will make expenditures of money and time to improve their health and reduce risks to their health. By observing people's behavior in well-developed

---

1. Cropper (1981) obtains estimates of valuation of health changes only under very specific assumptions. Gerking and Stanley (1986) do so more generally, estimating the value of a change in health as the cost of preventive activity times an estimated ratio of marginal products of inputs in the health production function.

markets for ordinary goods and services, values can be derived for health, which is not traded explicitly. Much of this type of evidence comes from the labor market in the form of estimates of compensating wage differentials for jobs with extraordinarily high risks to health and survival. Most of the studies focus on implicit values of changes in the risk of a fatal accident.

Consumption activity also can involve exchanges between health and safety and other desirables. Estimates of willingness to pay have been made based on analyses of residential housing site choice, automobile seat belt use, speed of travel on highways, and cigarette consumption.[2] This work, like that in the labor market, has focused on mortality risk. Inherent in this methodology of estimating implicit values of health risks is that individuals know and perceive differences in health risks associated with various jobs and consumption activity and that they can choose among various alternatives.

When investigating how workers and consumers make choices regarding risks to health, it is important to recognize that the utility individuals derive from consumption depends upon their state of health. Fatal risks pose the most extreme case, where one state of the world corresponds to the individual's death. In this case, expected utility depends upon consumption if alive, and the satisfaction from leaving bequests if death occurs. More generally, economists use the theory of state-dependent utility as applied to variations in health status by Zeckhauser (1970) and Arrow (1974). Viscusi (1979) was the first to apply the state-dependent approach to estimate the value of fatal risks faced by workers. Viscusi and Evans (1990) estimated state-dependent utility functions for the case of nonfatal job injuries and provided the first empirical evidence that the marginal utility of consumption is lower in the ill-health state. Below we use the state-dependent approach to model both mortality and morbidity risks.

A General Framework for Valuation

At this point there appear to be two disparate approaches to valuation of health and risks: cost of illness, perhaps inclusive of preventive expenditures, and willingness to pay. Research has proceeded using one approach or the other, but only limited effort has been made to compare and reconcile the approaches. A paper by Harrington and Portney (1987) is noteworthy in that they show that for morbidity, under certain conditions, the cost of illness values will be a lower bound on the theoretically preferred willingness to pay values. Below we develop an eclectic model with endogenous

---

2. For a review of labor market studies, see Smith (1979). For a comprehensive survey of the literature on willingness to pay and fatality risks, see Blomquist (1982) and Fisher, Chestnut, and Violette (1989).

health risks and derive the preference based values for changes in health risks. The model considers morbidity and mortality and allows the probabilities of various health states and survival to be influenced by preventive activity and exogenous factors such as environmental quality. Terms for preventive expenditures and costs of illness in the benefit expression are identified for purposes of comparison with the conceptually correct willingness to pay. The model provides a framework for comparing values of health risks estimated using various techniques.

2.3. Human Health Risk Reduction Benefit Model

Assume a person's utility depends on the consumption of goods and services and the state of health. Utility may be expressed as

$$U = U(C, q), \tag{2.1}$$

where U is utility, C is consumption, and q is a vector of health characteristics.[3]

A person does not know with certainty, however, what his or her health will be or, for a given state of health, whether he will survive the period in question. In order to incorporate these uncertainties into the model, we specify the probability of health characteristics and probability of survival functions. The probability density function for health characteristics can be represented as

$$h(q; X, E), \tag{2.2}$$

where X is preventive expenditures and E is any exogenous shift variable, such as environmental change. The health characteristic probabilities are not immutable but, rather, are influenced by preventive measures chosen by the individual person and exogenous changes such as environmental improvement.

It is reasonable to assume that the healthier a person is, the greater are the chances of survival of a given period. In other words, probability of survival can be expressed as a function of health characteristics:

$$p = p(q), \tag{2.3}$$

where p is the probability of surviving the period.

---

3. Consumption, C, consists of both expenditures on market goods and services and on time, combined in fixed proportions. If the value of time is constant at the market wage rate, then consumption time expenditures are simply the product of the wage and the amount of time spent in consumption activities. Preventive expenditures (X) and costs of illness (Z) introduced below are also assumed to consist of expenditures on time and market goods combined in fixed proportions.

A final element of the model facilitates comparisons with the cost of illness approach for valuing health risk reductions. When in poor health, a person incurs cost such as medical expenditures and earnings lost due to days not worked. These costs will vary according to the degree of illness malfunction that occurs:

$$Z = f(q), \qquad (2.4)$$

where Z is the cost incurred as a result of illness malfunctions. These expenditures reduce consumption and provide no utility on their own.[4]

In this framework, a person chooses preventive expenditures X in order to maximize the expected value of utility given the following income constraint:

$$M = C + X + Z, \qquad (2.5)$$

where M is money income in the absence of any costs due to illness malfunctions.[5]

Preventive expenditures influence the expected value of utility in three ways: (1) X increases the probability of being in good health, therefore increasing utility if alive; (2) at the same time, increasing the probability of being in good health also increases the probability of being alive; (3) finally, by increasing the probability of being in good health, X expenditures decrease malfunction costs Z that can be expected, increasing the amount of income expected to remain for consumption. These benefits must be weighed against the direct loss in consumption made necessary by the preventive expenditures.[6]

More formally, the consumer's problem can be stated as

$$\max E(U) = \int_{-\infty}^{\infty} U(C, q)p(q)h(q; X, E)dq, \qquad (2.6)$$

subject to the income constraint (2.5). Reexpressing the income constraint in terms of C and substituting it into (2.6), the consumer's problem becomes

---

4. Typically, the cost of illness approach only includes earnings lost or the value of time lost from work and excludes the value of time lost from consumption activities. Define $Z^\circ = Z - C_L$, where C_L is the value of time lost from consumption. In our empirical comparisons of the cost of illness and willingness to pay approaches in Section 4.5, we employ the more widely used Z° definition of the cost of illness.

5. Money income, M, is the sum of nonlabor income and potential earnings. Assuming the wage rate is constant, potential earnings are simply the product of the wage rate and the total time in the period. The individual's problem can be expressed in terms of the choice of X, rather than its goods and time components, because of the fixed proportions assumption for X, C, and Z.

6. Just as with Z expenditures, X expenditures provide no utility directly by themselves.

$$\max E(U) = \int_{-\infty}^{\infty} U[M - X - f(q), q]p(q)h(q; X, E)dq, \quad (2.7)$$

where U, p, and h come from equations (2.1), (2.3), and (2.2), respectively.[7]

The integral in (2.7) gives utility under different health outcomes weighted by the probability of the various outcomes. Since utility always depends upon health, the situation could be described as a continuum of state-dependent utility functions, the possible states being the possible health outcomes. Different attitudes toward risk are allowed for through the shape of each state-dependent utility function. When utility is expressed as $U[M - X - F(q), q]$, it becomes apparent that preventive expenditures X directly reduce the amount of income left over for consumption. The term $p(q)$ in (2.7) adjusts utility by the probability of being alive. Assuming no utility if dead, $U[M - X - f(q), q]p(q)$ gives expected utility conditional on the state of health. A more extended analysis might consider utility of heirs as affected by bequest. The density function $h(q; X, E)$ weights expected utility by the probabilities of different states of health. The integration over health states thus gives expected utility for the period.

The model as described does not specify fully the mechanisms available to the individual to adjust to risk such as market insurance. The only opportunity the individual has is to make ex ante preventive expenditures X that change the probabilities of the different states. Another extension of this analysis could be to carefully describe what opportunities are available to the individual to adjust expenditures made in each state of the world. Though these opportunities could easily be made explicit in the present model, this section retains the simpler framework in order to make the comparisons between preventive expenditures, cost of illness, and willingness to pay for risk reductions more straightforward. However, in general, willingness to pay values are affected by the opportunities available to adjust to risk, so it is vital to note the simplified framework used.

The problem also becomes more tractable if a single health outcome measurable as a zero-one condition is considered. An example is the occurrence of a specified type of cancer as affected by environmental irritants. Another example is the occurrence of traffic accidents due to poor visibility brought on by air pollution, provided the major cost is associated with frequency of accidents, all having about the same expected severity, rather

---

7. Although the consumer's problem as expressed in equations (2.6) and (2.7) is single period in nature, it can be generalized to allow for multiperiod planning as has been done by Cropper (1977). In particular, suppose the probability density function, the probability of survival function, and the utility function all vary over time. Assuming an infinite planning horizon, the consumer's problem can be restated as $\max E(U) =$ the integral from T to infinity of the integral from negative infinity to positive infinity of $U[M_t - X_t - F(q_t), q_t; t]p(q_t, t)h(q_t, X_t, E_t, t)dqdt$.

than the severity of an individual accident being importantly related to the degree of visibility. Tissue damage from contact with pollutants, such as liver damage, is another example as long as the principle effect is absence of unimpaired functioning rather than the degree of malfunctioning being associated with the degree of pollutant level.

A damage function, as might be the case for ozone, where the degree of discomfort rather than the presence or absence of discomfort is related to the level of pollution, requires a more extended analysis considering probabilities for more than two states of the world. Various degrees of symptoms along with their associated probability densities have to be considered, rather than just the presence or absence of symptoms. The integral in (2.7) would not simplify as it does in the case where there is only one malfunction state.

If health is a matter only of absence or presence of a deleterious condition, the probability density function $h(q; X, E)$ is discrete rather than continuous with probability concentrated at $q = 1$ for presence of the condition and $q = 0$ for absence of the condition:

$$\begin{aligned} h(q; X, E) &= H(X, E) & \text{if } q = 1, \\ h(q; X, E) &= (1 - H(X, E)) & \text{if } q = 0, \end{aligned} \tag{2.8}$$

where $H(X, E)$ is the probability of the absence of the condition.

In this case, the person decides at the beginning of the period what his or her preventive expenditures will be and then takes the resulting chance of what the health outcome will be for the period. A long planning period can be considered by letting consumption expenditures, illness costs, and preventive expenditures be average discounted present values, with the probabilities associated with survival and health status being averages of shorter-term probabilities, possibly allowing for cumulative exposure effects.

Because of the discreteness of q when health is a matter only of the absence or presence of a condition, the integral in (2.7) simplifies to a sum of two discrete states corresponding to $q = 0$ and $q = 1$. Using (2.8), the consumer's maximization problem is

$$\max E(U) = U_0 P_0 (1 - H) + U_1 P_1 H, \tag{2.9}$$

where

$U_0 = U(M - X, 0)$ is utility if free of the disease;

$U_1 = U(M - X - Z, 1)$ is utility with the disease;

$P_0 = p(0)$ is probability of survival if free of the disease;

$P_1 = p(1)$ is probability of survival with the disease; and

$H = H(X, E)$ is the probability of contracting the disease.

Equation (2.9) states that the expected utility to be maximized is the sum of utilities in the absence and the presence of the deleterious health condition, weighted by the probabilities of contracting and not contracting the disease and of surviving. As can be seen from the expressions for U_0 and U_1, utility depends both on the presence or absence of the disease; that is, there is state dependence. The income constraint has been substituted into the utility function just as in equation (2.7). In the discrete case, this constraint can be expressed as[8]

$$C = (M - X) \qquad \text{if } q = 0,$$
$$C = (M - X - Z) \quad \text{if } q = 1. \qquad (2.10)$$

Differentiating equation (2.9) with respect to preventive expenditures X and setting the result equal to zero gives the first-order condition for a maximum

$$F = U_0' P_0 (1 - H) - (U_1' P_1 H) - (U_0 P_0 H_X) + (U_1 P_1 H_X) = 0, \qquad (2.11)$$

where U_0' and U_1' are the marginal utilities of income when $q = 0$ and $q = 1$, respectively, and H_X is the change in the probability of contracting the disease resulting from an extra dollar spent on prevention. The first two terms give the decline in expected utility due to decreased consumption when an extra dollar is spent on defensive measures. The last two terms give the rise in expected utility due to decreased probability of contracting the disease as a result of the extra dollar spent on prevention. The first-order condition for a maximum is that the sacrifice of consumption given by the first two terms must just offset the gain from the reduced probability of contracting the disease given by the last two terms.

In order for the consumer to obtain a maximum, the second derivative of the expected utility function with respect to preventive expenditures must be less than or equal to zero. This second-order condition can be expressed as

$$\Delta = U_0'' P_0 (1 - H) + (U_1'' P_1 H) - (U_0 P_0 H_{XX}) + (U_1 P_1 H_{XX}) + 2H_X (U_0' P_0 - U_1' P_1) \le 0, \qquad (2.12)$$

where H_{XX} is the second partial derivative of $H(X, E)$ with respect to X, and U_0'' and U_1'' are the second derivatives of utility with respect to income when $q = 0$ and $q = 1$, respectively.

---

8. Note that, for any given individual, Z is fixed once the disease is contracted. In a more extended analysis, Z could be made to depend on other variables such as the price of medical care. Z could be made endogenous in the current framework if it were specified as a function of preventive expenditures.

2.4. Valuation of Changes in Risks to Human Health

Expressions for the marginal willingness to pay (WTP) for an exogenous reduction in health risks can be derived from this model. The totally differentiated expected utility function must be solved for the change in income that would be required to keep the expected utility constant when there is an exogenous change. The individual would be willing to pay the negative of this compensating variation for the exogenous improvements in health risks. Holding the expected utility constant by setting $dE(U) = 0$, we can solve for the WTP measure:[9]

$$-dM/dE = -[(U_0P_0 - U_1P_1)/m]H_E -$$
$$\{1 + [(U_0P_0 - U_1P_1)/m]H_X\}dX/dE. \quad (2.13)$$

The numerator of the first term on the right-hand side is the difference in expected utility between being healthy and being ill. This is divided by

$$m = U_0'P_0 (1 - H) + U_1'P_1H,$$

which is a weighted average of the expected marginal utility when healthy and the expected marginal utility when ill, with the weights being the probabilities of being healthy or ill. Thus m can be interpreted as the expected marginal utility of income.

So far, the analysis has neglected the fact that individuals choose the level of defensive expenditures so as to maximize expected utility. Rearranging the first-order condition given by equation (2.11) yields

$$(U_0P_0 - U_1P_1)/m = -1/H_X. \quad (2.14)$$

The left-hand side is familiar from the WTP expressions. As the dollar value of the difference in expected utilities between being healthy and ill, it can be interpreted as the marginal benefit of defensive expenditures that reduce the probability of illness. The right-hand side is the marginal cost of defensive expenditures.

Allowing the optimal choice of defensive expenditures as individuals adjust to the exogenous changes in health risks or the environment implies that equation (2.14) satisfies the first-order condition. Substituting the first-order condition as given by (2.14) into the WTP expression given in (2.13) results in

$$-dM/dE = H_E/H_X + [-1 + (H_X/H_X)]dX/$$
$$= H_E/H_X. \quad (2.15)$$

---

9. Terms involving the partial derivative of U with respect to q disappear since these terms are multiplied by dq, and $dq = 0$ since q is set at either zero or one. Similarly, recalling that the costs of illness Z are given by $Z = f(q)$, $dZ = f \mid (q)dq = 0$, since again $dq = 0$.

This simplification allows the WTP measure to be expressed, not in terms of the nonobservable utility function, but instead in terms of the health risk function H. In particular, equation (2.15) gives the WTP for a change in environment as a ratio of the marginal product of the environment in reducing health risks and the marginal product of preventive expenditures in reducing health risks. This result is very similar to the findings of others who suggest WTP for an environmental improvement can be expressed solely in terms of the production function (see Courant and Porter 1981; Needleman and Grossman 1983; Gerking and Stanley 1986; and Harrington and Portney 1987). One obvious difference is that, while in these models health is deterministically a function of the environment and defensive expenditures, in our model the probabilities of being healthy or ill are a function of these variables. Another difference is that our model considers mortality as well as morbidity.

Equation (2.15) is the basis for one approach to obtaining empirical estimates of willingness to pay. In principle, the health risk function $H(X, E)$ could be estimated, yielding the marginal products necessary to compute WTP. Gerking and Stanley (1986) use this strategy to estimate WTP for ozone reductions in a model with pure morbidity under certainty. (See Chap. 5 for a discussion of this and related studies.) However, Harrington and Portney (1987) and others emphasize the difficulties in correctly estimating a health or health risk production function.

The fundamental problem with the health production function approach is that it is hard to identify and measure all of the inputs that affect health. Harrington and Portney (1987) point out that typical epidemiological studies only explain a small fraction of the total variation in illness, suggesting that a number of important variables may have been omitted. Atkinson and Crocker (1992) explore the relative bias from omitted variables and measurement error when estimating health production functions. From the empirical example based on a widely used data set, they conclude that the production function estimates are likely to be the most sensitive to measurement error. Mullahy and Portney (1990) investigate an additional problem, the endogeneity of some health inputs. They use an instrumental variables approach to treat smoking as being endogenously determined, to estimate the effects of smoking and air quality on respiratory health. When estimating a health production function applicable to air pollution–induced morbidity, the health outcome is acute respiratory illness and not general health status. This could make the empirical estimation even more difficult since respiratory health is jointly produced with other aspects of health. Finally, equation (2.15) only holds as a marginal condition. Bockstael and McConnell (1983) show that it may also be very difficult to use the household production approach to estimate the value of nonmarginal changes. All of these problems indicate that the health production function approach to estimating WTP may be of limited usefulness. Below, other estimation strategies are investigated.

Equation (2.15) can be rewritten to allow for a more intuitive interpretation. Recalling that $H = H(X, E)$,

$$dH/dE = H_X(dX/dE) + H_E,		(2.16)$$

or, rearranging,

$$H_E = (dH/dE) - H_X(dX/dE).		(2.17)$$

Substituting this expression for the marginal product of the environment in reducing health risks into equation (2.15), we have

$$-dM/dE = [(dH/dE) + H_X(dX/dE)](1/H_X)$$
$$= (1/H_X)(dH/dE) - (dX/dE).		(2.18)$$

Writing this benefit expression in terms of utility by using the left-hand side of the equation (2.15), we have

$$-dM/dE = -[(U_0 P_0 - U_1 P_1)/m](dH/dE) - (dX/dE).		(2.19)$$

This form of the benefit expression states that a person's WTP for an environmental improvement can be expressed as the sum of two terms. The first term is the dollar value of the expected difference in expected utilities between being healthy and ill multiplied by the change in health risks due to the change in the environment or other exogenous factor. The second term is the change in preventive expenditures resulting from the exogenous change.

Our model yields an expression for willingness to pay that is ex ante in nature, that is, before it is known whether the individual is sick. The value is that amount of income we have to take away from both states to keep expected utility constant. The value is defined by

$$U_0 P_0(1 - H) + U_1 P_1 H - U(M - \hat{X} - dM/dE, 0)P_0 (1$$
$$- \hat{H}) - U(M - \hat{X} - Z - dM/dE, 1)P_0 \hat{H} = 0,		(2.20)$$

where the hat indicates the value of a variable after a change in E. In the context of uncertainty, our willingness to pay, $-dM/dE$, is similar to an option price (see Smith 1983) since it is a constant payment regardless of the state of nature that actually occurs. V. K. Smith (personal communication 1987) points out that, in the model described in this section, however, the framework in which individuals can purchase state contingent contracts is not fully specified, so it is difficult to restrict the payments to be constant across the states of nature. As explained earlier, the only opportunity for individuals to adjust to risk is the purchase of preventive expenditures. These features of the model mean that the willingness to pay measure,

$-dM/dE$, may not be consistent with conventional measures of option price. The measure is nevertheless a valid ex ante compensating variation for changes in risk.

Comparisons to Preventive Expenditures and Costs of Illness

It seems natural to assume that people will pay a positive amount for an environmental improvement. This means that to keep expected utility constant in the face of an exogenous improvement in the environment, an individual's income would have to be reduced; that is, $dM/dE < 0$, and positive willingness to pay is equal to $-dM/dE$. Inspection of the benefit expression given in equation (2.19) reveals that WTP could be positive if both terms, the utility value and the preventive expenditure value, are positive. Since the total derivatives, dH/dE and dX/dE, show how risk and expenditures change after optimizing behavior, however, the terms cannot be unambiguously signed. For the total derivatives, the general and plausible results and accompanying conditions are summarized in Table 2.1.

Preventive Expenditures

Consider the expenditure response of the individual to a change in the environment, dX/dE. Using the first-order condition, F, shown in equation (2.11) and the implicit function rule, it follows that

$$dX/dE = -F_E F_X = -F_E/\Delta, \tag{2.21}$$

where $\Delta < 0$ from the second-order condition given by equation (2.12). The sign of dX/dE then is the same as the sign of F_E. Differentiating F with respect to E we get

$$F_E = (U_0' P_0 - U_1' P_1)H_E - (U_0 P_0 - U_1 P_1)H_{EX}, \tag{2.22}$$

which cannot be signed unambiguously. The implication is that dX/dE need not be negative in that preventive expenditures could increase with an environmental improvement. Nonetheless, under plausible conditions dX/dE will be negative. If $H_{EX} > 0$, which is the case if H and E are substitutes, and if $(U_0 P_0 - U_1 P_1) > 0$, which is the case if expected utility when healthy exceeds the expected utility when sick, and if the difference between expected marginal utilities is small, then $F_E < 0$. If $F_E < 0$, then $dX/dE < 0$.

Change in Health Risk

The risk response to a change in the environment, dH/dE, depends in part on dX/dE, as can be seen from equation (2.16). The sign of dH/dE is negative if $dX/dE < 0$ and if H_E is larger in absolute value than $H_X dX/dE$; the sign of dH/dE is also negative if $dX/dE \geq 0$. In other words, the sign of dH/dE is negative except when $dX/dE < 0$ and, what seems to be unlikely, the direct effect (H_E) is less than the indirect effect $(H_E dX/dE)$. While it is

TABLE 2.1. Comparative Statics of the Health Risk Model

	General Result	Plausible Results	Sufficient Conditions for Plausible Results
Preventive expenditures	$dX/dE \gtreqless 0$	$dX/dE < 0$	$H_{EX} > 0$ and $(U_0 P_0 - U_1 P_1) > 0$ and $(U_0^1 P_0 - U_1^1 P_1) \geq 0$
Morbidity risk	$dH/dE \gtreqless 0$	$dH/dE < 0$	$dX/dE < 0$ and $H_E > H_X dX/dE$ or $dX/dE \geq 0$
Willingness to pay and preventive expenditures (eq. 2.19)[a]	$-dM/dE \gtreqless dX/dE$	$-dM/dE > -dX/dE$	$dX/dE < 0$ and $dH/dE < 0$
Willingness to pay and cost of illness (eq. 2.23)	$-dM/dE \neq -Z(dH/dE)$	$-dM/dE \neq -Z(dH/dE)$[b]	Many exist
Willingness to pay and preventive expenditures—pure morbidity case (eq. 2.24)	$-dM/dE \gtreqless -dX/dE$	$-dM/dE > -dX/dE$	$dX/dE < 0$ and $dH/dE < 0$
Willingness to pay and costs of illness—pure morbidity case (eq. 2.24)	$-dM/dE \neq -Z(dH/dE)$	$-dM/dE > -Z(dH/dE)$	$dH/dE < 0$ and $dX/dE < 0$ and $U(C, 0) > U(C, 1)$ and $U(Z) m^{\circ\circ} > Z$

[a] Willingness to pay is equal to $-dm/dE$.

[b] It is implausible that $-dM/dE = -Z(dH/dE)$. A set of sufficient conditions for this result is $dX/dE = 0$, U is not a function of q, $U(Z) m^{\circ} = Z$, and $P_0 = P_1 = 1$.

possible that the indirect effect can dominate even where there is evidence of counterproductive exogenous changes, alternative explanations are offered as being more plausible; for example, see Viscusi (1984*a*).

The upshot of this discussion is that, while the two terms in equation (2.19) taken together surely imply that a positive amount will be paid for an environmental improvement, it is not strictly true that the terms separately will each imply positive payments. It is the case, however, that the payments for reductions in risk and preventive expenditures will be positive under the plausible conditions that X and E are substitutes and the direct effect of E on H dominates the indirect effect through dX/dE. Under these conditions the willingness to pay for an environmental improvement is the sum of the utility value of the reduction in risk and the savings in preventive expenditures. Also under these conditions, the savings in preventive expenditures, dX/dE, is a lower bound on willingness to pay. If the conditions described above do not hold, then dX/dE is not necessarily a lower bound on WTP. Under no plausible conditions is dX/dE a special case of WTP.

COST OF ILLNESS. On the basis of the benefit expression, it is tempting to consider a value of exogenous improvement based solely on the costs of illness as special case of the general WTP measure. Indeed, there might appear to be conditions under which the expression approaches being a special case of WTP. For instance, if (1) defensive expenditures are nonexistent or unchanging, and if (2) health does not enter the utility function directly, the WTP expression shown in equation (2.19) collapses to the first term, and the difference in expected utilities between being healthy and ill only reflects the reduced level of consumption when ill due to the costs of illness incurred, Z. Even with these severe restrictions, however,

$$-ZdH/dE \neq \frac{U(M - X)P_0 - U(M - X - Z)P_1}{m^\circ} dH/dE, \quad (2.23)$$

where $m^\circ = U'[P_0(1 - H) + P_1 H]$. For Z to equal WTP, additional questionable restrictions are necessary. For example, sufficient conditions are that (3) the monetary value of the utility of consumption be equal to consumption expenditures, $Z = U(Z)/m^\circ$, and (4) the probability of survival be equal to one, $P_0 = P_1 = 1$ (see Table 2.1). In fact, there are no plausible assumptions that can be made to simplify the WTP measure to cost of illness. It is even less likely that WTP will equal Z°, the more commonly used cost of illness measure that excludes the value of lost nonwork time.

MORBIDITY RISK. For the sake of brevity and because considerable attention has been given to mortality risk in previous articles, we focus on valuing changes in morbidity risks.[10] For the pure morbidity case, there is no possibility of death whether healthy or ill, so $P_0 = P_1 = 1$. The general WTP expression, equation (2.19), simplifies to

$$-dM/dE_{P_0 = P_1 = 1}$$

$$= -\frac{U(M - X, 0) - U(M - X - Z, 1)}{m^{\circ\circ}} dH/dE - dX/dE$$

$$= -\frac{U_0 - U_1}{m^{\circ\circ}} dH/dE - dX/dE, \quad (2.24)$$

10. Although we concentrate on morbidity risk, we should note another implication of our model for the cost of illness approach. Typically cost of illness studies separately estimate the morbidity costs and the mortality costs and simply add them together (e.g., see Mushkin 1979, p. 385). From our model it is evident that willingness to pay for combined morbidity and mortality risks is not the sum of the willingness to pay for the special cases alone.

where $m^* = U_0'(1 + H) + U_1'H$, which is the expected marginal utility of consumption for the morbidity case.

The relationship between WTP and preventive expenditures is again, as in the case of morbidity and mortality, complex in that neither is unambiguously larger than the other. Again, however, under similar plausible conditions, dX/dE is a lower bound on WTP (see Table 2.1).

As in the case of morbidity and mortality, there is no reason to believe that WTP equals the savings in costs of illness, $-ZdH/dE$. Plausible conditions do exist, however, under which $-ZdH/dE$ is a lower bound on WTP. If $dH/dE < 0$ and $dX/dE < 0$, then WTP $> -ZdH/dE$ because ZdH/dE ignores the savings in preventive expenditures. One reason is that health enters directly in the utility function, and utility is enhanced by health; $U(C, 0) > U(C, 1)$. Another reason is that we expect the dollar value of utility lost due to losing Z dollars of consumption to costs of illness is less than Z. This relationship between the value of the utility of consumption and consumption expenditures, or labor earnings, has been explored in depth in the "value of life" literature. Conceptually it cannot be shown, strictly, what the empirical relationship should be (see Linnerooth 1979). Still, a representative theoretical conclusion is that the value of utility of consumption or earnings will "usually" exceed their dollar value; see Bergstrom (1982). Reviews by Blomquist (1981, 1982) and Chestnut and Violette (1984) of the estimates of the value of mortality risks are consistent with Bergstrom's conclusion. The implication for our case of morbidity is that $U(Z)/m^{**} > ZdH/dE$. This relationship, along with $U(C, 0) > U(C, 1)$, leads to WTP $> -ZdM/dE$. If also $dX/dE < 0$, then WTP exceeds $-ZdH/dE$ by a greater amount. So, while we cannot definitely conclude that cost of illness measures produce a lower bound for willingness to pay, the lower bound conclusion seems plausible. These results are summarized in Table 2.1.

Comparisons to Certainty Values of Morbidity

The willingness to pay expression in the pure morbidity case is shown in equation (2.24). The WTP holds expected utility constant in the face of an exogenous change in health risk. This can be compared to measures of certain changes in morbidity as follows.

Define consumer surplus (CS) as the dollar amount that holds utility constant in moving from the certainly sick to the certainly well state. For an irreplaceable commodity such as health this measure is what Cook and Graham (1977) call a "ransom." In terms of the model, CS is thus the difference between the utility in the healthy state and sick state $(U_0 - U_1)$ expressed in dollar terms by dividing by the marginal utility of income.

The expected consumer surplus associated with an exogenous change in the environment is the product of CS and the change in the probability of the certainly well state caused by the exogenous change:

expected CS $= -$CS dH/dE.

$$= \frac{-(U_0 - U_1)}{(\text{marginal utility of income})}dH/dE. \qquad (2.25)$$

Comparing equations (2.24) and (2.25), it is clear that the willingness to pay for changes in morbidity risks given by (2.24) is almost the expected value of consumer surplus, adjusted for changes in preventive expenditures. That is, equation (2.25) is almost the first term of equation (2.24). The only ambiguity in this comparison is that, in expressing the change in utility in dollar terms in equation (2.24), m^{**}, the *expected* marginal utility of income or money is used. Since m^{**} is a weighted average of marginal utilities when healthy and when ill, if we assume the marginal utilities are the same, the problem is resolved. In general, it is not clear when these two marginal utilities will be equal since differences in consumption levels and health status are involved. The relationship between the marginal utilities of income across states also depends upon the opportunities the individual has to adjust expenditures across states. For instance, with actuarially fair insurance available, the individual will equate marginal utilities across states, though this will not necessarily result in full insurance in the sense that levels of utility are equal across states (see Cook and Graham 1977). In any case, if the marginal utilities of income across states are close to each other, willingness to pay for a change in health risks is approximately equal to the expected value of consumer surplus, adjusted for changes in preventive expenditures.

Consumer surplus is what previous studies that address the pure morbidity case have measured in their valuation expressions since they have avoided the question of uncertainty. The empirical work in Parts 1 and 2 also makes use of consumer surplus. In particular, since it is difficult to appropriately incorporate uncertainty into the contingent valuation experiment, we measure consumer surpluses associated with certain changes in morbidity. However, we are able to approximate willingness to pay for risk changes by the expected value of these consumer surpluses as explained above.

2.5. Concluding Remarks

The main purpose of this chapter has been to compare preference-based willingness to pay measures for human health risk reduction with the main alternative approaches that are currently in use. After providing discussions of the various approaches, we construct an eclectic model from which we

derive preference-based (WTP) values for changes in health risks, which
are then compared with the alternative approaches. The model incorporates
partly endogenous health, uncertainty, mortality, and morbidity. In fact,
pure mortality and pure morbidity, to which previous studies have been
confined, are considered as special cases of the more general framework.

In the general case, we find that the preference-based willingness to pay
measure for reductions in health risks consists of two terms: a utility term,
which reflects the cost of illness as well as other factors, and a term reflecting preventive expenditures. It does not follow, however, that benefit measures involving the cost of illness alone or preventive expenditures alone are
special cases of our general willingness to pay measure. It is difficult or
impossible to specify truly reasonable assumptions under which the willingness to pay measure collapses to a cost of illness measure or a preventive
expenditures measure. Our emphasis is somewhat different from that of
Harrington and Portney's (1987) in that their willingness to pay measure for
a reduction in morbidity is reduced to the cost of illness measure under the
assumptions that there are no preventive expenditures and that health does
not enter the utility function directly.

Even the weaker result that the alternative benefit measures are lower
bounds to the willingness to pay measure does not necessarily hold for our
model. Without additional assumptions, we cannot establish any general
comparisons between the three measures. We do find a set of plausible
assumptions under which some comparisons of the alternative benefit measures can be made. First, it is necessary to assume that the environment and
preventive expenditures are substitutes in reducing health risks. Second, the
direct effects of a change in the environment on health risks must outweigh
the indirect effects, so $H_E > (H_X)(dX/dE)$. Third, the marginal utilities of
consumption when healthy and ill must be approximately the same.

If the above assumptions are made, for the special cases of pure mortality
and pure morbidity, both the cost of illness and the preventive expenditures
will plausibly be lower bounds to willingness to pay. The cost of illness
approach understates the true willingness to pay for several reasons. First,
it neglects the savings of preventive expenditures. Second, it does not allow
for individuals to enjoy health directly; that is, it implies in our formulation
that health q does not enter the utility function. Third, from the "value of
life" literature it seems reasonable to conclude that the value of the utility
of consumption will exceed consumption expenditures, so the utility lost
due to expenditures lost resulting from cost of illness is greater than the cost
of illness. It should be stressed that this result directly applies to the case of
mortality but would seem to be plausible for morbidity as well.

Preventive expenditures also are likely to be a lower bound to willingness
to pay. The preventive expenditures are not a complete measure of the
benefits of health risk reduction to an individual because the individual en-

joys gains in expected utility as well as the savings of expenditures. Our model does not suggest any necessary relationship between the cost of illness and preventive expenditures measures.

One additional result is that the benefit of an exogenous change that improves both mortality and morbidity risks is not the simple sum of the benefits of morbidity risk reduction and the benefits of morbidity risk reduction.

Our results come from a model of individual maximizing behavior that considers the private costs and benefits. Thus, our results cannot be immediately generalized to social costs and benefits. However, we are able to draw some conclusions. For instance, we find in the case of pure mortality that private WTP and private cost of illness are unrelated since the latter does not matter to an individual if he dies. Only if we were to build in bequests, or impose some constraint on the amount of debts that could be left at death, would cost of illness enter the pure mortality framework. But we know costs of illness are not necessarily zero for society. So society's willingness to pay for a reduction in mortality risk may exceed the willingness to pay of the individual.

Empirical research on mortality risks has tended to confirm the prediction that benefit measures based on cost of illness will be lower bounds to benefit measures based on a willingness to pay approach. Further empirical work is needed to substantiate or refute the theoretical result that for morbidity the cost of illness will be smaller than the willingness to pay. Work along these lines is reviewed in Chapter 4. In addition, future empirical work could shed some light on the case where both mortality and morbidity risks are present. Data that contain contingent value estimates of willingness to pay, estimates of direct and indirect costs of illness, and preventive expenditures could be highly useful. These data would enable us to further investigate the questions examined in this chapter.

3

Cost of Illness Approach

Donald Kenkel

3.1. Introduction

The cost of illness (COI) approach focuses on those aspects of the value of health that may be fairly directly measured: medical expenditures and forgone earnings due to illness. The basic idea of many COI studies is simply to convey in some quantifiable way the impact of illness on the U.S. economy. These studies range from comprehensive studies of the cost of all illness in the U.S. for a given year to studies dealing with a specific disease or group of diseases. The COI approach is also frequently used as a way to measure the benefits of a program or any change that improves health, for use in benefit cost analysis. The reasoning is clear: if illness imposes the costs of medical expenditures and forgone earnings, a reduction in illness yields benefits equal to the costs saved.

An example of an application of the COI approach is to value the health benefits resulting from a change in air pollution levels. Lave and Seskin (1977) combine their data with the Cooper and Rice (1976) estimates of the total cost of illness in the U.S. to find a value for a hypothetical change in pollution levels. This chapter mainly concerns using cost of illness estimates in policy applications such as this, but a fairly general appraisal of the approach is also undertaken.

The appeal of the COI approach is its seemingly straightforward estimation of clear, well-defined, and observable quantities. There is a large amount of information collected on medical expenditures and forgone earnings due to illness, and the sources are often good quality, national databases. Since the COI approach does not place a value on the more intangible aspects of health, notably pain and suffering, the approach is intuitively seen as estimating a lower bound to the true value of health.

As willingness to pay estimates for the value of reductions in mortality risks have become available, the COI approach is less frequently used to value these risks. However, alternative estimates for the value of morbidity are just becoming available, and the range of morbidity effects valued is still limited. The quality of the alternatives to COI values of morbidity is also questioned. For these reasons, the COI approach remains an attractive source of estimates for the values of a wide range of morbidity effects. In this chapter the COI approach is mainly applied to morbidity; mortality is discussed only incidentally.

A drawback to the COI approach as usually implemented is that it produces estimates of the total medical expenditures and forgone earnings due to illness in the United States. However, data linking policies to health are often on an individual basis. For example, an environmental policy that reduces air pollution can be related to the days an average individual spends ill in a year. There are two ways to conduct a benefit cost analysis of air pollution using aggregate cost of illness estimates and individual links between air pollution and health. First, the data linking individual health effects and air pollution could be used to extrapolate the total amount of illness caused by air pollution in the United States. This aggregate quantity of illness could then be valued using an existing COI estimate. (This is the procedure used by Lave and Seskin [1977].) An alternative route is to derive from the existing aggregate COI studies estimates of an individual's cost of illness. These individual estimates could then be directly combined with the data linking individual health effects and changes in air pollution. If the objective is to estimate the aggregate cost of illness due to air pollution, it would be necessary to make assumptions about the distribution of individuals and link them to the micro relationships. As V. K. Smith (personal communication, 1987) points out, this "bottom-up" approach is probably intuitively more appealing to many economists. To implement this approach, estimates of individual cost of illness are required.

Estimates of an individual's cost of illness are desirable for several other reasons. The theoretical models that suggest cost of illness measures may be a lower bound to the conceptually correct measure of the value of health apply to individual and not aggregate values. In addition, alternative approaches to valuing morbidity produce estimates of an individual's value of health. At present, direct comparisons of these individual willingness to pay estimates and the aggregate cost of illness estimates cannot be made.

The goal of this chapter is to express existing COI approach estimates on a basis that relates to what an individual would be willing to pay for a change in health. A number of studies' estimates are put on a per-case and a per-day basis. This procedure is not necessarily ideal since a "top-down" approach is still used in estimating the individual's costs of illness: the process begins with the aggregate costs and uses these to imply the individual costs. This approach was originally proposed as a means to avoid serious double-counting of costs (Rice 1966). Since the relative performances of the "top-down" versus "bottom-up" approaches is an open issue, some estimates based on individual observations of costs are also presented. Additional information on individual costs was obtained in the survey described in Part 2 of this book and is reported in Chapter 4.

Preceding the presentation of the empirical results obtained from existing COI studies, a general assessment of the usefulness of the COI approach is undertaken. The relationship between the COI approach and the conceptually correct willingness to pay approach is discussed. The discussion is extended to consider differences between individual and societal willingness to pay for health improvements. While this distinction is made in the context of the cost of illness approach, the difference between individual and societal values is important for all attempts to value the benefits of health improvements. Following these discussions of conceptual issues, there is a critical evaluation of the standard methodology of COI studies.

3.2. Linking the Cost of Illness Approach to Willingness to Pay

Researchers using the cost of illness approach have noted a number of shortcomings of the approach for benefit cost analysis. For instance, the COI approach makes no attempt to measure the benefits of reduced pain and suffering associated with health improvements, as noted above, but concentrates on more easily measured aspects of the cost of illness. Thus benefit cost analysis using this approach to valuing benefits may indicate that fewer resources should flow into cancer research, for example, than the public might desire because of the relatively high costs in terms of pain and suffering of cancer. (This example is suggested by Cooper and Rice [1976].)

A related problem is that it is possible for a policy to simultaneously make people better off and increase the costs measured in the COI approach. For example, treatment of AIDS patients with azidothymidine (AZT) is costly in itself and may increase medical expenditures in general by increasing life expectancy of AIDS patients. Clearly AZT and other innovations in AIDS treatment are making people better off, but a COI analysis could easily miss this or even conclude that the innovations are undesirable because the result is higher costs of illness.

Another general problem is that little value is placed on activities outside of the marketplace since the approach considers only forgone earnings. While recent studies have attempted to make adjustments to allow for value to be placed on the time of those individuals keeping house, leisure time in general—and thus much of the time of retired individuals in particular—is implicitly not valued at all. Programs that reduce the illnesses of the older members of society might be very difficult to justify using benefit cost analysis if the benefits are measured using the COI approach.

This list of troubling implications of benefit cost analysis using a COI approach could be extended, which suggests that the benefits of improved health that most people actually perceive may not be well estimated by the COI measures. The fundamental problem with the COI approach is that, though the quantities the studies estimate are clearly important aspects of the benefits of improved health, the methodology originally was not founded on any rigorous theoretical basis. This point is forcefully made by Mishan (1971), who particularly emphasizes changes in mortality risks—the "value of life." He points out that benefit cost analysis is based on the proposition that an action is judged by whether it represents a potential Pareto improvement, that is, whether the gains resulting from the action can be distributed so that at least one person is made better off and no one is made worse off. To use this criterion, it is necessary to look at the sum of what each member of society is willing to pay or accept for the change. The problem with the COI approach to measuring the "value of life" is that there is no a priori reason to believe that an individual's future earnings will be related to his willingness to pay for a reduction in mortality risks. Studies based on individual preferences for such reductions are now usually said to follow the willingness to pay (WTP) approach.

In one response to the criticisms of the COI approach, Robinson (1986) argues that the approach indeed has a strong theoretical background. He makes the case that the COI approach to valuing mortality and morbidity is based on assumptions that are similar to the propositions of the material welfare school, dominant in English economics between 1880 and 1940. He further claims that the COI approach is more consistent with a view of government as an active agent in society, while the WTP approach assigns government a more passive role. Some of his arguments suggest an overly restrictive view of the WTP approach. For instance, while the WTP approach emphasizes the importance of individual preferences in making decisions about health, it does not necessarily assume that all people are adequately informed. It may be appropriate for the government to take a very active role in providing health information, to allow individuals to make well-informed health decisions. Robinson also emphasizes that WTP estimates depend upon the existing distribution of income. On the most basic issue, Robinson and Mishan agree: the COI approach is not consistent with the approach of modern welfare economics. Robinson's discussion of the limitations and philosophical origins of modern welfare economics is beyond the scope of this chapter.

Another response to Mishan's and others' criticisms has been to focus on theoretically relating discounted future earnings to what an individual would be willing to pay for a small reduction in the risk of death. Two conclusions emerge from the theoretical work. First, there is no necessary relationship between future earnings and willingness to pay (see Linnerooth 1979; or Rosen 1981). Second, however, under certain restrictive conditions future earnings may be a lower bound to the willingness to pay measures (Usher 1971; Conley 1976).

Comparisons of empirical work following the COI approach to work following the WTP approach support both of these theoretical conclusions. Blomquist (1981, p. 162) in his review of existing empirical studies concludes that while "there is no close association of value of life with future earnings . . . there is a strong indication that the value of life is greater than future earnings." Thus, there is some theoretical and empirical justification for one element the COI studies estimate: the forgone earnings due to premature mortality. It must be stressed that the justification is weak. At best, these forgone earnings are only a lower bound to the conceptually correct WTP measure, so there is no reason to believe the measures will be close to each other.

Much less attention has been paid to justifying the remaining elements of the COI estimates: medical expenditures and forgone earnings due to morbidity. Ideally, the cases of mortality and morbidity should be considered together, to allow for possible interactions (see Chap. 2). The expressions derived from such a model are fairly complicated, but it is possible to show that for the case of pure morbidity, under certain plausible assumptions, the cost of illness will be a lower bound to the WTP measure.

In short, theoretical models suggest that WTP reflects four components: (1) lost wages, (2) additional medical expenses, (3) the dollar-value of the disutility of additional illness, and (4) the change in defensive expenditures. (For a more complete discussion and definition of all variables, see Chap. 2.)

In contrast, the COI measure only includes the lost wages (often called the *indirect costs*) and the additional medical expenses (the so-called *direct costs*). The amount an individual would be willing to pay is larger than the COI measure as long as the omitted quantities of the WTP measure are positive. People will always pay a positive amount to avoid the disutility of illness. While Courant and Porter (1981) emphasize that defensive expenditures may either increase or decrease in response to a decrease in pollution, the normal case is that a decrease in pollution saves defensive expenditures, and so these savings are a positive part of the WTP measure. In this case, the COI measure of the benefits of a reduction in morbidity is a lower bound to the theoretically correct WTP measure. However, as shown in Chapter 2, there are no plausible conditions under which the cost of illness measure is a special case of WTP.

The theoretical model does not suggest how close the COI measure will be to the WTP measure. Rigorous comparisons of these measures are undertaken in Chapter 4. Some idea of the difference between the measures can be gained by considering the aspects of benefits the COI measure neglects: the disutility of illness and the savings in defensive or preventive expenditures. While illness may decrease utility in many, possibly subtle, ways, probably the most important effect is the pain and suffering caused by illness. Mushkin (1979) attempts to estimate a dollar value on the total pain and suffering due to illness, basing her estimates partly on market revealed preferences, such as expenditures on painkillers, expenditures for medical care due to a pain symptom, and so forth, and partly on values given to pain and suffering in court awards. Her estimates for 1975 range from $25.8 billion to $228.6 billion, compared to a traditional COI measure of $322.6 billion. That is, allowing for pain and suffering could represent an increase of 8%–70% in the COI measures of the benefits of improved health.

Unfortunately, no comprehensive estimates could be found of the total defensive expenditures due to illness. The household production models of health (Grossman 1972) do suggest that a wide variety of activities and goods may play a role in the production of health, so the change in defensive expenditures is possibly large. As reported in Chapter 4, as part of the contingent valuation experiment, information was collected on individuals' purchase of items for health reasons (air conditioner and humidifiers), and it was found that nontrivial proportions of the sample had made such purchases. In relation to pollution-induced health risks, Smith and Desvousges (1985) find that households do make adjustments to reduce the risks of exposure to hazardous wastes through drinking water but are not able to measure the value of these actions. This evidence indicates that the change in preventive expenditures may be a significant determinant of how much individuals are willing to pay for a reduction in health risks. Thus, consideration of the elements of the WTP measure the COI measure neglects suggests a tentative conclusion that the COI measure seriously underestimates true willingness to pay for an improvement in morbidity.

The general conclusion of the work comparing the COI approach to valuing improvements in mortality and morbidity to the WTP approach is that the COI benefit measure is a lower bound to the WTP benefit measure, but not necessarily a very good approximation of it. Almost all three elements of the COI measure can be related to what an individual would be willing to pay for an improvement in health: medical expenditures due to morbidity, forgone earnings due to morbidity, and forgone earnings due to premature mortality are all elements of a theoretically derived measure. The omission is that medical expenditures due to fatal illnesses have not been related to the willingness to pay for a reduction in the probability of such an illness. In a nonrigorous argument, this seems plausible since an individual will not value these expenditures if he is not alive to pay them. The possibility of a bequest motive, though, implies that an individual does derive utility from his heirs' consumption possibilities, and so if the medical expenditures due to a fatal illness reduce the amount of the bequest, the individual may be willing to pay to avoid these costs. Other possible justifications for including the medical expenditures due to fatal illnesses arise from the consideration of societal, rather than individual, willingness to pay. The question is similar to the problem of whether "premature" funeral costs are of interest in valuing reductions in mortality risk.

A secondary problem stemming from the medical expenditures due to fatal illnesses is that in many studies where medical expenditures are used in benefit cost analysis, all medical expenditures are implicitly assumed to be due to morbidity. The impact of this incorrect assumption is difficult to assess. Clearly, on the one hand, most illness does not result in death; simple calculations show, for instance, that less than 1% of the total cases of pneumonia in a year result in death (National Center for Health Statistics 1979b). On the other hand, the treatment of a fatal case is certainly likely to be more expensive than the treatment of a nonfatal case (unless the fatal illness is very short), so fatal illnesses may still account for a significant proportion of medical expenditures. In this case, using total medical expenditures as an estimate of the benefits of reducing morbidity alone would overstate these benefits.

3.3. Individual versus Societal Willingness to Pay

The analysis so far has focused on COI measures as approximations of an individual's willingness to pay for improvements in his or her own health risks, but society might also have an interest in the individual's health. The problem of which viewpoint to use, individual or societal, has received attention in the cost of illness literature. Some early researchers, for instance, reported forgone earnings net of consumption, on the grounds that it is the net earnings that society lost due to an individual's morbidity and mortality (see, e.g., Weisbrod 1971). The common practice currently is to estimate total earnings forgone, which is justified by the relation between total earnings and individual willingness to pay, as discussed above.

In other ways, however, the COI studies have continued to try to consider the societal viewpoint. This can be seen in further details of the calculation of forgone earnings. Earnings are estimated gross of taxes, reflecting the value to society of the taxes that would be paid in the absence of illness, though what most likely matters to the individual's utility is his net of tax income. Nonlabor income is not included in COI measures of forgone earnings, however, because, though the individual does consume it, it would not be lost to society if the individual suffers morbidity or mortality. In general, the present status of the COI approach might be described as an uneasy compromise between the individual and the societal viewpoints.

Some attempts have been made to reconcile the differences between the individual and the societal viewpoints in measuring the benefits of improved health, though these seem to have concentrated on the case of mortality risks. Landefeld and Seskin (1982) develop an adjusted process to calculate forgone earnings, allowing for the individual's perspective in that earnings are computed net of tax, nonlabor income is included, an individual discount rate is used (as opposed to the social discount rate), and a risk-aversion factor is applied. These adjusted forgone earnings estimates are closer theoretically and empirically to the measures estimating individual willingness to pay for a reduction in mortality risks directly. Working in the opposite direction, Bailey (1980) attempts to adjust individual willingness to pay measures to allow for benefits to other persons from the reduction in the risk of an individual's death, and in some ways his methodology is closer to the methodology of the COI approach. He modifies a WTP measure to allow for future direct taxes on labor and future indirect business taxes on labor that would be lost due to an individual's premature mortality and to allow for direct costs associated with a fatality not borne by the family of the victim.

From the perspective of benefit cost analysis, however, many of the deeper conceptual problems in measuring the differences between individual and societal perceptions of the benefits of health improvement are not resolved and, in fact, seem to have received very little attention in this context. A number of problems involve the role of medical expenditures in benefit estimation when considered from an individual versus a societal point of view. In addition, the existence of paid sick leave allows the possibility of a difference between individual and societal valuations of forgone earnings due to morbidity. Finally, pure altruism plays a part when considering how society in general values an individual's health risks. Each of these problem areas is discussed below, but not at the length or with the rigorous analysis they deserve. It should also be noted that, in keeping with the general purpose of this section, only the case of morbidity is considered.

The role of medical expenditures in benefit estimation would be much clearer if the market for medical care were the textbook ideal of a competitive market in the absence of distortions. In this situation, Harberger's (1974, p. 5) basic postulates for benefit cost analysis would apply; in particular it could be assumed that "(a) the competitive demand price for a given unit measures the value of that unit to the demanders;" and "(b) the competitive supply price for a given unit measures the value of that unit to the supplier." For the last unit bought and sold, the price observed in the market will be the demand price and the supply price, in this ideal setting. So for a marginal change in the quantity of medical care, the market price represents the value both demanders and suppliers place on that unit, and the change in medical expenditures (price × quantity) is the value of that change appropriate for use in benefit cost analysis, from either an individual or the societal point of view. However, the medical care sector is far from the ideal nondistorted competitive market: there are reasons to believe the market price will not be a good approximation of the value of the last unit to demanders, and there are also reasons to believe that the market price of medical care may diverge from the value of the last unit to the supplier, that is, the value of the next best alternative use of the resources involved in the production of medical care.

The most obvious reason that the market price of medical care may not reflect the value demanders place on the last unit consumed is the existence of third-party payments. Recent figures show that over two-thirds of all personal health care expenses are paid for by third parties, including private health insurers, governments, private charities, and industry (Health Insurance Association of America 1989). Third-party payments drive a wedge between the demand price (the price the demander or consumer sees) and the market price. With third-party payments, the value the consumer of medical care places on the last unit may be fairly low, depending upon the portion of the cost he pays. The benefits of an improvement in health to the individual demander will relate only to the possibly small reductions in medical expenses he actually sees in the presence of third-party payments. Following the COI approach to measuring benefits, however, all medical expenditures are counted, not just those expenses the individual incurs. This means that a COI measure may not be comparable to a measure based on individual willingness to pay, unless the savings to a third-party payer resulting from an individual's reduced health risks are somehow passed on to the individual, as could be the case if healthier individuals receive reductions in their health insurance premiums.

Even if the individual does not perceive the total savings in medical expenditures, though, as a first approximation the COI benefit measure may represent the societal viewpoint since the third-party payer, or whoever does realize the savings in costs (such as other purchasers of health insurance), benefits. The sum of the savings to the individual directly involved and the savings to these others will equal the total medical expenditures estimated in the COI approach. This first approximation misses the more subtle effects of the wedge third-party payments drive between the demand price and the market price involving optimizing behavior on the part of the demanders. These effects cannot be successfully evaluated without developing a more rigorous analytical model of the demand and supply of medical care.

Other ways in which the medical care sector deviates from the ideal competitive market are the importance of nonprofit organizations in providing hospital services and the complicated role the physician plays as both a supplier of medical care and one who has a possible influence on the quantity of medical care demanded by patients. In the absence of the profit motive, hospital administrators may pursue other goals, such as a reputation for high quality medical care. If this is the case, hospitals may provide a higher-quality, and higher-priced, good than the demanders would prefer. The role of the physician could similarly result in patients consuming more medical care than they would judge optimal if they had full information. So both of these aspects of the medical care sector may drive further wedges between the value of the medical care to the demander and the market price. Again, a more rigorous analysis is required to make any conclusions about the importance of these possible effects.

A fairly standard analysis can be used in evaluating the importance of one final aspect of the medical care sector: the possible lack of competition in the supply of physician services. Various features of the market for physician services suggest that physicians may have a substantial degree of market power: the effective restriction of entry through the American Medical Association's control of the supply of medical students, the increases over time in the incomes of physicians relative to the incomes of what seem to be comparable professionals, and so forth. In this situation, the market price of medical care will be above the value of the next best alternative use of the resources used in the production of medical care. The difference is an economic rent, or monopoly profit, that is gained by the physicians. Now, a reduction in medical expenditures due to an improvement in health will release resources (physicians) that go to a use valued at less than the market price of medical care. The result is a reduction of the rents received by physicians. Thus, the decrease in medical expenditures is partly a transfer from physicians to patients. That this transfer is not a welfare gain for society as whole using the criterion of a potential Pareto improvement described earlier is clear: the gains by the demanders of health care are offset by the losses suffered by physicians. Distributional effects could be relevant, however.

To summarize the preceding discussion of the medical care sector, aspects of the demand and supply of medical care suggest that there may be differences in how the individual and how society value reductions in medical expenditures. Many of the effects are unclear, in the absence of a rigorous analytical model. The clearest result is that, if physicians do have some degree of market power, part of the reduction in medical expenditures will represent a transfer of income and not a gain to society as a whole.

Another case for which the value of a health improvement may be different depending upon the individual or societal viewpoint is the analysis of lost time due to illness if the individual receives paid sick leave. This case has been analyzed by Harrington and Portney (1987) as a variant of their general model. As they note, as a first approximation it might seem that lost time due to illness, though no longer a cost to the individual, still represents a cost to society as a whole: with paid sick leave the employers would perceive the costs associated with a worker's illness. Then if the COI approach estimates forgone earnings without allowing for paid sick leave, the COI benefit measure will diverge from the individual WTP measure, but it will still approximate society's willingness to pay for a health improvement. However, the presence of paid sick leave changes the individual's optimizing behavior; in particular it changes his optimal choice of defensive expenditures and his ability to trade off leisure time and time spent working. As a result, the formal analysis of Harrington and Portney concludes that, with paid sick leave, the COI measure is no longer necessarily a lower bound to the WTP measure. (This is the type of subtle effect that must be considered in a complete analysis of the issues raised earlier involving third-party payments and other distortions in the medical care sector.)

The final difference between individual and societal willingness to pay for a reduction in morbidity that will be considered is the possibility of pure altruism. In this case, other members of society are willing to pay for an improvement in an individual's health, and these amounts should be added to the individual WTP measure. Altruistic motives are clearly important, and in particular family members may be willing to pay a great deal to improve the morbidity risks of other members of the family. This explanation may relate to the values placed on decreasing morbidity risks to children, infant mortality risks, and even the value of prenatal care.

3.4. Quality of Cost of Illness Estimates

The analysis of the last two sections suggests there are conceptual problems with the cost of illness approach because costs of illness may not be closely related to either individual or societal willingness to pay for improved health. Despite these objections, the cost of illness approach remains widely accepted as a standard approach to valuing health. Often this acceptance is justified by the argument that, theoretical considerations aside, the COI benefit measures are easily and reliably estimated in practice. This section addresses directly the issue of the quality of cost of illness estimates, as usually implemented.

A comprehensive estimate of the total costs of illness in the United States is the study by Paringer and Berk (1977) for the fiscal year 1975. In addition, a comprehensive estimate of personal health expenditures by disease category has been completed by Hodgson and Kopstein (1984) for the year 1980. The health care expenditure estimates of the Hodgson and Kopstein study, combined with the estimates of forgone earnings due to morbidity from the Paringer and Berk study, will be an important source of estimates for possible use in benefit cost analysis. For this reason, a review of the quality of these estimates is in order. In addition, since these studies use a standard methodology, their weaknesses and strengths will be shared by a majority of the COI studies.[1]

1. The Paringer and Berk (1977) study is cited by Mushkin (1979). It is part of a series of estimates of the cost of illness for the years 1900, 1930, 1975, and projected for the year 2000, prepared at Georgetown University Public Services Laboratory. A study by Parsons et al. (1986) estimates the cost of illness in the United States using data from the 1980 National

First, the quality of the estimates of health or medical expenditures due to different diseases is reviewed. Following this is a discussion of the estimates of forgone earnings due to morbidity.

Estimates of Health Expenditures

To evaluate the quality of the COI estimates of health expenditures by disease category, it is necessary to review the methodology behind these estimates. The comprehensive studies such as that of Paringer and Berk (1971) follow fairly closely the methodology developed by Rice (1966). The starting point is a measure of total health-sector expenditures for a given year, E. Then, expenditures are broken down by type of service purchased, that is, hospital care, physicians' services, and so on. Letting E_i represent expenditures in the ith service category, where $i = 1, \ldots, n$, note that the sum of the E_i equals E. Estimates of the E_i are available from the Health Care Financing Administration (HCFA). (Before 1978, these estimates were prepared by the Social Security Administration.) Next, the COI studies must estimate a series of weights, v^j_i, which represents the percentage of expenditures in service category i accounted for by disease j. A variety of sources is used to estimate the different v^j_i. Finally, the expenditures necessitated by disease j, E^j, can be computed as the sum of the expenditures necessitated by disease j in each of the n service categories. The principle advantage of this methodology is that double counting is avoided since total expenditures are simply distributed to the different disease categories.

For the purpose of benefit estimation, it is the expenditures necessitated by a particular disease, E^j that are of interest. Since in general the weights for the jth disease will vary across the service categories, proper estimation of the expenditures by service category *and* the weights is required. In a recent review, Scitovsky (1982) finds problems in both parts of the estimation process.

A serious problem exists in the HCFA definitions of the service categories. The major categories of expenditures are (1) hospital care, (2) physicians' and other health professionals' services, (3) drugs and medical

---

Medical Care Utilization and Expenditure Survey. Some of the criticisms below will not apply to this study.

All details of the methodology of Hodgson and Kopstein (1984, p. 1) study are not described in the published article. They state that their "methodology follows closely that originally devised by Cooper and Rice (1976) to allocate expenditures among diagnoses, amended to include several additional sources of data." My discussion and criticism of the quality of the estimation of health care expenditures is based on the Cooper and Rice methodology, so most of it should apply to the Hodgson and Kopstein study. Since Hodgson and Kopstein do use new sources of data, it is expected that their estimates will be superior to earlier estimates, and some of the criticisms below may not apply.

sundries, (4) nursing home care, and (5) nonpersonal health care services, such as the prepayment and administrative expenses of insurance, medical construction, and so forth. Currently, the HCFA estimates of hospital expenditures include salaries and other payments to health professionals on hospital staffs and the expense of drugs dispensed in hospitals. So expenditures for hospital care are overstated, while expenditures for health care professionals' services and for drugs and medical sundries are understated. A similar problem arises in estimating expenditures on nursing home care: these estimates include the costs of drugs dispensed in nursing homes. Redefining the service categories to correct for these problems, Scitovsky presents conservative estimates of the errors in the 1978 HCFA estimates of health care expenditures by service category. She finds that expenditures for hospital services were overstated by 12.4%, and expenditures for nursing home care were overstated by 3.5%. Expenditures for dentists' services were understated by 1.8%, expenditures for physicians' services were understated by 9%, and expenditures for drugs and medical sundries were understated by 50%.

Scitovsky mentions other problems with the estimation of the size of the service categories but could not estimate the magnitude of these problems. For instance, expenditures for physicians' services may be further understated since the estimates are based on tax returns of physicians. Particularly for physicians in private practice, both the opportunity and a strong incentive to underreport income are present, so this is a source of potentially serious error. Another problem is that Scitovsky feels the quality of the data used to estimate expenditures for nursing home care is poor. Hodgson and Meiners (1982) point out a third problem: double counting of costs may be included in the estimates of expenditures for nonpersonal health care services. As an example, the costs of construction of new hospital facilities should be reflected in the prices charged for hospital care, so counting these costs in both categories is incorrect. This type of error is necessarily small, however, since expenditures for nonpersonal health care make up only a small percentage of total expenditures.

One category of expenditures is typically omitted: expenditures in the nonhealth sector necessitated by illness, such as transportation to and from medical providers, special diets, and so forth. These expenditures are conceptually medical expenses, not preventive expenditures, because they follow the incurrence of a disease and do not prevent or lessen the probability of illness. It would be quite difficult to make a comprehensive estimate of these expenditures since so many different types of goods and services could be involved. In an admittedly incomplete attempt to estimate some of these costs, Mushkin (1979, pp. 384–85) estimated that including the nonhealth-sector costs of illness would increase total expenditure estimates by 10%–16%.

The problems encountered in the estimation of the expenditures by service categories (the E_i) are probably not as serious as the problems of estimating the weights used to assign expenditures to specific illnesses. Based on the criticisms of Scitovsky (1982) and others, the most important problems seem to be those concerning the allocation of the two largest expenditure categories: hospital services and physicians' services.

Most hospital expenditures are for community hospitals. These expenditures are distributed by days of care for each diagnostic group, as estimated from the Hospital Discharge Survey, weighted by expense per patient day. However, several studies by the Institute of Medicine (1977) show that the hospital diagnosis data are imprecise, so the estimate of the days of care by diagnostic group will be imprecise. Another problem is that the inpatient/outpatient mix is not accounted for in the allocation of expenditures. All expenditures are allocated on the basis of days of inpatient care, but these expenditures include a substantial amount of outpatient care. To the extent that the case mix of outpatient care differs from that of inpatient care, costs will be misallocated: the weights v_1, where 1 = hospital expenditures, will be estimated incorrectly.

Computing the weights for allocating expenditures for physicians' services is also problematic. These weights are based on the distribution of physician visits by diagnosis, which is based on the National Disease and Therapeutic Index, a continuing survey of private medical practice in the United States. The quality of these diagnostic data is questionable. Scitovsky feels that these data are even less reliable than the similar data for hospitals, while the Institute of Medicine (1981, p. 89) describes the data as more reliable, but less precise due to the smaller sample used in the survey.

A larger problem is that the studies implicitly assume equal charges for all types of physician services. Since in fact a routine office visit is much less expensive than a visit requiring more extensive services or surgery, the weights will be incorrectly computed, and thus the costs of different illnesses incorrectly estimated. That this is a potentially serious problem can be seen by comparing several estimates of the expenditures due to cancer. Rice and Hodgson (1978) modify Paringer and Berk's assumption of constant costs by breaking down physicians' services into four types with four different costs. Using this procedure, they reach an estimate 85% higher than Paringer and Berk's, and they feel that their result is still an understatement. Based on actual observation of patients, Scitovsky and McCall (1976) estimate physicians' services for breast cancer as costing three times more than the Rice and Hodgson estimate. While it is not clear which is the best estimate, there is certainly a very large range in this case. In general, it must be concluded that the estimation of this set of weights, the v_m, where m = physicians' services, is also quite imprecise.

Problems also exist in the allocation of expenditures in the remaining smaller service categories: drugs and medical sundries, nursing home care, and nonpersonal health care services. Early studies' treatment of the expenditures for drugs and sundries is poor. The original Rice (1966) study does not allocate these expenditures at all, and the Cooper and Rice (1976) update allocates expenditures without distinguishing between prescription and nonprescription drugs. However, the Paringer and Berk (1977) study does make this distinction (Berk, Paringer, and Mushkin 1978). Without knowledge of the detailed methodology used in the Hodgson and Kopstein (1984) study, it is impossible to assess the accuracy of their estimates of the weights used in the allocation of expenditures for drugs and medical sundries. Scitovsky (1982) found no evaluation of the data in general, and so could not express an opinion regarding its reliability. In contrast, Scitovsky does judge the data used in allocating expenditures for nursing home care as poor, so the estimates of that set of weights are suspect.

Finally, some remaining personal health care expenditures may not be allocated at all; Hodgson and Kopstein (1984) were able to allocate all but 5.6% of these expenditures. However, no attempt is made to allocate expenditures for nonpersonal health care to specific disease categories. For 1980, this means that an additional 16% of total health care of expenditures are left unallocated. In effect, this final set of weights, v_n, where n = nonpersonal health care, have been arbitrarily set to zero. Hodgson and Meiners (1982) in particular emphasize that these expenditures are a cost of illness and should be allocated by disease category (to the extent they do not represent double counting; see above).

A serious problem that affects the estimation of all of the weights is the treatment of multiple conditions. The procedure is to allocate all of a patient's expenditures to his primary diagnosis, even though multiple conditions may be present. Multiple conditions seem fairly common. Scitovsky (1982, p. 479) reports studies that show that 52% of hospital patients have multiple conditions, 85.7% of all residents in nursing homes have more than one chronic condition, and 49.5% of the civilian noninstitutionalized population reported one or more chronic conditions; the average number of conditions per person with a chronic condition was 2.2.

In the context of benefit cost analysis, the proper treatment of multiple conditions will depend upon the exogenous change being considered. For example, Rice (1966) finds that cardiovascular conditions are often secondary causes of disability and, as such, increase the costs of treating other illnesses by necessitating longer hospital stays, and so on. Counting these extra expenditures as part of the costs of cardiovascular disease would add around 5% to Rice's original estimate. For a program that prevented or cured cardiovascular conditions, the savings of the expenditures due to cardiovascular complications would be a legitimate part of the benefit measure.

However, a program that prevented the primary illness might also prevent some of the secondary expense, so the expenditures saved could be counted as part of the benefit of that program also. Careful consideration of each program is necessary, to capture all the relevant benefits but to avoid double counting of benefits.

Proper treatment of the problem of multiple conditions is also necessary in the estimation of the lost wages caused by illness since these are commonly assigned only to the primary diagnosis as well.

Taken together, the above criticisms imply that the estimates of health expenditures by disease category are subject to numerous, possibly large, errors. Many of the different categories of expenditures, the E_i, are estimated incorrectly, as are the weights placed on the categories. The fact that several categories are omitted form the final estimate of expenditures by disease might be taken to imply that the estimates as a whole are conservative lower bounds. It is true that the estimates will sum to less than a true estimate of total expenditures. However, this does not imply anything about how the individual E^j as estimated will compare to the ideal true value. It is impossible to make any general statements even about the sign of the errors, much less estimate the magnitudes. Consider as an example the estimate of health expenditures created by a chronic illness that requires a great deal of routine care, but little hospitalization or surgery. Expenditures will be understated since such a condition would require relatively large nonhealth-sector costs, such as transportation. Since the care would be routine, however, the cost of each office visit would be overstated by the assumption of constant costs for all office visits. Considering the presence or absence of multiple conditions, whether the disease necessitates expenditures on drugs, nursing home care, and so on, further complicates the issue. All that can be concluded is that the estimate of the expenditures due to such an illness may be incorrect, but by how much or in what direction would be difficult to guess.

Estimates of Forgone Earnings

The estimation of forgone earnings due to different diseases is somewhat more straightforward than that of medical expenditures. The methodology of the Paringer and Berk (1977) study is fairly typical. First, the population is broken down into four groups losing wages due to illness: (1) currently employed individuals, (2) individuals keeping house, (3) noninstitutionalized individuals unable to work because of ill health, and (4) the institutional population. Within each group, detailed information is used to estimate the amount of earnings forgone and to allocate these losses to specific diseases.

A general problem of the forgone earnings estimates is that, following the human capital approach, the COI studies focus on output or production lost, be it market or nonmarket household production. Thus, the studies attempt to measure days lost from work, or days lost from housekeeping, as a result of illness. This measurement does not capture all the costs that an individual would be willing to pay to avoid. As in the models discussed above, an individual can be thought of spending his time working, at leisure, or ill. Utility-maximizing behavior implies that work and leisure will be traded off until at the margin leisure time is just as valuable as working time. Additional time spent ill, whether it comes out of leisure time or is lost from work, is valued at the wage rate by the individual. By only valuing the time actually lost from work or housekeeping, the COI measure of forgone earnings implicitly values leisure time at zero. Compared to the conceptually correct measure, COI estimates like Paringer and Berk's are incomplete.

There are also problems specific to the estimation of the forgone earnings of each of the four groups. The estimation of the forgone earnings due to illness of those currently in the workforce is probably the most problem-free. The Paringer and Berk (1977) study uses unpublished National Center for Health Statistics (NCHS) data on the number of work-loss condition days by age, sex, and diagnosis for individuals in this group. As the NCHS data are based on the National Health Interview Survey, a household survey, the first set of problems involves the accuracy of these estimates. In their general comments on the quality of data from the survey, NCHS cautions that the estimates are based on a sample, and not the entire population, so they are subject to sampling error, but adds that sampling errors for most of the estimates are small (see National Center for Health Statistics).

Another problem is that the results of the survey depend, of course, on how the respondents report their health status. While the National Health Survey is undoubtedly well designed, this type of problem is to some extent impossible to eliminate. Cooper and Rice (1976, p. 24) conclude that the use of survey data in estimating forgone earnings due to morbidity "undoubtedly results in conservative estimates for some diseases and overstatements for others" because of incorrect identification of the conditions actually present in the respondents.

A second set of problems encountered in the estimates of the forgone earnings of the currently employed is that it is the number of "condition days" that is reported. A condition day of work loss is a day of work loss associated with a certain condition, so that if an individual reports that he missed a day for two conditions, this would be reported as two condition days of work loss. In general, the sum of condition days of work loss may exceed the total number of person days of work loss. To avoid double counting of work-loss days, Paringer and Berk scale down all work-loss condition days by a constant, so the sum of adjusted work-loss condition days equals the total of person days of work loss. As they note, "this procedure may create a bias in the estimates of morbidity costs by disease class, since certain classes are more likely to be primary causes of work-loss or bed-disability than others" (Paringer and Berk 1977, p. 9).

A final source of error in the estimation of the forgone earnings of the currently employed is the specificity of the data used. While the data is age- and sex-specific, the Institute of Medicine (1981, p. 91) argues that even more specific data would be desirable. Consider their example that the better educated, who generally have higher earnings, may be healthier than the less well educated and less likely to fall ill from an exogenous threat such as pollution. Failure to control for education will result in an overstatement of the forgone earnings due to an increase in illness since the poorly educated with below-average earnings for their age/race/sex group will be affected disproportionately. Variables other than education may also be important, so additional bias may be present in the estimates of the earnings lost by those currently employed.

The estimation of the "forgone earnings" of individuals keeping house is less precise than the estimation for the currently employed. The Paringer and Berk (1977) study uses unpublished NCHS data on the number of bed-disability condition days for women keeping house, by age groups. Again, problems may be encountered because of the possible inaccuracies of the survey data. In addition, the bed-disability condition days are scaled down, so the estimates may be biased as with the work-loss condition days discussed above. Finally, the same biases may result because education and other possibly important variables are not controlled for.

There are further problems with the estimates of the value of housekeeping services. First, the procedure used to value these services is questionable. The values are based on what the Institute of Medicine (1981) describes as a "relatively small outdated sample." In addition, time spent housekeeping is valued according to the wage rates of workers in the marketplace performing similar services. What is relevant to the individual keeping house, however, is the wage rate she is giving up by staying out of the market. The Institute of Medicine suggests that this might be estimated "based on the earnings of working women with similar characteristics as housewives" (p. 91). Finally, the value of time spent by all individuals keeping house, not just women, should be estimated. While Paringer and Berk (1977, pp. 11–12) make a strong case that this should be done, they only estimate the value of men's housekeeping services (or household production in general) for the case of mortality. Estimates of the loss of household production due to morbidity are limited to estimates of women's loss.

There is less to say about the estimation of the forgone earnings of those unable to work because of illness and the institutional population. The key assumption made is that these groups would have had the same work and housekeeping experiences as the currently employed, controlling for sex and age. Whether this is a good approximation is not clear, but it is also not clear if any better assumption could be made. This assumption does imply that any biases in the estimation of the forgone earnings of the currently employed and of those keeping house will also exist in the estimates of the forgone earnings of those unable to work and the institutional population.

A study by Salkever (1985) includes several methodological refinements in the estimation of forgone earnings due to morbidity and so avoids some of the problems outlined above. Salkever develops estimates for forgone earnings for noninstitutionalized males aged 17–64 by combining data from the Health Interview Survey (HIS) and the 1976 Survey of Income and Education (SIE). To compute the earnings loss for each work-loss day reported in the HIS, a synthetic estimate of the respondent's hourly wage was computed. This entailed inserting data on the respondent's personal characteristics from the HIS into an hourly wage regression estimated with SIE data. The independent variables included measures of the individual's education, presence or absence of a chronic condition, region and urban or rural character of residence, industry where person was employed, and average earnings for the occupation in which the person was employed. Using such specific data on the individuals who suffer work-loss days implies that Salkever's estimates of forgone earnings are much less likely to suffer the bias problems the Institute of Medicine (IOM) described. To return to the IOM example, since education differences are controlled for in Salkever's estimates, forgone earnings will not be overstated even if the better educated earn more and are less likely to be sick, as the IOM suggests.

Salkever also estimates the earnings losses for persons unable to work because of illness. As in earlier studies, he assumes these persons lose income equal to the earnings of similar individuals without chronic health problems. Specifically, these forgone earnings were computed as the average earnings by persons in the SIE data, without chronic health problems, classified by age group, education level, race, and region of residence. Just as for valuing work-loss days, using more specific data on the individuals unable to work because of illness means that Salkever's estimates are less likely to be biased.

Salkever's estimates of forgone earnings due to morbidity represent important improvements in methodology, which should be reflected in improved accuracy. However, since Salkever only develops estimates for males aged 17–64 for certain conditions, his estimates are not directly comparable to the more comprehensive estimates of earlier studies reported below. As a result, it is difficult to judge the empirical importance of either Salkever's refinements or the inaccuracies implied by the earlier methodology.

In conclusion, the estimation of the forgone earnings due to illness may be straightforward, but the estimates still are not necessarily very close to the ideal true values. Most of the errors tend to understate forgone earnings due to morbidity, so in this case, unlike the health expenditures estimates, the existing estimates can be considered as conservative lower bounds to the true values.

3.5. Empirical Estimates of the Cost of Illness

Here I present estimates of medical expenditures and forgone earnings due to illness to be used as a measure of the value of improved morbidity risks. Particular emphasis is placed on the cost of illness estimates for diseases and disease categories that might be related to environmental quality. Then I present some estimates from existing COI studies of the total medical expenditures and forgone earnings to morbidity related to different disease categories. These estimates are put on a per-case basis, and additional per-case estimates are presented. The costs are also expressed on a per-day-of-illness basis for certain conditions.

Total Medical Expenditures and Forgone Earnings due to Morbidity

Reported in Table 3.1 are total figures for medical expenditures and forgone earnings due to morbidity caused by various diseases or disease groups. The totals have all been updated to August 1984 dollars, using the medical care component of the consumer price index (CPI) to adjust the medical expenditures and the general CPI to adjust forgone earnings. It is recognized that this procedure may introduce errors in the estimates, due to relative price changes in health care services and relative wage changes for different age/sex/race groups.

In addition to the comprehensive estimates of the cost of all illnesses of the Paringer and Berk (1977) and the Hodgson and Kopstein (1984) studies, Table 3.1 also reports the results of studies that estimate the costs of a specific illness or group of illnesses.[2] These studies are useful in two ways. First, the expenditures and earnings lost due to a specific illness (e.g., emphysema) can be found. Comprehensive studies only provide estimates relating to more general categories (e.g., all respiratory diseases). Second, the specific illness studies may employ a different methodology. This is particularly relevant for the estimates of health expenditures. While some studies use the came methods and data sources as the comprehensive studies, others estimate expenditures based on more disaggregated data, such as the observation of actual cases. For a review of the methodology and quality of

---

2. As explained earlier, the Paringer and Berk (1977) and Hodgson and Kopstein (1984) studies are used because they represent the most recent estimates of forgone earnings and medical expenditures due to illness that could be found.

TABLE 3.1.   Total Medical Expenditures and Forgone Earnings
due to Selected Illnesses (in Million $, August 1984)

Disease Category	Medical Expenditures	Forgone Earnings
All diseases:		
Hodgson and Kopstein (1984)	315,058	
Paringer and Berk (1977)		112,319
Infective and parisitic diseases:		
Hodgson and Kopstein (1984)	6,459	
Paringer and Berk		3,024
Neoplasms (cancer):		
Hodgson and Kopstein (1984)	19,563	
Paringer and Berk (1977)		2,144
Hartunian Smart, and Thompson (1980)	14,522	
Diseases of the circulatory system:		
All:		
Hodgson and Kopstein (1984)	47,652	
Paringer and Berk (1977)		16,963
Acton (1975)	14,557	10,557
Cerebreovascular disease (stroke):		
Hodgson and Kopstein (1984)	7,324	
Paringer and Berk (1977)		685
Hartunian Smart, and Thompson (1980)	5,364	
Acton (1975)	2,201	1,132
NHLI (1977)	3,789	735
Coronary heart disease:		
Hartunian Smart, and Thompson (1980)	5,642	
Acton (1975)	5,871	5,416
NHLI (1971)	7,912	1,157
Respiratory diseases:		
All:		
Hodgson and Kopstein (1984)	24,850	
Paringer and Berk (1977)		16,572
NHLI (1972)	6,385	4,284
Emphysema:		
NHLI (1972)	652	1,414
Freeman et al. (1976)	579	3,610

NOTE.—NHLI = U.S. National Heart and Lung Institute.

over 200 studies that estimate the costs of illness, see Hu and Sandifer
(1981). Briefly, the studies by the U.S. National Heart and Lung Institute
(1971, 1972) and the Acton (1975) study follow essentially the same methodology as the Paringer and Berk (1977) and the Hodgson and Kopstein
(1984) studies, as reviewed above in Section 3.4. The study by Freeman et
al. (1976) represents a slightly different methodology (and it is thus notable
the close correspondence of the Freeman estimates and the U.S. National

Heart and Lung Institute (1972) estimates of the cost of emphysema). The Hartunian, Smart, and Thompson (1980) study follows a methodology following an incidence-based approach to measuring medical expenditures.[3]

It is difficult to make many general statements concerning the range of estimates presented in Table 3.1. It is clear that the estimates from the Paringer and Berk (1977) and the Hodgson and Kopstein (1984) studies are much higher than comparable estimates from other studies. This seems to be part of a general trend that the more recent estimates are higher than estimates based on an earlier time period and scaled up for inflation. Two influences seem important. First, the use of the medical care component of the CPI and the general CPI in adjusting for inflation may somehow be biasing the earlier estimates downward. Second, the more recent studies may be a more complete accounting of costs, reflecting improvements in methodology and data sources. For instance, more expenditures are allocated by disease in the more recent studies, and more allowance is made for household production in the estimation of forgone earnings. For these reasons, it is likely that the more recent estimates are more accurate and, whenever possible, that the most recent study should be used to provide estimates for use in benefit cost analysis.

Per-Case Estimates of Medical Expenditures and Forgone Earnings due to Morbidity

Table 3.2 reports per-case estimates of medical expenditures and forgone earnings due to various illnesses. The estimates are based on the same sources as the totals of Table 3.1. In addition, independent per-case estimates by Scitovsky and McCall (1976) and Acton (1975) are presented. All estimates are updated to August 1984 dollars (see notes to Table 3.3 for details.)

In putting the total figures on a per-case basis, the basic procedure is simply to divide the total cost figure for a year by the appropriate number of cases of that illness in that year. The proper measurement of the appropriate number of cases is not simple, however. In defining what constitutes a "case" of an illness, the specific use of the per-case estimates in benefit cost analysis must be considered. For instance, it might be known from epidemiologic or health econometric studies that a reduction in pollution will reduce the number of serious cases of a particular disease, that is, only those cases that involve medical expenditures and forgone earnings. In this situation, in preparing per-case estimates it would thus be desirable to de-

---

3. The Hartunian et al. (1980) study reports forgone earnings due to morbidity and mortality combined, so the forgone earnings due to morbidity alone could not be derived easily. For this reason, only the estimates of medical expenditures from this study are reported in Table 3.1.

TABLE 3.2. Per-Case Medical Expenditure and Forgone Earnings (in $, August 1984)

Disease Category	Medical Expenditures per Case	Forgone Earnings per Case
Infective and parasitic disease:		
Hodgson and Kopstein (1984)	123	
Paringer and Berk (1977)		63
Neoplasms:		
All:		
Hodgson and Kopstein (1984)	8,780	
Paringer and Berk (1977)		962
Lung cancer:		
Hartunian Smart, and Thompson (1981)	15,687	13,404
Cancer of the breast:		
Scitovsky and McCall (1976)	7,605	
Disease of the circulatory system:		
All:		
Hodgson and Kopstein (1984)	773	
Paringer and Berk (1977)		275
Cerebreovascular disease (stroke):		
Hodgson and Kopstein (1984)	4,210	
Paringer and Berk (1977)		394
NHLI (1971)	3,708	1,318
Acton (1971)	1,561	803
Coronary heart disease:		
NHLI (1971)	2,393	350
Acton (1975)	1,406	1,297
Angina pectoris:		
Hartunian Smart, and Thompson (1980)	246	0
Myocardial infarction:		
Scitovsky and McCall (1976)	11,242	
Respiratory diseases:		
All:		
Hodgson and Kopstein (1984)	87	
Paringer and Berk (1977)		56
NHLI (1972)	25	17
Emphysema:		
NHLI (1972)	497	1,078
Freeman et al. (1976)	441	2,753
Pneumonia (nonhospital care):		
Scitovsky and McCall (1976)	253	

NOTE.—NHLI = U.S. National Heart and Lung Institute.

TABLE 3.3. Per-Case Medical Expenditures and Forgone Earnings: Background for Table 3.2.

Disease Category and Study	Total Costs (in Millions) (1)	Number of Cases (in Thousands) (2)	Per-Case Costs (Year Varies) (3)	Per-Case Costs (August 1984) (4)
A. Per-case medical expenditures:				
Infective and parasitic diseases:				
Hodgson and Kopstein (1984)	4,498	52,691	85.37	123
Neoplasms:				
Hodgson and Kopstein (1984)	13,623	2,228	6,114.5	8,780
Diseases of the circulatory system:				
All:				
Hodgson and Kopstein (1984)	33,184	61,652	538	773
Stroke:				
Hodgson and Kopstein (1984)	5,100	1,740	2,931	4,210
NHLI (1971)	971	1,534	633	3,708
Coronary heart disease:				
NHLI (1971)	2,072	3,307	627	2,393
Respiratory diseases:				
All:				
Hodgson and Kopstein (1984)	17,305	285,323	60.65	87
NHLI (1972)	1,672	258,473	6.47	25
Emphysema:				
NHLI (1972)	171	1,313	130.24	497
Freeman et al. (1976)	183	1,313	139.5	441
B. Per-case forgone earnings:				
Infective and parasitic diseases:				
Paringer and Berk (1977)	1,559	48,206	32.34	63
Neoplasms:				
Paringer and Berk (1977)	1,105	2,228	496	962
Diseases of the circulatory system:				
All:				
Paringer and Berk (1977)	8,744	61,652	141.8	275
Stroke:				
Paringer and Berk (1977)	353	1,740	203	394
NHLI (1971)	421	1,534	274	1,318
Coronary heart disease:				
NHLI (1971)	370	3,307	112	350
Respiratory diseases:				
All:				
Paringer and Berk (1977)	8,542	285,323	28.75	56
NHLI (1972)	1,370	258,473	5.3	17
Emphysema:				
NHLI (1972)	452	1,313	344.25	1,078
Freeman et al. (1976)	1,343	1,313	1,023	2,753

SOURCE.—National Center for Health Statistics (various issues).

NOTE.—Total costs (in millions) (col. 1) are the original estimates of the various studies of the total medical expenditures and forgone earnings. These estimates are for various years. Number of cases (in thousands) (col. 2) is the sum of the incidence of acute cases and the prevalence of chronic cases, for the year closest to the year the studies estimated that could be found. Per-case costs (col. 3) are the total costs divided by number of cases. These per case costs are for the years of the original studies. Per-case costs (August 1984) (col. 4) are the previous per-case costs expressed in current (August 1984) dollars; medical expenditures are adjusted using the medical care component of the consumer price index; forgone earnings are adjusted using the general consumer price index. NHLI = U.S. National Heart and Lung Institute.

fine a case as only a case of the disease that does involve medical expenditures and forgone earnings. Instead, it might be known only that the reduction in pollution will reduce the number of cases of a particular disease, without specifying if the cases are serious or not. Under these circumstances, a more general definition of case is desirable, allowing for cases involving varying amounts of medical expenditures and forgone earnings to be included. Essentially, the per-case estimates of medical expenditures and forgone earnings represent the average cost of a case of disease, but what population over which to average is somewhat ambiguous. The per-case estimates of Table 3.2 are prepared using a broad definition of the number of cases, so the average medical expenditures and forgone earnings due to a case of illness are conservative estimates.

The source of the data for the number of cases of acute and chronic illnesses (except neoplasms) is the National Health Interview Survey, as reported by the NCHS in various issues of *Vital and Health Statistics*. As described above, the estimates from the survey are subject to possible inaccuracies. Estimates of the number of cases of the different illnesses may understate the actual number of cases, in general. For acute cases, the estimates exclude all conditions involving neither restricted activity nor medical attention. For chronic cases, data are available on the degree of impact the illness had, so the number of cases could be adjusted downward so that only more severe cases are counted. However, the fact that chronic illnesses are generally underreported in surveys, and the likely use of the per-case estimates in benefit cost analysis of changes in all types of cases of illness, argue for the broader measure of chronic cases to be used.

An additional problem encountered in estimating the number of cases of chronic illnesses is encountered in that the prevalence of chronic conditions is not estimated for every year. The prevalence estimates used in preparing Table 3.2 are estimates from the survey for the closest year to the year used as a base for the different studies that report total medical expenditures and forgone earnings due to morbidity.

Estimating the number of cases of neoplasms (cancer) presents several special problems. Three different measurements are possible candidates. First, the incidence of cancer, that is, the number of new cases of cancer diagnosed in a given year, could be used. Second, the number of individuals under medical care for cancer is a possible measure of the number of cases of cancer existing in a given year. Third, by combining incidence and survival data, it is possible to estimate the number of people alive in a given year with a history of cancer. The incidence measurement is an understatement of the number of cases of cancer since in any given year there will be individuals with cancer that was incurred and diagnosed in an earlier year. The number of people alive with a history of cancer is an overstatement because it includes individuals who for all practical purposes have been totally cured of cancer. So the figure used in preparing Table 3.2 is the number of individuals under medical care for cancer, for 1974 (American Cancer Society 1974), though the measure is not exactly comparable to the broader definitions of cases used for other illnesses. Added to this figure is an estimate of the prevalence of neoplasms of the skin, from NCHS estimates. It should be pointed out that adding neoplasms of the skin doubles the number of cases of cancer and biases the per case estimates of the medical expenditures and forgone earnings due to cancer downward since neoplasms of the skin are likely to involve lower medical expenditures and forgone earnings than other cancers. This is an example of the inaccuracies involved in using estimates of the costs of broad groups of illness, such as cancer, as opposed to an estimate of the cost due to a more specific illness, such as a particular type of cancer.

The basic procedure for deriving per-case estimates described above is not applied to the totals from the study by Hartunian, Smart, and Thompson (1981). This study follows an incidence-based approach to estimating the costs of illness, while the other studies cited follow a prevalence-based approach. A problem of comparability results. On an aggregate basis, incidence-based estimates and prevalence-based estimates may be approximately the same; in fact, Hartunian, Smart, and Thompson (1980) find relatively small differences between the two approaches for some conditions. However, putting the prevalence-based estimates on a per-case basis yields estimates of the average yearly costs of a case of illness. In contrast, expressing incidence-based estimates on this same basis would yield estimates of the average lifetime costs of a case of illness. A second problem is that expressing the total incidence-based estimates of costs would entail dividing total costs by the incidence of the different conditions, and estimates of incidence are limited in scope and accuracy.[4]

The per-case estimates due to Hartunian, Smart, and Thompson reported in Table 3.2 are estimates of the average first-year costs of several conditions. The estimates are derived from the details given of the calculation of the total costs in Hartunian, Smart, and Thompson (1981, various chapters). Since detailed descriptions of the calculations were only given for selected conditions to be illustrative of the methodology, the number of conditions for which first-year costs can be estimated is limited.

In addition to the per-case estimates derived from studies estimating total medical expenditures and forgone earnings, Table 3.2 includes per-case estimates from two independent sources. Scitovsky and McCall (1976,

4. For a more complete discussion of the difference between prevalence-based and incidence-based estimates of the cost of illness, a report is available upon request.

as cited in Mushkin 1979) report average medical expenditures due to several conditions, based on the cost of care in the Palo Alto Medical Clinic in 1971 actually incurred by patients. Estimates of per-case medical expenditures and forgone earnings derived from Acton (1975, tables 7 and 9) are also presented. In what is described as an illustrative exercise, Acton puts his total estimates of the costs of various diseases of the circulatory system on a per-case basis using a procedure similar to that described above. The important difference is that Acton attempts to estimate the medical expenses and forgone earnings of an average person actively suffering the consequences of a disease. That is, Acton uses a narrower definition of a "case" of a disease than is used in the preparation of the other per-case estimates of Table 3.2.

While Table 3.2 may seem to include a very wide range of estimates, considering truly comparable diseases shows some agreement between the studies. The lowest estimates of medical expenditures and forgone earnings per case are for all respiratory diseases ($87 and $56, respectively) and for all infective and parasitic diseases ($123 and $63). However, the per-case figures for all respiratory diseases are influenced by the very large number of cases of upper respiratory tract infections that presumably involve relatively low medical expenditures and forgone earnings. The estimates of the medical expenditures and forgone earnings due to a more serious respiratory disease such as emphysema are substantially higher ($497 and $1,078 from U.S. National Heart and Lung Institute (1972), or $441 and $2,753 from Freeman, et al. 1976).

A similar result holds when comparing the cost of cases of diseases of the circulatory system. The per-case estimates for all diseases of the circulatory system are much smaller than the per-case estimates for specific, more serious diseases, such as cerebreovascular disease (stroke), coronary heart disease, and myocardial infarction. The different estimates for these specific diseases show more agreement between studies, but there is still a fairly wide range. For instance, Acton (1975) estimates the medical expenditures due to a stroke as $1,561, while the per-case estimate based on Hodgson and Kopstein (1984) is $4,210. As noted above, Acton uses a lower estimate of the number of cases in expressing his results on a per-case basis, which implies that, if the Acton and the Hodgson and Kopstein estimates were computed in exactly the same manner, the difference would be even greater. This difference in the medical expenditures due to a case of stroke is the most extreme difference found in Table 3.2 for a specific disease; in general, the per-case estimates based on different studies' estimates of the medical expenditures and forgone earnings for a specific illness are much closer together.

To sum up, in using the per-case estimates of Table 3.2 in benefit cost

TABLE 3.4.   Costs of Illness per Day Spent Ill (in $, August 1984)

Disease Category	Costs per Case (1)	RADs per Case per Year (2)	Costs per RAD (3)
Infective and parasitic diseases:			
Combined values, Hodgson and Kopstein (1984) and Paringer and Berk (1977)	186	4.06	46
Diseases of the circulatory system:			
Coronary heart disease:			
NHLI (1971)	2,743	43.1	64
Acton (1971)	2,703	43.1	63
Respiratory diseases:			
All:			
Combined values, Hodgson and Kopstein (1984) and Paringer and Berk (1977)	143	4.1	35
NHLI (1972)	42	4.1	10
Emphysema:			
NHLI (1972)	1,575	35.8	44
Freeman et al. (1976)	3,194	35.8	89
Pneumonia (nonhospital care):			
Scitovsky and McCall (1976)	253	18	14

NOTE.—RAD = restricted-activity day. NHLI = U.S. National Heart and Lung Institute.

analysis, two considerations should be kept in mind. First, just as for the estimates of the totals in Table 3.1, the per-case estimates in Table 3.2 based on the most recent studies are judged as generally superior in quality. Second, the estimates of the costs of a specific disease should be used, rather than the estimates of the costs of a group of diseases, whenever possible.

Estimates of the Costs of Illness per Day Spent Ill

The third column of Table 3.4 presents estimates of the costs of various illnesses per day spent ill. These estimates are derived by dividing the per-case costs developed above by the average number of days spent ill per case of illness per year. In the first column of Table 3.4 are per-case costs of illness (medical expenditures plus forgone earnings) from Table 3.3. Estimates of the average number of restricted-activity days (RADs) are available from the Health Interview Survey for most acute conditions and certain chronic conditions. These estimates are presented in column 2 of Table 3.4.

Costs of different illnesses per day spent ill present a fairly narrow range, from $10 to $81. This reflects the fact that a great deal of the difference between a minor and a serious illness is simply the average number of days spent ill: the number of days per condition varies from about 4 for an average case of acute infective and parasitic disease or for an acute respiratory disease, to over 40 days spent ill due to heart disease. Another possible difference is the degree of disability on the day spent ill. A restricted-activity day is defined as "one on which a person substantially reduces his normal activity for the whole day due to an illness or injury" (National Center for Health Statistics); this can range from reduced activity alone to a day of work loss to a day of bed disability. The RADs for the more serious conditions may reflect a greater restriction of activity than the RADs for the minor conditions.

3.6. Concluding Remarks on the Cost of Illness Approach

This chapter has been concerned with the problems of valuing changes in health risks as reduction in health expenditures and forgone earnings, that is, the cost of illness approach. A contribution of the present project has been to put aggregate costs of illness on an individual per-case and per-day spent ill basis. Results indicate that a typical case of acute respiratory disease involves $87 of medical expenditures, and $56 of forgone earnings. A case of emphysema involves $441 of medical expenditures, and $2,753 of forgone earnings. A day spent ill due to a typical case of acute respiratory illness costs $35, while a day spent ill due to emphysema implies costs of $89. Estimates of this kind—that is, based on an individual basis—that are needed to evaluate policy changes have not been available heretofore.

The cost of illness approach is an important source of estimates for the value of health because it is commonly accepted by many researchers in the health care fields, and it provides estimates for the value of a wide range of health effects. Therefore, this chapter included a careful evaluation of the approach to assess its usefulness and accuracy.

This evaluation reveals that the approach suffers from conceptual and methodological shortcomings that limit its usefulness. One set of issues essentially raises the problem that the cost of illness benefit measure is not well related to the conceptually correct willingness to pay measure. The discussion of this problem suggests that a cost of illness measure may be a lower bound to a willingness to pay measure. It is not necessarily a good approximation to the willingness to pay measure, however. In addition, the distinction between individual and societal willingness to pay has been treated unevenly in the cost of illness approach and deserves further consideration.

The review of the methodology of the cost of illness approach leads to the conclusion that the estimates of medical expenditures and forgone earnings due to morbidity are not particularly precise or reliable. This is especially significant since it is the presumed practical advantages of calculating medical expenditures and forgone earnings, instead of calculating willingness to pay, that is often the stated reason for preferring the cost of illness approach.

4

Contingent Valuation of Health

Donald Kenkel, Mark Berger, and Glenn Blomquist

4.1. Introduction

One approach to valuing a nonmarket good is to conduct a survey and ask people directly what they would pay for the good, hypothetically assuming (contingent upon) the existence of a market for the good. This approach is termed the contingent valuation method and has been applied to a variety of nonmarket goods, including health.

The purpose of this chapter is to review the applications of the contingent valuation method to the problem of valuing health, including the new survey described more completely in Part 2. Since the goal is to find useful empirical evidence on the value of health, both methodological issues and actual results are discussed. Major methodological issues arising in contingent valuation are discussed in Section 4.2. Section 4.3 reviews empirical estimates of the value of health from six contingent valuation studies. Section 4.4 compares estimates of the value of health from contingent valuation studies with estimates based on the cost of illness approach discussed in Chapter 3. Section 4.5 concludes.

4.2. Major Issues in Contingent Valuation

Contingent valuation is an established research method for valuing nonmarket goods. Since it is a fairly flexible approach providing a conceptually correct and complete measure of willingness to pay, it has been applied to a wide variety of nonmarket goods, especially in the area of environmental economics. Studies have also compared the results to indirect market methods for valuing such goods. Many methodological issues concerning the contingent valuation method have been addressed as well. For comprehensive reviews of the literature, see Cummings, Brookshire, and Schulze (1986) and Mitchell and Carson (1989). In the brief discussion that follows, the focus is on the accuracy that can be expected for values from contingent studies.

Biases and Contingent Valuation

The basic reason contingent valuation results may be inaccurate is the possibility that the responses are biased away from the unobservable true maximum willingness to pay (or accept). Types of bias often mentioned include hypothetical bias, strategic bias, starting point bias, vehicle bias, and information bias, though these categories can overlap.

Hypothetical bias and strategic bias can be understood as a dilemma for contingent valuation. On the one hand, if respondents believe the questions to be entirely hypothetical, they have little incentive to give accurate information concerning their maximum willingness to pay. On the other hand, if they see the exercise as playing an important role in future policy making, and not hypothetical, respondents may have incentives to strategically misrepresent their values.

Other biases stem from the structure of the contingent valuation questionnaire. If a bidding process is used that begins by asking whether the respondent is willing to pay a certain amount, respondents may view this figure as appropriate and so bids would be biased toward the starting point. An alternative questionnaire structure, the dichotomous choice contingent valuation, avoids the starting point bias. In a dichotomous choice questionnaire, respondents are presented with a policy and a randomly chosen policy price and asked to respond yes or no to a close-ended value elicitation question (Hoehn and Randall 1987).

A more general problem is the vehicle by which the contingent payment is made. If it is suggested that the payment will occur through a concrete vehicle such as an increase in taxes, respondents who dislike taxes may underreport their values or protest the exercise by giving zero bids.

Finally, the values reported by respondents in a contingent valuation experiment may be sensitive to the information provided them during the questioning, and even the order of questions asked may be important.

Various studies shed light on the importance of the possible biases to which the contingent valuation method may be subject. The fundamental problem—that contingent valuation is hypothetical—has been investigated by conducting experiments that include both hypothetical payments and actual cash payments. Bishop and Heberlein (1986) conducted surveys of hunters who had received free early season goose-hunting permits. For actual cash payments, the mean willingness to sell was $63, while for hypothetical payments the mean willingness to sell was $101. Mitchell and Carson (1986) dispute this finding: in a reanalysis of Bishop and Heberlein's data they find no statistically significant difference between the hypothetical and actual values. However, Bishop and Heberlein defend their original methodology and present preliminary results from a new survey that supports the finding that hypothetical bias exists. For a discussion of this debate, see the chapter by Bishop and Heberlein and the appendix by Carson and Mitchell in Cummings, Brookshire and Schulze (1986).

Other sources of bias can also be more or less directly tested by varying the starting point, payment vehicle, or information given or by changing the incentives for strategic behavior. Results to date are somewhat inconclusive, though Cummings, Brookshire, and Schulze (1986) tend to minimize the importance of strategic bias and starting point bias, while noting that payment vehicle and information may be more important sources of bias. No strong consensus seems to have been reached in this area, and in particular a number of researchers believe starting point bias may be quite significant. For a discussion of the various studies' results that relate to these biases, see Cummings, Brookshire, and Schulze (1986, chap. 3).

In short, existing reviews of the contingent valuation method suggest that bias problems are not insurmountable and that careful design of the survey can minimize them in many cases. This points to the need to carefully consider the design of the survey that produces any contingent valuation results. Of particular concern are the trade-offs faced in survey design. For instance, it may be possible to reduce hypothetical bias by using more concrete payment and delivery vehicles, but only at the cost of increasing the chances of strategic behavior. The trade-offs chosen in designing a particular survey need to be explicitly recognized and discussed.

Willingness to Pay versus Willingness to Accept

Both the *willingness to pay* (how much a respondent is willing to pay to acquire a nonmarket good) and *willingness to accept* (how much compensation is required by the respondent to give it up) are theoretically definable measures of a person's valuation of a nonmarket good. Practical application in contingent valuation surveys, however, has made it evident that willingness to pay responses yield more realistic results under most survey conditions used until now. Cummings, Brookshire, and Schulze (1986), citing this evidence, include the use of willingness to pay questions as one of four reference operating conditions that form the basis of reliable contingent valuation.

Theoretically, valuations should be about the same for increases or decreases in a nonmarket good about a given base, especially for small changes. Willingness to accept valuations, however, have proved to be appreciably larger in most survey applications. This effect has been studied in the literature of both psychology and economics. Brookshire and Coursey (1987) report experiments in which subjects are given repeated questionnaires in one approach and participate in repeated sealed auctions in another approach. In both approaches, it is found that subjects appear to learn, and willingness to accept bids converge to willingness to pay levels.

The studies reviewed in this chapter and the original study reported in Part 2 of this book elicit willingness to pay measures.

Accuracy of Contingent Valuation

Aside from issues of survey design and bias, the basic question remains, however: in a properly designed contingent valuation study, how accurate are the values reported? In a sense, the question is unanswerable since the true values are unobservable. Several types of evidence can suggest a range of accuracy.

First, as Tolley and Fabian (1988) point out, studies have found that contingent values are systematically related to income, availability of substitute goods, and other variables that economic theory suggests should be important. This implies that the contingent market is to some extent similar to an actual market and that the values reported are not random but are reasonable subjects for economic analysis.

Second, a number of studies have compared the contingent valuation method to alternative indirect market methods of valuing nonmarket goods. Cummings, Brookshire, and Schulze (1986) review these studies and stress that the results can not establish the accuracy of contingent valuation. But, "Assuming that, within the range of plus or minus 50%, value estimates derived from indirect market methods include 'true' valuations by individuals, these results suggest that CVM [contingent valuation method] values may yield 'accurate' estimates of value in cases where individuals have had some opportunity to make actual previous choices over that commodity in a market framework" (Cummings, Brookshire, and Schulze, p. 102).

Based on their comprehensive review of the methodology and practice of contingent valuation, Cummings et al. (1986) suggest a range of accuracy for carefully designed contingent valuation studies. (These suggestions are linked to a set of reference operating conditions that the study must meet for the accuracy range to apply.) At the least, "the method produces *order of magnitude* estimates—but we think one can argue that error ranges are much smaller" (Cummings, Brookshire, and Schulze, p. 233). At the best, "one might tentatively conclude that, given the current state of the art, the CVM is not likely to be more accurate than plus or minus 50 percent of the measured value" (p. 99). This plus-or-minus 50% range is a suggested reference accuracy, and though it is a somewhat arbitrary figure, it seems reasonable.

4.3. Applications of Contingent Valuation to Health

Scope of the Review

We turn to a critique of studies that use the contingent valuation method to value health symptoms related to air pollution. This section first briefly refers to a number of contingent valuation studies that have served to develop the method and demonstrate its ability to obtain estimates of willingness to pay, but they do not yield values directly comparable to those sought in this study, mainly because of the definition of the good being valued. The section then goes on to consider studies more narrowly focused on health values. The first three studies mainly concern acute symptoms. The original motivation for these studies was to value symptoms linked to air pollution, but the symptoms valued are also of much more general interest. Loehman et al. (1979) used a mail questionnaire of the general public, while Dickie et al. and the new study reported in Part 2 used personal (telephone or household) surveys of the general public. The second set of studies concerns more serious, chronic illness. The earliest is Rowe and Chestnut (1984), which provides estimates of the value of a reduction in asthma symptoms, using personal interviews of a group of individuals suffering asthma. Viscusi, Magat, and Huber (1991) and Krupnick and Cropper (1992) both estimate the value of reductions in the risk of chronic bronchitis. Viscusi, Magat, and Huber use a sample from the general population. Krupnick and Cropper apply the same survey to a sample of people who are presumably more familiar with the "good" sold in the contingent market because they have a relative with chronic lung disease.

At the outset, the limited scope of this section should be explained. In line with the overall purpose of Part 1 of this book, the focus is on empirical estimates of the value of health. As a result, no attempt is made to report and review all of the findings of the studies in question. In particular, for our purposes the values of health are best summarized by simple statistics such as the median and mean values for the sample. Other statistical analyses, including the estimation of bid functions based on the contingent valuation responses, are not reviewed, though they are important parts of these studies. In addition, questions of methodology and survey design are only addressed in the context of evaluating the usefulness and accuracy of the value estimates produced.

Several important studies that use the contingent valuation method to value changes in air quality, including the health effects, are quite comprehensive: in two of them (Brookshire et al. 1979, Loehman, Boldt, and Chaiken 1981) respondents were asked separately about their values for the visibility and health effects of air pollution. The sum of these values may be the most meaningful estimate, and we have not attempted to use the health values because of a concern over the ability of respondents to disentangle the two values. The values of health alone may be overstated, reflecting part of the value of visibility, or understated if part of the value of health is included in the reported value of visibility.

A third study by Schulze et al. (1983) concentrates on health effects of ozone. Respondents were provided with descriptions of the health effects likely to result from air pollution levels and then asked for their values for a change in pollution levels. The descriptions are of the general form: for a given level of pollution, some people (or a certain percentage of people) experience these effects. Respondents might identify the general population risk as their own risk. So if they are told that 50% of people will experience a symptom, they may view this as a 50% chance they will experience the symptom. Another interpretation is that the information provided helps remind the respondents of their experiences with air pollution. In this case, respondents will bid for a change based on their prior subjective probability estimates of experiencing a symptom given varying levels of pollution. Or, they may adjust their prior beliefs on the basis of the information given. In either case, the commodity the respondents are valuing is a change in risks (probabilities of symptoms) that is not strictly observable to the researcher, and for the purposes of this book these changes are not useful in attempting to establish individual health values.

Shechter et al. (1988) and Shechter and Kim (1991) employ a comparative approach to the valuation of health damages caused by air pollution in an urban environment. Both studies use data from the same sample of individuals to derive empirical results by means of different analytic methods. Contingent valuation is employed in these studies to give direct estimates of the health value of environmental improvement. Indirect estimates are obtained by deriving an expenditure function or a household production function in which the demand for housing services or medical services leads to a measure of the benefits of cleaner air. In these and other studies, Shechter and his colleagues introduce stress, anxiety, and personality variables in the theoretical and empirical investigations of the role of psychological factors in the demand for environmental quality (Zeidner and Shechter 1988; Shechter and Zeidner 1990).

The analysis of these studies is highly complementary to the approach of the present volume, although the empirical results are not directly comparable. The reason is that the dependent variable employed by Shechter and his colleagues is air quality rather than health status. The health status variables used as regressors (e.g., asthma, bronchitis) are grouped together, so it is not possible to infer the health value of a specific condition.

The studies reviewed up to this point help establish contingent valuation as a useful approach to valuing health and environmental quality but do not yield estimates of the value of health directly comparable to the approach of this book. We now turn to studies that provide such estimates.

Loehman et al. (1979)

STUDY DESIGN. The study by Loehman et al. (1979) concerns the benefits of controlling sulfur oxides in Florida. A mail contingent valuation survey was sent to 1,977 residents in the Tampa Bay area, resulting in 432 returns. Willingness to pay questions were asked about the following three groups of symptoms: shortness of breath/chest pains; coughing/sneezing; head congestion/eye/ear/throat irritations. Values were elicited for minor and severe symptom days, which were defined briefly. Respondents were asked to value 1 day, 7 days, and 90 days of relief. No mention was made of any specific underlying disease, nor were causes such as air pollution mentioned. No specific delivery vehicle, such as a pill, was employed, and a simple, abstract payment vehicle—"tell us how much you would pay"—was chosen. The means of payment was a checklist, or payment card, ranging from $0 to $1,000 per year in 10 increments.

The Loehman et al. study design is similar to our seven-symptom survey described in Part 2. In both cases a pure health attribute approach was used. The Loehman et al. study carefully avoided the introduction of redundant information in its introductory letter, its symptom narrative, and in its delivery and payment vehicles. One difference between the design of our survey and the Loehman et al. survey is the large number (24) of similar willingness to pay questions of the latter survey. Our approach was to employ fewer questions on any survey instrument in order to avoid taxing the respondents' concentration and the extent of their information and preference review, a problem that might account for the relatively low return rate (22%) encountered by Loehman et al. It also could imply a reduction in the accuracy of their estimates of the value of health.

The major difference between Loehman et al. and the other contingent valuation studies reviewed below is that the Loehman et al. study used a mail questionnaire. The advantage to using this approach is that the lower cost per survey completed allows a larger sample size. There are several disadvantages. An obvious question is whether the respondents are representative of the general population. Loehman et al. test for this and find that the sample seems to be more or less representative, at least in terms of standard demographic characteristics.

Another problem with using a mail survey is that in a contingent valuation experiment there will be some protestors, or people who either refuse to participate in the contingent market or do not understand the nature of the exercise. In a personal interview, follow-up questions and interviewer comments can help identify respondents who are protestors. A mail questionnaire gives no indication of the identity of protestors, except for the bids themselves. Loehman et al. note the presence of bids from respondents who gave values of $1,000 (the highest amount on the payment card). These bids were statistically outlyers, and the respondents exhibited intransitivity of preferences. It seems reasonable that these respondents were protestors. However, it is also possible that these individuals simply had high values for health. The limited information from a mail questionnaire means this problem is difficult to resolve.

A final disadvantage of using a mail questionnaire is that a payment card is often used. Such a card lists the possible amounts people might be willing to pay, and the respondents choose among the different amounts. Designing a card that covers a wide range of low to high values and allows small but important differences between values to be reported is difficult. In addition, some have questioned whether such a card elicits *maximum* willingness to pay responses. Cummings, Brookshire, and Schulze (1986) suggest that, if a payment card is used, it should be followed with iterative bidding, but this is not feasible in the context of a mail questionnaire. These problems indicate that the values from the Loehman et al. study may be inaccurate, and in particular they may be underestimates of the maximum willingness to pay for health.

RESULTS. Table 4.1 lists the median and mean bids found by Loehman et al. All bids are expressed in terms of 1984 dollars, to insure comparability

TABLE 4.1. Contingent Values of Health from
Loehman et al. (1979) (in $)

Symptom	Median Bid	Mean Bid
1 day of:		
Shortness of breath/chest pains:		
Mild	8	78
Severe	18	127
Coughing/sneezing:		
Mild	4	42
Severe	11	73
Head congestion, eye, ear, throat irritation:		
Mild	6	52
Severe	13	85
7 days of:		
Shortness of breath/chest pains:		
Mild	22	118
Severe	57	218
Coughing/sneezing:		
Mild	13	71
Severe	32	116
Head congestion, eye, ear, throat irritation:		
Mild	15	66
Severe	33	129
90 days of:		
Shortness of breath/chest pains:		
Mild	56	233
Severe	156	403
Coughing/sneezing:		
Mild	37	138
Severe	81	236
Head congestion, eye, ear, throat irritation:		
Mild	40	145
Severe	99	288

with other estimates of the value of health discussed in this book. The bids were adjusted using the consumer price index and were rounded to the nearest dollar.

The bids cover a fairly wide range. For one day of relief, the lowest median bid is $4 for mild coughing/sneezing, and the highest median bid is $18 for severe shortness of breath/chest pains. However, the mean bids for 1 day of symptoms are often an order of magnitude larger, ranging from $42 for mild coughing/sneezing to $127 for severe shortness of breath/chest pains. There is generally a smaller difference between median and mean bids for 7 days of relief and 90 days of relief.

The large difference between median and mean bids results from properties of the distribution of bids. As Loehman et al. describe it, the distribution is clearly not normal but includes a large number of relatively low bids, with a few bids in the upper tail of the distribution. These bids were for $1,000, the highest bid possible, and represent the possible protestors discussed above. The mean bids are much more sensitive to these outlyers than are the medians, and so the means are much larger than the medians.

In their analysis, Loehman et al. use only the median bids. One justification for this use is normative. They argue that the median is "indicative of majority voting since it indicates the bid which at least 50 percent of the population would agree to pay" (Loehman et al. 1979, p. 232). Though this majority voting criterion is certainly reasonable, it represents an alternative to the standard methodology of applied welfare economics, where programs are evaluated using the criterion of a potential Pareto improvement. Using this criterion, all individuals' values are given equal weight, including the very high values. It is possible that a program that represents a potential Pareto improvement would not be favored by over 50% of the population. Potentially, though, payments by gainers could compensate the losers by enough that all would favor (or at worst be indifferent to) the program. If this standard of applied welfare economics is accepted, the correct summary statistic is the mean, which puts equal weights on all, and not the median.

Loehman et al. also justify their use of median bids by noting that the median is less likely to be biased due to the outliers. V. K. Smith (personal communication 1987) explains how this problem could justify use of median bids even if the potential Pareto improvement criterion is accepted as relevant. If a distribution of individuals' true values of health in a population is known, the mean value is the correct summary statistic as explained above. Applying this reasoning to a distribution of values resulting from a contingent valuation experiment is not necessarily correct. To do so requires the assumption that all contingent valuation responses are judged as equally good estimates of each individual's willingness to pay. Arguments that have been made in the contingent valuation literature for the use of the median implicitly assume that not all responses to contingent valuation questions are equally good estimates of each individual's willingness to pay. In particular, there is a presumption that very large or very small responses are more likely to have large errors associated with them. Since the mean value is more affected than the median, the mean would be a less robust estimate of the "average person's" willingness to pay. In this case, if outliers are a problem, the median bid may be preferred.

Accepting the criterion of a potential Pareto improvement as the relevant welfare guideline, the choice of using median or mean values from a contingent valuation study depends upon the informational content assumed for different responses. Reporting median bids avoids overstating values due to the effect of very high bids, which may be inaccurate in the sense that they are not a true reflection of willingness to pay. At the same time, legitimately high bids are also given little weight. In addition, though the very high bids may be inaccurate, they probably do indicate that these individuals are actually willing to pay an amount higher than average. Finally, the argument is symmetric with respect to low bids. While very low bids probably do indicate that these individuals have lower than average willingness to pay values, the true values may not be as low as the values reported in the contingent valuation experiment.

To rigorously account for all of the considerations discussed above requires a model of how people respond to contingent valuation questions. In chapter 15 there are the beginnings of such a model, but it does not allow any definite conclusions to be made regarding the mean versus median question. In practice, both mean and median values are important pieces of evidence. Inferences of the informational content of very high and very low bids can be drawn from careful consideration of the study design and the distribution of bids found. For the Loehman et al. results, the problems inherent in a mail survey and the distribution of bids suggest that the high bids are not accurate reflections of willingness to pay. Thus the median may be a more robust summary statistic.

It is interesting to note the relationships between the bids for 1 day, 7 days, and 90 days of relief found by Loehman et al. Using mild coughing/ sneezing as an example, the bid for 1 day is $4, while the bid for 7 days is $13, roughly three times as large. The bid for 90 days is $37, about nine times as large as the bid for 1 day. Roughly similar results are found for other median bids. For mean bids the ratios are even smaller; the bid for 7 days of relief from mild coughing/sneezing ($71) is less than twice the bid for 1 day ($42), and the bid for 90 days ($138) is only about three times the 1 day bid.

Two explanations for these relationships are possible. The marginal disutility from sickness (symptoms) could be diminishing rapidly, so that extra days of symptoms do not matter much and the individual is willing to pay increasingly less for relief from the symptoms. This does not seem plausible, especially since decreasing marginal disutility from sickness implies increasing marginal utility from health, which is not consistent with the assumptions of economic theory. A second possibility is that the respondents had trouble valuing large changes in health because these changes were outside of their experiences. That bids for unfamiliar commodities may be inaccurate has been suggested by users of the contingent valuation method (see Cummings, Brookshire, and Schulze 1986). This explanation seems to be more powerful in explaining why bids for 90 days of relief (an unfamiliar commodity to most people) are so small compared to the bids for 1 day of relief (a more familiar commodity within the range of most people's experiences). It is less powerful in explaining the ratio of bids for 1 day and 7 days of relief since both are probably familiar experiences to most people.

Dickie, et al. (1987)

STUDY DESIGN. Dickie et al. (1987) conducted a telephone survey of 221 residents of Glendora and Burbank, California. The most important contingent valuation results are for nine symptoms related to ozone pollution: sinus pain, cough, throat irritation, tight chest, could not breathe deep, pain on deep breath, out of breath easily, wheezing/whistling breath, and headache. The careful survey design clearly encouraged and guided respondents to think carefully about the health symptoms to be valued. Following a set of questions on standard socioeconomic measures, respondents were asked about their experience with a list of symptoms. Focusing on their most bothersome symptoms, respondents were asked about the frequency, duration, and severity of symptoms, as well as averting actions taken in response to the symptoms.

The next step was to determine their willingness to pay for 1 day of relief. Respondents were asked to value up to three symptoms. Only respondents who experienced a symptom were asked to value it. One hundred sixty-five respondents reported having had at least one symptom and so answered one or more contingent valuation questions. Respondents who had experienced more than three of the symptoms were asked about the three most bothersome. The number of respondents providing willingness to pay bids for the nine ozone symptoms varied from 11 for wheezing/whistling breath to 61 for headache.

Dickie et al. consider in detail the reliability of the contingent valuation method, and this is reflected in both the survey design and in the analysis of the results. As part of the survey, respondents were given an opportunity to revise their bids, after being presented information about their implied total monthly bid for avoiding symptoms. There was particular concern about unrealistically high bids. Dickie et al. note that half of the symptoms distributions include at least one value of $5,000 or more to eliminate 1 day of symptoms. In two cases the implied monthly bids initially totaled $899,910, which exceeded not only the respondents' monthly incomes but even their annual incomes by substantial margins. Given the opportunity to revise their bids, the highest monthly total was in the range $501–$600.

While there is an obvious concern about the reliability of the initial bids, Cropper and Freeman (1991, p. 203) point out that the procedure used by Dickie et al. is also problematic. If average willingness to pay is less than marginal willingness to pay, the total monthly bid as calculated in the Dickie et al. survey exceeds total willingness to pay. Presenting information about the total monthly bid to the respondents may then be misleading and may cause the revised bids to be too low (i.e., to be below true willingness to pay).

RESULTS. Table 4.2 presents the main results of the Dickie et al. contingent valuation survey. The authors' attention to reliability issues is again reflected in the detailed presentation of results. The first part of Table 4.2 presents the median and mean initial bids, and the median and mean bids after respondents were given the chance to revise their bidding. The second part of Table 4.2 presents mean bids after the responses were subject to trimming and consistency checks, as described below. The range of values reported in Table 4.2 is extremely wide, making it imperative to develop some judgments as to which values are the most reliable.

As in other contingent valuation studies, a small number of bids in the upper tail of the distribution of bids have a pronounced influence of the sample means reported in Table 4.2. To explore this problem further, Dickie et al. subject the contingent valuation bids to trimming and consistency checks. In trimming, either 5% or 10% of bids from each tail of the distribution are arbitrarily eliminated. In the consistency checks, bids were excluded for a number of different reasons. First, bids were excluded if the implied total monthly bid to eliminate a symptom exceeded monthly household income. Additional checks excluded bids if the bid for symptom relief was inconsistent with other information provided in the survey. An example of an inconsistency is if the respondent bid a large amount (defined as over $100) for a symptom that he or she judged to be of low severity and was a symptom for which he or she took no averting action. Zero bids were similarly excluded if other information suggested the symptom was important to the respondent.

All three methods used to improve reliability—allowing respondents to revise bids, trimming the samples, and subjecting the bids to consistency checks—result in substantially lower means, as extremely high bids are removed from the sample. Using the initial bids, the mean value placed on a

TABLE 4.2.   Contingent Values of Health from Dickie et al. (1987) (in $)

A. Initial and Revised Values

	Initial Value		Revised Value	
Symptom	Median	Mean	Median	Mean
Sinus pain or discomfort	3.50	239.50	1.00	4.53
Cough	1.00	355.10	.00	1.61
Throat irritation	3.00	15.00	1.00	3.74
Chest tightness	5.00	813.72	.80	3.55
Could not breathe deep	1.00	1,139.58	.00	2.78
Pain on deep breath	3.50	954.13	.00	4.67
Out of breath easily	.00	7.88	.00	1.94
Wheezing/whistling breath	2.00	54.36	.00	2.53
Headache	1.00	178.39	1.00	3.24

B. Trimming and Consistency Checks

	Trimmed Means (in $)		Consistency Check
Symptom	5%	10%	Means (in $)
Sinus pain or discomfort	10.98	9.42	13.15
Cough	9.96	8.65	11.46
Throat irritation	12.08	7.00	16.60
Chest tightness	449.74	18.11	19.60
Could not breathe deep	567.74	213.20	14.74
Pain on deep breath	376.21	22.25	26.70
Out of breath easily	5.43	2.16	6.91
Wheezing/whistling breath	15.78	15.78	11.50
Headache	12.42	8.33	18.80

day of relief is often above $100 and, in one case, is above $1,000. While there are still a few cases of means in excess of $100, after trimming most of the means are below $20. The highest mean value placed on a day of relief in the sample subjected to consistency checks is $26.70. The highest mean value in the sample of revised bids is $4.67.

The results just reviewed document the influence a few high bids have on the sample means for the value of symptoms. The substantial differences between medians and means also stem from this feature of the distribution of bids. The question as to whether the high bids are reliable indicators of individual willingness to pay is harder to resolve. The trimming procedure is obviously arbitrary, although Dickie et al. begin to develop a model of symptom value formation that could justify some procedure along these lines. The problem noted by Cropper and Freeman (1991) applies to both the consistency checks and the bid revision process. A person could legitimately report a high marginal value on a day of relief but be unwilling or unable to pay 30 times that for a month of relief. Both of the other contingent valuation surveys of light symptoms reviewed in this section provide some evidence in support of this conjecture, although it is not clear why this relationship between marginal and average valuations should exist.

It should also be noted that the sample includes a number of unrealistically low values. Dickie et al. report that, for six of the nine symptoms, the modal bid for relief was zero. In the sample of revised bids, in five cases the median bid was zero, implying that half of the sample bid zero for relief. If respondents fully understand the nature of the contingent valuation survey, zero bids literally mean these respondents place no value on symptom relief. Any evidence that the symptoms caused discomfort or averting actions suggest a nonzero value. More realistically, zero bids are probably best interpreted as representing very low values that respondents have approximated as zero. Since replacing zeros with very low bids would not dramatically change the means reported, this problem is of less practical importance.

Given the problems noted, it is probably inappropriate to look for very precise estimates of the value of symptom relief from the Dickie et al. results reported in Table 4.2. The trimmed samples, the samples subjected to consistency checks, and the revised bids provide useful evidence on the lower bound to placed on the value of symptom relief: in the range from $2.00 to $5.00 a day. However, each of the methods used to improve reliability also systematically removed high bids from the sample. While the actual bids reported may be unrealistically high, the respondents making these bids probably placed a higher than average value on symptom relief. The procedures used by Dickie et al. therefore tend to create a downward bias in the estimates of the average value of symptom relief.

Original Contingent Valuation Study

STUDY DESIGN. Part 2 of this book contains a detailed description of the design of our original contingent valuation experiment and the considerations involved in this design. The experiment consists of four surveys valuing (1) 1 day of relief from seven light symptoms, such as coughing, and so on, (2) 30 days of relief from these same seven symptoms, (3) relief from mild and severe angina (chest pain) given that the respondent already suffered from 10 days of this symptom, and (4) relief from mild and severe angina given that the respondent already suffered from 20 days of this symptom. Separate surveys were used to keep the length of the survey at a level where reasoned responses could be reached, but respondents' patience and concentration were not overtaxed. A total of 199 interviews were completed, roughly equally divided among the four types of surveys. The surveys were personal interviews of a randomly selected sample from Chicago and Denver.

Of the total of 199 completed surveys, 23 surveys were removed from the sample. Several criteria were used to determine which responses to remove. First, protestors who refused to give any bids were removed from the sample. Protestors are distinguished from those who wished to bid zero. Zero bidders were left in the sample on the grounds that the bids were felt to be legitimate. A second group excluded from the sample were those respondents who indicated that they would pay any amount for the improvement in health or exorbitantly high amounts (two or three times their yearly income). The last group of respondents removed from the sample were random bidders whose bids bore no logical relationship to each other. Interviewer comments were used in all cases to help identify individuals unwilling or unable to participate in the contingent market.

A great deal of care was taken in the creation of the contingent market. The contingent commodities were described to the respondents, and the structure of the survey encouraged respondents to think about the commodities before bidding began. A form of iterative bidding was used. Abstract payment vehicles and delivery vehicles were chosen to avoid protests and to avoid distracting respondents from giving reasoned values. Finally, interviewer comments and analysis of the bids were used to identify protestors.

For the two surveys concerning the seven light symptoms, the structure of the survey instrument first helps the respondent to recall his own experience with these common symptoms and then establishes a standardized hypothetical product (relief from symptoms) to be valued. As a result, the respondent should be familiar with the commodity of the contingent market, an important prerequisite to obtaining accurate value estimates.

The procedure described above could not be exactly followed for the two surveys concerning angina since most respondents had little or no experience with this symptom. Standard questions on health status help the respondent to begin to think about his or her health and its importance. The contingent valuation section begins with a general two-paragraph introduction that asks the respondent to imagine having mild or severe angina and includes a brief statement about the extent of angina in the United States. The actual contingent valuation includes a description by the interviewer of the specific symptoms to be valued, and a card summarizing of this description is then handed to the respondent. This approach to survey structure was used to minimize the problems associated with respondents being unfamiliar with angina. While the value estimates resulting may not be as accurate as for the more familiar seven symptoms, it is felt that most respondents did give reasoned bids.

RESULTS. Table 4.3 presents the values for symptoms from the four surveys. Part A. of Table 4.3 presents median and mean bids for relief from 1 additional day of seven individual light symptoms and two combinations of symptoms. Part B. of Table 4.3 presents the same statistics for relief from 30 additional days of the same individual and combined symptoms. Parts C. and D. of Table 4.3 present bids for relief from angina. The number of additional days of angina, the severity of the angina, and the endowment that respondents were asked to assume described their situation are varied to provide a range of values.

The median bids for relief from 1 additional day of the seven light symptoms range from $11 for relief from a day of coughing to $20 for headaches. Mean bids are roughly two to three times larger, ranging from $25.20 for a coughing day to $50.28 for relief from a day of nausea. Relief from combinations of three symptoms is more highly valued than relief from one symptom alone but is not the simple sum of the values of the individual symptoms. For instance, a day of cough, throat, and sinus symptoms combined is valued at $65.60 The sum of the bids for relief from these symptoms individually is $89.22.

The difference between the median bids and the mean bids is substantially less than that found for the Loehman et al. (1979) results. As described above, the excessively large bids resulting from respondents who explicitly or implicitly protested the contingent market were removed from our sample. This shows one advantage of the personal interview structure compared to mail surveys: interviewer comments can help identify protestors. Since all responses were subject to the editing process, and the distribution of bids shows the smaller impact of the largest bids, the mean seems to be the most robust summary statistic for this sample. In other words, the assumption seems justified that all responses, even the very large and very small bids, have roughly equivalent informational content.

For relief from 30 days of the seven light symptoms, the median bids range from $95 for 30 days of coughing to $135 for 30 days of sinus problems. Again, mean bids are usually about two or three times larger than the medians, ranging from $166.50 for 30 days of coughing to $488.20 for 30 days of headaches. The same relationship between the bids for combinations of symptoms and the sum of the bids for relief from the individual symptoms is found as in the 1-day survey. A combination of three symptoms is valued more than any one symptom alone, but not as much as the sum of the bids for the three individual symptoms.

Just as in the Loehman et al. (1979) results, a somewhat surprising relationship is found between the bids for different days of relief. The mean bids for 30 days of relief from the light symptoms are not 30 times larger than the mean bids for 1 day of relief. The 30-day bids are closer to 10 times the size of the 1-day bids. Though these bids result from two different

TABLE 4.3.   Contingent Values of Health from Original Study (in $)

A. Survey 1

1 Additional Day of Symptom	Median Bid	Mean Bid
Coughing	11	25.20
Sinus congestion	14	35.05
Throat irritation	13	28.97
Eye irritation	12.50	27.73
Drowsiness	15	31.49
Headaches	20	40.10
Nausea	17.50	50.28
Cough, throat, and sinus congestion	30.50	65.60
Drowsiness, headaches and nausea	25	95.08

B. Survey 2

30 Additional Days of Symptom	Median Bid	Mean Bid
Coughing	95	166.50
Sinus congestion	135	265.62
Throat irritation	100	206.26
Eye irritation	100	235.53
Drowsiness	100	317.98
Headaches	132.50	488.20
Nausea	100	186.02
Cough, throat, and sinus congestion	200	624.98
Drowsiness, headaches and nausea	300	868.89

C. Survey 3

Relief from Angina, Given Days of Endowment of Angina	Median Bid	Mean Bid
1 mild day:		
Given 1 mild day	53	66.08
Given 10 mild days	50	83.95
1 severe day:		
Given 1 severe day	100	123.59
Given 10 severe days	100	144.74
5 mild days:		
Given 10 mild days	55	96.18
5 severe days:		
Given 10 severe days	150	192.90
10 mild days:		
Given 10 mild days	100	154.36
10 severe days:		
Given 10 severe days	200	261.84

TABLE 4.3. (*continued*)

D. Survey 4		
Relief from Angina, Given Days of Endowment of Angina	Median Bid	Mean Bid
1 mild day:		
Given 1 mild day	53	90.24
Given 20 mild days	40	99.05
1 severe day:		
Given 1 severe day	75	278.88
Given 20 severe days	60	208.78
10 mild days:		
Given 20 mild days	100	287.63
10 severe days:		
Given 20 severe days	125	506.25
20 mild days:		
Given 20 mild days	100	486.25
20 severe days:		
Given 20 severe days	200	844.38

samples of individuals, in terms of observable characteristics, the samples seemed similar. Another possible explanation is that the results reflect diminishing marginal disutility from sickness, but this explanation implies increasing marginal utility from health, which seems implausible. In addition, other results from these surveys support the more standard relationship of increasing marginal disutility from sickness. Finally, it could be argued that 30 days of sickness are a more unfamiliar commodity to most individuals, so they are undervaluing it. This possibility points to the continued need for a formal model of how respondents react to contingent valuation questions since it is not obvious why bids for an unfamiliar commodity would be systematically biased downward.

The third survey concerns the value of relief from angina (chest pain), given an endowment of up to 10 days of severe angina. Median bids range from $50 for relief from 1 mild day given an endowment of 10 mild days, to $200 for relief from 10 severe days given an endowment of 10 severe days. The mean bids are fairly close to the median bids, ranging from $66.08 for relief from 1 mild day given an endowment of 1 mild day to $261.84 for 10 severe days given an endowment of 10 severe days. For comparable endowments, median and mean bids for mild days are always less than bids for severe days, as would be expected. Comparing across endowments, it is generally true that relief from a given number of days of angina is valued more highly as the endowment increases. This is consistent with increasing marginal disutility of illness and is the expected relationship.

The fourth survey also concerns angina, but the endowment ranges up to 20 days of mild and severe angina. Median bids range from $40 for relief from 1 mild day given an endowment of 20 mild days to $200 for relief from 20 severe days given an endowment of 20 severe days. Mean bids show a larger difference between the value of 1 day and 20 days of angina. The mean bid for relief from 1 mild day given an endowment of 1 mild day is $90.24, while the mean bid for 20 severe days given an endowment of 20 severe days is $844.38. Again, as expected, relief from severe days of angina are valued more highly than relief from mild days. However, comparing bids across endowments, the results do not always support that increasing the endowment increases the bid for a given number of days of relief. For example, the mean bid for relief from 1 severe day given an endowment of 1 severe day is $278.88, while the mean bid for relief from 1 severe day given an endowment of 20 severe days is only 208.78 This difference may not be highly significant. Closer examination of the bids reveals that some respondents bid a large amount to be completely free of angina while placing a small value on a day at the margin given a large endowment. Though this behavior is not consistent with increasing marginal disutility of illness, it is not necessarily irrational. Whether individuals with actual experience of angina would bid in this way is an interesting and open question.

It is possible to compare the results of the two surveys on angina in a few cases where identical commodities were valued by the different samples of individuals. The mean bid for relief from 1 mild day given an endowment of 1 mild day is $66.08 for survey 3 and somewhat larger for survey 4 at $90.24. A larger difference is found for the only other case in which the surveys are directly comparable. In survey 3, the mean bid for relief from 1 severe day given an endowment of 1 severe day is $123.59, while in survey 4 the mean bid is $278.88. This larger mean bid in survey 4 reflects the influence of a few very high bidders who bid a large amount to be completely free of angina. In fact, the median bid from survey 4 for relief from 1 severe day of angina given an endowment of 1 severe day ($75) is less than the median bid from survey 3 ($100). These results show the effect a few bids can have on the summary statistics and suggest that the values reported for relief from angina may not be highly accurate.

Rowe and Chestnut (1984)

STUDY DESIGN. The study by Rowe and Chestnut (1984) provides estimates of the value of a reduction in asthma days for people with asthma. The economic research supplemented research under way at the University of California, Los Angeles, School of Medicine concerning the effects of air pollution on asthmatics. The UCLA project included over 90 subjects from Glendora, California (in 1983); the general questionnaire that included the contingent valuation questions was completed by 64 adults and 18 parents of children under 16 years of age. Of this total sample of 82, there was only one refusal. After evaluation of the bids, including checking for protestors and other respondents whose bids were judged to be inaccurate on the bias of consistency checks, 65 bids were retained. The fact that asthmatics were sampled instead of the general population is arguably a strength, not a weakness, since people with asthma are a group likely to be affected by pollution who may value the change differently than the general population. Unfortunately, the sample was not chosen so as to be representative of asthmatics in general.

Contingent valuation bids were obtained by asking the respondents, "If federal, state, or local governments set up programs that could reduce pollens, dusts, air pollutants, and other factors throughout this area that might reduce your (and your household's) bad asthma days by half, but would cost you increased tax dollars, what would be the *maximum increase* in taxes each year that you and your household would be willing to pay and still support such a program?" A number of aspects of this contingent market deserve comment. First, the good or commodity being bid on is a reduction by half of the respondent's and his household's bad asthma days. Given the respondent's experience with asthma and the earlier questions in the questionnaire, it seems reasonable that the respondents understood the commodity and by this point in the experiment had prior valuation and choice experience with respect to consumption levels of it. The major drawback of this definition of the commodity is that it is different for each respondent. What constitutes a "bad asthma day" is subjective, and since the number of bad days varies across respondents, so does the number of bad days removed implied by the 50% reduction.

Second, it was made clear that the reduction in asthma days would be the result of a governmental program and paid for by an increase in taxes. That is, relatively concrete vehicles for the delivery of and payment for the good are used. Though this makes the contingent market more realistic, the added realism is purchased at the cost of increasing the possibility of problems such as strategic bias or protestors (either at the idea of increased taxes or the impossibility of such a program). In addition, experience in focus groups in Chicago showed that mentioning the environment as a cause of health condition seemed to distract the respondents from providing reasoned bids. This problem may not have existed for the asthma patients, however, since other results of the project showed that they had a good understanding and accurate perceptions of the effects of pollution on their conditions.

Third, an element of uncertainty is introduced into the market since it is stated that the program improving air quality "might" reduce bad days by half. This wording raises difficulties in interpreting the bids. Is one respondent bidding a small amount because the reduction in asthma days is not worth much to him or because his subjective probability that the program will work is relatively low? The extensive analysis of the bids supports the former interpretation, but the issue can not be entirely resolved.

Two more general problems of the structure of the contingent market should be mentioned. First, there is the problem of the bidding format. The Rowe and Chestnut study used a payment card format. It was designed to eliminate some of the problems associated with this format; they note that problems may remain.

The second problem is the treatment of protest bids and extreme values (either zero bids or very large bids). The ideal is to retain all bids that reflect the true value, no matter how extreme, and to remove bids that do not. To be a useful bid, the respondent must be willing to participate in the contingent market and fully understand the nature of the exercise. Rowe and Chestnut carefully examine the zero bids and subject bids to a consistency check. This process necessarily involves some rather ad hoc procedures and is to a certain extent subjective. It would be interesting to know how sensitive the bid results are to the editing process. As mentioned earlier, this process results in 17 of 82 bids being rejected, or roughly 20%.

RESULTS. The results of the Rowe and Chestnut study relevant for this review can be very easily summarized. They found a mean bid for a 50% reduction in bad asthma days (for 65 observations) of $401 per year, with a standard deviation of $85. This is for an average number of bad days reduced equal to 19. Thus, on average a bad asthma day is worth about $21. Of course, this average value cannot in general be used to value a marginal change of 1 bad asthma day.

Viscusi, Magat, and Huber (1991)

STUDY DESIGN. Viscusi, Magat, and Huber (1991) extend contingent valuation methodology to measure willingness to pay for reductions in the risk of developing chronic bronchitis. Chronic bronchitis risk reduction differs substantially from the health improvements considered by the other contingent valuation studies reviewed in this chapter. It is a lifelong illness with much more serious respiratory symptoms than those considered by the light symptom contingent valuation studies (Loehman et al. 1979; Dickie et al. 1987; and the original contingent valuation study in Pt. 2). Since Viscusi, Magat, and Huber focus on the most severe form of chronic bronchitis, it is also a much more serious condition than the chronic asthma in Rowe and Chestnut (1984). In addition, where Rowe and Chestnut use a sample of asthmatics who were quite familiar with the symptoms to be valued, Viscusi, Magat, and Huber use a sample of healthy individuals. Finally, they measure the value of a reduction in the risk of chronic bronchitis rather than the certain changes considered in the other studies. In light of these differences, Viscusi, Magat, and Huber make a number of innovative changes in the design of the contingent valuation survey.

A central problem faced by Viscusi, Magat, and Huber is the difficulty of communicating chronic disease effects to potential sufferers. To address this problem, the contingent valuation questionnaire is administered via an interactive personal-computer program. The program includes several tests to determine whether the respondent understands the valuation task being asked of him or her. If the respondent fails the tests, the program provides additional information before proceeding with the questionnaire. Responses were also subject to a set of consistency checks, and subjects were excluded from the sample if their responses could not be used or indicated that they did not fully understand the valuation task. Viscusi, Magat, and Huber discuss in detail the consistency checks and the number of subjects who failed the various tests. This discussion should be very useful to future contingent valuation studies facing similar problems.

Viscusi, Magat, and Huber employ another innovative design feature: their approach measures the rates at which people are willing to trade off chronic bronchitis risk reduction in terms of the risk of an automobile fatality (risk-risk trade-off) as well as in dollars (risk-dollar trade-off). The approach is partly motivated by the suspicion that consumers may be more willing and able to specify the rates of trade-off of one risk with another. Viscusi, Magat, and Huber note that, when faced with risk-dollar trade-offs, some subjects cannot envision that they would voluntarily subject themselves to higher risks for a finite amount of money. The risk-risk form of the morbidity valuations can be converted into dollar values by placing dollar values on the fatality risks as in the empirical literature on the value of a statistical life.

The study uses a sample of 389 shoppers from a blue-collar mall in Greensboro, North Carolina. Three series of valuation questions were asked. The first series yielded the risk-risk trade-off, specifically, the rate of trade-off between chronic bronchitis risk reductions and increases in the risk of an automobile fatality. The second series yielded the risk-dollar trade-off. The third series yields a dollar measure of the value of reducing the risks of an automobile fatality. Using this measure, the risk-risk form of the valuation can be converted and compared to the risk-dollar responses.

RESULTS. Viscusi, Magat, and Huber develop a range of estimates of the dollar value of reducing the risk of chronic bronchitis. As is often done when valuing mortality risks, the results can be expressed as the dollar value of a statistical case of chronic bronchitis. This form is a convenient way to convey results about the dollar value of small changes in risk, but care must be taken when interpreting the results. Valuing a statistical case of chronic bronchitis at, for example, $883,000 does not mean that an individual is willing to pay that sum to avoid a case of chronic bronchitis with certainty. Instead a large number of individuals are each willing to pay a much smaller amount to reduce the risk of chronic bronchitis. Summing over the individuals, they are willing to pay $883,000 for a risk reduction that in a statistical sense is expected to result in one less case of chronic bronchitis.

From the risk-dollar trade-off questions, the mean value of a statistical case of chronic bronchitis is $883,000, with an associated standard error of $114,000. As is the case in the other contingent valuation studies reviewed in this chapter, the distribution of responses is skewed so that the mean is substantially larger than the corresponding median value of $457,000.

Viscusi, Magat, and Huber also convert the risk-risk results into dollar values, using several different estimates of the value of a statistical life. If a statistical life is valued at $2 million, using the mean of the risk-risk results implies that a statistical case of chronic bronchitis is worth $1,360,000. Using the median of the risk-risk results, a statistical case of chronic bronchitis is worth $640,000. If the value of a statistical life is higher than $2 million, the implied value of a statistical life is higher than $2 million, the implied value of a statistical case of chronic bronchitis increases accordingly. If the value of a statistical life is $5 million, the implied values for a statistical case of chronic bronchitis are $3,400,000 (mean) and $1,600,000 (median).

Krupnick and Cropper (1992)

STUDY DESIGN. Krupnick and Cropper (1992) study whether people's familiarity with chronic lung disease affects their willingness to pay for risk reductions. They accomplish this by administering the survey designed by Viscusi, Magat, and Huber to a sample of people who have a relative with chronic lung disease. The sample of 189 subjects responded to newspaper ads in the Washington, D.C., area. Each subject had a relative with chronic lung disease but did not have a chronic respiratory condition himself or herself.

The design and use of the computer-interactive survey was identical to Viscusi, Magat, and Huber, with two exceptions. First, a set of questions was appended to the end of the survey, asking about the respondent's familiarity with his or her relative's disease and about the severity of that disease. Second, Krupnick and Cropper randomly assigned the respondents to two versions of the survey instrument. The second version was modified to elicit valuations of "a case of chronic respiratory disease like your relative's." In the first version, a case of chronic bronchitis was described as in the Viscusi, Magat, and Huber survey.

RESULTS. As in Viscusi, Magat, and Huber, the value of a statistical case of chronic bronchitis can be estimated directly based on responses to the risk-dollar trade-offs and inferred based on responses to the risk-risk trade-offs. From responses to the first version of the survey, based on the risk-dollar trade-offs the mean value of a statistical case of bronchitis is $2.08 million. The mean of the responses to the second version of the survey is $1.84 million. Based on a $2 million value of a statistical life, the mean risk-risk trade-off results imply values of a statistical case of bronchitis of $1.34 million from the first survey version and $1.76 million for the second version.

Krupnick and Cropper also analyze the results to determine if the respondents' familiarity with the disease significantly affected the reported valuations. They do this by comparing their results to those of Viscusi, Magat, and Huber. To control for differences in sample characteristics, they estimate regression models that predict responses to the trade-offs as functions of respondent characteristics. Krupnick and Cropper test the hypothesis that the predicted mean of responses from the estimated models are the same across samples, conditional on respondent characteristics. They find that for the risk-dollar trade-offs, the respondents more familiar with chronic lung conditions reveal a statistically significantly higher mean willingness to pay to reduce the risk of chronic bronchitis. No statistically significant difference is found for the risk-risk trade-offs. Based on these results and additional analysis, they suggest that the answers to risk-risk trade-offs are more stable than answers to risk-dollar trades.

4.4. Comparing Cost of Illness and Contingent Valuation

Introduction

The cost of illness (COI) approach and contingent valuation (CV) are two important methods that allow a dollar value to be placed on a change in morbidity or sickness. A direct comparison of values based on these methods is undertaken in this section. This comparison is especially interesting because the methods are in some sense complementary. The cost of illness approach, focusing on medical expenditures and forgone earnings, uses widely available data and straightforward empirical techniques, so it is generally accepted on a practical level by many health professionals. However, there is no strong theoretical basis for using COI values in benefit cost analysis. That is, there are serious questions whether a COI value associated with a given change in morbidity will be close to what an individual would be willing to pay for that change. In contrast, contingent valuation experiments can be designed to directly estimate what an individual would be willing to pay for a certain change in morbidity. So CV values are estimates of the conceptually correct benefit measures for benefit cost analysis under certainty. Unfortunately, the proper design of CV experiments is difficult and still controversial, and some economists tend to be skeptical of the actual values given by individuals in a CV experiment. On a practical level, COI values are often judged superior to CV values, while on a theoretical or conceptual level, CV values are preferred.

Due to the perceived practical advantages of the cost of illness approach, recent theoretical work has investigated the relationship between COI values and an individual's true willingness to pay (WTP) for changes in morbidity. Harrington and Portney's (1987) theoretical analysis supports the conclusion that a COI value is a lower bound to the true WTP, for the certainty case. The more general model presented in Chapter 2 also implies that under plausible conditions, COI < WTP under certainty; the model also allows the analysis to be extended to the case of uncertainty.

Contingent valuation studies of the value of morbidity have considered changes in health status that occur with certainty. This seems justified since the costs of adding uncertainty seem large in light of the problems encountered in surveys that deal with concepts of uncertainty and the benefits of adding uncertainty in the context of nonserious morbidity may be small. In this section, only the relationship between willingness to pay and cost of illness for certain changes can be directly addressed.

The empirical evidence presented in this section is used to test the hypothesis that the cost of illness values are lower bounds to the true willingness to pay values. Values reported in CV experiments are used to represent the true WTP values for a change from being certainly sick to being certainly well. On the assumption that the CV values are reasonable proxies for the true WTP, the empirical results support the hypothesis that COI < WTP. Alternatively, the fact that this reasonable relationship holds between COI- and CV-reported WTP can be seen as additional evidence on the usefulness and reliability of contingent valuation methods.

Next, previous work comparing cost of illness and contingent valuation is reviewed. The results of a new contingent valuation experiment are presented to test the hypothesized relationship. The analysis is extended to a preliminary discussion of the relationship of COI and WTP values under certainty, and the amount an individual would be willing to pay for a change in health risks. No direct evidence is available on willingness to pay for morbidity risks, but the analysis suggests an approximation from the evidence on certainty values is possible.

Previous Work Comparing COI and CV

Two contingent valuation studies on the value of morbidity contain some evidence on the relationship between cost of illness values and CV values. The first study, reported in Loehman et al. (1979), estimated median willingness to pay bids for reductions in air pollution–related symptoms. They note that the bids "are probably low compared to out-of-pocket costs of illness" (p. 233). As an example, the income loss per day for a person with an average income would be $65, while the highest median reported for 1 day of relief from severe symptoms (shortness of breath) is $10.92. Including the value of medical expenditures would cause COI to exceed the CV bid by a larger amount. The difference may be in part due to paid sick leave and medical insurance causing out-of-pocket expenses to be low. Another problem is the use of median CV bids. In order to avoid overstating WTP because of the influence of a few very large bids on the means, they instead used the much smaller medians. This might have resulted in an understatement of WTP, however, which might explain why the CV bids are small relative to reasonable COI values. At least, the median CV bids should be compared to median COI values. In any case, Loehman et al. do not collect the data that would allow a direct comparison of individuals' CV bids and their experienced or expected costs of illness. Thus, their results seem to be only a weak indication that WTP is less than COI; that is, this is weak evidence against the hypothesis that COI is a lower bound to WTP.

A second CV study, by Rowe and Chestnut (1984) on the value of asthma, is more suitable to a direct comparison of CV bids representing WTP and the cost of illness. The first body of evidence on WTP compared to COI is the respondents' rankings of the importance of the benefits they might receive from reduced asthma. Based on statistical analysis of the rankings, Rowe and Chestnut conclude that discomfort and effects on leisure and recreation activities, which are part of WTP but not part of COI, clearly ranked above medical costs and work lost, which are the only components of WTP that a COI value includes. So according to these rankings, COI estimates do not include the most important benefits of reduced morbidity. This indicates that WTP should therefore exceed COI.

The second body of evidence from the Rowe and Chestnut study is a comparison of the total WTP bid and a constructed COI value. This method reported yields a ratio of WTP/COI of 1.6, supporting the hypothesis that WTP is greater than COI. Other approaches to measuring this ratio examined in their larger study suggest a ratio as high as 3.7.

Unfortunately, the data collected do not include forgone earnings, so to construct the COI value Rowe and Chestnut had to assume that the earnings forgone were equal to the medical costs. The assumption is justified on the grounds that the respondents' rankings of the importance of forgone earnings and medical expenditures were nearly identical. The comparison of WTP to COI does not seem sensitive to any inaccuracies inherent in this assumption.

Another problem in the construction of the COI value is that it includes only variable medical expenditures, such as medicine or doctor visits. The asthmatics interviewed also had significant fixed cost expenses on onetime goods such as intermittent positive pressure breathing machines. From Rowe and Chestnut's (1984) table 1, the total (household) fixed cost expenses were $713, compared to total (household) variable expenses per year of $528. Clearly, the entire sum of fixed costs expenditures should not be compared to the willingness to pay for an improvement in morbidity. However, since the improvement would change individuals' marginal decisions on the purchase of a onetime good, ideally some (unknown) portion of the fixed expenses would be included in a COI value. It does not seem likely that doing so would change the result that WTP is greater than COI.

In general, while the Rowe and Chestnut study is not the ideal test of the hypothesis that WTP exceeds COI, it does offer strong support of that relationship. The final caveat is that the study involved only a relatively small sample of individuals with a chronic condition, asthma, and may not be relevant for the general population.

Comparisons of COI and CV values from the Loehman et al. (1979) and Rowe and Chestnut (1984) studies are thus somewhat inconclusive. The first study contains very weak evidence against the hypothesis that WTP exceeds COI. The second study contains much stronger evidence that supports the hypothesis, but problems with the study may limit its applicability.

Comparing COI and CV—New Results [1]

The contingent valuation study described in detail in Part 2 of this book was designed to collect the necessary data for a direct comparison of CV willingness to pay bids for changes in health status with certainty and experienced cost of illness. Only the surveys on seven light symptoms (coughing spells, stuffed-up sinuses, throat congestion, itching eyes, drowsiness, headaches, and nausea) are used for this comparative analysis. The surveys on angina could not be used because few of the respondents had experience with angina and its related cost of illness.

The total sample of the seven light symptom surveys used in the analysis was 131, using door-to-door and mall-intercept interview methods. Out of this sample, nine observations were unusuable because they were incomplete. Because of the limited scope of the sample, we view this empirical study as illustrative.

Table 4.4 compares the mean WTP and private COI for each of the seven symptoms in the contingent valuation survey. The comparison is made among those who have experienced the symptom in the previous year, that is, those for whom we have COI data. The private COI calculated consistent with the prevailing measure in the COI literature. It is the expenditures on medicine and doctor visits less any insurance payments plus any

---

1. The material in this subsection originally appeared in M. Berger, G. Blomquist, D. Kenkel, and G. Tolley, "Valuing Changes in Health Risks: A Comparison of Alternative Measures," *Southern Economic Journal* 53, no. 4 (April 1987): 967–84. Reprinted with permission.

TABLE 4.4. Willingness to Pay and Private Cost of Illness Comparisons
of Means

Symptom	Sample Size[a]	Mean Daily Willingness to Pay (in $)[b]	Mean Daily Private Costs of Illness (in $)[c]	t-Value[d]
Coughing spells	27	105.34	11.29	2.12*
Sinus congestion	43	38.84	6.79	2.22*
Throat congestion	24	43.93	14.27	1.59
Itching eyes	16	172.23	14.56	1.24
Heavy drowsiness	6	173.89	21.50	2.57*
Headaches	48	173.21	3.33	2.07*
Nausea	18	91.24	2.36	2.03*

[a]Only those experiencing the symptom are included.
[b]Willingness to pay to avoid one extra day of the symptom.
[c]Calculated as expenditures on doctor visits and medicine net of insurance reimbursements plus lost earnings, expressed on a daily basis.
[d]Test of the null hypothesis that willingness to pay is less than or equal to private costs of illness.
*Indicates hypothesis rejected at 0.05 level of significance in a one-tailed test.

lost earnings. Both the individual WTP and COI measures are expressed on a daily basis.[2]

Out of the entire sample of 122 individuals, the subsamples of those who had experienced the various symptoms in the previous year ranged in size from six for drowsiness to 48 for headaches. Within each of these subsamples, the mean WTP always exceeded the mean cost of illness. The last column of Table 4.4 indicates that in five of the seven cases, the differences were significant at the .05 level in a one-tailed test.

Another way to test the equality of the private COI and the WTP is through the use of a nonparametric sign test (see Hoel 1971, pp. 310–15). This type of test is less sensitive to extreme WTP or COI values than is the t-test. For the sign test, the 192 WTP-COI pairs across all seven symptoms are compared. In 174 cases, the WTP exceeds private COI. If the WTP-COI pairs had in fact come from the same distribution, we would expect that in only 96 cases would WTP exceed COI. We can then test whether 174 is significantly greater than 96 by using the binomial approximation to the normal distribution.[3] The resulting value of the test statistic is 11.26,

2. The contingent valuation experiments were conducted for both 1-day and 30-day changes in the experience of the various systems. Implicit in the normalization to 1-day changes is the assumption of constant marginal costs in the case of cost of illness and constant marginal utility in the case of willingness to pay.
3. The standard deviation for calculating the normal distribution test statistic is constructed under the null hypothesis that the WTP-COI pairs come from the same distribution. In this

which is significantly different from zero at a .001 level of significance, further adding to the empirical evidence that WTP exceeds COI.

There are two types of additional evidence that support the finding that WTP exceeds COI. First, we asked individuals to rank the reasons for their values for symptom relief. Focus group feedback led to development of a five-item list that covered most reasons. The reasons and the percentage of the 122 respondents who ranked the reason as the most important are comfort (67%), loss of work at home (6%), loss of work away from home (12%), loss of recreation (2%), reduction of medical expenses (11%), and other (2%). So, as in the Rowe and Chestnut (1984) study, the components of the value of health included in COI are ranked as less important than the components COI omits.

We also estimated simple ordinary least squares regressions of WTP on the private COI.[4] In each case the intercept is positive and, in most cases, is significantly different from zero. The slope term is never significantly different from zero. However, in the cases in which it approaches significance, it is positive. Thus, the regression results are consistent with the above finding that in general WTP exceeds COI, although there does not appear to be any strong tendency for the two to move together. This suggests that it is not possible to predict WTP based on COI. So while WTP/COI ratios could be computed based on the means reported in Table 4.4, yielding ratios of about 3 to over 50, the regression results suggest that these ratios are not particularly meaningful.

Implicit in our WTP-COI comparison is the assumption that the symptoms that people experienced in the previous year are the same as those that they are bidding on in the contingent valuation experiments. For the light symptoms included in the survey, the differences are rather inconsequential. When the samples are limited to those who reported that their symptoms were the same, not worse, or less severe than the contingent symptoms, the mean of WTP is still greater than the mean of COI for each symptom, and although the dollar differences are greater for four of the seven symptoms, only two of the t-values are significant at the .05 level due to the smaller sample sizes. The nonparametric sign test yielded a test statistic of 8.77, and the regression results are similar to those described above.[5]

---

case the probability that WTP > COI is 1/2, and the standard deviation for the binomial approximation to the normal distribution is $174 \times 1/2 \times 1/2 = 43.5$.

4. These and other results not reported in this chapter are available upon request.

5. A final piece of corroborating evidence is contained in the survey. Individuals were asked how much they would be willing to pay to avoid all the symptoms they had experienced in the previous year. Of the 46 individuals who did not experience symptoms in combinations with one another, 41 had WTP > COI, yielding a nonparametric sign test statistic of 5.3, which

Our empirical evidence suggests that the private COI, defined by excluding time lost from consumption, is less than WTP. Is it the exclusion of these time expenditures that is driving the result? In order to investigate this question, we use other information available from our contingent valuation survey to construct an expanded COI measure that can then be compared to the WTP values. This measure is the cost of medicine and doctor visits net of insurance reimbursements plus the value of time lost from any activity (e.g., market, work, school, work at home).[6] This increases the measured COI and is more compatible with theoretical models of COI. A comparison of the mean COI and WTP for the various symptoms indicates that WTP is greater than COI in six of seven cases (the exception is throat congestion), although the significance levels of the t-statistics are lower than before (they range from $-.165$ to 2.08). The nonparametric test produces a test statistics of 5.48, which is again significant at the .001 level, indicating WTP > COI. Regressions explaining WTP again produce positive (although smaller) and mostly significant constant terms and insignificant COI coefficients. So overall, the exclusion of lost consumption time does not appear to be the reason for our earlier result. Our empirical results are consistent with the hypothesis that consumer surplus exceeds the private COI, whether or not the value of lost consumption time is included. It should be noted, though, that our earlier measure, excluding the value of lost consumption time, is more consistent with that used in COI studies.

The next step is to generalize our results to the relationship between willingness to pay for a change in morbidity risks and the expected COI. From the theoretical model of Chapter 2, if exogenous change that lowers the probability of contracting an illness causes individuals to reduce their preventive expenditures (i.e., if dX/dE is negative), then willingness to pay for a change in risks exceeds expected consumer surplus (CS). This is true since individuals would also be willing to pay their preventive expenditure savings to avoid increases in health risks. While our survey contains no direct evidence on the sign of dX/dE, fortunately, it contains some indirect evidence. Individuals are asked whether they have made various defensive

---

is highly significant. The mean WTP greatly exceeded the mean COI, and a simple regression yielded results similar to those described previously.

6. The value of time lost from market or nonmarket activity is measured by multiplying the number of days lost by the daily wage (hourly wage $\times$ 8). This reduces the sample somewhat since not everyone in the sample worked in the previous year and thus reported a wage rate. We also expanded the definition of cost of illness even further to include days of market and nonmarket activity "hindered." This cost of illness measure is the same as above except that it also includes the number of days hindered multiplied by one-half the daily wage. The means test, sign tests, and regressions were all recalculated, and the results are very similar to those described for the first expanded cost of illness measure.

expenditures for health reasons: whether they have purchased air conditioners, air purifiers, humidifiers for their home or car, or made other preventive expenditures. Nontrivial proportions of the full sample have made some
type of preventive expenditure. But more interesting are the differences
between those who have and have not experienced at least one of the seven
light symptoms.[7] While the percentages of the two groups are almost equal
for the purchase of humidifiers, those who have experienced at least one of
the seven symptoms are more likely to have made expenditures in the other
three categories than those who have not. The difference is most pronounced for air conditioners. No one in the group not experiencing any
symptoms purchased on air conditioner for health reasons, but 19 of those
having at least one of the seven symptoms did so.

What does this pattern of preventive expenditures tell us about the sign
of dX/dE? The pattern is consistent with a negative dX/dE in the following
way. Assume that those having experienced the symptoms also experience
worse exogenous environmental conditions. This results in a higher probability of experiencing the symptom. In looking across the sample, we observe an increase in the quality of the environment $(dE > 0)$ in moving
from those who have experienced at least one of the symptoms to those who
have not. The resulting change in preventive expenditures then appears to
be negative. It should be stressed that the above explanation is only consistent with $dX/dE < 0$. The data in the survey do not allow for a strict test of
hypothesis.

However, if it is true that $dX/dE < 0$, then our empirical results are also
consistent with willingness to pay for a change in morbidity risks being
greater than the expected COI. This allows us to make statements about
our theoretical model with uncertainty from our empirical results, which by
practical necessity are couched in terms of certainty, and yield only estimates of willingness to pay under certainty, in other words, an estimate of
consumer surplus.

One final illustration will help show the usefulness of our empirical consumer surplus estimates. From the theoretical model, it is plausible that the

---

7. The proportions of the full sample having made various preventive expenditures, and
the proportions among those who have and have not experienced at least one of the seven light
symptoms, are as follows:

Preventive Expenditure	Full Sample	No Symptoms	One or more Symptoms
Air conditioner	.151	.000	.188
Air purifier	.110	.044	.126
Humidifier	.311	.318	.309
Other	.074	.056	.078

expected change in consumer surplus is a lower bound on willingness to pay for a change in health risks. Since the contingent valuation experiment measures CS, if we assume some value for the change in probabilities of becoming sick, we can estimate a lower bound for the value of the reduction of health risks. For example, in Table 4.4 we report that, among those having experienced coughing spells in the previous year, the mean CS for avoiding 1 extra day of cough with certainty is $105.34. These individuals had on average approximately 48 days of coughing spells in the previous year. If we assume that the probability of having a coughing spell on any given day is constant throughout the year, the mean individual faces approximately a .13 probability of having a coughing spell each day. A lower-bound estimate of the willingness to pay for a 10% reduction in the risk of a coughing spell on any given day for the mean individual is simply $- CS \, dH/dE$ or $\$105.34 \times .013 = \$1.37$. The willingness to pay for a whole year's worth of 10% reductions is $\$1.37 \times 365 = \$500.05$. Lower bounds on the values of changes in the risks of the other symptoms can be similarly calculated. It should be stressed, however, that our lower-bound estimates, while useful for comparisons among approaches, should be used for policy purposes with caution. Our small sample is probably not representative of the entire U.S. population. In addition, it should be recalled that the contingent valuation experiment contained no direct evidence on the value of morbidity risks, and the lower-bound estimates depend upon the theoretical model used in chapter 2.

Conclusion about Comparisons

Our empirical work provides evidence on WTP and COI for seven light symptoms in the certainty case: coughing spells, stuffed-up sinuses, throat congestion, itching eyes, heavy drowsiness, headache, and nausea. The WTP values that are obtained are equivalent to consumer surpluses. The results suggest that WTP exceeds COI, but there is no strong indication that WTP and COI move together in any systematic fashion. Assuming that exogenous changes affecting health risks reduce preventive expenditures, our results also imply that the WTP for reduction in health risks that arises from our uncertainty-based model exceeds expected COI. We then provide an illustrative lower-bound estimate of the value of a change in health risks from our contingent valuation survey.

The results of the new empirical work thus tend to confirm Rowe and Chestnut's (1984) preliminary results that WTP exceeds COI. It should be noted that this relationship is also found in the experimental mail survey completed (see Chap. 13), but the results are for a very small sample. So there is a growing body of evidence that suggests that contingent valuation responses on WTP exceed COI, as predicted by several theoretical models. The major limitation is the small sample sizes of the studies.

4.5. Conclusions and Summary of Contingent Valuation

An assessment of the contingent valuation method suggests that with careful design the resulting value estimates may be fairly accurate. With this in mind, this chapter reviewed six studies that applied the contingent valuation method to the problem of valuing health: Loehman et al. (1979), Dickie et al. (1987), and the study described in Part 2 address the value of light symptoms; Rowe and Chestnut (1984), Viscusi, Magat, and Huber (1991), and Krupnick and Cropper (1992) address the value of asthma and bronchitis. Each of these studies seems to be carefully designed, though certain problems are noted. Future work could focus on two general problems: (i) the treatment of extremely large bids that are statistical outliers, and (ii) the relationship between bids for a marginal day of relief, compared to the average value per day of relief when a larger change in health is being contemplated.

While the health effects valued are not exactly the same, certain comparisons can be made between the results of four of the six studies. Each of the four studies implies a value for one day of respiratory symptoms, though not always of the same symptoms. From the Loehman et al. (1979) study, 1 day of coughing/sneezing has a mean value of $138 (mild day) or $236 (severe day). In terms of the initial bids, the mean value placed on a day of coughing from the Dickie et al. (1987) study is $355.10, but the mean falls to between $1.61 and $9.96 after alternative methods to improve reliability are applied to the sample of bids. Our study finds that relief from 1 day of coughing, throat, and sinus problems has a mean value of $65.60. The Rowe and Chestnut (1984) study implies that relief from 1 day of asthma symptoms is worth on average about $20.

These different values can be reconciled, to some extent. First, the Rowe and Chestnut value is not a value for a marginal day of relief but an average value for 1 day, given an average of 19 days of symptoms relieved. Thus, it is not really comparable to the other estimates. The Loehman et al. study is more directly comparable to Dickie et al. and our study. In general, somewhat different values result. But if we compare median bids across the studies, or compare mean bids across the studies, the values are closer. The range of values is narrowed further if, as argued above, the results from the Dickie et al. study are best viewed as lower-bound estimates.

5

Household Health Production, Property Values, and the Value of Health

Richard Clemmer, Donald Kenkel,
Robert Ohsfeldt, and William Webb

5.1. Introduction

Although public policies and other external factors are important determinants of health, health remains at least partially under the control of the individual consumer. By analyzing the decisions consumers make when faced with trade-offs between health and other economic goods, it is sometimes possible to infer the value of health to the consumer. This chapter reviews two approaches used in empirical studies that concern such trade-offs: the household health production framework, and the hedonic analysis of housing markets. The main focus is on developing useful empirical estimates of the value of health based on these approaches.

In the household production framework, the individual is seen as producing the commodity health by combining his or her own time and effort with purchased goods such as medical care, diet, and so on. Some recent theoretical and empirical work has used this framework to derive expressions for what an individual would be willing to pay for an exogeneous improvement in health or health risks. The theoretical studies, such as the model developed in Chapter 2 and the references therein, investigate how the conceptually correct willingness to pay measure will be related to observable quantities, namely, the cost of illness and preventive expenditures (averting behavior). Since health is not the only commodity produced by the household, the approach can also be used to value environmental benefits more generally; see Smith (1991).

In keeping with the focus on empirical value estimates, Section 5.2 examines several empirical studies that use the household production approach to estimate willingness to pay for health directly. Cropper (1981) estimates willingness to pay for health risks related to an index of air pollutants. Gerking and Stanley (1986) estimate willingness to pay for health risks related to ozone exposure, and Dickie and Gerking (1991) develop estimates of the value of chest, throat, and other relatively minor symptoms. Each of these studies are reviewed to investigate the usefulness and comparability of their empirical estimates of the value of health.

This chapter also explores the possibility of deriving meaningful information about the value of health risks from the literature relating property values and air pollution. Hedonic analysis of housing markets frequently has been employed in an effort to estimate the benefits of improved air quality. Presumably, individuals reveal their willingness to pay for environmental quality through their location choices in housing markets and the corresponding housing premiums for various locational attributes, including air quality. The benefit estimates thus obtained, if accurately measured, represent the total benefits to individuals of improvements in air quality, including improvements in health status, reduced property damage (soiling costs), as well as less tangible psychic benefits such as improved visibility. As such, estimates of the aggregate benefits of improved air quality obtained from hedonic analysis of housing markets may be viewed as upper-bound estimates of the benefits of improved health status attributable to improved air quality.

Section 5.3 considers the hedonic analysis of housing markets in detail. After noting a number of econometric problems that have not been fully resolved in the literature, some estimates of willingness to pay for air quality implied by a number of studies are presented. It should be noted that the review does not attempt to attack or defend the basic methodology of applying hedonic analysis to the problem of property values and environmental quality. Bartik (1987) and Epple (1987) address the basic methodology in more detail. Given the existing state of knowledge, it seems premature to attempt to make judgments about the appropriateness of housing market hedonic studies or to attempt the derivation of a consensus or best estimate of the value of air quality as revealed in housing markets. Instead, a number of methodological concerns and a range of empirical values are presented to explore the robustness of the method.

5.2. Review of Household Production Studies

Cropper (1981)

Cropper (1981) postulates a dynamic health capital model in which pollutants affect health expenditures only through wealth maximization. Pollution increases the rate of health capital decay—changing the margin between the net rate of return on health capital and other investment goods—and increases the number of days ill. But because the consumer's utility does not directly depend on either pollution or health, the consumer optimization problem can be formulated as a two-stage maximum: the individual first chooses a schedule of health to maximize the present value of lifetime wealth, and then uses capital markets to shift consumption over time so as to maximize utility. For a small change in the pollutant level in some period t, Cropper defines the willingness to pay (WTP) as

$$WTP = [s(dS/dP)p + b(dI/dP)P]e^{-rt},$$

where w is the wage rate, S the number of sick days, P the level of pollution, b the costs of a unit of health investment, I the extent of health investment, and r the discount rate. The first term represents costs of illness (COI), the second the change in health investment expenditures.

In the course of working through the dynamic wealth maximization, Cropper makes three restrictive assumptions that allow the WTP expression to be simplified considerably; the relationships between the pollutant level and the depreciation rate, and between health status and days ill, are assumed to be of constant elasticity, and the health production function is defined as constant returns to scale. Given these assumptions, it can be shown that the change in averting expenditures exactly equals the COI costs; the first-order conditions for the wealth maximization insure that the marginal costs of sickness and health investment will be equated, but, given the constant returns to scale—which insures constant prices—and the constant elasticity relationships, the equilibrium margins are constant irrespective of the scale, and hence total costs are also equated. Thus to calculate the WTP one merely needs to calculate COI and multiply by two, or, to calculate the change in averting expenditures, one just needs to measure the COI.

Cropper illustrates her analysis by calculating COI and WTP from Michigan Panel Study of Income Dynamics data. Given the estimated elasticity of sick time with respect to pollution, an average person in the 1976 sample earning $6.00 per hour would be willing to pay $7.20 annually for a 10% reduction in the mean of sulfur dioxide.

Since WTP is always twice the forgone earnings in this model, it is also possible to say that this average individual would be willing to pay $96 to avoid the loss of an 8-hour workday. Putting this in 1984 dollars implies a value of $176 per work-loss day.

Gerking and Stanley (1986)

The Gerking and Stanley (1986) study formulates a household production model where environmental quality enters as a factor in the production of health, which is in preferences, and which affects the number of days sick. Thus the WTP for an environmental quality improvement can be derived:

$$WTP = dY/dA \mid (dU = 0) = -H_A(S, A, D)/H_S(S, A, D),$$

where H is a multidimensional health production function, S is averting activity—in this case visits to a doctor—and D represents individual characteristics that parameterize individual productivities of S and A in producing H; for example, D will include the existence and length of a chronic health condition. Given that the assumptions of the implicit function theorem hold, $H = H(S, A, D)$ may be expressed as $F(H, A, D)$, and thus

$$S_A = -F_A/F_S = -(F_A/F_H)/(F_S/F_H) = -H_A/H_S.$$

Gerking and Stanley measure $dS(A, D)/dA$ using a cross-sectional survey of 2,594 households in St. Louis, Missouri, over the years 1977–80, which is combined with air quality data from the Regional Air Pollution Study matched to each data point. Because two of the independent variables in the regression—the existence and length of the chronic condition—are determined under the formulations of the model simultaneously with the health decision, a two-stage logit procedure is followed; the health variables are regressed on the other explanatory variables, and from this, predicted values are entered into the final logit regression.

Of the four pollutants considered in the model—ozone, sulfur dioxides, total suspended particulates, and nitrous oxides—only ozone has a coefficient significantly different from zero, at the 1% level of significance. None of the other pollutants are significant at the 10% level. By multiplying this coefficient by the mean cost of a medical visit and by a posited change in ozone levels, Gerking and Stanley calculate the change in new first medical visits expenses due to a 30% reduction in ambient ozone levels. The reduction in expenditures range from $18.45 to $24.45 per capita, annually.

As a result of the order of their two-stage estimation process, Gerking and Stanley do not directly estimate the effects of ozone on health, so it is impossible to specify what change in health results from a given ozone reduction. Thus, these values of WTP for an ozone reduction do not unambiguously imply a value for WTP for health. However, Gerking and Stanley do suggest that it might be reasonable to assume that each medical visit is associated with a day of restricted activity due to illness. If this is true, the value of preventing a restricted activity day is equal to the full price of the medical visit, which they estimated at about $40.

Another approach is to use an independent estimate of the effect of ozone on health and calculate what change in health individuals are purchasing when they purchase a given change in ozone. Portney and Mullahy (1986) present a range of estimated effects of ozone on health. When combined with the Gerking and Stanley values for a 30% reduction in ozone, these estimates imply values not inconsistent with the $40 per restricted activity day value above.

Two problems noted by Gerking and Stanley that may affect the robustness of this study are the choice of the dependent variable and the possible sample selection bias created by the use of a relatively small subset of the entire sample. First, whether an individual has ever visited a doctor within a year just does not seem very sensitive to the particular health care needs created by high ozone levels. It does not capture additional medical trips made by those already visiting doctors for other reasons and, similarly, does not reflect the intensity of care related to a particular ozone-related health problem. Second, because the model is formulated using the full price of medical care—which equals the direct price of medical care plus the time cost of receiving such care—the need for wage information to value time suggests that only the 824 households who list their primary occupation as employed, and who had reported a wage rate, be included in the regressions. The WTP calculated from a regression using data only on employed individuals may not be generalizable to the population at large. Employees may experience different exposures to air pollution levels than those not employed—for example, they may work in an air-conditioned office. Employees may also face different medical costs because of employment-related health insurance. Gerking and Stanley do report, however, that regression results run on the full sample do not differ much from the sub-sample regression.

Dickie and Gerking (1991)

The study by Dickie and Gerking (1991) estimates household production relationships between health attributes, private goods, and air quality. An important contribution of this study is to generalize previous research by allowing for certain types of jointness in household production. In their model, a private good can be an input into the household production of more than one health attribute. As they show, this clearly realistic extension has important implications for developing an expression for the willingness to pay for an improvement in health.

In particular, Dickie and Gerking show that it is sometimes but not always possible to express willingness to pay for a marginal improvement in a health attribute as a function of prices and production parameters. Since in principle prices are observable and production parameters are estimable, when this is possible the household production approach can be used to value health. But there are circumstances where it breaks down. The technical condition established by Dickie and Gerking requires that the number of private good inputs is at least as great as the number of health outputs. An important practical implication is that it may be impossible to value a large number of detailed attributes of health, unless an even larger number of inputs are used in the household production processes. Instead, Dickie and Gerking suggest aggregating detailed health attributes into a smaller number of rather broadly defined health outputs. For instance, based on their empirical analysis, they cannot calculate separate values of chest and throat and other light symptoms, but they can calculate a common value for symptom relief.

Dickie and Gerking estimate their model using data from surveys of 226 residents of two Los Angeles communities. Each respondent was contacted between three and six times in 1985 and 1986, yielding a panel dataset based on 1,147 contacts. A very useful feature of the sample is that it included 126 respondents with respiratory impairments. A straightforward hypothesis is that the marginal willingness to pay for a health improvement will be higher in the impaired subsample than in the normal subsample.

The outputs of the household production functions, the health attributes, were measured according to the number of symptoms experienced in the 2 days before the contact. The private inputs into the symptom production functions included central air conditioning in the home, an air-purifying system in the home, use of fuel other than natural gas for cooking, and the use of air conditioning in the automobile. The production functions were estimated using a random effects tobit model for panel data.

The detailed results of the household production functions estimated by Dickie and Gerking will not be presented since the focus here is on the implied values of health. Based on their results, Dickie and Gerking calculate that the daily willingness to pay for relief of symptoms is $1.12 in the impaired subsample and $0.73 in the normal subsample. While the expected relationship between willingness to pay in the two subsamples is found, the magnitudes are extremely small.

The estimates by Dickie and Gerking of willingness to pay for symptom reductions are much smaller than estimates from other studies using a variety of approaches. For instance, the two other studies that value health by using a household production approach reviewed above suggest the value of a day of illness is between $40 and $176. The contingent valuation studies reviewed in Chapter 4 suggest that the daily willingness to pay for similar symptoms is closer to $50 or $100. Even the daily costs of illness estimates, which are intuitively a lower bound to willingness to pay, exceed the values calculated by Dickie and Gerking (see Chap. 3 and Sec. 4 of Chap. 4).

Dickie and Gerking suggest one explanation for the difference between their estimates and results based on contingent valuation studies. They speculate that, when asked to value individual symptoms, respondents instead report their willingness to pay for broader health concerns. This behavior is consistent with Dickie and Gerking's findings that independent technologies for producing reductions in symptoms do not exist. If consumers cannot produce reductions in certain symptoms separately, they may be unable to answer contingent valuation questions about separate symptoms in a meaningful way. However, it is not clear that this type of problem in the contingent valuation studies is enough to explain the magnitude of the differences in the two sets of estimates. In addition, it does not explain the discrepancy between the Dickie and Gerking estimate and estimates from other studies using either the household production approach or the cost of illness approach.

At this point, no convincing explanation for the surprisingly low willingness to pay estimates of Dickie and Gerking is apparent.

5.3. Property Values and the Value of Health

Introduction

Ideally, to find the value of the health effects of air pollution we need estimates of the parameters of the demand function for improved air quality and an estimate of the initial height of the demand curve. The benefits of a given improvement in air quality can be measured as the integral under the compensated demand curve, from the initial level of air quality to the level of air quality that is attained with the improvement. In Figure 5.1, the initial level of air quality is shown by A_1, and the augmented level A_2. The initial level of marginal benefits as perceived by the consumer are shown as B_1, and the level of marginal benefits corresponding to level A_2 are shown as B_2. The value of the improvement to the consumer is shown as the shaded area $B_1 B_2 A_1 A_2$ and corresponds to the equivalent variation of income of the change. This is a measure of the dollar equivalent of the welfare improvement (Hicks 1979).

The earliest hedonic analysis of housing markets concerns the construction of housing price indices. This literature is motivated by an interest in

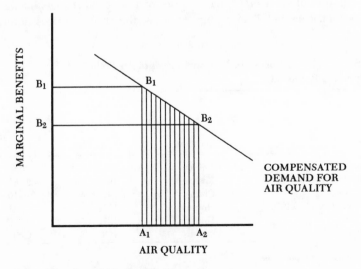

Figure 5.1.   Benefits of Air Quality Improvement

accurately estimating changes in housing price. Following Adelman and Griliches (1961), the primary emphasis in the housing price index literature is the development of a time-series (or cross-standard-metropolitan-statistical-area) housing price index holding housing "quality" constant. In some of these studies, the sales price of a particular house at different points in time is used to estimate a price index (e.g., Palmquist 1983). In most of the remaining studies (Palmquist 1984 is typical), the sale price is regressed on the characteristics of the house, with the housing price index computed as the change over time (or across areas) in the predicted sales price of a typical housing bundle (i.e., a bundle with the sample mean level of each attribute).

Related to the housing price index literature is the early hedonic demand literature. Studies of this type were primarily interested in estimating the shadow prices of housing characteristics—that is, the contribution of particular characteristics to total value—rather than an overall housing price. Studies concentrating on the impact of air quality on housing values include Ridker and Henning (1967), Anderson and Crocker (1971), Smith (1978), and Wieand (1973). A summary of the results from these studies and others are provided in Table 5.1. The marginal price estimates vary considerably across studies, ranging from zero to $422.

In many of these studies, marginal prices are assumed to reveal the consumer's willingness to pay for various units of a particular characteristic. However, these are not estimates of the consumer's entire willingness to pay schedule and may not reveal the marginal evaluations of different classes of consumers, except as an overall average. Instead, these estimates are measures of the average market price of a marginal change in a particular locational amenity—clean air. At most, the shadow prices determine

TABLE 5.1.   Estimates of Marginal Prices of Air Pollution
(Suspended Particulates)

Study	Location	Year	Estimated Marginal Price (1980 Dollars/ mm^3)
Diamond (1980)	Chicago	1969–71	422
Li and Brown (1980)	Boston	1971	2–8[*]
Smith (1978)	Chicago	1971	91–108
Smith and Ohsfeldt (1979)	Houston	1970	4–21
	Houston	1976	14–68
Wieand (1973)	Census	1960	0–9[*]

[*] Not statistically different from zero.

only the height of the demand for this characteristic but do not throw any light on the shape of the demand function.

An additional problem of using single-state hedonic regression concerns the implicit nature of housing characteristics. Consider an ordinary good that is supplied in a competitive market. A consumer faces a constant market-determined price and adjusts quantity purchased to the point where the person's marginal evaluation of the good (demand) is equal to the market price. If the good is sold in such a way that the price facing the consumer varies with the quantity purchased, the single hedonic estimate of the marginal benefit to the consumer will be a weighted average of marginal evaluations of consumers in different circumstances. If air quality is a normal good, higher-income consumers will have a higher demand for it, and their demand curves will intersect the nonconstant price schedule at different points. It is still true that consumers equate marginal evaluation with price, and measures of benefits to improved air quality can be estimated as the area under the compensated demand curve, but these measures will vary with consumers. One may conclude that a proper measure of benefits should segment consumers by different income levels and other characteristics, or alternatively one may accept that the average marginal evaluation, shown by the hedonic estimate, might be used for an overall estimate of benefits to the typical consumer. The single-stage hedonic estimate still will not provide evidence as to the shape of the demand curve, however.

Hedonic Prices and the Demand for Characteristics

There have been many attempts to estimate the demand for housing characteristics directly, either as a system of demand equations or with each equation treated separately. Among the earliest studies of this type are Kain and Quigley (1975), Straszheim (1974), and King (1976). Unlike Kain and Quigley, both Straszheim and King include price information in their estimating equations (specifically, the "hedonic" price of the attribute). Since both studies assume a linear housing price structure (i.e., a constant marginal price of the attribute), it is necessary to invoke a "segmented-markets" assumption to insure variation of the hedonic prices within an urban area at a single point in time. That is, a separate hedonic regression is estimated for each market segment, and the resulting coefficient estimates are used as the price variable in the demand function.

It is important to note that the segmented-markets hypothesis arose from the observation that point estimates of marginal price differ across areas within an urban area. If markets were not segmented (or separated), it was (implicitly) assumed that arbitrage between markets would insure price equality across the urban area. Although this argument may be applicable to the literature on racial discrimination in housing, the segmented-markets hypothesis, in general, represents a failure to recognize the implicit nature of characteristics markets. The fact that characteristics are purchased jointly in indivisible bundles limits arbitrage possibilities, resulting in a nonlinear price structure. Differences in point estimates of marginal price are to be expected, and do not constitute evidence of segmented markets.

Rosen's Model of Implicit Markets

A general model of implicit markets for characteristics was developed by Rosen (1974). In this model, the interaction of supply and demand produces a market clearing price function, $P(Z)$, which relates the price of a hetero-geneous good to Z, the characteristics of the good. Rosen defined equilib-rium as the state at which the marginal bid price for Z_i, θ_i, equals the marginal offer price for Z_i, ϕ_i for all i in Z. The bid curve relates the maxi-mum price a consumer is willing to pay for an additional unit of Z_i, holding income (and other exogenous demand variables) and utility constant (U^0). The offer price curve relates the minimum price a producer is willing to accept for an additional unit of Z_i, holding exogenous supply variables and profits constant (Pi^0). Notationally, an implicit market is in equilibrium when

$$\theta_i(Z, Y_1, U^0) = P_i = \phi_1(Z, Y_2, Pi^0)$$

for all i, where Y_1 represents income and other exogenous demand vari-ables, Y_2 represents exogenous supply variables, and P_i is the equilibrium implicit marginal price of Z_i.

In Rosen's model, the derivatives of θ_i form a set of compensated (in-verse) demand functions, and the derivatives of ϕ_i form a set of profit-compensated supply functions. The intersections of the demand and supply functions trace out the price function P_i, which will not in general be linear and will not imply a constant marginal price. (The usual hedonic technique and the competitive model for an ordinary good both imply constant mar-ginal prices.) If the price function P_i can be determined, then taking its derivative at various levels of Z_i will yield a set of implicit marginal prices, which in turn may be used to estimate the compensated demand function needed in the estimation of benefits to improved air quality. In essence, since the price function relating the marginal price and the quantity of an attribute is composed of intersections of demand and supply, it is neither demand nor supply itself. What results is an identification problem.

Rosen suggested a two-step estimation procedure, where a hedonic mar-ket equation, $P(Z)$, is estimated in the first step using the best-fitting func-tional form and omitting Y_1 and Y_2. In the second step, the derivatives of the equation estimated in the first step, evaluated at each observation's level of Z, are used in the estimation of a system of supply and demand equations:

$$P_i = \Theta_i(Z, Y_1) \quad \text{(demand)},$$
$$P_i = \phi_i(Z, Y_2) \quad \text{(supply)},$$

where P_i = the partial derivative of $P(Z)$ with respect to Z_i, evaluated at each observed Z.

Rosen's Model: Applications to Demand for Air Quality

Studies that apply Rosen's technique to the analysis of the demand for air quality are Harrison and Rubinfeld (1978), Nelson (1978), Bender, Gronberg, and Hwang (1980), and Ohsfeldt (1983). Harrison and Rubinfeld are primarily interested in a single characteristic, air quality. They estimate a single demand equation (1) using ordinary least squares and (2) with an instrumental variable for air quality. Nelson estimates a supply and demand function for clean air using two-stage least squares. In both cases, the variation in P_i in the system is entirely attributable to the nonlinearity of the price structure and the subsequent differences in point estimates of marginal price. Bender, Gronberg, and Hwang estimate the demand for air quality giving special attention to the choice of functional form for both the demand function and the hedonic price equation. Ohsfeldt estimates the demand for three housing neighborhood characteristics including quality (of which air quality is a major component) for three cities using the longitudinal Annual Housing Survey for the years 1974–79.

In all of these studies, with the exception of Ohsfeldt (1983), the market price function, $P(Z)$, contains a greater number of characteristics variables than the demand (or supply) equations. One reason why the empirical models have this structure, although it is never explicitly stated as such, is to reduce the severity of a problem that is immediately apparent in Rosen's suggested empirical technique. That is, if P_i is linear in Z and ϕ_i is linear in Z, then in the second step of the estimating procedure, Z will explain all of the variance in P_i and the coefficients of Y_1 will be zero. The only way to avoid this result using Rosen's technique is to assume that P_i and ϕ_i have different functional forms with respect to Z, of which including linear fewer Z_i's in ϕ_i is a special case. In other words, with a single market area at a particular point in time, all of the variation in the estimated marginal price, P_i, can be attributed to the nonlinearity of the price structure, $P(Z)$. In estimating demand (or supply), restrictions on the functional forms must be imposed to avoid duplicating the marginal price function. Even with multiple market data, substantial exogenous price variation is necessary to avoid the effects of spurious correlation (see Ohsfeldt and Smith 1985). It seems likely that all of these studies suffer, to some degree, from inadequate exogenous price variation. Thus, the benefit estimates obtained from these analyses are not very reliable.

TABLE 5.2.   Estimates of Elasticities of Demand for Clean Air

Study	Location	Year	Price Elasticity	Income Elasticity
Bender, Gronberg, and Hwang (1980)	Chicago	1972	−.516	.609
Harrison and Rubinfeld (1978)	Boston	1970	−.850	.957
Nelson (1978)	Washington, DC	1970	−1.250	1.000
Ohsfeldt (1983)	Houston	1974–79	−1.111	.081
	Chicago	1974–79	−.113	.139
	Philadelphia	1974–79	−.382	.123

Another basic flaw in most of these studies is that they accept Rosen's view of the identification problem. The object of an implicit market analysis is the individual consumer (or producer). Since the market price structure, $P(Z)$, is exogenous to the individual, there is no direct interaction between *individual* supply and *individual* demand. The relevant simultaneity problem in an implicit market analysis results from the quantity dependence of marginal prices.

With these limitations in mind, we provide summary of demand elasticity estimates from these empirical studies in Table 5.2. These estimates, to the extent they are accurate, indicate that the demand for clean air is probably price inelastic and that clean air is a normal good.

In terms of benefit estimates, Bender, Gronberg, and Hwang (1980) suggest that a permanent 10% reduction in suspended particulates would result in a $700–$1,800 benefit (present value) per household. A permanent reduction of 20% would create $1,500–$3,000 in benefits (present value) per household. Similarly, Harrison and Rubinfeld (1978) estimate that a 2 pphm (parts per hundred million) reduction in nitrogen oxides would create benefits of $800 per middle-income household, while a 9 pphm reduction would result in benefits of $2200 per middle-income household. But because of the econometric problems outlined earlier, these estimates should be used cautiously.

5.4. Conclusions

This chapter reviewed studies following the household production approach to valuing health and studies concerning air quality and property values. The common element to the two sets of studies reviewed is that they concern observable trade-offs consumers make between other goods and services and health.

Studies by Cropper (1981), Gerking and Stanley (1986) and Dickie and Gerking (1991) attempt to estimate what an individual would be willing to pay for an improvement in air quality related to health effects only. The implied values for health are about and $176 for a work-loss day in the Cropper study, $40 for a day of restricted activity from the Gerking and Stanley study, and $1 a day of symptoms from the Dickie and Gerking study. Since a work-loss day is a more severe effect than a day of restricted activity (as defined in these studies), it is not unexpected that the Cropper estimate is larger than the Gerking and Stanley estimate. The extremely small estimate from the Dickie and Gerking study remains puzzling.

As noted at the outset, the estimates of the value of air quality derived from hedonic analysis of housing markets can be viewed as providing upper-bound estimates of the benefits of improved health status. In addition, these values should reflect the value of both morbidity and mortality related to air pollution. For these reasons, the estimates are not comparable to the empirical morbidity value estimates reviewed in this and other chapters of this book.

6

The Qualy Approach

Robert Fabian

6.1. Introduction

Applied welfare economics provides the theoretical foundation for the willingness to pay measures of health values reported in this book. Dollar values provide the common denominator that links together the quantity or length of life with the many dimensions of quality of life into a single health measure. Because health changes often involve several of these dimensions, willingness to pay measures are an ideal tool for the analysis of health policy programs.

Another method of measuring health status has developed, which is referred to in this book as qualy analysis. ("QALY" is the expression that is frequently used. The terms mean quality-adjusted life year.) Qualy analysis provides a common unit of measurement capable of describing the complicated interplay of quantity and quality of life. It rejects the idea of monetary valuation of health status or health change, however, and differs from the applied welfare approach in some fundamental ways. This chapter examines the common foundations of the two methods and some theoretical and empirical differences that separate them. The purpose is to clarify the nature of the synthesis of empirical research results in Chapter 15 and to suggest that the methods can constructively be viewed as complementary rather than antagonistic—as has sometimes been the case in the past. Exploiting the common elements of the two frameworks constructively would greatly expand the stock of health values and their quality.

Zeckhauser and Shephard, in their seminal article, "Where Now for Saving Lives?" (1976) inaugurated the quality-adjusted life year analysis by developing a framework whose fundamental shape is clearly recognizable in theoretical and empirical research being done today. They observe that different health assessments frequently arise because "we have no commonly accepted measures for the outputs of alternative policies." They say that the guiding principle should be to select measures "that would predict the choices that an informed individual would make for himself." Accordingly, they view the person as "choosing among alternative lotteries on quality and quantity of life" (p. 11). Von Newmann–Morgenstern utility is assumed. Respondents are offered life-death lotteries with varying probabilities as an alternative to a certainty health state to be measured. Indifference probability determines utility as an expected lottery value. This approach remains the standard measure of qualy-based health utility to the present day, although alternatives have been devised to permit simpler responses.

Zeckhauser and Shepard make a set of assumptions that enable them to aggregate health benefits in terms of qualys. One of these is the assumption "that QALYs returning to different individuals should be weighted equally" (p. 15). This has come to be known as the egalitarian assumption in the qualy literature (Torrance 1986) and is discussed below. They dismiss the alternative of aggregating in terms of dollar values because "we would not substantially improve performance on our implicit objective function" (pp. 15–16). This decision, and their reservations about value-of-life measurements on which dollar valuation of qualys rest, have evidently created a strong tradition in the public-health literature of health-status measurement. (See Zeckhauser for a critique in his essay, "Procedures for Valuing Lives" [1975]. The position against "calibrating and valuing health benefits in dollar terms" is restated in Shepard and Zeckhauser [1982], p. 276. "QALY optimization per dollar of expenditure" is endorsed on p. 279.)

Zeckhauser and Shepard apply the qualy approach to four health-promoting interventions—mobile cardiac units, diet control of cholesterol, auto air bags, and lower speed limits. The health policy objective is framed in terms of maximizing quality-adjusted life years saved for various levels of expenditure by an intervention or set of interventions. The versatility of their approach is made evident by the fact that qualys are able to measure a very heterogeneous group of quality- and quantity-of-life outcomes. In particular, persons saved by the cardiac unit remain at very high risk and have correspondingly lower quality of life, whereas diet prevents or postpones heart attack among lower-risk people. The authors adjust their life-cycle scenarios to take account of these effects (p. 23). (Shepard and Zeckhauser [1982] discuss the measurement of benefits where populations are heterogeneous with respect to risk. Qualy, rather than a willingness to pay criterion, remains the benefit measure.)

6.2. Description of the Qualy Approach

A qualy is a measure of health based on people's attitudes toward symptoms or different levels of pain or of impairment to functioning in day-to-day life. People are asked during interviews to rate different health states according to the strengths of their preferences for or aversions to the conditions described in the questionnaire. A scale is used to portray health states, ranging from zero for death (or numbers less than zero for something worse, such as severe brain damage) to one for unimpaired health.

Respondents are presented with an array of impairment descriptions and asked to locate them on a 0–1 scale so that the distance between the health states reflects the differences in the utilities of those health states to the respondent. Average responses for each health state give an estimate of health preferences for the population represented in the sample. The result is an index of utility for the different health states, measured on an interval scale. Torrance (1986) illustrates the interpretation of qualys with an example: "If a programme improves the health of individual A from a 0.50 utility to a 0.75 utility for one year and extends the life of individual B for one year in a 0.50 utility state, the total QALY's gained for that year would be 0.25 for individual A plus 0.50 for individual B for a total of 0.75" (p. 8). Weinstein uses the following example: "Symptomatic improvement is assumed to provide the equivalent of 0.01 quality-adjusted year of life for each year on treatment. This figure reflects a judgment on the part of the patient that living 1.00 year with the symptoms . . . is as desirable as living 0.99 year without the symptoms, i.e., a willingness to sacrifice one percent of life to get rid of the symptoms during those years" (Weinstein 1980, p. 311). The examples illustrate the close relationship between the quantity and quality of life captured by the qualy measure.

Extensions of qualy analysis have been made through the use of multiattribute utility functions. This approach stresses that preferences can be complex and that program effects can affect many aspects of a person's well-being. For example, health effects could be defined in terms of the following attributes (Kaplan, Bush, and Berry 1976, pp. 486–90):

mobility (e.g., driving a car);
physical activity (e.g., walking with physical limitations);
social activity (e.g., needing help with self-care); or
symptom/problem complex (e.g., having a headache, dizziness, or ringing in the ears).

Each of these attributes is defined in personal, functional terms—for example, from having no physical impairments to not being able to move about without help.

By defining a person's preferences in terms of several attributes or dimensions, it becomes possible to examine these preferences in easily describable parts. This greatly aids communication with respondents. The ability to convey and elicit more information comes at the price of considerably increased analytic complexity, however. (Torrance, Boyle, and Harwood [1982] give a thorough discussion of the analysis.)

Program-cost information is readily introduced into this framework, as the Zeckhauser and Shepard (1976) study demonstrates. Programs, or groups of programs, are ranked according to utility gain per dollar of expenditure. The qualy method provides a utility-based cost-effectiveness analysis, often called cost-utility analysis. Dollar cost per qualy is the unit of measurement by which programs, evaluated by different authors during different periods of time, can be compared in the public health literature.

6.3. Comparison of Methods

Qualy analysis, discussed in this chapter, and benefit analysis, used in much of the rest of this book, have a number of common characteristics. First and most important is the fact that both methods approach the problem of health program evaluation on the basis of individual preferences. The major contribution of the preference-based approach is that programs are judged on the strengths of people's expressed wants and needs as well as on the scarce resources used up in achieving them. A second advantage of the preference-based approach is the common denominator in which program values are expressed—utility units or dollars. The common unit of measure permits comparison of program effects that may be highly different when expressed in physical terms.

Another similarity between qualy analysis and willingness to pay based on contingent valuation, seldom noted, is their common foundation in eliciting answers to hypothetical questions from interviewees, as opposed to observing behavior in real situations. Torrance (1986) is a basic source on qualy literature and method. Cummings, Brookshire, and Schulz (1986) is a comprehensive treatise on contingent valuation. In addition to the extensive use of contingent valuation in this book, Tolley and Fabian (1988) and Mitchell and Carson (1989) are examples of theoretical developments and further empirical applications in a rapidly expanding literature. Most of these developments that have occurred in the context of contingent valuation are also applicable to qualy analysis, which, however, has apparently not attempted to incorporate them.

Contingent valuation is the use of hypothetical or contingent markets to elicit values from respondents during interviews. Contingent-market products are used to describe goods not ordinarily traded in real markets that are difficult or impossible to value using data from ordinary transactions. The essential features of the process are provision of an orientation period during which respondents research their own preferences, careful and plausible framing of the contingent product, neutral elicitation of values or utilities, and background explanatory information concerning the respondent.

Qualy analysis entails construction of hypothetical health-status situations and obtaining comparable, quantitative responses to hypothetical changes in health status. Alternative degrees of sickness or wellness are described to respondents in terms of the way they function in their day-to-day lives. Initial health status is defined, along with relevant background variables such as age. Aggregation issues are addressed, such as the perspective of the analysis (patient, society) and standardization of program outcomes.

The health states, in addition to being described to the respondent practically in terms of symptoms and human functions, correspond to changes that can be brought about by public health policies. The qualy is thus a versatile measure that can be adapted to diverse policy requirements with complex health outcomes. A qualy index can be used to evaluate the reduction of light symptoms such as headaches caused by ozone air pollution, or threats to life caused by exposure to toxic substances. Relative evaluations of morbidity and mortality effects can be made, as well as effects that are delayed in time because of latency periods.

6.4. Eliciting Qualy Values—Three Approaches

The most widely used qualy-elicitation techniques are the rating scale, the standard gamble and the time trade-off. The simplest, or rating-scale approach, presents respondents with a line, one point of which is marked zero, death; and one, corresponding to a year of perfect health. The symptoms for a disease—for example, severe bronchitis—are described, and the respondents are asked to mark on the line how they rate the desirability of that health state along the 0–1 scale. If they do not mind the symptom very much, the rating will be not far below one, whereas, if they have extreme aversion to the symptoms, the rating will not be far above zero. The distance of the point from zero is the estimated qualy value.

A second approach is the so-called standard gamble. Respondents are asked what odds they would take of dying that would make them indifferent to having the symptoms. These odds provide another estimate of the qualy value. In the third, or time trade-off approach, respondents are asked how many healthy years at the end of life they would be willing to give up to avoid the symptoms. Each method produces utility measures on an interval scale. Utility differences can be compared, but not ratios of utility values. The 0–1 endpoints are arbitrary. By setting the difference in utility between death and life equal across people, part of the basis for utility aggregation is established (Zeckhauser and Shepard 1976, pp. 11, 14–15; Torrance 1986, pp. 16–17.)

The three approaches may be discussed in relation to Figure 6.1, which shows utility, displaying its usual diminishing marginal characteristic, scaled so that utility is zero for the death state and one for the perfect-health state. Utility is plotted in the y direction, and an unobservable physical measure of health, representing a set of symptoms described in the questionnaire, is plotted in the x direction.

In the first approach, when the symptoms are described, the respondent mentally, perhaps subconsciously, places the symptom along the x axis and then reads up to point A on the utility curve, finding the point U_s on the y

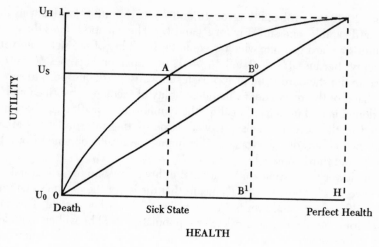

Figure 6.1.   Utility of Health States

axis, which is the utility level achieved when the symptoms are present. The point U_S is what the respondent is supposedly marking down on the 0–1 line in the first approach.

Regarding the second approach, any point along the straight diagonal line between zero and the point on the utility curve corresponding to perfect health represents the value of a gamble that the person will die. The standard gamble gives the respondent's odds at point B^0, which, reading over to the utility curve, gives the same utility level as the symptoms. Point B^1 is the health state with the standard-gamble risk of death that has the same utility as sick state with certainty.

To discuss the third approach, let T denote the years of life remaining, so that total utility over remaining life, as yearly utility level times number of years, is $T \cdot U_s$ if one has to endure the symptoms. The respondent is asked how many remaining years T_H he would be willing to accept and still be as well off as living T years with the symptoms. That is, $T \cdot U_S$ is equated to $T_H \cdot U_H$, where utility in the healthy state U_H is scaled to one, or in solving, $U_S = (T_H/T)U_H$.

In the third approach, then, the qualy value is the number of healthy years that will be accepted (perhaps stated as years remaining minus years one is willing to give up) divided by years remaining. Conceptually, the three approaches gives the same answer, though a shortcoming of the third approach, not usually pointed out, is that it assumes no discounting of future years.

Note that from the second approach we have $P_D \cdot U_D + P_H \cdot U_H = U_S,$

where P_D is the probability of death and U_D is the utility of death in the standard gamble, and similarly for P_H and U_H. The equation states the equilibrium standard gamble, which is equal to the utility of the sick state with certainty. Because $U_D = 0$ and $U_H = 1$, the equation becomes $U_S = P_H$. Because the standard-gamble approach simply uses risk questions to reveal the shape of the respondent's marginal utility of income curve (income being denominated in units of health), the equilibrium equation can be interpreted in the certainty sense, as well as permitting interpretations about differing degrees of risk aversion. Combining the results obtained from the second and third approaches, we have $U_S = T_H/T = P_H$.

The lower the respondent's marginal utility of income (or risk aversion), the lower is P_H. Hence $U_S = P_H$ means that the lower the person's marginal utility of income, the lower is U_S, the utility of the sickness state. This suggests, for example, that less risk-averse populations will be willing to undertake more dangerous medical interventions to avoid sick states than would more conservative populations.

From the point of view of the third approach, a lower marginal utility of income means a lower T_H/T, or a willingness to give up a greater amount of life expectancy to enjoy a healthy remaining life. The respondent is giving up low-income-yielding years (in units of health) to achieve higher utility during the remaining T_H years.

6.5. Distinctive Features of the Qualy Method

The Egalitarian Assumption

The egalitarian assumption is a fundamental feature of the qualy approach. It is both a statement of social philosophy concerning the unique importance of health in people's lives and a technical step designed to permit the aggregation of utilities. Different authors have emphasized one or another aspect of the egalitarian assumption.

Emphasizing the social-values perspective, Chen and Bush (1976, p. 225) say "that days and well-years in everyone's life are of equal value, regardless of the individual's age, sex, socioeconomic status, or other characteristics." Kaplan and Bush (1982, p. 65) state that an "egalitarian basis for comparing the lives and preferences of different persons . . . treats days in all lives as of equivalent social value." (These authors also recognize the role that their position plays in aggregation.)

Emphasizing the role of the egalitarian assumption in the adding up of utilities, Torrance and Feeney (1989, p. 567) say, "The central basis for the aggregation is that the difference in utility between these two outcomes is set equal across people. In this way the method is egalitarian; a full healthy life for each individual carries the same weight." The authors also state that this aggregation approach embodies a "fundamental ethical judgment" (p. 560). Zeckhauser and Shepard (1976) adopt the egalitarian assumption as an explicit principle of aggregation ("QALYs returning to different individuals should be weighted equally"; p. 15). They add that a health state may affect different years differently, so that the utilities would have to be scaled separately. Age is cited as an example (pp. 11–12).

A person's economic position is, of course, a circumstance that may not be permitted to influence the importance of a person's health status in comparison with others. The irrelevance of economic position is underscored by a corollary to the egalitarian assumption. Torrance (1986) says "the utility measurement should be unconfounded by the subject's economic well-being. Thus, it is important to assure the subject that all treatment and all outcomes will be costless to him and to his family" (p. 18). The corollary on cost is particularly important in that it ensures that poor people have an equal voice and weight in the determination of health policy. It also illustrates that calibrating or scaling utilities to account for income or other variables to satisfy the egalitarian assumption is not an easy matter.

Qualy Elicitation and Contingent Valuation

Willingness to pay to prevent imminent, painless death is an impossible contingent-valuation question. But the qualy response is easy: qualy loss = 1. Likewise, people can rate severe head injury at qualy loss = 1.16 (Table 15.6) or cognitive disfunction (defined in Table 15.3) at qualy loss = 0.34. The nature of the question enables people to detach themselves from the problems, at least in many cases, when they give their ratings. Elicitation of monetary values, in contrast, eliminates detachment. We get around this by asking people to respond in terms of changes in small probabilities. Such responses are realistic because they resemble decisions that are made in everyday life. The key to obtaining responses in both situations is keeping dread at bay.

Contingent valuation of dreadful health problems can obtain dollar values directly. They are then applied to interventions involving changes in small probabilities. A great strength of willingness to pay responses is that they apply in a straightforward way to a wide variety of policy interventions where there is a small probability of benefit to a population of people. Lowering levels of potentially cancer-producing air pollutants is an example. Industrial safety procedures to lower the likelihood of head injury is another. Research into the cure or attenuation of Alzheimer's disease is another example. Increasing the availability of trauma facilities reduces any individual's probability of death in an accident. Framing willingness to pay questions in behaviorally meaningful ways that fit the method contributes to good policy.

A distinguishing feature of willingness to pay responses is that they fully reflect the influence of income and prices on the individual's valuation. Because they are regarded as an essential part of the individual's or household's choice, economic variables are emphasized, whereas in qualy analysis they are submerged.

In 1976 Chen and Bush advocated a "universal egalitarian conversion factor" that would convert their well-year measure to a monetary value (p. 225). They sought "one egalitarian social norm rather than varying the benefit computation for the same health output by arbitrary socioeconomic distinctions" (p. 225). This proposal never took hold in the literature; the cost per qualy criterion became the standard measure. A population statistical value of life year, however, might approximate their objective. Anonymity and equal representation would contribute to the egalitarian norm, and calculation of net monetary benefit would be possible, as Chen and Bush recommended.

An alternative is to use age-specific life-year values to monetize qualys. This approach holds constant some socioeconomic characteristics that influence valuation. It utilizes the utility measurement of qualy analysis but departs from the spirit of the egalitarian assumption. The approach is a step in the direction of willingness to pay analysis. If we had an ideal reduced-form equation in which willingness to pay is regressed on explanatory variables, we could predict values on the basis of these variables. Age-specific value of life is a simple approximation of this regression.

Thus there are two ways to employ the statistical value of life year in monetizing qualys. One is to use a population average value, in the spirit of the egalitarian assumption. The other is to employ measures that are tailored to the population, such as age-specific measures, in order to approximate willingness to pay responses.

Benefit analysis does not offer any egalitarian assurances. People's values are weighted by their ability to pay for benefits received. Contingent valuation in a benefit framework imitates actual markets as closely as possible. There is no egalitarian assumption in benefit analysis first because people differ in the way they value health improvements. The evidence of this book concerning light-symptom reduction is that there are wide disparities in values among people, although it turns out that they are not particularly related to income. The great differences among people at the other end of the scale, near death, are underscored by the wide range of differences in risk aversion that people reveal by their behavior. These differences mean that people trade off prospects of death for other goods at widely different rates. In light of this behavior, it seems difficult to give meaning to the idea that death means the same thing to people in general.

The objective of imitating actual markets as closely as possible leads to the rejection of the cost corollary of qualy analysis. Benefit measurement is applied demand analysis. This means maximization of utility subject to a budget constraint at the individual level. Contingent valuation is a demand-revealing process because respondents are carefully prepared to think about the value of program effects within the limits of their ability to pay for them. In short, benefit analysis treats health as a good like any other good that is traded in the market. Qualy analysis treats health as a preeminent condition of life, transcending any economic or social conditions at the individual level. How far the two traditions diverge in the guidance that they offer in practical, quantitative terms is an entirely different question, and one that deserves to be investigated. Additional comments along these lines are made in Section 6.6. Comparative analysis should be carried out at the theoretical level to sharpen understanding of differences at the quantitative level.

Empirically, there is a need for theoretically grounded regression studies that measure the importance of socioeconomic differences with some precision. These results are not available from either approach. When adequate regression results are available, controlled simulations and calibrations will be possible by adjusting income, social, and demographic variables. These adjustments should permit comparisons under conditions made similar experimentally and should permit experimental investigation of changes in health values with respect to the most important control variables. In the meantime, good mean-value results are available from both approaches, and preliminary comparisons can be made. Furthermore, the value-of-life literature, discussed in the next section, provides a sound theoretical and empirical basis for integrating results.

Health and the Value of Productive Time

Health is demanded for two reasons—for utility and for its value as an investment good. Health is valued for its own sake. People also invest in health because it yields healthy time that is used to produce market goods and nonmarket productive time. Utility is *derived* from the output of the investment good, which is used in the production of utility-yielding consumption commodities.

Health is to an important extent produced by the people who enjoy it and yields utility both directly and indirectly. It is a produced good that competes in consumption with other goods and is subject to a downward-sloping demand curve. The quantity demanded is negatively correlated with its shadow price, which depends on many variables, including the price of medical care (Grossman 1972, p. 225).

These elements of the theory that underlies empirical studies of health values provide guidance in estimating the utility and value yielded by public health programs. In particular they illuminate the problem of measuring program effects on people in the labor force and those outside it because of choice, age, or other considerations. This latter problem is empirically a difficult one, but it is capable of measurement because all people do make these decisions more or less frequently throughout their lives.

This theoretical orientation does not, however, provide guidance to the qualy researcher because of the egalitarian assumption, which places program costs to the individual, as well as differences in individual preferences and productivity, off of the research agenda.

An example of the kind of problem that can arise is found in the multiattribute health state classification system of Torrance et al. (1982, p. 1045). They define the attribute "role function," which involves various degrees of "limitations when working, going to school, playing or in other activities." The first problem with the role function attribute has already been addressed; the Grossman framework makes it clear that working and playing bear conceptually different relationships to health. A second problem relates to the definition of the contingent-market product, usually so carefully considered by qualy researchers. Because work and play (to continue that example) are so different, it is important that respondents be carefully prepared to take account of the differences by explicitly explaining the meaning of the various attribute levels. Only then can the researcher be confident that all respondents have similar things in mind when they answer. Without proper advance framing of the contingent market product, different respondents are likely to notice and emphasize different aspects of the attribute. The resulting ambiguity increases unexplained variances and reduces the interpretability of the results. The Kaplan, Bush, and Berry (1976, pp. 486–90) function and symptom categories are largely neutral with respect to utility-yielding and work-enhancing activities. They do, however, refer to work, housework, and other activities in the social activity function. Neutrality may be the best approach; introducing the distinction would put added burden on respondents. It holds promise, however, of providing valuable information and would make it possible to tailor questionnaires to the special circumstances of respondents.

One way of introducing productivity effects into a multiattribute qualy framework is to include a health dimension related to work impairment in the questionnaire. The responses might add valuable knowledge about work-health relationships. The next step is to link productivity effects to utility. This step could be approached, directly, using the survey approach, or indirectly, by drawing on economic models of health behavior that incorporate both utility and productivity effects.

As an example of the utility-productivity problem, consider throat soreness and congestion. The general population would state that their quality of life had been reduced because of discomfort and the inconvenience of taking medicine. A professional singer, however, would experience some loss of livelihood from the condition, in addition to the problems experienced by the general population. The Grossman framework emphasizes that the loss of livelihood does not affect utility directly. Rather, it reduces the ownership of resources that are used to produce a wide variety of utilities. As a practical matter, qualy research, which resembles contingent valuation, needs to recognize this distinction and carefully build it into questionnaires that elicit utilities from respondents. Otherwise, respondents will not be adequately prepared to sort out these matters, and their responses will be ambiguous. A challenge to qualy analysts, therefore, is to develop an enhanced theoretical framework to guide empirical studies in this area. The problem is an inherent one, whether one recognizes differences in individual preferences, or whether program costs are allowed to enter at the level of individual choice.

Aggregation Problems

The method of evaluating the social value of a public-health program follows from the way the problem is formulated at the level of individual choice. Qualy explicitly keeps considerations of cost out of the problem at the individual level. Qualys and costs are aggregated separately, and results are typically reported in terms of program cost per qualy. It is a matter of judgment as to whether the empirical research favors the program or not. Kaplan and Bush suggest that programs with a cost per well year of less than $20,000 are "cost-effective by current standards"; those in the range of $20,000–$100,000 are "possibly controversial, but justifiable by many current examples"; and those over $100,000 are "questionable in comparison with other health care expenditures" (Kaplan and Bush 1982, p. 74; see Table 6.1, where values are expressed in 1991 dollars).

By contrast, economic measures of willingness to pay reflect a downward-sloping demand curve for health and hence bring cost in at the individual level. Aggregate willingness to pay measures can be compared with aggregate cost estimates in the form of a net present value figure. Aggregate net present value, while requiring informed interpretation and judgment rather than mechanical interpretation, is directly interpretable in terms of social benefit evaluation. Qualy analysis, in contrast, regards individual differences in preferences and willingness to pay as extraneous and hence yields results that are more difficult to interpret at the aggregate level.

TABLE 6.1.   Policy Implications of Qualy Values

Cost per Well Year (Qualy)	Policy Implication
< $30,000	Cost-effective
$30,000–$140,000	Possibly controversial, but justifiable by many current examples
> $140,000	Questionable

The fact that good health also produces utility indirectly by adding to healthy time gives rise to aggregation problems. We have discussed the introduction of a work attribute as a separate dimension in the multiattribute setting. People in the market- or nonmarket-employment phases of their life cycles could rate program effects on this dimension. Children would also score zero on the work dimension in the case of light health problems, but problems arise in measuring the long-term benefits of programs that will affect the productivity of their later working years. But in utility terms, problems must be solved in aggregating scores on this dimension with scores on other dimensions that yields utility directly. Retired persons would presumably score zero on the work attribute, but far from zero on direct utility attributes.

Health Effects over Time—the Discounting Problem

Various decisions about health have different time horizons. Some decisions have immediate, short-term consequences, such as taking medication to relieve cold symptoms or taking defensive measures to fend off the cold discomforts in advance. Other decisions are made with much longer time horizons in mind. Moderating fat intake and alcohol consumption and engaging in regular exercise reduce the probability of heart disease over the entire remaining life span. By avoiding airborne asbestos fibers, one can reduce the danger of contracting cancers that have latency periods as long as 50 years or more.

Public health policies involve a diversity of time-horizon effects that are just as complicated as health decisions made by the individual. Evaluating the benefits of public health policies thus raises difficult problems of theory and measurement. Two aspects of qualy analysis are of particular interest in connection with the issue. The first, already discussed, pertains to the health utility derived by persons engaged in market work compared with others—typically children, older people, and those engaged in household activities. The second is related to the measurement of utilities that will accrue only in the future. The public health professional must deal with these utilities now, in connection with policies or practices presently employed that will produce them. Qualy analysts ask the question, Should future benefits be discounted or not? This is a controversial question in the public health literature. Weinstein says, "In cost-effectiveness analysis from the societal prospective, it has been argued, benefits in terms of years of life gained should be discounted, but this approach is still controversial" (1980, p. 309). Drummond, Stoddard, and Torrance (1987, p. 82) say that "the weight of the argument is for discounting health effects occurring in the future." They go on to say that "the current state of the art would suggest that effects should be treated in the same way as costs, and discounted at the same rate." Weinstein and Stason (1977, pp. 719–20) develop this argument in a widely cited study. For a fundamentally different approach to the discounting problem, Sjaastad and Wisecarver (1977) develop a framework that addresses the major schools of thought on social discounting and the opportunity cost of public spending. Horowitz and Carson (1990) present a model of discount-rate estimation and an experimental method for use in empirical measurement of the statistical value of life. An outline of suggested work in the context of public health is found in Chapter 16.

This volume places individual health choices involving time in a life-cycle decision-making framework. The theoretical basis for this approach is developed in Chapter 11. The life-cycle framework is applied to life-threatening illnesses in which symptoms occur years in the future and in which both length and quality of life are affected. To implement the life-cycle framework, entire life paths involving differences in quantity and quality of life are formulated. Certainty and uncertainty scenarios are both explored. A strong result, both theoretical and empirical, is that people discount future health problems. Young people in particular heavily discount health problems that are postulated to occur late in life. Time preference is involved, and more research is needed on the problem.

Fuchs notes the importance that differences in time preference can have on health. People with lower rates of time preference would invest more heavily in health because they are more forward-looking than others. His research strategy in "Time Preference and Health: An Exploratory Study" (1982) is to measure time preference in a questionnaire survey of 508 respondents and relate responses to socioeconomic characteristics. Survey questions utilize interest rates, dollar trade-offs, and other monetary questions. Fuchs reviews a number of other studies that explore time preference using similar contingent valuation frameworks. He notes that these studies of time preference rely on the assumption of imperfect capital markets—that is, people cannot borrow and lend without limit at a single market rate of interest. This being the case, people may have different discount rates related to health behavior and health status (p. 96).

In the course of this discussion, Fuchs makes a critical observation that is not pursued in his own research or the studies he reviews: if capital markets were perfect, "differences across individuals in time preference might still result in differences in nontradable health-related activities, but these would not be predictable from the replies to interest rate questions" (p. 96). The problem with this research is that interest-rate questions, or other kinds of capital-market questions, might not measure people's behavior in the critical nontradable health-related goods and activities. This is the realm of the lifestyle variables—diet, exercise, and so forth—that are such important determinants of health.

It would therefore be useful to focus survey research directly on health behavior that involves intertemporal decisions. Several approaches are possible. One is to develop alternative life-cycle scenarios, as in Chapter 13. Preferences that people express for appropriately constructed alternative life paths would reflect differences in time preference that might exist among respondents. The discount rate might remain implicit.

Another approach is to derive discount rates explicitly from contingent market experiments. One way of doing this would be to derive qualy estimates for several health conditions that explicitly pertain to the present. The second step is to arrange these health states in various plausible life-path scenarios. The sum of the qualys is a quality-adjusted life for each scenario. The implicit discount rate is zero. The next step is to present these scenarios to respondents with the time dimensions clearly stated. The disability time paths would differ considerably among scenarios. The respondent would compare them with each other and with a base-case scenario in which none of the disabilities appeared. Respondents would first rank the scenarios according to their preferences. They would then evaluate the scenarios in qualy terms. For the base case, having n years of life, the sum of qualys equals n, which assumes a zero discount rate. For the other scenarios, the quality-adjusted life has a value less than n. One would not attempt to elicit qualys for individual years for these scenarios. The implicit discount rate would be obtained by comparing the quality-adjusted lives with the life path constructed by adding together the timeless qualys into corresponding life paths. The discount rate that emerged could be used to evaluate qualys in the traditional way. This work could of course be carried out in willingness to pay terms as well as qualys.

Moore and Viscusi (1988) derived a discount rate of 10%–12% endogenously in a study that focused on wage premiums paid to workers who engaged in jobs with fatality risks. Another approach to the discounting problem, favorable to a zero discount rate, is suggested by the egalitarian assumption. Qualy researchers may wish to reject the life-cycle framework on the grounds that later health years are equally deserving as present years. This is the egalitarian assumption on intertemporal grounds, applied to a single person. Justification for this approach could include the evidence that people have great difficulty thinking about health matters that are deferred for many years and that they come to regret decisions made in the past, even when those decisions were informed ones.

This application of the egalitarian assumption seems to stand on the same ethical footing as the interpersonal application, which holds all people equal with respect to health states. Indeed, both versions of the principle are already being applied to an extent. The reason is that treating different people equally entails treating different age groups equally because people affected by public health policies occupy all age groups. It is a small step to treat all age groups equally for each person. It follows that succeeding generations would be treated the same way as well. A practical problem that arises is that program benefit estimates, in qualy or dollar terms, become sensitive to the planning horizon that is used. Indeed, with a zero discount rate, benefits are simply proportional to the horizon and become indefinitely large (infinite) as longer horizons are assumed.

The hard fact is that health state in later years is only a part of what people get out of life. If their desires are heeded, a positive discount rate will be used. The relevant question, on which additional serious effort is needed, would appear to be what positive discounting procedure should be followed.

6.6. Comparison and Synthesis of Methods

Qualy analysis is achieving widespread attention among health professionals. Because it is a preference-based approach to assessing the merits of health care programs, it is closely related to conventional economic analysis. Benefit analysis has also made considerable progress in achieving application to health-care programs. Progress in effectively formulating contingent markets has greatly extended capabilities for valuing nonmarket health benefits. Theoretical formulation of utility-yielding and productivity-enhancing aspects of health improvements has clarified the valuation process. The two areas of research can be merged by calibrating existing findings from both fields.

At the same time, the qualy approach to the measurement of health values is in some respects fundamentally different from the economic approach, even though they are both rooted in an analysis of utility. As demonstrated in Chapter 15, however, they can be brought together in a consistent way to greatly extend the range of health values available to health care professionals and policy makers.

The economic concept of the statistical value of life provides a key to empirically calibrating the qualy literature with the willingness to pay literature. The value-of-life calculation is made by estimating people's willingness to pay for changes in small levels of risk. This can be accomplished in several different ways. Bailey (1980) discusses a number of important studies in this field. Derivation of the value of a life year from the statistical value of life is the step that brings together the qualy with the economic approach to measuring health values. The value of a life year is obtained by discounting the remaining expected years of a statistical life. The result is an estimate of the dollar value of a qualy.

For example, Miller, Calhoun, and Arthur (1990) use a statistical value of life of $1.95 million, derived from a synthesis of 25 willingness to pay studies. The average respondent is 38 years old with a life expectancy of

39 years. A 6% discount rate yields a value of life year of $120,000. The effect of different discount rates is considered. Moore and Viscusi (1988), in a study of wage premiums for risky jobs, estimate the value of a life year to be $175,000. A discount rate of 10%–12% is estimated endogenously. Mauskopf and French (1989) used the dollar value of a qualy, assuming a $5 million value of life. Using a 3% discount rate and 36 years of life expectancy, they arrive at a life-year value of $220,000.

These examples illustrate important work of others in quantifying and applying the relationship between the qualy and the economic approach to health values that we pursue in Chapter 14. An aspect of this synthesis should be studied in future research, however. Value-of-life-based estimates can vary considerably depending on discount rates and other assumptions. On the qualy side, a widely cited guideline in the public health literature (Kaplan and Bush, 1982, p. 74), updated in round numbers from 1982 to 1991 dollars, is shown in Table 6.1. The judgments are based on a comparison of programs and medical interventions that are considered more or less justifiable in terms of costs and qualy returns. The ranges in life-year values and acceptable cost per qualy overlap to a considerable extent. They are not very well calibrated, however. In the first place, the acceptable range of cost-per-qualy values tends to be lower than that implied by the value of a life year. Second, the range of values within each approach is large. Consequently, their combined effect is to leave considerable ambiguity in policy implications when they are considered together. Additional research in both areas could bring the two approaches closer together and narrow the ranges of uncertainty. Ranges of uncertainty will always exist, but policy decisions for or against a particular action are greatly strengthened if they are supported by evidence from both approaches.

Various kinds of research could be undertaken to improve the calibrations. One could set up a contingent market for a health improvement that would be evaluated both in qualy terms and willingness to pay terms. If qualy respondents gave an average response of .033 qualys gained and the average yearly willingness to pay for the program was $5,000, then the implied value of a qualy is $150,000. Different programs, having greater and lesser values, could be evaluated this way to arrive at a qualy value.

A second approach involves contingent-market experiments to directly measure the value of a statistical life. These experiments are difficult to design, but the following example illustrates the idea. A person faces imminent death unless treated for a condition. Two treatments exist. Both offer the patient a normal life expectancy in good health, except that treatment 1 carries a .01 probability of death this year, while treatment 2 carries a .01 probability of death next year. How much more is treatment 2 worth than treatment 1? Suppose the patient is willing to pay $1,200 more for treatment 2, which in expectation terms provides .01 of a qualy. Then the implied value of a qualy is $1,200 divided by .01—that is, $120,000.

Implementing the value-of-life approach in a contingent valuation framework involves problems of plausible framing of the product, avoidance of undue complication, respondent understanding of probabilities, risk aversion, discounting, and other matters. But the problems are probably not insuperable.

Research along these lines would facilitate the synthesis of empirical findings that would further contribute to the body of common knowledge available to policy makers and health professionals. Care and judgment would be required because of the different theoretical foundations underlying the studies. But, as already suggested, this diversity can be a virtue in that policy problems can be evaluated from different perspectives, strengthening the evidence for or against policy decisions. The work underlying the tables of health values in Chapter 15 illustrates the complexity of the task. In addition to enlarging the body of common useful knowledge, the effort is capable of providing many plausibility checks concerning both dollar and utility magnitudes. It would also enlarge the common domain of theoretical underpinnings by bringing the separate research efforts closer together.

The willingness to pay analysis of light symptoms reported in this book might be useful to qualy researchers in extending their results near the perfect-health end of the utility scale. The reason is that contingent market questions are easy and natural to answer in willingness to pay terms, whereas they might be more difficult to frame in terms of the 0–1 utility scale. For example, a willingness to pay $145 per year to relieve 30 days of symptoms implies a qualy improvement of $145 divided by value of qualy divided by 12, which is something like .00012 qualys. Framing contingent valuation questions directly in quality-of-life terms is likely to be difficult in this range of values. Dividing a qualy by 12 or by 365 to get the value of a month or a day of symptoms is less desirable than direct measurement. Calculations of qualy values for light symptoms can be made from mathematically expressed utility functions. These results, however, often extend values beyond the range of directly obtained contingent values. They are less satisfactory because of this.

6.7. Conclusion

The qualy literature discussed in this chapter is a major source of empirical values for health policy analysis. It has been developed by public health professionals who have made specialized applications of the economic theory and measurement of utility. These studies complement the willingness to pay studies developed for this book and for a still modest number of other economic studies of health values. I have attempted in this chapter to highlight and critique some of the similarities and differences between the work being published in the public health literature and in economics. The major theoretical similarity is that both approaches are grounded in the preferences of individuals as represented by the utility function. The major empirical similarity is the use of contingent valuation to obtain quantitative measures of preferences. The major difference between the two methods is a theoretical one. The willingness to pay studies of the economic approach are grounded in the theory of demand, which recognizes that value is meaningful only if expressed relative to other things that must be given up, as accomplished in demand theory through explicit introduction of a budget constraint reflecting the fact that resources are limited. The qualy approach excludes resource constraints from the analysis of preferences. To be useful for our purposes, qualys must be expressed in terms of what people would be willing to pay to obtain them. The unit of a qualy is a life year. The economic literature on the value of life gives estimates of the total value of life, which is the sum of a person's life years. Using the idea that the value of life is the discounted sum of the value of each year of life, we are able to solve for the implied value of a life year, thus enabling qualys to be translated into dollar values. In this way, qualy results and the willingness to pay results reported elsewhere in this book are integrated into a common empirical framework.

Valuation of Common Symptoms

Overview of Part Two

The purpose of this part of the book is to further explore methods for estimating the value of reducing common, or light, symptoms. Knowledge about the value of light symptom reduction is a major element of policy analysis that has not received adequate attention. It is important to know the value of smaller benefits received by a large number of people.

While the value-of-life literature has provided analytic constructs for valuing mortality benefits, economic analysis has offered no such ready construct for measuring the benefits of reduced illness. Most morbidity analyses have measured benefits in terms of reduced work-loss days and reduced medical expenditures. Those measures, however, do not provide a conceptually satisfactory measure of morbidity benefits because they neglect the value of comfort and other benefits of health, such as leisure and the productivity of nonmarket work.

Contingent valuation offers a technique capable of getting at values that are extraordinarily difficult to measure by other means, such as property value or revealed behavior methods. Health and aesthetic values of air and water quality, recreation, and power plant siting are among the topics that have been addressed by contingent valuation. Our objective is to establish a contingent market in symptom reduction that encompasses all essential aspects of symptom disutility. Expressions of willingness to pay are designed to reflect the total value of symptom reduction, unlike payments in existing markets, which provide only partial measures of value.

Contingent valuation has become an established research method during the last 15 or 20 years. Considerable advances have been made in overcoming methodological shortcomings and eliciting high-quality information. The present study builds on this progress by applying contingent valuation to a neglected area of empirical economics.

Chapter 7 deals with the design of the contingent valuation instrument. It begins with an overview of major issues in contingent valuation and describes how these issues are handled in this study. Chapter 7 then goes on to review in more detail experiences with focus groups that influenced the design of the survey instrument. Chapter 7 concludes by presenting the

139

structure of the contingent valuation instrument used in this study. A representative questionnaire is included as an appendix.

After a discussion of the sampling design, Chapter 8 presents the empirical results from household personal surveys conducted in two cities. Summary statistics on bids and characteristics of respondents are given. Regression results explaining the bids are presented.

Finally, in Chapter 9, the results from a corroborative mail questionnaire are presented.

7

Issues in Questionnaire Design

Robert Fabian and George Tolley

7.1. Major Issues in Contingent Valuation

Contingent valuation has become a widely accepted source of empirical values in economics, though some economists continue to question it. Methodological studies of contingent valuation, as well as empirical applications of the technique, are widely published in the literature of economics. Cummings et al. (1986) and Mitchell and Carson (1989) provide extended critiques of the role and state of development of contingent valuation. In building upon this work, we have given greatest attention to three methodological areas. These are the information and preference context of contingent valuation, which frames the problem for respondents and helps them research their preferences; the structure of the contingent market, which defines the good to be valued in a clear, concise, and quantitative manner; and the bidding-game process, which assists respondents in arriving at carefully thought-out, unbiased values. This study builds on progress in dealing with those issues, and it considers the new problems they raise when dealing with morbidity.

Information and Preference Context

The quality of answers is affected by the fact that information is imperfect and thinking requires effort. If people are asked out of the blue how they value hypothetical situations, their answers may be nearly random unless considerable thought is given. Contingent valuation must give effort to helping respondents invest in information and explore background information on the subject matter—for example, their health status and the various health costs and disutilities they have borne, such as loss of work, doctor bills, and discomfort. In this way they are helped to invest in thought about the considerations that go into a reasoned answer. Questions arise as to the optimum degree of investment and as to the content of the investment. Tedium is a major limit on the amount of time that can be taken. Attempts to help respondents think about the problem will be counterproductive if they become bored. Manageable total length of the questionnaire becomes an extremely important consideration.

Questions of optimum content involve, first, focusing on most important matters in view of the limited time available, and, second, avoiding imparting bias by overstressing certain effects and understressing others. Helping the respondent invest in information raises unique problems in the case of morbidity because of the variety of ways that health affects a person. Guidance from economic theory is needed that sorts out the roles of work, medical costs, discomfort, and defensive measures. These subjects must be introduced in commonsense terms but still be consistent with the economic theory of utility maximization and consumer surplus. The theoretical framework for the information and preference context is given in Chapter 12.

Structuring the Contingent Market

It is essential that the contingent market good be presented to respondents in a natural, believable way so that they can reach a valid judgment about it. It is equally important, however, that the good be defined in a precise way that is amenable to quantitative analysis. Reconciling these objectives required much experimentation.

Everyday language is an important part of the description of symptoms. Descriptions of the frequency, duration, and severity of symptoms must be included in a natural way that assures as much as possible that all respondents are thinking about the same thing when they express their willingness to pay.

In the case of light symptoms, the problem is simplified by the fact that most people have firsthand experience. This makes it possible to keep the description of the contingent market good fairly short and still fulfill both major objectives.

For severe symptoms, out of range of ordinary experience, more difficult problems are raised. The angina questionnaires posed these problems. A special effort must be made to help the respondent imagine what it would be like to live with extreme and recurrent pain—in the case of severe angina—or recurrent pain of less intensity in the case of mild angina.

Respondents are asked to imagine having a specific angina health problem, in contrast to the light symptoms surveys, in which they simply recall their own endowment from their information and preference contexts.

After the contingent market good has been established, it is necessary to devise a vehicle for delivery of the good to the respondent and a vehicle of payment. The payment vehicle problem has received much discussion in the literature. The vehicle for delivery has received less discussion, but will be important in future contingent valuation studies of health.

Much experimentation was devoted to devising an effective method of conveying the good—better health—to the respondent. An example is to attribute all light symptoms to allergy and to postulate a new prescription drug, one easy to take with no side effects, that would deliver a specified amount of relief. This delivery vehicle is expressed in tangible, concrete terms in the interest of achieving realism. But its realism proves to be a drawback: numerous respondents were found to object to the idea of taking medicine; they did not accept the allergy; and the necessary specification of ease of use and no side effects introduced abstractions that caused respondents to balk. Because efforts to achieve tangibility in the vehicle of delivery introduce distractions of this sort, use of pure willingness to pay questions is regarded as an advantageous approach.

The payment vehicle presents similar problems. Tangibility can be achieved by making payment come through higher prices or taxes. Public goods have been paid for through higher utility bills. Tangibility, however, is often found to be accompanied by suggestions of other matters of concern to respondents that distract them from making bids that reflect the true value of the contingent market good. As in the case of the vehicle for delivery of the good, there are strong reasons for using an abstract payment vehicle that simply asks "How much would you be willing to pay for this good?"

Bidding Game

Bidding formats have received extensive analysis in the literature. Drawing upon this literature, as well as extensive previous experimentation with alternative formats, we chose the iterative bidding procedure. A major virtue of iterative bidding is the focusing of attention it demands of respondents. No bidding format is perfect, however, and several problem areas must always receive special attention. Strategic bidding and limited investment in the information needed to bid serve as a convenient two-way classification of concerns.

Because normal precautions were taken, strategic bidding did not pose difficult problems, although one problem is worth mentioning. It is very important that the interviewer not suggest in any way what answer is being sought. There is a tendency among some respondents to try to please the interviewer with their answers or to demonstrate their wisdom by giving the answer they believe the interviewer thinks correct.

The information-investment problem was much greater, however, and considerable research was devoted to it. Anchoring is a frequently encountered problem in bidding behavior with insufficient information.

"Anchoring" means that people seize upon a convenient, easy bid amount and stick to it across bids because they have little information-based incentive to do otherwise. Starting point bias, often seen as a weakness of iterative bidding, is probably more fundamentally a problem of limited investment in information and inadequate researching of preferences on the part of the bidder. Focus group experience teaches that, as questionnaires are enriched in their information and preference review, aspects anchoring at or near the starting point cease to be a problem.

As more and more bid questions are asked about similar contingent market goods, it becomes increasingly difficult for respondents to recognize meaningful variations in value. Careful preparation enhances the respondents' ability to handle more questions, but experience teaches that splitting the questionnaire or sacrificing information becomes a necessity. Excessive variation across respondents to a question often indicates problems. Variation is expected because respondents do not have perfect information about the good or their preferences. Problems arise when the respondents' understanding of the good and the market and of their own preferences is so limited that extraneous information predominates in determining bids.

There are two important cases—extremely high bids and extremely low bids. Take the high-bid case. Respondents may be thinking of the increase of their well-being due to greater comfort without thinking of the food, clothing, housing, and other goods they must give up if they bid high, or they may simply forget about their budget constraints. With regard to respondents who bid too low, there may be a high threshold of preception due to the cost of thinking. For example, eliminating a cough will really be worth something to them, but they bid zero because they have relegated cough to an unimportant category where they do not bother to make comparisons.

Previous Contingent Valuation Work on Morbidity

Some previous work has included morbidity as a part of other effects, as, for example, the study by Schulze et al. (1985), where air pollution effects, including both morbidity and visibility, were asked about. Previous contingent valuation studies concerned with morbidity as such are rare. One is an asthma study reported in a paper by Rowe and Chestnut (1984).

Another research project by Loehman and associates (1979, 1981) concerns the benefits of controlling sulfur oxides. In the 1979 study, a mail contingent valuation survey was sent to 1,977 residents in the Tampa Bay area, resulting in 432 returns. Willingness to pay questions were asked about the following three groups of symptoms: shortness of breath/chest pains; coughing/sneezing; head congestion/eye/ear/throat irritations. Values were elicited for minor and severe symptom days, which were defined briefly. No mention was made of any specific underlying disease, nor were causes such as air pollution mentioned. No specific delivery vehicle, such as a pill, was employed, and a simple, abstract payment vehicle—"tell us how much you would pay"—was chosen. The means of payment was a checklist, ranging from $0 to $1,000 per year in 10 increments.

The Loehman et al. study is similar to our seven-symptom survey in a number of respects. First of all, there is a close correspondence between the symptom lists. In both cases a pure health attribute approach was used. The Loehman et al. study carefully avoided the introduction of redundant information in its introductory letter, its symptom narrative, and in its delivery and payment vehicles. (Our mail survey, unlike the much more extensive door-to-door versions, used a medication to deliver the contingent market good.) The Loehman et al. return rate—22%—is much lower than our 48%, which reflects the effectiveness of the procedures followed in our mail survey. A major difference between the two approaches is the large number (24) of similar willingness to pay questions in the Loehman et al. survey. Our surveys employed much fewer questions on any survey instrument in order to avoid taxing the respondents' concentration and the extent of their information and preference review.

7.2. Focus Group Experience and Questionnaire Design

Focus groups were the basic research tool employed in the development of the seven-symptom and angina questionnaires. Many alternative versions of the questionnaires were administered to participants during the first half of focus group sessions, followed during the second half by discussions among participants and researchers. These sessions were followed by weekly meetings of the research team devoted to discussing strengths and shortcomings of the test questionnaires, discussing problems and new insights derived from the sessions, and formulating revised versions for testing with the next focus group.

Two seven-light-symptom questionnaires and two angina questionnaires resulted from this process. The following discussion outlines the major issues that received the greatest clarification and development as a result of the focus group process.

Contingent Valuation Product

Establishing a standard contingent market good to be purchased (in various quantities) by all respondents was a basic requirement. For analytic purposes, a well-defined regressor is essential. Realism or concreteness was a complimentary objective because respondents feel more comfortable bidding on tangible goods.

Early focus group experience confirmed a prior hypothesis that any mention of environmental pollution as a cause of symptoms, for example, would distract respondents from expressing their values. No mention of pollution is made in the final versions. Early versions of single-light-symptom questionnaires achieved concreteness by postulating the existence of an allergy that caused the symptom and a new prescription medicine that relieved it. The medicine was declared safe by the doctor, and the allergy was declared to pose no underlying threats to health.

Use of variants of this approach with several focus groups, however, eventually convinced the research team that concreteness was purchased at the expense of distraction from the nature of the values being sought. Some respondents expressed disbeliefs in allergy as a source of some symptoms. They thought in terms of more serious disease as the source of difficulty, suggesting that people were not bidding purely for symptom relief. Some respondents related the cost of symptom discomfort to the price they spend on medicines to obtain relief. Maximum willingness to pay was thus confused with market price, causing misstatement of the correct values. In several focus groups, a frequent explanation for zero bids was that the experience is a common event in everyday life and that it is best simply to live with it until it passes. The zero bids of these respondents are thus interpretable as "I usually don't spend money on medicines in these situations."

Introducing the judgment of the doctor into the contingent valuation (CV) narrative appeared to have a similar unintended effect. Its purpose was to help the respondent accept the narrative as authentic and bid on the basis of best available information. One apparent result, however, was to increase the number of zero bids because people took account of the fact that they usually do not visit the doctor because of these symptoms. The CV narrative implied a visit to the doctor, which would be costly in terms of both time and money.

Thus the attempt to construct a tangible, real-life situation in terms of allergy, medicine, and implied doctor visit created an information overload that biased responses away from true willingness to pay for symptom relief. The solution to the problem was to use a more abstract narrative that abandoned these devices. In the final version of the questionnaire, respondents were reminded of the various ways they might deal with the symptoms— buy medicine, go to the doctor, or simply wait for them to go away. Then they were asked to notice that a cure might be worth even more than the price they had to pay for medicine or doctor's assistance and might be valuable even if they just waited for relief to come on its own accord. The CV questions that follow this general introduction are of the form, "If you were faced with 30 additional days of coughing in the next 12 months, would it be worth $100 to completely get rid of these coughing days?"

This version of the light-symptom questionnaire was field tested before being adopted and was found to be effective. The relatively abstract nature of the contingent market good proved to be acceptable to respondents.

Bidding Framework

SYMPTOM SELECTION: LIGHT SYMPTOMS. Because policy application was the research objective, a set of individual symptoms and symptom combinations had to be a selected that would be affected by environmental policy. At the same time, contingent markets in symptom reduction had to be established in a manageable bidding framework. At the outset, the choice was between restricting each questionnaire to one or two symptoms, on the one hand, or, on the other hand, constructing more inclusive questionnaires that spanned the set of policy consequences.

The former route initially appeared to permit more intensive iterative bidding and the attainment of more points on the bid functions of each of the symptoms. Accordingly, one-symptom questionnaires were developed and tested in focus groups. The result, however, was that respondents quickly tired of concentrating at length on the symptom problems. Iterative bidding, while helpful in getting the bidding process focused on reasonable values, proved to be redundant after several applications.

The final seven-symptom questionnaires contained the solutions to these problems. Tedium was reduced by introducing a variety of symptoms. Before money bids for symptom reduction were asked, respondents ranked the symptoms in order of bothersomeness to them. This led them to establish relations among their own preferences first. Iterative bids were obtained on the least—and most—bothersome symptoms. Bids for each of the intermediate symptoms were then directly obtained without iteration.

SYMPTOM SELECTION: ANGINA. Angina symptoms were included in the light symptom surveys during early focus groups. It was decided to use them in a separate set of surveys to reduce the length and complexity of these explanatory survey forms. Angina symptoms were seen as being qualitatively different from the light symptoms. Consequently, they required individually tailored sections to prepare the respondent for bidding. First, a longer, more detailed set of symptom descriptions was necessary because most people are unfamiliar with angina. Second, the health status part of the questionnaire had to be related to angina in order to establish the appropriate health endowment and serve as an effective respondent warm-up.

The angina questionnaires represent a step in the direction of the study of life-threatening health problems. Severe angina introduces anxiety and extreme pain. The narrative carefully excludes danger of death, however, and is thus purely symptom oriented. A risk-of-death question was included in early versions of the angina questionnaires but was dropped when it was recognized that careful preparation of respondents in probability interpretation was necessary. It was hoped that the angina responses would be useful in understanding health problems involving the anxiety and response of risk bearing associated with serious illness and death.

FREQUENCY OF SYMPTOM OCCURRENCE IN QUESTIONNAIRES. Much focus group experimentation was devoted to determining the proper number of bids to elicit from respondents. Progress in the solution of this problem complimented work in determining the number of symptoms feasibly investigated in one questionnaire. Several issues were involved. A purely practical problem was how many bids a respondent could make before losing concentration and giving mechanical answers. This question was discussed in numerous meetings following focus group sessions. Various devices were developed to discourage mechanical bidding.

Another issue was the necessity of representing both normal and sensitive populations. Bids representing both small- and large-symptom responses to environmental change were necessary in order to estimate benefits among all affected groups. Getting people to take small-symptom changes seriously required major experimentation. A third issue was the desirability of having an adequate number of points to econometrically estimate bid or demand functions for symptom reduction.

Both the angina and the seven-symptom surveys were split into two versions—identical except for frequency of symptom occurrence and number of symptom-days reduction to be valued.

Health Status

The health status module of the seven-symptom survey underwent considerable evolution as a result of focus group experience. The basic challenge was to obtain a substantial amount of detailed information about the background and experience of the respondent with each of the seven symptoms and information about expenditures for medicine and professional care on the symptoms. Early attempts proved to be cumbersome and time-consuming, and much of the individual symptom detail was removed. When it became evident that too much analytically valuable information was being lost, further attempts were made to include it, and an efficient format, originally developed for an experimental mail survey, was successfully adopted.

Respondent-Interviewer Interaction

As expected, some respondents had difficulty concentrating on the survey for more than a few minutes. To combat this problem, a number of handout cards were developed for use throughout the interview. Some of these cards simply list the respondents' choices of answers. Others play a more active role in the survey. Ranking of symptoms was introduced into the seven-symptom survey primarily to avoid mechanical or inadequately thought-out bidding. People tended to bid the same amount for several symptoms without too much thought in early focus groups. The ranking approach required them to consider carefully which symptoms were more or less bothersome. (Ties were allowed.) Greater variation in bids resulted in later focus groups. Respondents arranged the symptom cards from least to most bothersome. They were asked to think carefully about the role of these symptoms in their own lives. The resulting card order determined the order of bidding.

The tally sheet was filled out by respondents to keep track of bids. They were given an opportunity to revise bids and symptom rankings, in case they had second thoughts about these judgments as the contingent valuation was carried out.

Experience indicated that respondents could be kept involved in the interviews for up to about 40 minutes. All final questionnaires fall within that time limit.

7.3. Structure of the Contingent Valuation Instrument

The structure of the health survey is reflected partly in the organization of the questionnaires and partly in the relationship of the questionnaires to each other. Internally, the four questionnaires have essentially the same organization. Their major features are questions on health endowment in the beginning, followed by contingent valuation questions, and ending with questions on socioeconomic characteristics. A major structural feature of all questionnaires is that they contain a high degree of interaction throughout between interviewer and respondent. Pairs of angina and seven-symptom questionnaires were used in the field in order to obtain responses on a range of symptom severities. This contributes greater precision to econometric estimation and assures that contingent market symptom avoidance spanned an adequately wide range of experience to be useful in policy analysis. Pairs of questionnaires were used rather than single versions in order to keep interview time within acceptable bounds. Responses were pooled during analysis into single datasets for the seven-symptom and for the angina questionnaires.

Details of the questionnaire structure are given in the remainder of this section, using the 1-symptom-day version of the seven-symptom questionnaire for discussion. Differences in the other questionnaires are then discussed briefly. The 1-day version is presented in the Appendix to this chapter.

SEVEN-SYMPTOM HEALTH QUESTIONNAIRE: 1 DAY. The first part of the questionnaire introduces the interviewer, briefly explains the purpose of the visit, and seeks an eligible respondent. Some general respondent and interviewer identification is recorded.

Respondents are then asked to subjectively rate their own health. This is followed by questions on perceived degree of control over own health and frequency of illness or physical discomfort during the last month.

These three questions orient the respondent to thinking about the subject of health, about which detailed hypothetical and experience-based questions will be asked. They are also intended for use as explanatory variables in the analysis.

The next section of the survey focuses on the respondent's experience with the seven symptoms during the previous 12 months. It is difficult to get accurate recall over a yearlong period, but a shorter period was ruled out because responses would likely be unrepresentative because of seasonal effects.

In the first question, people are simply asked if they have experienced any of the seven health problems during the last year. They are handed a card that lists the problems. A series of questions is then asked concerning the problems experienced by respondents. First, they are asked to recall about how many times they have experienced each problem. Next, they rank problems from most to least bothersome. These three initial questions are increasingly specific—eliciting more and more recall and thought.

The next questions quantify symptom severity in physical terms. They obtain information on the numbers of days of activities of various kinds that were lost or interfered with by each of the symptoms. If workdays were lost, they are asked how much earnings fell as a result.

The following questions pertain to purchase of medicine or use of professional health care related to the symptoms. First, respondents are asked if they have purchased medicine or visited a health professional. Then they are asked how many times and, last, how much it cost (net of insurance payments). Last, respondents are asked if they have experienced any of the symptoms in combination. If so, they are asked to name the combination of symptoms they have experienced most frequently.

Health status was one of the most extensive and time-consuming sections of the questionnaire. The principal reason for obtaining such extensive health status information is to provide the database for the comparison of the health expenditures and contingent valuation analyses. Less detailed databases originally considered would have greatly restricted the comparative analysis.

The other purpose of the health status data is that they, together with the health evaluation responses, determined the health endowment of the respondent. It is important to know respondents' initial health condition because it is hypothesized to be an important influence on willingness to pay for additional symptom avoidance.

The next major section of the survey concerns defensive measures. Respondents are asked if they have purchased any air-quality control equipment for their home or car for health reasons. They are asked if they avoid smoking and if they have changed location of residence for health reasons.

Money spent on equipment to reduce the risk of health problems is an important part of what some people are willing to pay to avoid the seven questionnaire symptoms. Avoiding smoking is not money expenditure, but it represents an expenditure of effort for many people that is probably equivalent to a large monetary expenditure. Moving for health reasons reflects willingness to pay both in terms of dollar amount and effort.

The role of defensive measures, or averting behavior, was given considerable theoretical attention during the time that the survey was being prepared and administered in the field. That work is reported in Chapters 2 and 4. The abridged list of defensive measures included in the questionnaires had the purpose of giving a preliminary indication of the direction and extent of their influence on willingness to pay for symptom avoidance.

The survey next turns to the ranking of symptoms, as a preparation for the bidding of the contingent valuation section. It establishes the standardized hypothetical product to be valued. Each symptom is described in a brief statement read by the interviewer. Cards are handed to respondents, summarizing the main points of each symptom description. Respondents are asked to suppose that their health endowment during the next 12 months will be exactly as it was in the past 12 months, except for 1 additional day of each of each of seven symptoms in turn. Thus, while the additional symptom day is the same for all, nevertheless the situation for each is unique because it is based on own individual experience. Several objectives are accomplished with this approach. First, a standard product is established, making it clear for purposes of quantitative analysis what is being valued by the bids. Second, realism is achieved by relating the contingent valuation problem to the respondents' personal experience. (Respondents have, of course, just spent quite a bit of time recalling that experience.) Third, it permits analytic exploration of the entire demand surface of the population by giving measures of willingness to substitute symptom-free days for other goods over a wide range of health endowments.

The ranking procedure accomplishes the additional objective of establishing relative valuations among the symptoms in physical terms. It requires respondents to think carefully about the symptoms in personal terms before bidding. Symptoms and symptom cards are presented one by one, as described above. After each card is presented, they are asked to arrange the cards in a stack with the more bothersome symptoms toward the bottom. Ties are permitted. The interviewer records the rankings on a tally sheet, in the order determined by the respondents.

To further prepare respondents for bidding, a household spending card is presented. This card lists six categories of household spending together with amounts and percentages spent by a typical family. Each respondent is urged to think about the actual amounts pertaining to his or her own family and to think specifically where symptom bids would affect the family budget.

After discussing the spending card, a paragraph is read that gives some instructions about how to think of the contingent markets about to be examined. The problem addressed is that people often think about willingness to pay in terms of what they actually pay in the market for remedies. In cases where they are accustomed to suffering through a problem until it goes away without buying medicine or going to the doctor, people often declare their willingness to pay to be zero. Respondents are asked to set aside their actual behavior in these situations and enter a simpler kind of hypothetical market in which a monetary payment could be exchanged for a cure. The contingent market is structured this way in order to avoid the larger number of zero bids that were found to result from alternative structures. An important feature of the contingent market structure is that it abstracts from visits to the doctor, purchases of medicine, or similar activities usually associated with curing health problems. A straightforward, abstract market involving a simple expression of willingness to pay was adopted and found, with suitable preparation, to be acceptable to respondents. The advantage of this approach over more tangibly constructed markets is that it avoids the equation of "I usually do nothing to treat this symptom" with "I am willing to pay zero."

Bidding then proceeds for each of the seven symptoms. For each symptom, the respondents are asked to suppose that their health will be the same during the next year as last, except for 1 additional day of the symptom in question. Bidding begins with the least bothersome problem identified by the symptom card at the top of the stock. The second contingent valuation is given for the most bothersome problem, corresponding to the bottom card.

These two bids are obtained by means of iterative bidding. An arbitrary starting point of $100 is used. Bidding proceeds up—doubled—or down—halved—depending on whether the respondent says yes or no to the opening offer. Once a no answer is received after an opening yes bid, half the difference between the last no answer and to most recent yes answer is asked. Bidding concludes with the last yes answer or zero. Answers are recorded on the tally sheet.

Having bracketed the dollar values on the least and most bothersome symptoms, the respondent is asked to decide the values for avoiding symptoms of intermediate bothersomeness. No bidding game is utilized; the respondent simply enters the values on the tally sheet. The respondent is encouraged to change bids or even alter the original rankings if desired.

The next part of the contingent valuation section is devoted to combinations of symptoms. One combination consists of an extra day of cough, sinus, and throat problems. Another consists of an extra day of headache, nausea, and drowsiness symptoms. As an approach to valuing the avoidance of a day of these symptoms, the respondent is asked to add respective individual bids and compare the sum with the value of avoiding all three together.

The next contingent valuation question asks the willingness to pay for a day of symptom relief for the respondent's entire household, using the first three-symptom combination: cough, sinus, and throat problems. The last question extends the day of relief from the three symptoms to everyone in the entire United States. The bid is for relief over and above that already bid for the respondent's own family.

In the last section of the survey dealing with health valuation, respondents distinguish loss of activity in the market (work away from home, medical expenses) and activities outside the market (comfort, work at home, recreation). They rank as many of the six categories (including "other," which they are asked to specify) as pertain to them. One intended use of the rankings is a descriptive tabulation that provides a qualitative summary of the importance of the symptoms to the general population. Another use is to provide additional information for the comparative analysis of willingness to pay versus health expenditures in valuing symptom reduction.

Respondents are also asked to compare the severity of the hypothetical symptoms described to them in the contingent market with the severity of corresponding symptoms they actually experienced. Then the respondents are asked how much they would pay to completely get rid of the symptoms they have actually experienced. The question helps to quantify the product being offered by linking it to the hypothetical symptom descriptions in terms of severity. Information on frequency has already been gathered in the health status section.

While the contingent value question on actual symptom experience logically belongs in the prevention section, including it here gives the respondent a little relief and variety and permits proper preparatory questioning.

Finally, an opportunity is given to change many of the bids and rankings about which they may have had second thoughts.

Socioeconomic information, together with the health endowment data collected at the beginning of the survey, quantifies the explanatory variables in the willingness to pay regressions. Socioeconomic questions comprise general demographic household information, various measures of household market activity, and general measures of human capital. The health endowment information is complementary in that it quantifies important specific human capital variables.

The first three questions deal with past and expected change of residence. The next question identifies the respondent's occupation. A question on respondent aptitudes is included partly as a general human capital measure and partly for the purpose of gauging ability to respond to the questionnaire. The remainder of the socioeconomic section gathers household data on age, race, education, family size and structure, current and permanent income, wealth, and savings. At the end of the questionnaire, the interviewer records comments that may be helpful in identifying problems that call into question the quality of the responses.

SEVEN-SYMPTOM HEALTH QUESTIONNAIRE: 30 DAYS. This version of the seven-light-symptom survey is identical to the 1-day version, except that avoidance of 30 additional days of symptoms, instead of 1 additional day, are ranked and valued in the ranking and CV sections.

ANGINA HEALTH QUESTIONNAIRE: 10 DAYS. The angina questionnaires are identical to the seven symptom questionnaires in the following sections: introduction, health evaluation, defensive measures, reasons, socioeconomic questions, and interviewer evaluation. The content of the remaining sections is modified as described below.

In terms of health status, the first group of questions pertains to respondents who have been diagnosed as having a heart condition of any kind. First, they are asked if they know the name of their condition. Next, they are asked to list the symptoms they have experienced and to rank them according to how bad they have been. Frequency of occurrence is then recorded. For those respondents who experienced some curtailment of normal activity, information similar to that in the seven-symptom survey is obtained. They are then asked about types and extent of health care they have received for their condition during the past year and associated expenses. The health status section concludes by asking all respondents, including those without heart condition, if they are familiar with the subject of the survey (angina pectoris), whether they know anyone with the condition, and how they are related to these people.

As in the seven-symptom surveys, the health status section establishes the respondent's health endowment most closely related to the concern of the questionnaire, as well as relevant health expenditure data. The questions about familiarity with the health problem are an important addition to the angina questionnaire because they address the question of the importance of familiarity and semantic effects.

The contingent valuation sections of the 10-day and 20-day angina questionnaires are structured identically. The 10-day questionnaire is described in detail here, followed by a brief comparison with the 20-day version.

The section begins with a general two-paragraph introduction that asks the respondent to imagine having the angina problems about to be described—first a relatively mild problem, then a severe one. The introduction concludes with a brief statement about the extent of angina pectoris in the United States.

Contingent valuation begins with an endowment of 1 day of mild angina symptoms a month, on the average. The problem is described by the interviewer and summarized on a card handed to the respondent. Willingness to pay to avoid the problem is elicited in some cases by means of an iterative bid with a starting point of $53. The odd number was chosen to avoid tempting the respondent to settle for a round number at the beginning.

The next question supposes an endowment of 10 mild symptom days a month. Willingness to pay pertains to eliminating one of these days. Iterative bidding is again employed, starting at twice the value determined by the respondent on the previous answer. The third question pertains to eliminating all 10 symptom days. The fourth question eliminates 5 of the 10 symptom days. No iteration is employed in the third and fourth questions.

The second half of the contingent valuation section pertains to severe angina, which is described by the interviewer and by the summary card handed to the respondent. Endowments, levels of avoidance, and bidding strategy are the same as for mild angina. The starting bid for avoidance of the 1 day per month of severe angina is twice the corresponding bid for mild angina. Twice this bid is the starting point for eliminating 1 day of 10 severe angina days.

ANGINA HEALTH QUESTIONNAIRE: 20 DAYS. This version of the angina survey is identical to the 10-day survey, except that the endowment of angina the respondents were asked to imagine they experienced, and the number of days of relief bid for, ranged from 1 day to 10 days to 20 days of mild and severe angina.

Appendix to Chapter 7

Contingent Valuation of Health: The Questionnaire

This appendix presents the seven-symptom, 1-day questionnaire, which is one of four versions used in our survey. The socioeconomic questions, which conclude the questionnaire, are omitted. The questionnaire was prepared by Lyndon Babcock, Anthony Bilotti, Glenn Blomquist, Michael Brien, Robert Fabian, Gideon Fishelson, Austin Kelly, Donald Kenkel, Ronald Krumm, George Tolley, and Wallace Wilson.

Seven-Symptom Health Questionnaire: One Day

Hello. I'm _____ from the University of Illinois School of Public Health. We are visiting with people in your area as part of a research project about risks to your health. We have scientifically selected a sample of households to represent your area and your household has been chosen as part of the sample.

Are you the [male/female] head of the household?

[If not, ask to speak to the head and start over.]

Your opinions are very important and we hope you will help us. Please be assured that this is purely a research project and we do not represent any business or product. No sales call will result by your participation in this study. The information you provide us will remain confidential.

The questionnaire will take about 30 minutes.

A. Health Evaluation
[Interviewer: circle numbers.]

A-1. Would you describe your overall health as being
1. Excellent
2. Good
3. Fair
4. Poor

A-2. Please look at this card and tell me which statement best describes the control you have over your health.
[Interviewer: hand out card on ABILITY TO CONTROL HEALTH.]
1. There is little I can do because it is beyond my control.
2. I can do some things, but they have little effect.
3. My actions have moderate effect.
4. My actions have a great effect.
[Interviewer: take card from respondent.]

A-3. How often were you bothered by any illness, bodily disorders, aches, or
     pains during the last month?

Every day	1
Almost every day	2
About half of the time	3
Now and then, but less than half of the time	4
Rarely	5
None of the time	6

H. Health Status

Now we are going to talk about whether you have certain health problems and how
they have occurred. Most people have difficulty remembering how many times they
have experienced these problems, but it is important that you try to remember
about how often you have had them. The health problems are listed on this card.

[Hand respondent Health Problem card.]

H-1. Which of the health problems on the card have you experienced in the last
     12 months?

[For any health problem named, circle the number at the top of the column corresponding to the symptom. Remember to turn the page to complete each question.]

Questions	Coughing Spells	Stuffed up Sinuses	Throat Conges- tion	Itching Eyes	Heavy Drowsi- ness	Headache	Nausea
H-2. About how many days have you had this in the last 12 months?	__days	__days	__days	__days	__days	__days	__days
H-3. Which of these both- ered you the most? 1 = most, 7 = least	_____	_____	_____	_____	_____	_____	_____
H-4. During the last year did this health prob- lem cause you to miss 1 or more days of usual activity such as work, school, or work at home? Write H for housework, N for no activity missed, S for school, W for work away from home.	_____	_____	_____	_____	_____	_____	_____
H-5. About how many days of work or other usual activity did you lose because of this?	__days	__days	__days	__days	__days	__days	__days

	Coughing Spells	Stuffed up Sinuses	Throat Conges-tion	Itching Eyes	Heavy Drowsi-ness	Headache	Nausea
H-6. Were there 1 or more days during the last year when this health problem caused you to greatly reduce your normal activities? Enter number of days.	__days	__days	__days	__days	__days	__days	__days
H-7. During the last year did you purchase any medicine for this health problem, either over the counter or with a prescription? Check for yes.	_____	_____	_____	_____	_____	_____	_____
H-8. About how much did you spend for this medicine?	$___	$___	$___	$___	$___	$___	$___
H-9. How much of this cost (if any) was paid by insurance or any other health plan?	$___	$___	$___	$___	$___	$___	$___
H-10. During the last year did you visit a doctor, clinic, hospital, or other source of professional medical care for this problem? Enter number of visits.	_____	_____	_____	_____	_____	_____	_____
H-11. About how much did these visits cost during the last year?	$___	$___	$___	$___	$___	$___	$___
H-12. About how much of this cost was paid by insurance or any other plan?	$___	$___	$___	$___	$___	$___	$___
H-13. [If workdays were lost in H-5] About how much earnings were lost because of workdays missed?	$___	$___	$___	$___	$___	$___	$___

H-14. Do you have any of the symptoms in combination? [Check one]

Yes___   No___ [Skip to section M.]

H-15. What combination did you have most often? [1 = coughing spells. 2 = stuffed-up sinuses. 3 = throat congestion. 4 = itching eyes. 5 = headache. 6 = heavy drowsiness. 7 = nausea. For example, a combination of stuffed-up sinuses, itching eyes, and headache should be recorded as 2, 4, 5.]

Combination _____

M. Defensive Measures

Now I would like to ask you some questions about your day-to-day living that are related to the symptoms we have been discussing.

M-1. Do you have any of the following in your home or car, purchased for health reasons?

Air conditioner	Yes____	No____
Air purifier	Yes____	No____
Humidifier	Yes____	No____
Other (_____)	Yes____	No____

M-2. Do you smoke? Yes____ [Skip to M-3]
                    No____

    (a) Did you ever smoke? Yes____ No____ [Skip to M-2(c)]
    (b) Did you quit for health reasons? Yes____ No____
    (c) Would you smoke if smoking Yes____ No____
        were not damaging to your
        health?

M-3. Have you ever changed the location of your residence for health reasons?

Yes____ No____ [Skip to Section R]

M-4. Where did you move from?_____

M-5. To?_____

M-6. What health problem prompted the move?_____

R. Ranking of Symptoms

In this next set of questions, I'm going to describe several symptoms of discomfort that are common to many people. The symptoms will not necessarily describe what you experience. I would like you to put yourself in the position of having these symptoms, however.

I want you to suppose that your health in the next 12 months is going to be like it was in the past 12 months, except that you will experience an additional day of a given symptom.

First we're going to talk about which of the symptoms you consider to be worst, and which you would be bothered by the least.

Everyone has experienced coughing. Please look at this card, which describes a particular coughing experience.
[Hand respondent coughing days card]

The card describes the 1 additional day on which coughing occurs. You will cough about twice an hour in spells that last 10 to 20 seconds. You will feel the cough in your chest, but it is not severe enough to make you red in the face.

I am going to pause briefly to let you think about how much you would mind the 1 additional day of coughing.
[Interviewer: pause for 15 seconds]

Now suppose that, *instead of* having the 1 additional day of coughing, you will have one additional day of sinus problems in the next 12 months. In other respects, your health will be exactly as it has been in the last 12 months.

A day of sinus problems is described on this card.

[Interviewer: hand respondent Days of Sinus Problems card]

You will have congestion and pain in your sinuses and forehead all day. You will be bothered by a feeling of stuffiness in your head, accompanied by sinus drainage in your throat. You will need to blow your nose every few minutes. You will have to breathe through your mouth most of the time.

Please think over how much you would be bothered by the 1 additional day of sinus problems and compare it to the day of coughing. Think about which symptom you mind the least and which the most.

When you have decided, please tell me which bothers you more.

[Check one]

___One coughing day
___One day of sinus problems

Place that card under the other card.

[Wait for respondent to arrange cards]

Another problem that bothers people is throat congestion. Here is a card describing a day of throat congestion.

[Hand respondent card on Day of Throat Congestion]

On this day, you will have congestion in your throat and upper respiratory tract. You will make repeated efforts to clear your throat. The throat clearing is annoying to you and those around you. Your throat will be scratchy. Your voice will be hoarse, and you will have some difficulty speaking.

Suppose that instead of either the coughing or the sinus problems, you will have 1 additional day of throat congestion, as described on the card.

Please rank the three symptoms. The question is which day bothers you the least, which the next least, and which bothers you the most.

Take your time.

Place the three cards in the order you have decided on.

[Interviewer: check to see cards are in proper order. If respondent has difficulty in ranking the days, read the following three indented paragraphs. If respondent has difficulty in ranking later on in the questionnaire, return and read these paragraphs. Otherwise, do not read the indented paragraphs to the respondent.]

> If there are symptoms that bother you the same, cards for those days should be next to each other in the deck. It does not matter which comes before the other.

> For example, if you don't care whether you have coughing or sinus problems, either of the two cards may be on top.

[Interviewer: be sure that the cards for any group within which there is indifference are in their proper place in the deck, showing how this group ranks relative to the other days.]

> Symptoms that you mind less than coughing and sinus problems should be on the top, symptoms that you mind more should be on the bottom.

[Resume text if indented paragraphs were not read]

Let's go on to eye irritation. Here is a card describing a day with this type of problem.
[Hand respondent card on Days of Itching and Smarting of Eyes]
Watering and smarting of your eyes on this day forces you to interrupt what you are doing every 15 minutes or so. You rub your eyes and close them. Stinging of your eyes brings tears three times during the day—bad enough to cause you to use a handkerchief or Kleenex around your eyes.
We want to proceed as before. Please think about how much you mind 1 additional day of this symptom and how you rank it with the others.
[Wait until respondent has finished arranging cards]
Next we consider a day on which you have headaches. Here is the card that describes the headache experience.
[Hand respondent Headache Day card]
Two rather painful, splitting headaches will strike some time during the day. Each period of headache will last 2 hours.
Please proceed as before. Think about how much you mind the additional day of headaches. After you have decided, put the card in its proper place in the deck.
[Wait until respondent is through]
We have a couple of more symptoms to consider. The next one is drowsiness. Here is a card describing a day when you are bothered by heavy drowsiness.
[Hand respondent Heavy Drowsiness card]
You will have extreme difficulty staying awake during 6 of the hours when you are normally awake. Sometimes your eyelids will flutter. You will doze off for an instant now and then. The drowsiness will interfere with your social activities and other leisure. You will find the drowsiness dangerous if it comes over you while you are driving or working with tools, appliances, or other machinery.
After thinking about 1 additional day when you have drowsiness, add the card to the deck to reflect where it comes in your ranking.
[Wait for respondent to finish, and then proceed]
The last symptom is nausea. Here is a card about it.
[Hand respondent Nausea card]
Throughout the day, you will have a lingering urge to vomit, but you will not be able to do so. Stomach distress will be strong. There will be no actual pain.
As before, think about how you rank 1 additional day of nausea, and place it in the deck.
Thank you. I'm going to record your answers for use later. Let's keep the deck sitting there. We'll use it in a minute.
[Interviewer: record rankings on Tally Sheet.]

CV. Contingent Valuation

In this next set of questions, I'm going to ask you how much it would be worth to you to avoid the symptoms we've been talking about.
The answers in this part are for yourself alone and not for any other members of your household.
Before we start, please look at this card showing how a typical family spends its take-home income.

[Hand respondent Household Spending card]

When you pay to avoid symptoms, the money will have to come out of one of the categories shown. We'll leave the card here so that you can think about where the money comes from that you would spend to avoid the symptoms. Keep in mind, however, that your situation is probably different from this one.

Let's think about ways we normally deal with health problems. One way is to go to the doctor, another way is to buy medicine at the drugstore. Oftentimes we don't do anything at all—we just suffer through the problem until it goes away. It might be that the price of a bottle of medicine or a visit to the doctor measures the value of a cure. But if we stop to think about it, the cure might be worth much more to us than that—if we really had to pay it. A cure might be valuable to us even when we just suffer with the problem until it goes away. In such cases we might ask ourselves "How much would I be willing to pay to get rid of this problem right now, even if I don't want to take medicine or visit the doctor?"

With these thoughts in mind, please try to give the largest dollar value a cure would be worth to you when answering the next few questions.

Now look at the card at the top of the deck—[symptom]—which is the symptom you mind least.

CV-1. If your health symptoms in the next 12 months were the same as in the last 12 months, except that you would also be faced with 1 additional day of [symptom], would it be worth $100 to you to completely get rid of these days of symptoms? [Circle one]

Yes   No

CV-2. [If answer to CV-1 is yes, ask if getting rid of the day would be worth $200, $400—doubling each time until a no response is obtained. Then subtract half the difference between the two previous answers. Continue adding or subtracting half the difference between the last two answers until respondent no longer wants to change.]

[If answer to CV-1 is no, ask $50, $25—decreasing by half until a yes response is obtained. Then add half the difference between the two previous answers, continuing with the half difference procedure until respondent no longer wants to change.]

[Record final bid at top of tally sheet.]

Next look at the card at the bottom of the deck which is the symptom you mind the most.

[Interviewer: for the following two questions, you will need a calculated bid for CV-3. The calculated bid for CV-3 is the bid to get rid of the least bothersome day given in the answer to CV-2, multiplied by two.]

CV-3. If your health symptoms were the same in the next 12 months as in the last 12 months, except that you would also be faced with 1 day of the symptom you mind the most, would you be willing to pay [calculated bid for CV-5] to completely get rid of the symptoms on that day? [Circle one]

Yes   No

CV-4. [If the answer to CV-3 is yes, ask if respondent would be willing to pay double the calculated bid for CV-3. Proceed by further doubling until a no answer is obtained. Then subtract half the difference between the first no amount and the last yes amount. Continue increasing or decreasing by half the difference until a final bid is obtained.]

[If the answer to CV-3 is no, ask if respondent would be willing to pay half the calculated bid for CV-3. Proceed by halving until a yes answer is obtained. Then add half the difference between the first yes amount and the last no amount. Continue increasing or decreasing by half the difference until a final bid is obtained] [Record Final bid at bottom of tally sheet.]

I have here a tally sheet for you to keep track of your answers. [Interviewer: hand respondent Tally Sheet]

Here is a pencil. [Interviewer: hand respondent a pencil]

The first column of the Tally Sheet is called "Symptom Days Ranked from Least to Most Bothersome." In this column, I have written the symptoms in the correct order from the deck of cards you have arranged.

The second column of the Tally Sheet is your bid to avoid the additional symptom day. The dollar amounts you have given are for the first and last lines in this column.

At this point, think about how much you would be willing to pay to avoid 1 additional day of the other five symptoms that you placed between the least and most bothersome.

Take as much time as you need to decide on the amounts you would be willing to pay to avoid each symptom day. As you decide on the amounts, record them.

People often find that they want to change the bids originally given for the least and most bothersome days. They often take several tries at each entry in the column.

Feel free to change any of the amounts as much as you want. In this part, people find themselves using the eraser a lot.

Tally Sheet

Ranking of Symptoms from Least to Most Bothersome	Bid for 1 day of Relief in the Next 12 Months
1)_____	$_____per year
2)_____	$_____per year
3)_____	$_____per year
4)_____	$_____per year
5)_____	$_____per year
6)_____	$_____per year
7)_____	$_____per year

[Interviewer: wait for respondent to complete the tally sheet. Avoid any appearance of impatience]

CV-5. So far we have been considering the symptoms individually. Sometimes, however, they occur together.

Suppose you faced 1 day in the coming year in which you had the three following symptoms on a single day. [Interviewer: hand respondent cough, sinus, throat card.] You would have coughing, stuffed-up sinuses, and throat congestion on that day.

Look at your bids for these three individual symptoms on the Tally Sheet. Let's add them up.

[Interviewer: compare sum with respondent: Record sum]

         Sum of individual bids:

         _____dollars

Think about whether you would be willing to pay more or less than this sum to get rid of 1 day on which all three of the symptoms occur together. When you are ready, please tell me how much are you willing to pay to get rid of the 1 day of combined symptoms.

         Bid to get rid of 1 day of combined cough, sinus,
         and throat symptoms:

         _____dollars

CV-6. Now suppose that you faced 1 day in the coming year of these three symptoms. [Interviewer: hand respondent Headache, Nausea, Drowsiness card.] You would have headache, nausea, and drowsiness.

Once again, let's add up your bids for the individual symptoms.
[Interviewer: compare sum with respondent. Record sum.]

         Sum of individual bids:

         _____dollars

How much would you be willing to pay to get rid of 1 day on which all three of the symptoms occur together?

         Bid to get rid of 1 day of headache, nausea, and
         drowsiness:

         _____dollars

CV-7. Your answers so far have been about how much you would pay for relief of yourself alone.

Look again at the five Combined Symptoms card. How much would your household be willing to pay to relieve the 1 day of combined symptoms for yourself and every other member of your household?

         Bid for relieving household of one day of com-
         bined symptoms:

         _____dollars

CV-8. I have one final question on amounts you are willing to pay. Suppose that everybody in the United States faced 1 additional day of the five combined symptoms. How much extra would your household be willing to pay for everybody's symptoms to be eliminated on this day? This is in addition to the amount you just stated for your household alone.

Addition to household payment to get rid of day of combined symptoms for everybody in the United States:

_____dollars

RE. Reasons

The value questions are now complete, but before we move on, would you tell me what the major reasons were for your answers? Here is a card that list some reasons:

[Interviewer: hand respondent Reasons card]

[Interviewer: The following list will be needed to record the ranking of reasons in question RE-1]

___Comfort

___Loss of work at home

___Loss of work away from home

___Loss of recreation

___Reduce medical expenses

___Other (specify)

RE-1. Please look at the card and tell me the most important reason for the amounts you were willing to pay.

[Interviewer: enter "1" beside the reason given as answer]

Please continue with the next most important reason, the one after that, and so forth, for all the reasons that influenced your bid.

[Interviewer: enter "2" beside the next most important reason, "3" beside the one after that, and so forth, for all reasons mentioned by respondent]

RE-2. [This question is for respondents who have experienced one or more of the health problems as reported in H-1. For respondents who didn't experience any of the health problems, skip to RE-4.]

Could you tell me how the symptoms you actually experienced during the last 12 months compared with the symptom days described in this questionnaire? Please indicate whether your symptoms were worse than, about the same, or less severe than those described.

[W = worse.   S = same.   L = less severe.   Make no entry if respondent did not have the symptom]

___Coughing

___Sinuses

___Throat congestion

___Itching eyes

___Headaches

___Heavy drowsiness

___Nausea

RE-3. Concerning the seven symptoms we have been discussing, how much would you be willing to pay to completely get rid of the symptoms you have actually experienced?

___dollars

RE-4. Because we want your best answers, I am asking you once again
whether you would like to go back and change any of your bids or
rankings given in your responses to previous questions.

Do you want to change any of your answers? [Circle one]

Yes   No

[Allow respondent to change any answers. Record all changes made by respondent
in appropriate places on questionnaire.]

Please give me back all the cards you have. These include the symptom cards,
the family spending card, and the reasons card.

Also please give me the Tally Sheet you have filled out.

[Interviewer: take back cards and Tally Sheet. INSERT TALLY SHEET INSIDE THIS
QUESTIONNAIRE IMMEDIATELY AFTER THE FIRST PAGE]

8

Empirical Results from Household Personal Interviews

Michael Brien, Donald Kenkel, Austin Kelly, and Robert Fabian

8.1. Introduction

This chapter presents the detailed empirical results of the contingent valuation surveys of the value of health. As described in Chapter 7, there are four versions of the surveys. Two versions address the value of either 1 day or 30 days of relief from light symptoms such as coughing and sinus congestion. The other two versions address the value of different amounts of relief from a more serious problem, angina pectoris (chest pain). Since the four versions of the surveys ask respondents to value quite different changes in health, each version is analyzed separately.

Two types of empirical results are reported below. The first type includes descriptive statistics on both the characteristics of the survey respondents and their answers about the value they place on the changes in health. The average values placed on the health symptoms are particularly useful for policy. The second type of empirical findings includes the results of multiple regression analyses. Multiple regression analysis was used to investigate the relationship between the contingent valuation bids for improved health and various socioeconomic and health status measures. The goal was to determine how much of the variation in individuals' bids could be explained by differences in observed characteristics. These results are relevant to economic models of the demand for health, as well as for contingent valuation methodology.

The next section presents the main hypotheses to be tested about the determinants of the contingent valuation bids for health. After describing the household sampling, summary statistics and the results of the regression analyses are reported in the remainder of the chapter. The regression techniques are also discussed in detail. The chapter concludes with a summary of the results of the analyses and a discussion of the implications for valuing health.

8.2. Hypotheses about the Determinants of the Valuation Bids

The dependent variables in the multiple regressions are contingent valuation bids reflecting the respondents' willingness to pay for the changes in health specified in the surveys. Before reporting the results, this section reviews the hypothesized relationships between these bids and the explanatory variables used in the analysis.

The socioeconomic measures used as explanatory variables in the regressions are income, education, race (white/nonwhite), age, and sex. Assuming health is a normal good, it is expected that higher-income respondents would bid larger amounts. Since wealth or permanent income may be more relevant to the individual's willingness to pay than his or her current income, a variable indicating whether the respondent owns or rents was included in an earlier set of regressions as a proxy for wealth. However, this variable had an unexpected sign and is not included in the regressions reported below. There is no obvious explanation for the anomalous results, except that the own/rent variable may be a poor proxy for wealth, perhaps because door-to-door sampling may result in an atypical mixture of owners and renters.

The remaining socioeconomic measures used as explanatory variables are motivated by the literature on the demand for health and medical care. For a review of this literature, see Feldstein (1983); a standard reference is Grossman (1972). Studies have found systematic differences in demand for health and medical care according to education, race, age, and sex. These same patterns may appear in the contingent markets for health defined in the four surveys. If so, the better-educated individuals are expected to bid more for improvements in health. Whites are expected to bid more than nonwhites, older individuals are expected to bid more than the young, and females are expected to bid more than males. Much of the previous empirical work in this general area concerns the effect of health insurance on the demand for medical care (Manning et al. 1987). However, health insurance coverage should have no direct effect on the demand for health (as opposed to the demand for medical care), so it is not included as an explanatory variable in the analysis.

Differences in the expected costs of illness (out-of-pocket medical expenses and forgone earnings) might also help explain differences in bids to avoid illness. Measurement of these expected costs is difficult, however. For those individuals who had experience with the light symptoms, past costs may be used as an estimate of expected costs, but this limits the sample. For these smaller samples, willingness to pay bids were regressed on experienced cost of illness, as described in Chapter 4. The costs of illness were measured as the sum of medical expenses and forgone earnings, adjusted for health insurance coverage and paid sick leave. The coefficients on the costs of illness terms were not significantly different from zero, indicating that in these small samples the willingness to pay bids and cost of illness show no strong tendency to move together in a systematic fashion. Costs of illness measures were not used in the regressions using the full samples reported below.

A set of health status measures were included in the regressions as explanatory variables for the willingness to pay bids. For all four surveys, a measure of general health status was included, indicating whether the respondent judged his own health to be excellent or other—that is, to be only good, fair, or poor. For the seven-symptom surveys, the individual's previous experience with the symptom was included. For the angina surveys, a dummy variable indicating whether the individual had a heart condition or not was included. Individuals in bad health, as indicated by these measures, are expected to bid higher amounts for improvements in their health, reflecting increasing marginal disutility of bad health.

The concept of increasing marginal disutility of bad health can be seen to be the converse of the more familiar idea of decreasing marginal utility. Following Grossman (1972), it is assumed that what people care about—that is, what provides utility—is the amount of healthy time available. The standard assumption of diminishing marginal utility of good health means that the more healthy days an individual experiences, the less he is willing to pay to obtain an additional good day. The case at hand does not deal directly with healthy days but, rather, with the change in symptom days experienced. As symptom days increase, healthy days decrease, so the marginal utility of health increases. Thus, the hypothesis that people are willing to pay more for an extra day of relief the more symptom days that they have already experienced is consistent with standard economic theory.

8.3. Household Sampling

Sampling Procedures

The basic objective of the sample design was to obtain a representative cross section of households on which to base inferences about health behavior. Two metropolitan areas were sampled—Chicago and Denver. The personal interviews were administered throughout the Chicago and Denver metropolitan areas in the winter of 1984–85. The data were collected from the field interviewers by an area supervisor and were returned to the University of Chicago for coding, inputting, and analysis.

Random sampling was employed. Census tracts within each metropolitan area, and starting points within each tract, were chosen randomly. The sample in each metropolitan area was drawn using 1980 census tract maps and census statistical tables. First, all of the n census tracts in the urban portion of the metropolitan area were assigned numbers one through n. Then about 30 numbers between one and n were drawn from a table of random numbers and matched with the corresponding census tracts. Eight interviews were to be taken within each tract, in the order drawn, until an adequate city sample was obtained. Extra tracts were drawn in case eight interviews could not be obtained in some of the tracts. The sampling order of the random draw had to be followed, however; no interviewer discretion was allowed in tract choice.

Random selection of households within each tract was achieved in a similar way. Every block within each selected tract was assigned a number between one and m, which was determined by counting the blocks shown on the census tract maps. A random number between one and m was chosen to determine the block where interviewing started. Additional blocks were determined by going to the next-higher numbered block as indicated in the tract maps (returning to the lowest-numbered block if necessary).

The interviewer's starting point on each block and the direction to proceed around the block were uniformly specified in advance for all interviewers. The procedure continued until eight interviews were obtained within a tract.

Copies of census tract maps were provided to all interviewers, with starting blocks clearly indicated. Field supervisors in each city worked closely with interviewers and monitored their work. Contact between the field supervisors and the University of Chicago survey coordinator was maintained throughout.

Sample Size and Editing

One hundred ninety-nine interviews were completed, approximately equally divided between two cities. Twenty-three of these interviews had to be removed from the sample. The reasons for removal were infinite bids (respondents who said they would pay any amount), random bidders, whose bids bore no logical relationship to each other, and protestors.

Similar to other personal interviewer surveys employed in the past, a few incomplete and inconsistent responses were a problem in the analysis. It was occasionally necessary to extrapolate existing information to fill the gaps left by respondents who were unwilling or unable to provide consistent or thorough information. In the present surveys, two areas required particular attention: willingness to pay bids, and values of household income.

The bids are crucial to the contingent valuation framework, and it was necessary to assure their validity. "Protestors," respondents who refused to give any bids, were removed from the sample. The protestors were determined by the lack of any contingent valuation bids or an interviewer comment and were distinguished from those who wished to bid zero. Zero bidders were left in the sample on the grounds that the bids were felt to be legitimate by the interviewer and by the consistency of other information provided.

Equally important to the respondent being willing to participate in the experiment (i.e., not being a protestor) is that the respondent fully understood the nature of the exercise. A lack of understanding of the willingness to pay concept led to the exclusion or editing of two other groups of respondents. First are random bidders, the several respondents who bid dollar amounts that were grossly out of sequence for the manner in which they had ranked the symptoms. They were entirely excluded. As should be clear by the description of the survey instruments, this was a problem only in the seven-light-symptom versions. A second and somewhat more important group was the few respondents who bid infinite amounts (a willingness to pay "any amount") or exorbitantly high amounts (two or three times their yearly income) for the relief of the symptoms. As was stressed in the survey, it is important for a contingent valuation experiment to have bids that are consistent with the household budget constraint. In most cases, respondents offered unrealistic bids for only one or two endowments. The various combinations of symptoms, the additional amount to relieve the entire United States, and 20 days of severe angina were the conditions that occasionally induced unrealistic bids. Allowing those respondents' other, more reasonable, bids to be included, we set the questionable bids equal to missing values. Exclusion of the very high bidders may have produced some downward bias on the summary statistics and the regression results because the actual, although unknown, values of these bidders may have been higher than others in the sample.

The final determination of household income also needed additional work. To gather this figure, the survey used a direct question on yearly income and a variety of questions concerning hours, weeks, and months worked and hourly, weekly, and monthly wages of all members of the household. If income was still undetermined, a default mechanism allowed the respondent's median census tract income to be used.

8.4. Seven Symptoms: One Day

Summary Statistics

Reported in Table 8.1 are the means and standard deviations for all variables that were included in the regression analysis of the seven symptoms, 1-day relief questionnaire.

Presented first are the bids to relieve 1 day of each of the seven light symptoms. The mean values range from $50.28 to relieve 1 day of nausea to $25.20 to relieve 1 day of coughing. The ranking of the symptoms from most bothersome to least bothersome, according to mean bid values, is nausea,

TABLE 8.1. Means and Standard Deviations for Seven Light Symptoms: 1-Day Survey

Variable Label	Description	Mean	SD
BIDCGH1	Bid to relieve 1 additional day of coughing	25.20	38.66
BIDSNS1	Bid to relieve 1 additional day of sinus problems	35.05	42.32
BIDTHT1	Bid to relieve 1 additional day of throat congestion	28.97	42.29
BIDEYE1	Bid to relieve 1 additional day of itchy eyes	27.73	33.01
BIDDRW1	Bid to relieve 1 additional day of drowsiness	31.41	45.69
BIDHED1	Bid to relieve 1 additional day of headaches	40.10	61.23
BINAS1	Bid to relieve 1 additional day of nausea	50.28	102.41
BID1231	Bid to relieve 1 additional day of coughing, throat congestion, and sinus problems	65.60	77.13
BID5671	Bid to relieve 1 additional day of drowsiness, headaches, and nausea	95.08	158.84
BIDCOMB1	Bid to relieve 1 additional day of coughing, congestion, and sinus symptoms for entire household	113.65	148.48
BIDUS1	Bid to relieve 1 additional day of coughing, sinus problems, and congestion for entire United States	137.97	297.96
PERSBID1	Bid to relieve symptoms actually experienced last year by respondent	614.09	1,356.96
INCOME	1983 income of household (dollars)	28,583.30	24,371.50
EDUC1	Education of person 1 (years)	14.25	4.57
AGE1	Age of person 1 (years)	44.49	15.77
WHITE	1 if white, 0 otherwise	.73	.45
SEX	1 if female, 0 if male	.55	.50
NOEXHLTH	1 if not in excellent overall health, 0 otherwise	.65	.48
DAYSSYM1	Number of days of coughing	7.65	20.94
DAYSSYM2	Number of days of sinus problems	14.08	32.75
DAYSSYM3	Number of days of throat congestion	6.83	20.94
DAYSSYM4	Number of days of itchy eyes	19.75	69.93
DAYSSYM5	Number of days of drowsiness	2.50	10.50
DAYSSYM6	Number of days of headaches	15.88	62.88
DAYSSYM7	Number of days of nausea	1.30	4.98

headaches, sinus problems, drowsiness, throat congestion, itchy eyes, and coughing. The next set of variables presented are the bids to relieve a combination of the symptoms for the individual and the United States and to relieve the symptoms that are actually experienced by the respondents.

Following the bids are the independent variables used in the analysis. The central tendencies for income and education are high for a random sample, but not very different from those obtained in other door-to-door surveys. There is a substantial spread in these variables.

The WHITE, "SEX," "NOEXHLTH," and the various health status variables are zero-one dummy variables as indicated. Seventy-three percent of those interviewed answered "white" to the race question. The health status variables disclose the respondents' general perception of their personal health.

The last set of variables used in the analysis indicates the respondents' experience with each of the seven symptoms over a 12-month period. The mean symptom days range from 19.75 days of itchy eyes to 1.3 days with nausea. The mean values may appear slightly large. This is primarily due to the respondents who claim to have experienced a symptom extremely frequently. The two largest values, for example, headaches and itchy eyes, each had one respondent who claimed to have experienced the symptom virtually every day of the year in question.

Regression Analysis

Using the 1 day relief data, ordinary least squares regressions were performed. Household income, age, sex, education and race of the respondent, as well as home ownership, various measures of health status, and experience with the seven symptoms were used as the explanatory variables. Equation (8.1) is the equation that was estimated:

$$Y_{in} = a_i + b_{i1}X_{in} + b_{i2}x_{2n} + \ldots + b_{ik}X_{kn}, + U_{in} \qquad (8.1)$$

where

Y = bid i of person n (i refers to a symptom or combination of symptoms, and n refers to the respondent);

a_i = intercept;

b_{ij} = effect of independent variables j on the ith bid;

X_{jn} = independent variable j for person n; and

U_{in} = Stochastic error on bid for person n on the ith bid.

The results of the ordinary least squares regressions are presented in Table 8.2. In general, the results offer little support for the expected relationships between the different socioeconomic variables and the amounts bid. The effects of income on bids tended to be small or even negative, and the estimated coefficient is never statistically significantly different from

TABLE 8.2. Seven Light Symptoms: 1-Day Survey Regression Results

A. Symptoms

	Coughing	Sinus Problems	Throat Congestion	Itchy Eyes	Drowsiness	Headaches	Nausea
Intercept	-103.79	-56.73	-46.75	-95.05	45.40	47.84	-101.20
	(-2.84)	(-1.48)	(-1.00)	(-2.69)	(.93)	(.74)	(-1.62)
INCOME	-.000026	.000036	-.00051	-.000023	-.00018	-.00081	-.00019
	(-.10)	(.14)	(-1.57)	(-.11)	(-.54)	(-1.82)	(-.45)
EDUC1	2.85	2.72	2.51	4.22	-2.24	1.21	3.53
	(1.91)	(1.71)	(1.33)	(2.79)	(-1.10)	(.45)	(1.38)
WHITE	22.41	-3.47	21.21	19.02	3.62	39.18	43.93
	(1.47)	(-.21)	(1.13)	(1.42)	(.18)	(1.46)	(1.77)
AGE1	1.56	.74	.46	.64	.74	-1.88	.77
	(3.23)	(1.46)	(.83)	(1.65)	(1.16)	(-2.15)	(1.06)
SEX	-20.77	10.57	-10.98	4.91	-28.63	29.87	-4.24
	(-1.62)	(.77)	(-.69)	(.42)	(-1.61)	(1.27)	(-.20)
NOEXHLTH	4.58	8.95	31.53	20.36	-2.22	73.32	47.05
	(.30)	(.59)	(1.86)	(1.65)	(-.11)	(2.83)	(2.08)
Days of dependent variable	1.43	.71	1.12	.15	3.25	-.006	16.91
	(3.43)	(3.23)	(2.14)	(1.79)	(2.93)	(-.03)	(8.23)
F-value	3.23	2.83	2.00	2.07	2.11	2.84	18.22
R^2	.48	.45	.37	.38	.38	.45	.84

B. Bids

	BID1231	BID5671	BIDCOMB1	BIDUS1	PERSBID1
Intercept	-15.64	-80.74	-73.16	-369.45	172.38
	(-.21)	(-.52)	(-.45)	(-1.01)	(.11)

INCOME	.000062	−.00066	.00046	.0039	.0081
	(.12)	(−.67)	(.42)	(1.57)	(.75)
EDUC1	3.77	3.46	9.74	14.36	−19.91
	(1.33)	(.61)	(1.41)	(.92)	(−.30)
WHITE	−21.98	75.34	17.42	56.94	1,178.75
	(−.77)	(1.37)	(.25)	(.36)	(1.73)
AGE1	−.21	.06	−2.13	1.56	−17.08
	(−.2288)	(.03)	(−1.07)	(.35)	(−.88)
SEX	45.21	−2.22	135.96	66.80	−447.45
	(1.87)	(−.04)	(2.29)	(.50)	(−.77)
NOEXHLTH	3.99	85.52	94.24	83.11	1,135.23
	(.14)	(1.60)	(1.49)	(.58)	(1.84)
DAYSSYM1	.91	...	...	...	...
	(.57)				
DAYSSYM2	1.14	...	...	...	...
	(1.49)				
DAYSSYM3	1.04	...	...	...	...
	(1.31)				
DAYSSYM5	...	−18.01	...	...	...
		(−1.27)			
DAYSSYM6	...	2.59	...	...	...
		(1.38)			
DAYSSYM7	...	23.24	...	...	...
		(4.98)			
F-value	4.28	5.82	2.28	1.09	1.10
R^2	.64	.70	.35	.21	.21

NOTE.—t = values are in parentheses.

zero. As expected, the more-educated did tend to bid more. The coefficient on education is positive in nearly all of the regressions but is only significantly different from zero at the 95% confidence level in one case. It approaches statistical significance in several other cases. In most cases, whites bid more than nonwhites, as expected, but the effect is never statistically significant. In general, older individuals bid more than the young, but of the estimated coefficients that are positive, only one is significantly so. In addition, in the regression explaining the bids to relieve a day of headaches, age had a negative and significant coefficient. Finally, no systematic relationship between the sex of the respondent and the amount bid is found. In about half of the regressions females tended to bid more and in about half females bid less; most of the time these coefficients are not significant in the statistical sense.

More support is found for the expected positive relationship between poor health and amount bid, reflecting increasing marginal disutility of illness. Being in other than excellent health had a positive effect on the amount bid in all but one regression. The estimated coefficients are significant at the 95% confidence level in two cases and significant at the 90% level in two more instances. In addition, a strong relationship exists between the respondents' actual experiences, with a symptom and their bids to relieve that symptom. The parameter estimate is usually positive and significantly different from zero. This result holds better for the individual symptom bids than for the bids to relieve combinations of symptoms.

Bids to relieve 1 symptom day of each of the seven symptoms were also estimated using Zellner's seemingly unrelated regression technique. This procedure will account for any correlation across the bids by individuals. Beginning with the ordinary least squares equation (8.1), this method allows for a correlation in the error terms, giving more efficient estimates. The results (not presented) were parameter estimates that are consistent with the ordinary least squares method. In addition, this technique shows the relationship that exists between the regressions for each of the seven symptoms. It should be noted that all values of correlations among equation errors are positive and occasionally quite close to one. There appears to be a strong correlation between the bids for headaches and nausea and a lesser but still strong relationship between itching eyes and both nausea and headaches.

8.5. Seven Symptoms: Thirty Days

Summary Statistics

Table 8.3 shows the means and standard deviations for the variables in the 30-days of relief surveys.

TABLE 8.3. Means and Standard Deviations for Seven Light Symptoms: 30-Day Survey

Variable Label	Description	Mean	SD
BIDCGH3	Bid to relieve 30 additional days of coughing	166.50	230.27
BIDSNS3	Bid to relieve 30 additional days of sinus problems	265.62	359.82
BIDTHT3	Bid to relieve 30 additional days of throat congestion	206.26	284.88
BIDEYE3	Bid to relieve 30 additional days of itching eyes	235.53	458.94
BIDDRW3	Bid to relieve 30 additional days of drowsiness	317.98	593.00
BIDHED3	Bid to relieve 30 additional days of headaches	488.20	833.21
BIDNAS3	Bid to relieve 30 additional days of nausea	186.02	256.02
BID1233	Bid to relieve 30 additional days of coughing, throat congestion, and sinus problems	624.98	879.87
BID5673	Bid to relieve 30 additional days of drowsiness, headaches, and nausea	868.89	1,343.36
BIDCOMB3	Bid to relieve 30 additional days of coughing, congestion, and sinus symptoms for entire household	1,250.00	2,165.51
BIDUS3	Bid to relieve 30 additional days of coughing, sinus problems, and congestion for entire United States	483.46	1,013.62
PERSBID3	Bid to relieve symptoms actually experienced last year by respondent	1,169.07	2,369.27
INCOME	1983 income of household (dollars)	30,109.70	18,359.90
EDUC1	Education of person 1 (years)	13.83	4.10
AGE1	Age of person 1 (years)	42.15	15.72
WHITE	1 if respondent is white, 0 otherwise	.81	.40
SEX	1 if female, 0 if male	.49	.51
NOEXHLTH	1 if not in excellent overall health, 0 otherwise	.70	.46
DAYSSYM1	Number of days of coughing	4.96	14.05
DAYSSYM2	Number of days of sinus problems	9.64	28.39
DAYSSYM3	Number of days of throat congestion	1.89	4.82
DAYSSYM4	Number of days of itchy eyes	33.15	112.74
DAYSSYM5	Number of days of drowsiness	6.74	43.75
DAYSSYM6	Number of days of headaches	24.23	62.54
DAYSSYM7	Number of days of nausea	1.96	4.52

As before, the means and standard deviations of the bids for each of the seven symptoms and combinations of symptoms are presented first. The mean bids for each of the seven symptoms range from $488.20 to relieve 30 days of headaches to $166.50 to relieve 30 days of coughing. Drowsiness, sinus problems, itching eyes, throat congestion, and nausea is the order of the remaining middle symptoms. This ranking is different from that in the 1-day version, with only sinus problems, coughing, and throat congestion occupying the same position.

The 30-day results are also not 30 times larger than the 1 day even though the added endowment is 30 times larger. The differences between the 1-day and 30-day bid values appear to be on the order of 10. Comparison of the bids from the two different survey instruments thus does not support the hypothesis of increasing marginal disutility of symptom days. This is in contrast to the results of the regressions explaining the 1-day bids. Most of the independent variables are consistent with those found in the 1-day experiment.

Regression Analysis

The analysis of bids for 30 days of symptom relief is similar to the analysis of the 1-day bids already discussed. The results of the ordinary least squares regressions are presented in Table 8.4. The results are not supportive of the expected relationships between the socioeconomic variables and the amount bid. Income had a generally positive effect on bids, but the estimated coefficients were never significantly different from zero. In fact, virtually none of the estimated coefficients on the socioeconomic variables differed significantly from zero in the statistical sense. In addition, for many of the variables the signs of the coefficients were not consistent across regressions explaining bids for different symptoms.

The results of the regressions explaining the 30-day bids are also not supportive of a positive relationship between poor health as indicated by a general health status variable or the number of days of a symptom the individual actually experienced. There was some tendency for the individuals who had experienced more days of a symptom to bid more for 30-days of relief. However, the estimated coefficients were not significant, and the signs of the coefficients were not always consistent across regressions.

The seemingly unrelated regressions (not repeated) again yielded comparable, but more efficient, parameter estimates than the ordinary least squares regressions. The correlation across models is considerably stronger than was found in the 1-day results. A correlation greater than .9 is found across the same models as in the 1-day sample as well as across many other models.

8.6. Angina: Ten Days

Summary Statistics

Table 8.5 presents the means and standard deviations for the data collected in the angina 10-day surveys. The first eight values are the dependent variables used in the regression analysis. The bids vary from $261.84 to relieve 10 days of severe angina when the respondent is endowed with 10 severe days to $66.08 to relieve 1 mild day when only afflicted with 1 mild day. The bids can be seen to vary according to the severity and duration of the endowment, and according to level of relief provided. The relationships found between different bids are supportive of the hypothesis of increasing marginal disutility of illness. In general, the more severe or the greater duration of the angina the respondent was asked to suppose he was endowed with, the greater the amount bid. The mean bid for 1 day of relief from mild angina when the respondent was endowed with 10 mild days is greater than the mean bid for the same amount of relief when the respondent was endowed with only 1 day ($83.95 and $66.08, respectively). The same holds true for the bids for relief from one severe day when endowed with either ten or one days.

The independent variables that follow are similar to those found in the light-symptom surveys. A major difference is the replacement of symptom days experienced with the variable, HEARTCON, that indicates whether or not an individual respondent has experienced a heart condition. This new variable should permit similar explanatory effects on the magnitude of the bids as well as allow for testing the existence of increasing marginal disutility of this symptom. About one-quarter of this sample had ever experienced a heart condition.

The other independent variables are equivalent in nature to those found in the earlier tables. It should be noted that a slightly lower income figure and a higher average age are found in this version.

Regression Results

For both angina surveys, ordinary least squares and seemingly unrelated regressions were performed to estimate equation (8.1). Results for the 10-day survey are presented in Table 8.6. As in the seven-light-symptom results, there is little support for the expected relationships between the socioeconomic variables and the amounts bid for relief from angina. Income always has a positive coefficient, but it is never significantly different from zero. The signs of the coefficients on other variables tend to vary. None of the estimated coefficients is significantly different from zero.

The angina regression results do not provide support for the existence of increasing marginal disutility of symptom days. Neither the measure of

TABLE 8.4. Seven Light Symptoms: 30-Day Survey Regression Results

A. Symptoms

	Coughing	Sinus Problems	Throat Congestion	Itchy Eyes	Drowsiness	Headaches	Nausea
Intercept	365.02	258.35	322.28	135.52	449.52	615.88	159.09
	(1.45)	(.59)	(.96)	(.23)	(.60)	(.57)	(.59)
INCOME	.00007	.00002	.00095	.062	.0072	.007	-.00013
	(.31)	(.05)	(.30)	(1.16)	(.99)	(.73)	(-.05)
EDUC1	-3.98	2.93	6.91	29.50	-18.35	55.30	7.91
	(-.37)	(.15)	(.48)	(1.20)	(-.56)	(1.23)	(.61)
WHITE	-197.72	-133.96	-324.37	-723.34	5.85	-1,027.00	-100.50
	(-1.74)	(-.66)	(-2.22)	(-2.39)	(.02)	(-2.13)	(-.88)
AGE1	-.10	1.56	1.07	5.61	5.48	-2.65	.24
	(-.03)	(.32)	(.29)	(.88)	(.65)	(-.23)	(.08)
SEX	-15.11	-20.76	49.26	-85.52	-194.53	-375.92	-187.54
	(-.19)	(-.15)	(.47)	(-.47)	(-.82)	(-1.11)	(-1.98)
NOEXHLTH	-19.17	-26.44	-52.72	-71.30	-377.89	56.40	56.48
	(-.22)	(.18)	(-.22)	(-.78)	(-1.46)	(.16)	(.58)
Days of dependent variable	6.93	.08	-2.22	-.74	3.07	1.17	10.42
	(1.79)	(.01)	(-.22)	(-.78)	(1.11)	(.38)	(1.03)
F-value	1.51	.14	.84	1.37	.92	1.27	.90
R²	.28	.04	.18	.26	.19	.25	.19

B. Bids

	BID1233	BID5673	BIDCOMB3	BIDUS3	PERSBID3
Intercept	147.26	1,057.77	-52.83	1,051.17	-1,267.41
	(.14)	(.32)	(-.02)	(.81)	(-.55)

	(1)	(2)	(3)	(4)	(5)
INCOME	.0014	.0051	.017	−.009	.03
	(.14)	(.32)	(.72)	(−.75)	(1.34)
EDUC1	52.42	33.55	180.75	.10	30.27
	(1.15)	(.42)	(1.62)	(.002)	(.30)
WHITE	−500.35	−789.38	−2,670.97	−118.13	−210.71
	(−.99)	(−.92)	(−2.37)	(−.21)	(−.21)
AGE1	6.90	.20	27.80	−9.37	30.57
	(.58)	(.01)	(.97)	(−.66)	(1.19)
SEX	−211.81	−810.01	−574.83	−235.54	207.12
	(−.62)	(−1.32)	(−.71)	(−.58)	(.29)
NOEXHLTH	21.16	53.06	−465.29	495.77	−324.67
	(−.62)	(.09)	(−.52)	(1.11)	(−.41)
DAYSSYM1	40.23	...	...	...	...
	(1.46)				
DAYSSYM2	−18.57	...	...	...	...
	(−.84)				
DAYSSYM3	−57.01	...	...	...	...
	(−1.29)				
DAYSSYM5	...	11.53	...	...	...
		(1.95)			
DAYSSYM6	...	.80	...	...	...
		(.17)			
DAYSSYM7	...	62.32	...	...	...
		(1.02)			
F-value	.67	1.40	1.53	.46	.67
R²	.19	.33	.25	.09	.12

NOTE.—t-values are in parentheses.

TABLE 8.5.   Means and Standard Deviations for Angina: 10-Day Survey

Variable Label	Description	Mean	SD
BIDTEN1	Bid to relieve 1 mild day when afflicted with 1 mild day	66.08	55.68
BIDTEN2	Bid to relieve 1 mild day when afflicted with 10 mild days	83.95	102.30
BIDTEN3	Bid to relieve 10 mild days when afflicted with 10 mild days	154.36	165.21
BIDTEN4	Bid to relieve 5 mild days when afflicted with 10 mild days	96.18	103.87
BIDTEN5	Bid to relieve 1 severe day when afflicted with 1 severe day	123.59	101.63
BIDTEN6	Bid to relieve 1 severe day when afflicted with 10 severe days	144.74	145.72
BIDTEN7	Bid to relieve 10 severe days when afflicted with 10 severe days	261.84	244.80
BIDTEN8	Bid to relieve 5 severe days when afflicted with 10 severe days	192.90	195.03
INCOME	1983 income of household (dollars)	25,531.00	18,842.70
EDUC1	Education of person 1 (years)	13.20	3.43
AGE1	Age of person 1 (years)	50.33	17.79
WHITE	1 if respondent is white, 0 otherwise	.85	.36
SEX	1 if female, 0 if male	.50	.51
NOEXHLTH	1 if not in excellent overall health, 0 otherwise	.70	.46
HEARTCON	1 if heart condition exists, 0 otherwise	.25	.44

general poor health status or the heart condition experience variable had a significant positive effect on the willingness to pay bids.

The insignificant effect of having a heart condition on willingness to pay for angina relief may be partially due to the definition of the variable. Unlike the symptom variables in the seven-symptom analysis, HEARTCON stems from a general question concerning the respondent's experience with any heart condition. The endowments that are suggested here may be out of the range of experience of most respondents. Therefore, even those who do indicate having a heart condition may have never experienced symptoms similar to those described. On the whole, experience with the seven light symptoms is expected to explain bids better than experience with a heart condition. The reason is that the light-symptom experience pertains exactly to the light-symptom bids, whereas heart condition experience at best bears only a partial relationship to the angina bids.

The results of the seemingly unrelated regressions (not reported) are extremely similar to the ordinary least square results but may be considered

TABLE 8.6. Angina: 10-Day Survey Regression Results

	BIDTEN1	BIDTEN2	BIDTEN3	BIDTEN4	BIDTEN5	BIDTEN6	BIDTEN7	BIDTEN8
Intercept	114.32	8.71	153.69	37.34	171.14	260.26	455.45	321.29
	(1.43)	(.08)	(.85)	(.26)	(1.16)	(1.29)	(1.56)	(1.24)
INCOME	.00023	.00026	.00078	.00017	.00046	.0015	.0038	.0044
	(.30)	(.25)	(.45)	(.12)	(.33)	(.79)	(1.31)	(1.79)
EDUC1	-2.37	.85	-5.01	-1.14	-1.42	-8.11	-21.11	-18.19
	(-.55)	(.15)	(-.51)	(-.14)	(-.18)	(-.74)	(-1.33)	(-1.29)
WHITE	-5.07	3.90	57.70	45.16	-18.85	-17.09	60.69	2.04
	(-.15)	(.09)	(.77)	(.75)	(-.31)	(-.20)	(.50)	(.01)
AGE1	-.69	.10	-1.21	-.51	-.50	-.007	-2.00	-.0086
	(-.85)	(.09)	(-.66)	(-.35)	(-.33)	(-.004)	(-.68)	(-.003)
SEX	12.41	39.19	23.88	38.67	-5.34	17.11	28.99	54.97
	(.55)	(1.28)	(.46)	(.94)	(-.13)	(0.30)	(.35)	(.75)
NOEXHLTH	14.03	23.17	55.75	62.38	13.37	-63.43	16.88	-30.08
	(.53)	(.64)	(.92)	(1.28)	(.27)	(-.94)	(.17)	(-.35)
HEARTCON	6.99	23.17	-21.65	-10.17	-17.04	-1.26	-22.32	-57.80
	(.23)	(.57)	(-.32)	(-.19)	(-.31)	(-.02)	(-.20)	(-.59)
F-value	.25	.48	.36	.45	.12	.22	.66	.68
R^2	.06	.11	.08	.10	.03	.05	.14	.15

NOTE.—t-values are in parentheses.

a more efficient estimate. A strong correlation between models was found, with correlation values consistently in the range of .8 or .9.

8.7. Angina: Twenty Days

Summary Statistics

Table 8.7 presents the means and standard deviations for all variables used in the analysis of the survey that incorporated an endowment of 20 days of angina. In this version, the bids ranged from $844.38 to relieve 20 days of severe angina to $90.24 for eliminating 1 day of mild angina a month.

For a given number of days of relief from angina, the mean bids tend to vary directly with the severity and duration of the endowment. As explained above, this is seen as evidence of an increasing marginal disutility of illness.

Two points should be raised concerning the size of the bids. First, and most notably, is the difference between BIDTEN1 (see Table 8.5) and

TABLE 8.7. Means and Standard Deviations for Angina: 20-Day Survey

Variable Label	Description	Mean	SD
BIDTWT1	Bid to relieve 1 mild day when afflicted with 1 mild day	90.24	103.56
BIDTWT2	Bid to relieve 1 mild day when afflicted with 20 mild days	99.05	179.78
BIDTWT3	Bid to relieve 20 mild days when afflicted with 20 mild days	486.25	923.90
BIDTWT4	Bid to relieve 10 mild days when afflicted with 20 mild days	287.63	506.59
BIDTWT5	Bid to relieve 1 severe day when afflicted with 1 severe day	278.88	776.35
BIDTWT6	Bid to relieve 1 severe days when afflicted with 20 severe days	208.78	339.09
BIDTWT7	Bid to relieve 20 severe days when afflicted with 20 severe days	844.38	1,609.94
BIDTWT8	Bid to relieve 10 severe days when afflicted with 20 severe days	506.25	1,000.27
INCOME	1983 income of household (dollars)	29,950.10	23,723.70
EDUC1	Education of person 1 (years)	14.15	3.02
AGE1	Age of person 1 (years)	48.13	18.46
WHITE	1 if respondent is white, 0 otherwise	0.74	0.44
SEX	1 if female, 0 if male	0.69	0.47
NOEXHLTH	1 if not in excellent overall health, 0 otherwise	0.67	0.48
HEARTCON	1 if heart condition exists, 0 otherwise	0.14	0.35

BIDTWT1 (see Table 8.7) as well as between BIDTEN5 and BIDTWT5. As described above, the first and fifth bid requests are the same for each survey. While BIDTEN1 and BIDTWT1 are relatively close, $66.08 and $90.24, respectively, BIDTEN5 and BIDTWT5 are quite far apart, $123.59 and $278.88, respectively. A small part of the difference may be explained by the differences in income in the two samples. The 10-day sample mean income was $25,531.00, while the 20-day mean was higher at $29,950.10. This explanation assumes that income has a strong positive effect on bid values. The regression analysis presented below adds some support to this proposition. The difference in value can also be explained by the outliers in the bids. Some respondents bid considerably higher than others but offered no grounds for being removed from the sample. The importance of these bids can be seen by observing the large standard deviation for BIDTWT5.

It should be noted that the 20-day results represent more than a twofold increase in bid values over the 10-day results. This point is consistent with increasing marginal disutility since respondents on average are willing to pay proportionately larger amounts for relief when confronted with larger endowments.

Regression Analysis

The ordinary least squares results are presented in Table 8.8. Income tends to be a significant factor in the determination of the bids. The estimated coefficient is positive in all regressions and significant at at least the 95% confidence level in all but two of the regressions. No strong relationships are found between the bids and the other socioeconomic variables or health status measure.

The seemingly unrelated regressions (not reported) behaved in a manner similar to those found in the 10-day version and gave results equivalent to the ordinary least squares method. The correlation across models tended not to be as strong as the angina 10-day results. While many values were in the range of 0.8 and 0.9, there were also many values considerably lower or even negative.

8.8. Summary and Implications

Health Values

This chapter presents results from contingent valuation surveys that elicited from respondents their willingness to pay for varying amounts of relief from seven light symptoms and angina. As is discussed in more detail in Part 4, the average value placed on these health symptoms is an extremely useful input for a variety of policy decisions.

Since they were first presented to the U.S. Environmental Protection

TABLE 8.8. Angina: 20-Day Survey Regression Results

	BIDTWT1	BIDTWT2	BIDTWT3	BIDTWT4	BIDTWT5	BIDTWT6	BIDTWT7	BIDTWT8
Intercept	-3.11	487.85	-873.41	-130.71	-430.43	710.20	-1,031.89	-581.14
	(-.03)	(2.30)	(-1.06)	(-.28)	(-.50)	(1.77)	(-1.13)	(-.76)
INCOME	.0027	.00029	.012	.0082	.023	.0049	.03	.03
	(3.48)	(.19)	(2.06)	(2.44)	(3.76)	(1.73)	(3.80)	(5.28)
EDUC1	-2.45	-11.77	54.70	10.36	-34.23	-24.92	25.14	-30.14
	(-.40)	(-.98)	(1.17)	(.39)	(-.70)	(-1.09)	(.39)	(-.70)
WHITE	40.40	-114.07	77.97	2.40	212.08	95.36	447.37	293.35
	(1.02)	(-1.47)	(.26)	(.01)	(.67)	(.65)	(1.06)	(1.05)
AGE1	.02	-1.53	6.81	2.55	-1.86	-6.64	5.88	2.83
	(.02)	(-.79)	(.90)	(.59)	(-.24)	(-1.81)	(.56)	(.42)
SEX	-26.75	-150.99	-212.20	-218.65	407.64	-58.57	125.71	78.58
	(-.71)	(-2.03)	(-.73)	(-1.31)	(1.35)	(-.42)	(.31)	(.29)
NOEXHLTH	24.80	37.89	-185.22	8.36	176.86	-94.12	-133.95	189.73
	(.72)	(.56)	(-.70)	(.05)	(.64)	(-.73)	(-.36)	(.78)
HEARTCON	92.80	29.20	98.89	22.75	-785.21	-688.51	2,534.89	906.58
	(1.82)	(.29)	(.25)	(.10)	(.96)	(1.73)	(.77)	(.81)
F-value	2.56	1.44	1.66	1.81	2.22	1.37	2.73	4.62
R^2	.39	.27	.29	.32	.36	.25	.41	.54

NOTE.—t-values are in parentheses.

Agency and elsewhere in 1986–87, there have been both informal reactions and a few explicit criticisms of the contingent valuation results. The most common comments are that the average values placed on 1 day of relief from light symptoms seem "too high." We are taking this opportunity to respond to these comments, not only because we believe the values presented here are reasonable, but also in the interest of furthering methodological improvements in contingent valuation.

The informal reactions are based on introspection: in conversations about the results, some people (and perhaps some readers of this book) express doubts that they would be willing to pay, for instance, $40 to relieve a day of headaches. This is not surprising, once it is recalled that there is a good deal of variance in the willingness to pay bids in the sample surveyed. If the variance in the entire population is similar, it will be common to find people whose maximum willingness to pay is below the average. In fact, due to the distribution of bids, most people surveyed were willing to pay less than the average bid: the averages reflect a few very high, but apparently legitimate, bids. The median bids reported, which are lower, probably accord better with most people's introspection. Values of $40 or higher may be reasonable for people who cannot take aspirin or other analgesics because of allergic reactions or other undesirable side effects. For example, some pregnant women will not take any medication if at all possible to avoid effects on the fetus. Finally, it should be pointed out that casual introspection will be less reliable than a properly executed contingent valuation survey that encourages respondents to give careful, well thought-out answers.

In addition to the informal reactions, there are some more formal criticisms of the contingent valuation methodology as applied to valuing light symptoms. Cropper and Freeman (1991) and Cropper and Oates (1992) argue that there are two important problems encountered in our study and other similar studies. One problem is whether respondents carefully considered their budget constraints and the opportunity cost of their responses. The second problem concerns whether respondents considered opportunities for defensive or averting behavior when valuing the change in health.

In terms of the first problem, we believe most respondents did carefully consider their budget constraints and gave reasoned answers to the contingent valuation questions. Obviously, the possibility that respondents do not take the hypothetical exercise seriously is an inherent problem in contingent valuation experiments. However, in studies comparing hypothetical payments to actual payments, average willingness to pay bids were fairly similar (Mitchell and Carson 1989, pp. 204–9).

Our surveys were carefully designed to encourage thought about budget constraints and opportunity costs. Just prior to the willingness to pay questions, respondents were handed a card showing how a typical family spends its take-home income. Respondents were then told, "When you pay to avoid symptoms, the money will have to come out of one of the categories shown. We'll leave the card here so that you can think about where the money comes from that you would spend to avoid the symptoms. Keep in mind, however, that your situation is probably different from this one." With these instructions, we believe most respondents tried to take into account their budget constraints. However, there were still a few bids that clearly exceeded the respondent's income. As is explained earlier in Section 8.1, these bids were judged to be "protest bids" that indicated the respondent did not fully understand the nature of the exercise. Accordingly, these bids were removed from the sample and are not reflected in the summary statistics presented.

The second potential problem is whether the respondents, when placing a value on the symptoms, considered their opportunities for defensive or averting behavior. Using a model similar to that developed in Chapter 2 of this book, Cropper and Freeman (1991) show, as we do, that willingness to pay for symptom relief consists of two terms: a first term that reflects the disutility of illness after mitigating actions have been taken, plus a second term that reflects the cost of the mitigating activity. They conclude that "a day of headache should be valued after mitigating actions have been taken and should include the cost of the mitigating activity" (p. 202). If respondents fail to consider the possibility of mitigating actions, they might place unrealistically high values on symptom relief. Consider the case of aspirin as an example of a mitigating action in response to a headache. If aspirin is close to a perfect cure for a headache, the disutility of illness after aspirin has been taken may be close to zero. Then the true value of relief is simply the cost of aspirin. But if the respondent fails to consider the possibility of aspirin, the value he or she places on relief from a headache might be much higher.

Two parts of the contingent valuation questionnaire design address the role of defensive or mitigating actions and should help prevent the problem Cropper and Freeman mention. First, prior to the valuation questions, respondents were asked about their defensive measures. Specifically, respondents were asked if they had made the following purchases for health reasons: air conditioner, air purifier, humidifier, or other. They were also asked if they had given up smoking or moved for health reasons. This set of questions should have served to remind applicants of these and other opportunities for averting or mitigating behavior.

Just before the valuation questions, the surveyors read the following text:

> Let's think about ways we normally deal with health problems. One way is to go to the doctor, another way is to buy medicine at the drugstore. Oftentimes we don't do anything at all—we just suffer

through the problem until it goes away. It might be that the price of a bottle of medicine or a visit to the doctor measures the value of a cure. But if we stop to think about it, the cure might be worth much more to us than that—if we really had to pay it. A cure might be valuable to us even when we just suffer with the problem until it goes away. In such cases we might ask ourselves "How much would I be willing to pay to get rid of this problem right now, even if I don't want to take medicine or visit the doctor?" With these thoughts in mind, please try to give the largest dollar value a cure would be worth to you when answering the next few questions.

In the final analysis, we believe the respondents were encouraged to think carefully about the possibility of mitigating actions and to consider these actions when placing a dollar value on relief from symptoms. However, in designing this survey and future surveys, there is a trade-off in reducing the different types of errors respondents might make. Future work might investigate how sensitive responses are to the amount and type of information about mitigating actions provided in the survey instrument.

Determinants of Individual Willingness to Pay for Health

Two conclusions can be drawn from the empirical investigation of the determinants of the willingness to pay bids for relief from light symptoms and angina. The first finding is that various pieces of evidence support the hypothesis of increasing marginal disutility of illness. As shown, this hypothesis follows from the more standard assumption of decreasing marginal utility from health. In the 1-day and 30-days light-symptom surveys, respondents were asked to bid for 1 day or 30 days of relief given their previous experience with the symptom. It was notable in the 1-day survey that those respondents who had experienced more days of a symptom tended to bid more for the marginal day of relief. This offers support for the hypothesis of increasing marginal disutility, though support was not found in the regression analyses of the 30-day surveys. However, considerable additional support was found for the hypothesis in the angina surveys. In these surveys, the respondents were asked to suppose they experienced different endowments of angina and were then asked to bid for relief. Again, the results are seen as consistent with the hypothesis of increasing marginal disutility of illness: respondents tended to bid more when they were given endowments of increased severity or duration.

Second, the regression analyses did not show strong relationships between various socioeconomic variables and the willingness to pay bids. In a number of regressions, certain socioeconomic variables were significantly related to willingness to pay; a case in point is the consistent and significant positive impact of income on the bids for angina relief in the 20-day survey.

However, income was not always an important explanatory variable in other sets of regressions.

As described in Chapter 4, one further finding of the surveys was that the most important reason given as explanation of the willingness to pay bids was to avoid the discomfort of illness. This suggests that a respondent's taste for health, or distaste for illness, will dominate the amount he or she is willing to bid. In this situation it is not surprising that no strong relationship was found between the socioeconomic variables and the willingness to pay bids, especially in the small samples analyzed. This pertains to a final point on the methodology of contingent valuation. Some researchers have argued that evidence that contingent values are systematically related to socioeconomic variables such as income tends to support the validity of the method. The converse is not necessarily true: failure to find systematic relationships is not necessarily indicative that contingent valuation methods are faulty. The empirical analyses of the results of the four surveys is entirely consistent with individuals making rational choices over the value of health and reporting those values accurately in a contingent valuation experiment. Unobservable differences between individuals accounted for much of the variation in bids.

To sum up, we believe the contingent valuation estimates of the value of light symptoms and angina are reasonable and useful for policy analysis. Although the average values reported may seem high, the much lower median values probably accord well with most people's introspection. (The median values are presented in Chap. 4, which also contains comparisons of these results with other contingent valuation studies.) In terms of methodology, the survey instrument carefully incorporated material to encourage respondents to give consideration to their budget constraint and the opportunities for mitigating behavior. Given this care, we believe this and other well-designed contingent valuation studies can provide very useful information when analyzing policies that affect health.

9

Empirical Results from Mail Questionnaires

Wallace Wilson

9.1. Background

It is clear that the personal interviews on which contingent valuation was based produced the most complete and highest quality data. Personal interviews are also much more expensive than telephone and mail interviews. Realizing that greater accuracy in estimation of willingness to pay could be obtained through a larger number of interviews, we considered these less costly modes of survey research.

Telephone interviews, which are intermediate in cost between personal and mail interviews, were not chosen because the relatively brief interviews required for telephone surveys would not allow adequate time for thoughtful bidding. Also, we saw a strong possibility that advance mailing of the tally sheet, use of which by the respondent was essential to generation of a reasoned set of bids, would significantly lower the response rate. Instead, we decided that a mail survey would be used.

9.2. Design of the Mail Survey

The mail survey was based on six common light symptoms, which could be caused, for example, by air pollutants such as sulfur dioxide, nitrogen dioxide, ozone, and carbon monoxide. The mail survey was based on two questionnaires, A and B. Questionnaire B included a set of comparative questions concerning lost earnings and expenditures for physician visits, medicines, and other medical expenses for each symptom. The B questionnaire was identical to the A except for omission of these comparative questions. This was done because we anticipated that the additional time and effort required to answer these memory-based comparative questions might significantly lower the response rate to the mail survey.

The symptoms in the mail questionnaires included painful headache, coughing spells, stuffed-up sinuses, itching eyes, and heavy drowsiness when driving. Respondents were asked about their willingness to make monthly payments for an excellent medicine that would eliminate a certain endowment of 3 symptom days each month of each symptom. The medicine would only have to be taken once a month, and it would be safe and have no side effects. Respondents were also told that their bids for the different symptoms would not be added to any multiple symptom monthly total, that each symptom and the bid associated with it would occur separately, without the other symptoms.

The common questions in the two mail surveys asked whether the respondents had ever experienced each symptom (to establish interest and focus, question 1), the degree to which each symptom bothers them (to encourage thoughtful variation in bids, question 2), and reasons for choosing the amounts of the bids (question 3). Demographic information was also collected. The demographic variables included sex and age of respondents, highest level of education, number of persons per household, and household income.

We decided that the mail survey methodology used would be the Dillman method. This method indicates that an approximately 70% response rate of the general public could be achieved in a mail survey (Dillman 1978).

9.3. Sample Construction and the Response Rate

Reverse telephone directories for the Chicago metropolitan area were used to draw a sample of 103 names and addresses, using interval sampling with a random start. Business addresses were excluded. Addresses without the name of the resident and those with unlisted telephone numbers were included and addressed to "Resident." The cover letter asked that the adult who usually pays the bills complete the questionnaire. Questionnaire types A and B were alternated, producing an almost equal number of mailings. Of the 103 mailed questionnaires, 15 were returned to sender, indicating that the subject has moved since publication of the reverse directories. This yielded 88 possible mail interviews. Of this number, 42 completed questionnaires were returned, a response rate of 48 percent. This is a reasonably high response rate, but below that suggested by Dillman. Forty-two questionnaires do not form a large sample, but it is adequate for an exploratory survey and analysis. The response rates for the two questionnaires were exactly equal. The addition of the comparative expense questions to questionnaire B did not lower the response rate of the longer questionnaire.

9.4. Results of the Survey

The first question in the type A survey asked whether the respondent had ever experienced each symptom. The results are shown in Table 9.1. A

TABLE 9.1. Whether Respondent Ever Experienced Symptom

Symptom	% of Respondents Who Ever Experienced the Symptom
Painful headache	71
Coughing spells	55
Stuffed-up sinuses	81
Irritated throat	69
Itching and smarting of eyes	50
Heavy drowsiness when driving	43
Number of cases	42

TABLE 9.2. How Much Symptom Bothers the Respondent

Symptom	"Does not bother me" (in %)	"Bothers me some" (in %)	"Bothers me a lot" (in %)	"Bothers me a great deal" (in %)	Mean Score °	Number of Cases
Painful headaches	30	47	17	6	3.8	30
Coughing spells	35	48	13	4	2.9	23
Stuffed-up sinuses	22	40	19	19	3.4	37
Irritated throat	20	57	20	3	3.1	30
Itching eyes	22	56	22	†	3.0	23
Heavy drowsiness when driving	35	40	10	15	3.1	20

NOTE.—Percentages per symptom sum to 100.
° The mean score is based on "Does not bother me" = 2, "Bothers me some" = 3, "Bothers me a lot" = 4, and "Bothers me a great deal" = 5.
† Less than 1%.

majority of the respondents reported having experienced every symptom except drowsiness when driving, which was reported by 43%. The most commonly experienced symptom was stuffed-up sinuses.

Question 2 asked the degree to which each symptom bothered the respondent. Only those who had experienced a symptom were asked how much it bothered them. The results are shown in Table 9.2. All of the symptoms centered on "Bothers me some," but both the percentage distributions and the mean scores based on the percentage distributions showed stuffed-up sinuses to be the symptom which bothered the respondents the most, averaging about midway between "Bothers me some" and "Bothers me a lot."

TABLE 9.3. Respondent's Willingness to Pay per Month to Eliminate 3 Symptom Days per Month

Symptom	Mean Dollar Amount Respondent Is Willing to Pay		Number of Cases
	Per Month	Per Year°	
Painful headache	9.39	113	33
Coughing spells	8.87	106	30
Stuffed-up sinuses	9.68	116	34
Irritated throat	8.42	101	31
Itching eyes	8.63	104	27
Heavy drowsiness when driving	5.41	65	27

° Calculated by multiplying the mean monthly bid by 12.

Question 3 asked about willingness to pay each month to eliminate 3 symptom days of each symptom per month through purchase of a safe, effective, side-effect-free medicine. The results are shown in Table 9.3. Mean bids for personal discomfort symptoms were in the $8–$9 per month range, representing yearly bids of about $100–$115. The average willingness to pay to eliminate heavy drowsiness when driving was about $5.40 per month, or $65 per year. The highest willingness to pay was expressed for two symptoms: stuffed-up sinuses ($116 per year), which is consistent with the answers to question 2, in which stuffed-up sinuses were reported to be the most bothersome symptom, and headaches ($113 per year to eliminate headache days).

About 20% of the respondents did not bid on each symptom because they had never experienced the symptom. The question was not structured to exclude those who had never experienced each symptom. Instead, most of those respondents who had reported never having experienced a symptom spontaneously decided not to bid on elimination of the symptom. A few of those who had never experienced a symptom did make a bid, typically zero.

Question 4 asked about the reasons for willingness to pay in question 3. The data on reasons are shown in Table 9.4. The most common basis for willingness to pay bids was personal comfort. About 84% of all respondents who bid listed personal comfort as a reason for their bids. To avoid loss of work or other usual activity was the next most frequently mentioned reason; it was reported by 32% of the respondents. The other reasons ranged between 10% and 20% of the total.

The fact that only 14% of the respondents mentioned the amount of their monthly income as being a basis for their bids might suggest lack of realism in bidding. However, the modest level of the bids, typically less than $10

TABLE 9.4.   Reasons for Willingness to Pay Amounts

Reasons	% Respondents Mentioning Reason
For comfort	84
To avoid loss of work or other usual activity	32
Amount of monthly income allows it	14
To spend less for other medicines	16
To spend less for doctor bills and other medical care	11
To not have to take other medicines	19
Other	11
Number of cases	37

per month, suggests that the budget constraint was taken into consideration when bidding.

Question 5, which appeared only in the type B questionnaire, asked about the symptom days experienced in the last 12 months for each symptom, the days of work or other usual activity lost, earnings lost, and medical care expenses induced by the symptom. Although 12 months may be too long a period for accurate recall, it is also true that the symptoms included in this question and elsewhere in the questionnaire are quite seasonal in their incidence. This would imply that the use of a time period of less than 1 year would have produced considerable variation according to the month of the year in which the survey was conducted. On balance, the data produced by this question should be viewed as being approximate in accuracy.

The question about medical care expenses did not ask for expenses net of any health insurance reimbursement. The phrasing of the question suggests out-of-pocket expenditure. It should be noted that costs of over-the-counter medications, doctor office visits, and prescription drugs measured here are not covered by most health insurance policies.

The findings from question 5 are shown in Table 9.5. Mean data are presented both for respondents who experienced each symptom (symptom respondents) and across all 20 respondents, which includes those who did not report the symptom.

Of the 21 type B questionnaires that were returned, one was not completely ascertained with respect to question 5, leaving 20 usable cases. This is not a large number of cases, but a sample worthy of exploratory analysis. The number of cases of the last three symptoms—irritated throat, itching eyes, and drowsiness—was quite small. The data for these symptoms should be viewed as being merely suggestive.

The most frequently reported symptom was stuffed-up sinuses, reported

TABLE 9.5. Mean Incidence of Symptom Days, Mean Days Lost, Mean Earnings Lost, and Mean Medical Care Expense, Last 12 Months

Symptom	% of Respondents Who Had Symptom during the Last 12 Months	Mean Symptom Days		Mean Days Work or Other Lost		Mean Earnings Lost (in $)		Mean Medical Expenses (in $)		Number of Cases
		Symptom Respondents	All Respondents	Symptom Respondents	All Respondents	Symptom Respondents	All Respondents	Symptom Respondents	All Respondents	
Painful headache	60	28	17	1.9	1.1	179	108	100	60	12
Coughing spells	50	9	4	0.6	0.3	67	31	4	2	10
Stuffed-up sinuses	80	34	27	0.9	0.8	22	18	15	12	16
Irritated throat	60	8	5	0.3	0.2	8	5	5	3	12
Itching eyes	35	9	3	0.3	0.1	0	0	0	0	7
Heavy drowsiness when driving	20	7	1	0.3	0	0	0	0	0	4

NOTE.—Symptom respondents: the mean is taken across all those reporting the symptom in the last 12 months. All respondents: the mean is taken across all 20 type B questionnaire respondents.

by 80% of the respondents. The least frequently reported symptoms were itching eyes (35%) and heavy drowsiness when driving (20%). Stuffed-up sinuses also had the highest average number of symptom days—34 days per year for those experiencing the symptom and 27 days averaged across all respondents. Headaches were next most frequently reported, averaging 28 days for those experiencing headaches and 17 days averaged across all respondents. Itching eyes and heavy drowsiness when driving were the least frequently reported symptom days.

In terms of days of work lost or other usual activity lost, headaches produced the greatest mean number of days lost—1.9 days per year for those experiencing headaches and 1.1 days averaged across all respondents. Stuffed-up sinuses produced the next greatest number of average days lost—0.9 days for those experiencing stuffed up sinuses and 0.8 days averaged over all respondents. No days of work or other usual activity lost were reported for itching eyes and heavy drowsiness when driving. Headaches also produced the greatest mean loss of earnings—averaging $179 per year for those experiencing headaches and an average of $108 for all respondents. Coughing caused the next highest average loss of earnings—$67 per year for those experiencing coughing and an average of $31 for all respondents. Stuffed-up sinuses produced an average of $22 in earnings lost for those experiencing this symptom and $18 for all respondents. Headaches similarly produced the highest average medical expenses averaged across all respondents. The next highest mean medical expense was for stuffed-up sinuses—averaging $22 per year for those experiencing stuffed-up sinuses and an average of $17 per year for all respondents.

In terms of comparison of willingness to pay with earnings lost and medical care expenses, for those respondents reporting each symptom it is clear that mean willingness to pay, shown in Table 9.3, greatly exceeded both mean earnings lost and mean medical expense, both separately and in combination, for all symptoms except headache, where both mean earnings lost and mean medical expense were of the same general magnitude as mean willingness to pay. For headaches, the mean earnings loss was $179, the mean medical expense $100, and the mean willingness to pay $113.

9.5. Demographics

Respondents were more or less evenly divided between male (56%) and female (44%) respondents. The age distribution of the respondents appears to be reasonably representative of the age distribution among adults. There is a somewhat higher rate of representation among those with more education and higher household incomes. The distribution of respondents according to size of household shows that about half (51%) of the respondents lived in a two-member household, 15% in single-member households, and about one-third (34%) in households of three or more persons.

9.6. Summary of Results

A mail survey was conducted to determine whether it would be feasible to greatly expand the number of cases on which the contingent valuation estimates could be based. As in the personal interview questionnaires, the symptom-based approach to willingness to pay was adopted, using six common air pollution–caused symptoms, including those caused by general air pollution, ozone, and carbon monoxide. Two questionnaires were developed, identical except that one questionnaire, type B, added a set of comparative questions that measure earnings lost and medical care expenses occasioned by the symptoms. The Dillman mail survey method was employed for this survey.

An equal probability sample of 103 names and addresses representing the Chicago metropolitan area adult resident population was drawn from reverse telephone directories. Discounting 15 addresses that had changed, a response rate of 48% of the 88 possible interviews was achieved, forming a database of 42 cases.

The symptom that was reported to be the most commonly ever experienced and most bothersome was stuffed-up sinuses.

The willingness to pay question was based on a certain endowment of 3 symptom days per month for each symptom. The bids were for an effective, safe, side-effect-free medication that would be taken only once a month. The mean bids to eliminate the personal discomfort symptoms of headache, coughing, stuffed-up sinuses, irritated throat, and itching eyes ranged between $9.42 and $9.68 per month, or $101 and $116 per year. The mean willingness to pay to eliminate heavy drowsiness when driving was $5.41 per month, or $65 per year.

By far the most common reason underlying the amount of the bids was personal comfort. Next most frequently mentioned was to avoid loss of work or other usual activity.

The comparative set of questions again showed stuffed-up sinuses to be the most commonly experienced symptom, followed by headaches, irritated throat, and coughing, which also were common. Stuffed-up sinuses showed the highest mean number of symptoms per year—27 averaged across all respondents, with headaches showing a mean 17 symptom days per year. However, in terms of days of work or other usual activity lost, headaches produced the largest mean number of days lost, 1.1 per year averaged over all respondents. Earnings lost because of headache was by far the largest—averaging $108 per year across all respondents. Medical care expenses were also by far the largest for headaches—averaging $60 per year over all respondents. Coughing caused the next highest mean level of earnings loss, and stuffed-up sinuses the next highest mean medical expenses. For most symptoms, mean willingness to pay greatly exceeded the sum of mean earnings loss and mean medical expenses. For the exception, headaches, mean willingness to pay was somewhat lower than the sum of lost earnings and medical expenses.

Analysis of the demographic characteristics of the respondents showed male respondents to be slightly more common than female respondents, the age distribution to be approximately representative, and the educational distribution to be somewhat skewed toward those with higher levels of education. Size of household proved to be mostly two-person households, with a third of the households having three or more persons. The distribution of household incomes showed overrepresentation of those with higher levels of income.

As a final note, the results from the mail survey can be compared to the data gathered through the personal interviews. The most direct comparison involves the seven-light-symptom 1-day and 30-day surveys. In Chapter 15, where the estimates of this study are expressed in common 1991 dollars, the mean bids for the mail survey, which considers the relief of 3 symptom days per month, are mostly intermediate in value between the 1-day and 30-day means for a comparable symptom. They are not, however, three times the 1-day mean bids or one-tenth of the 30-day means.

When examining the mail data, we also find a positive relationship between the mean bid for a symptom and the number of days the symptom was actually experienced. The same relationship was also clearly observed within the seven-symptom 1-day data. This observation adds further evidence to the proposition of increasing marginal disutility when a particular symptom is experienced.

Valuation of Serious Illness

Overview of Part Three

Part 3 extends the analysis of health valuation to life-threatening illness. Chapter 10 considers alternative definitions of health useful for the study of serious illnesses and concludes that a definition in terms of absence of symptoms should be used. Specific measures of health status are evaluated, including symptom description, self-assessment, health risk appraisal, health indexes, and multiattribute utility functions.

Chapter 11 develops a life-cycle explanatory framework for valuing reductions in life-threatening illness that guides the remainder of the study. Within this framework, longevity (i.e., mortality) and quality of life (as affected by morbidity) are considered together in a unified context. Young people, presented with improved prospects for greater health and longevity only after a long period of time, will discount the benefits and may pay little, even though aware that their preferences many years hence will be different. Policies that promise a near-term benefit will be valued more highly by people of any age. If people can easily substitute near-term consumption for deferred consumption, they will place less value on additions to life expectancy. The capacity for consumption changes over the life cycle. An added year of life accompanied by high income or accumulated wealth, together with a high quality of leisure time, will be valued relatively highly. Latency is modeled within the life-cycle framework.

Chapter 12 develops a model of choice under uncertain preferences, bringing utility theory to bear on the problem of valuing small changes in events that are thought of only infrequently and may involve low probabilities of occurrence. The model is applicable to contingent valuation approaches to serious illness. The model assumes that most health risks are unfamiliar to most people and that, because people seldom have occasion to think carefully about them, they are uncertain about their preferences concerning them. The model leads to 12 theorems for stimulating people to obtain improved knowledge about their preferences and to state valid, consistent risk-reduction values.

Chapter 13 applies the preceding sections to contingent valuation of life-threatening illness. A structure for an intensive interviewing process is developed, based on techniques of in-depth interviewing.

The proposed interview structure contains four modules. The first module concerns the respondent's health experiences. The defensive-measures module is the second module. The third module pertains to risk perception and risk behavior. This module teaches respondents basic notions of probability and conveys information about probabilities involved in health. Information is obtained about respondent perceptions and attitudes toward risks.

Contingent valuation questions form the fourth module. The module begins with simple questions involving certainty scenarios and mortality only, after which serious illnesses are introduced. Then life-path scenarios are introduced that combine morbidity and mortality in a life-cycle setting. Respondents are asked to choose among and value the scenarios, first in a certainty and then an uncertainty setting.

Areas of future research suggested by this volume are discussed in Chapter 14. These include defining units of health to be valued, which depends on the purpose for which they are to be used. Investigations of ways to improve willingness to pay estimates are suggested, including relating valuations to the prior stock of health, dread, risk aversion, and values of one person's health to other people. Among remaining issues in using a life-cycle framework for health values are effects of age on the valuation of health in an intertemporal setting and discounting health effects to present values within and between generations.

10

Defining and Measuring Health over Life

Lyndon Babcock and Anthony Bilotti

10.1. Overview

Health measurement is an essential part of any analysis of the values that people derive from policies affecting health. Several different methods of health measurement have been employed in the literature. Self-assessment is the most widely used measure of health status. People are asked to rate their own health as excellent, good, fair, or poor. This approach has been used in national surveys conducted by the Center for Health Administration Studies of the University of Chicago and in many smaller household surveys.

Other frequently used approaches include reports of restricted activity days, bed disability days, number and severity of symptoms experienced, number of chronic conditions, and the amount of pain experienced by the respondent during the past year. A variety of attitude questions have also been used, such as perceived effectiveness of health care (Fuchs 1982, pp. 144–45). Studies of the demand for health care have utilized these measures of health status. These studies have included nonmarket health-related activities as well as expenditures on medical care consumption. They have focused on such topics as price and income elasticities of demand and the effects of insurance on medical care consumption. Health status is often an important variable in explaining the demand for health care.

Recent work has emphasized that health is a multidimensional condition whose complexity should be represented in health studies in order to avoid bias in the measurement of price and income elasticities and other important variables. The multiattribute utility function is an example of the multidimensional approach. A study of Torrance, Boyle, and Horwood (1982) represents health according to four dimensions: morbidity and physical activity; self-care and role activity, emotional well-being and social activity, and health problems (Chestnut and Violette 1984).

In studying values associated with life-threatening illness in this study, it is necessary to define and measure health, choosing among the previous

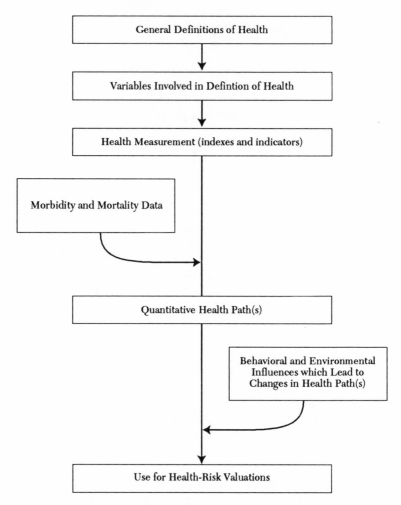

Figure 10.1   Health Definition: Steps Toward Quantification

approaches and building on them where necessary. Figure 10.1 depicts the progression from health definition, to use of morbidity and mortality data and knowledge about influences on health, to measurements for health risk valuations. Drawing on this schema, this section provides a critique of previous approaches and suggests extensions, giving attention to conceptual adequacy and practical considerations in valuing serious illness.

This chapter begins first with considering alternative health definitions. Attention is given first to definitions that consider the dimensions of health in terms of various attributes that may be good and desired or alternatively may be bad and undesired. Definitions of varying broadness are examined. Second, attention is given to definitions of health that focus in detail on symptoms or on departures from good health, rather than on desired attributes.

The chapter then takes up the questions of the relevance to the measurement problem of the causal factors that affect health. Attention to heredity, lifestyle, and environment as causes of disease helps to arrive at judgments as to which health attributes should be emphasized. The view we take is that definition and measurement should depend on the purpose at hand. In this study, the major purpose is to consider serious illnesses.

Health measurement per se is discussed next. Self-rating of health, the health risk appraisal approach, and various approaches to measuring specific symptoms are considered in detail.

Finally, this chapter considers the implications of the preceding sections for empirical work on values associated with serious illness. We give a critique of approaches to health measurement from the point of view of their adequacy for the valuation of serious illness. Criteria include familiarity of respondents with symptoms, ability to encompass risk, adequacy in terms of the effects of serious illness on life-cycle experiences, brevity, and simplicity. Refinements and extensions to previous approaches to health measurement are suggested.

10.2. Alternative Health Definitions

Health is a key determinant of the quality of life. Central to the valuation of health is an understanding of the nature of health and the forces that influence it. Essential to this effort is the definition of human health such that deviations from the conditions it describes can be quantitatively described. While most people have an instinctive comprehension of what constitutes "health," few explicit working definitions are in common use. A multitude of biological, behavioral, cultural, and social factors combine to shape human health—factors that act in both favorable and unfavorable ways to determine the level of well-being of a person at any point in time. "Death" is easily and explicitly defined as the end or extinction of life. "Morbid" indicates that one is diseased, sick, or unhealthy. But the definition of health itself is much more elusive, particularly when quantification is desired. Webster defines health as "physical and mental well-being," "soundness," "vitality," "prosperity," and as a "flourishing condition." Health is thought of also as simply the absence of illness or morbidity, that is, a biological state dependent upon biological factors. As Banta (1981) points out, other more recent definitions of health also stress life functioning, mental state, and self-fulfillment. In fact there is no single definition of health, although many definitions have been developed and are currently in use."

Carroll, Miller, and Nash (1976, p. 1) state that health goes beyond absence of disease or discomfort to the ability "to function effectively, happily, and as long as possible in a particular environment." The constitution of the World Health Organization describes health as a "state of complete physical, mental and social well-being, and not merely an absence of disease or infirmity," though this may be regarded as a statement of goals rather than a definition (Hanlon and Pickett 1984, p. 5). The Great Britain Royal Commission on the National Health Service (1979, p. 8) aptly summed up the debate by declaring that "health itself is not a simple or precise concept." Clearly, health is much more than mere absence of disease, and it has extremely great value.

Another related concept that is undergoing a change in meaning is that of "medical care," which traditionally has meant the provision of medical services by, or under the direction of, physicians. In recent years, the emphasis of such care has broadened to include preventive, as well as strictly curative, measures to preventive actions—albeit care is still provided by the physician in a clinical setting.

Broader still is the term "health care," no longer the exclusive province of the clinical physician. The term "health care" has come to replace "medical care" in many instances. Other new terms such as "health promotion," "health maintenance," and "disease prevention" have come into use (often interchangeably) to characterize the new preventive focus of health care that includes measures to be undertaken by individuals themselves. The Surgeon General's Report (U.S. Public Health Service 1979) describes disease prevention as the protection of people from the harmful effects of health threats (e.g., diseases, environmental hazards). Health promotion measures are aimed at well, as well as ill, people (e.g., the promotion of activities to improve lifestyles).

Perhaps the most far-reaching of the new health concepts are "wellness" and "high-level wellness" (Ardell 1977; Travis 1977), which can be defined as "active processes through which the individual becomes aware of and makes choices toward a more successful existence" (Hettler 1980, p. 77). Indeed, individuals are becoming increasingly aware of the merits of promoting their own health; sizable investments in time and other resources are being made.

Given the array of similar terms and definitions introduced above, an attempt to visualize these conceptual relationships suggests a health continuum described by Brubaker (1983). From this point of view, illness and death lie at one end, wellness at the other, while an individual's state of health is characterized by any degree of illness or wellness. Hettler (1981, p. 78) offers a somewhat expanded representation of the health continuum, adding terms to describe social well-being and the ability to function within a society.

10.3. Role of Causal Factors

Background

Causal factors in health include hereditary, lifestyle, and environmental factors. The causal factors are relevant to the definition and measurement of health, primarily because they determine the strength of various health attributes, which helps to distinguish the important from the unimportant. For example, if environmental change affects the incidence of cancer, then cancer symptoms, and not the entire range of health attributes, will be a principal focus in a study related to the environment. Among cancer symptoms, the degree of refinement of measurement of physical pain versus mental anguish will be determined by the relative strength of these attributes among cancer victims. Furthermore, the causal factors determine how greatly a policy will affect health attributes, which in turn determines the range of change in health attributes that need to be studied. As noted, health is influenced by a great number of forces, which can be described as hereditary, lifestyle, and environmental. Health can be seen as a process of continuous adaptation to the effects of these forces. The nature of these influences and their relative importance to human health have been described by Hettler (1980) and by Blum (1980). Health is described as an indivisible whole composed of somatic (physical), social, and psychic (mental) well-being: illness in any one of the three facets affects the other two.

Of primary concern to the valuation of risk reduction are the environmental and behavioral influences on health and, to a limited extent, medical or health care. Heredity, though important, will not be given further attention here. Furthermore, the definition of environment outlined by Blum (1980) encompasses education, culture, and politics, factors beyond the scope of this study. For our purposes, environment consists of the interaction between human health and physical factors, such as air and water quality stressors, toxic substances present in the ambient environment, workplace hazards, radiation exposure, and accidents. We assume that these aspects of the physical environment are partly under the control of an individual. Behavioral factors are under even greater control of the individual and demonstrably influence personal health (Somers 1980).

Some generally accepted conclusions are:

1. Everyone is endowed with certain health assets at birth. These may be above or below average for the population in general. Regardless of initial birth endowment, however, the health of an individual is subject to change.

2. Interventions can influence the health of each individual either positively or negatively. Some interventions will have an immediate effect on health level (e.g., an automobile accident); the effects of other interventions

may not manifest themselves until years after the intervention (latent effects of cigarette smoking, for example).

3. Health changes can be temporary and reversible, such as those associated with a common cold or exercise, or the health change can be permanent, such as loss of a limb or contraction of emphysema.

4. Interventions may be voluntary, involuntary, or something in between. Cigarette smoking clearly is voluntary, but subjecting oneself to the risks of living near a hazardous chemical facility may be either voluntary or involuntary, depending on the amount of information available to the risk taker.

5. The health path will, at some point, terminate in death. For an individual, this termination can occur at any age, regardless of health.

Role of Behavior or Lifestyle

The influence that behavior can have on health has been long recognized, but systematic study and measurement of the implications of human actions on health are recent developments. Behavior patterns, or lifestyles, are at least partly under individual control. Lifestyle is intimately tied to social class and culture—complex concepts describing characteristics of human interactions whose effect on health are not easily quantified. Nonetheless, it is clear that intervention against lifestyle-induced risk factors can reduce the probability of dying from the major causes of death (Klein 1980; Somers 1980; Berkman and Breslow 1983; Mausner and Kramer 1985).

As Somers (1980) affirms, the links between behavior and health can be summarized in three statements: (1) The major causes of death, serious illness, and disability in the United States today are chronic disease and violence (see Table 10.1); (2) Most chronic disease, disabilities, and premature deaths are related to a variety of environmental and behavioral factors,

TABLE 10.1.   Death Rates: Leading Causes of Death, United States, 1979

Cause	Rate/100,000 Population	% of All Deaths
Disease of heart	333	38
Malignant neoplasms	183	21
Cerebrovascular disease	77	9
Miscellaneous chronic diseases°	56	7
Accidents, including motor vehicle, suicide, and homicide	70	8
Other	151	17
All causes	870	100

SOURCE.—National Center for Health Statistics (1979a), vol. 2, pt. A.
   NOTE.—Figures are rounded.
   ° Diabetes, cirrhosis of liver, arteriosclerosis, bronchitis, emphysema and asthma, nephritis and nephrosis, and peptic ulcer.

which may be preventable; (3) Lifestyle pattern is the major behavioral risk factor involved in chronic disease contraction and disability (Somers 1980).

No matter how comprehensive a nation's programs of environmental monitoring, or how extensive its health care services, the individual is ultimately responsible for minimizing threats to his or her health (Mechanic and Cleary 1980). Factors such as smoking, alcohol and drug abuse, lack of exercise, reckless driving, and failure to use seat belts can have considerable effects on health status and life expectancy (Breslow 1978; Breslow and Enstrom 1980; Mechanic and Cleary 1980). This is not to say that people can easily correct negative behavior because they are a part of the larger society and influenced by its institutions, which offer ambiguous messages about what is advisable behavior (U.S. Public Health Service 1979; Blum 1980). Nonetheless, a willing individual can take steps which will measurably affect health status.

Role of Environment

Several approaches that relate environmental stressors to health effects have been considered. While the present research is concerned with valuing health consequences, and not with environmental cause-effect relations as such, some attention to cause-effect relations is needed.

In what follows, we describe the source-receptor-effects system, and present inventories of some of the pollutants receiving considerable study and public attention during the past 15 years. The extreme uncertainty of cause-effect relationships is indicated. This chapter then turns to the study of light symptoms. It becomes more quantitative and has greater depth on a narrower range of pollutants than the introductory part of the chapter, thereby serving as an introduction to a wider range of pollutants needed for the study of serious illness.

With few exceptions, the existence of causal relationships between pollution in the ambient environment and disease is difficult to quantify. Problems arise in attempting to relate exposure to a suspected agent with the development of illness, particularly if the illness is preceded by a long latency period (U.S. Environmental Protection Agency, 1982).

Figure 10.2 summarizes the complex path between a source of pollution and a variety of possible health effects, including death. Moving down the diagram, the source of pollution may be industrial, residential, natural, and so on. The emission may be from air, water, land, or a combination of media. The pollutants are likely to be diluted, transformed, and partially decayed before reaching exposed human receptors.

Note that defensive measures may be applied at the source to reduce the amount of, or entirely eliminate, the emission; other personal defensive measures may be applied prior to exposure (migration, air conditioning, etc.).

After or during continuous exposure, it is likely there will be a finite

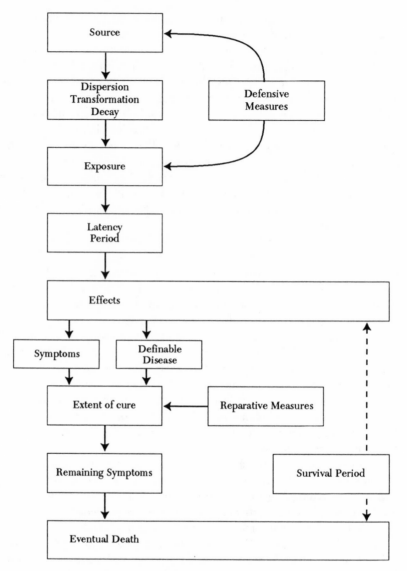

Figure 10.2   Pollution–Health Relationship

latency period before adverse health effects, if any, appear. Uncertain and often lengthy latency periods make exposure-effect determinations very difficult.

The adverse effects, by definition, include any departure from optimal health. They range from almost imperceptible discomfort to terminal lung cancer. These adverse effects might be defined either as groupings of symptoms or as a clearly identified disease. Defensive and/or curative measures may reduce the effect of disease, but the adverse environmental effects may still be present. Adverse effects are not discretely divided into morbidity and mortality, but, rather, the effects are seen to influence a health continuum that begins with optimal health (that existing in the absence of pollution) and ending with death.

Even prior to exposure, however, health can be adversely influenced by factors other than pollution, such as age and previous medical history. Each person exposed, at a different point on a different route, will die. The challenge is to define the environmental influence on each path of mortality.

There is uncertainty at each linkage. Rosen (1981, p. 245) concludes, "The most pressing need is for better estimates of risk valuations. That will require much better data than are currently available."

In summary, the complexities involved in establishing direct cause-effect relationships include: (a) exposure to a toxic substance may occur through direct contact with contaminated soil, water, air, food, or in the workplace; (b) the substance may be absorbed through the skin, ingested, inhaled; (c) contact may be brief or prolonged on single, multiple, or continuous occasions; (d) the effects may be manifested very shortly after exposure or, as in the case of carcinogens, many years later; (e) the substance may act synergistically with other agents to produce illness, such as asbestos exposure combined with cigarette smoke; and (f) the existing health status of the exposed person may affect the development of illness.

Of the hazards to human health arising from toxic substances, cancer is the target of most concern. It is the only major cause of death that has continued to rise since 1900, and it is responsible for the loss of 400,000 lives each year. Some of the increase in cancer mortality since 1900 is a function of the greater average age of the population and the medical progress made against infectious diseases. But even after correcting for age, both mortality rates and incidence of cancer are increasing.

It is extremely difficult to assess the role that environmental factors play in causing human cancer because people are exposed to multiple stressors of both physical and chemical natures, some of which are related to their own behavior. Some early estimates of the proportion of cancers directly attributable to environmental agents were as high as 85%–90%, but more recent analyses suggest that the role of environmental health pollutants is minimal (U.S. Environmental Protection Agency 1982). This finding is supported by Doll and Peto (1981) who compare environmental and behavioral risks and conclude that the environmental and occupational risks are relatively minor.

Much of what is known about the acute and chronic health effects of chemical substances has come from studies of workplace exposure. Many workers die each year as a result of physical and chemical hazards at work, but the exact magnitude of the long-term health effects of occupational conditions is unknown (Toxic Substances Strategy Committee 1980).

Complex human epidemiology over a lifetime seems essential if progress at unraveling the cause-effect complexities is to be made. Animal studies, with their high pollutant concentrations of short duration, are a poor substitute for actual lifetime human exposures to low ambient concentrations of toxics. Long latency periods cloud the exposure response. In addition, animal studies cannot be used for annoyance symptoms (e.g., cough, headache). The kinds of research needed to define environmental health risks are described in depth in a report for Environmental Protection Agency (Babcock and Allen 1983).

10.4. Health Measurement

Measurement in Terms of Ill Health

Levels of morbidity are commonly classified as a series of five "D's": disability, discomfort, discontent, disease, and death. Available evidence argues that trace environmental pollutants have their greatest impact on the first four "D's," although they may contribute to premature death as well.

Nationwide U.S. surveys provide information on prevalence of diseases and various health indicators. For example, the National Health and Nutrition Examination Survey (NHANES) clinically examines 20,000 different people every 4 years. A variety of health, nutritional, and disease prevalence information is obtained.

The National Health Interview Survey (NHIS), which provides data concerning the prevalence of disease, surveys more than 100,000 people per year, but it is restricted to question-answer interviews rather than examinations. These tabulations do not specifically indicate numbers of people who suffer from more than one malady or from the same malady more than once in a year. Likewise, there is no information about numbers of people who escape all the diseases. These surveys are cross-sectional; they do not follow individuals through life. However, such information is useful for construction of likely scenarios that exhibit certain diseases during a lifetime.

In practice, many health status measurements are based on functional classification or therapeutic considerations involving diseased or disabled persons, not those who are well. That is, the definition is in terms of ill health, not good health.

Mausner and Kramer (1985, p. 6) point out that "the development of disease is often an irregularly evolving process, and the point at which a person should be labeled 'diseased' rather than 'not diseased' may be arbitrary." Left untreated, a disease may extend over time with symptoms changing in stages. This pattern may be termed its "natural history" or "clinical course." In relation to age, "factors favoring the development of chronic disease are often present early in life, antedating the appearance of clinical disease by many years." The Mausner and Kramer framework for analysis of disease history follows (pp. 6–9):

Stage of susceptibility: Prior to the presence of a disease, factors which may increase the probability of its development may be present. These are termed risk factors. Age, sex, and race are examples which are not susceptible to human intervention, but alcohol or tobacco use can be subject to change. The presence of risk factors does not ensure disease development nor does their absence ensure freedom from disease.

Pre-symptomatic stage: Pathogenetic changes begin to occur, but the changes are not manifested in symptoms or signs which can be diagnosed.

Clinical stage: Recognizable signs and symptoms occur. It is at this point that classifications of health status based on functional or therapeutic considerations are made. Examples for categorization of cardiac disease appear below.

Functional Classification[1]

Class I	No limitation of physical activity because of discomfort;
Class II	Slight limitation of physical activity; patient comfortable at rest but ordinary activity produces discomfort;
Class III	Marked limitation of physical activity; comfortable at rest but less than ordinary activity causes discomfort;
Class IV	Inability to carry out physical activity without discomfort;
Class V	Progression of disease where a residual effect of varying duration may occur, resulting in limitation of a person's activities.

Therapeutic Classification

Class A	Physical activity need not be restricted in any way;
Class B	Ordinary physical activity need not be restricted, but patient is advised against severe efforts;
Class C	Ordinary physical activity should be moderately restricted;
Class D	Ordinary physical activity should be markedly restricted;

1. These classifications originated with the New York Heart Association (1964). We have taken them from Mausner and Kramer (1985), pp. 7–8.

Class E   Complete bed rest advised; patient confined to bed or chair.

Descriptions of the natural history of the disease can be incorporated into indicated health effects. Lung cancer provides an example as follows: (1) the time when an individual is at no risk: the individual either has not been exposed to the disease-causing agent (e.g., does not smoke or work with asbestos) or has been exposed to the agent but is not vulnerable to it (e.g., even in the presence of smoke, newborn infants are not vulnerable to, and will not develop, lung cancer); (2) when one is vulnerable due to genetic propensities or a change in age or environment and therefore does not have an immune status; (3) when the damaging agent is present, at which time the exposed individual is in danger of acquiring the disease (e.g., anyone who smokes); (4) when an actual sign of disease is observable by a physician, though not apparent to the victim (e.g., an abnormal chest X ray); (5) when symptoms appear (severe coughing, chest pains, blood in sputum), and the individual, who knows that something is wrong, may tell a physician or other health worker; or (6) when disability, partial or complete, occurs.

The natural histories of many diseases are still unknown. In addition, some people never develop a disease despite the presence of a number of risk factors.

The listed functional classifications might be expanded into health indexes by defining various levels of minor discomfort and pain and minor limitations of physical activity. Some health problems attributed to environmental interventions include learning impairment, peripheral neuropathy, and birth defects.

More simply, however, the history of the diseases provides descriptions of symptoms and consequences that could be quantified to a more or less exact degree depending on considerations of measurement feasibility in view of a particular study purpose.

Health Indexes

The health definitions discussed above suggested that a person has neither absolute health nor absolute illness (except death) but is in an ever-changing state and that one can be at any point on the continuum at any point in life. For some purposes it would be useful to quantify a health continuum, numerically and in terms of economic valuation of small increments of change. Initially, efforts could focus on the simpler Brubaker (1983) health continuum, but the expansions by Hettler (1981) into risks and education might also possibly be useful in contingent valuation studies.

Pulmonary function tests are used to measure lung capabilities (Babcock and Nagda 1976). These and other physiological tests (exercise, work level, physical education performance, etc.) might provide another type of index.

Multiattribute Utility Functions

Researchers in the field of decision analysis have devised techniques for the characterization or prediction of health status (Katz et al. 1983; Wolinsky et al. 1984), usually for the evaluation and comparison of health care treatment alternatives or medical policy decisions. Quantitative methods, such as multiattribute utility functions (Keeney and Raiffa 1976) or linear analog scales (Sutherland, Dunn and Boyd 1983), are employed to evaluate the nature of trade-offs between quality of life and longevity (Pliskin, Shepard, and Weinstein 1980) or to measure a patient's preference for certain health states (Torrance, Boyle, and Horwood 1982). Such analytical methods may involve complex, lottery-based measurement techniques to determine probabilistic outcomes.

Boyle et al. (1982) employ a multiattribute health state classification system for use in a cost-effectiveness analysis of neonatal intensive care. Health status is defined by physical function, using measures of mobility and physical activity; role function, or self-care, such as the ability to eat, dress, or bathe with or without help; social-emotional function, measures of emotional well-being and social activity; and health problems, such as the presence or absence of a disability.

Self-rating of Health

As noted earlier, self-assessment is the most widely used measure of health status. The simple ranking of one's health (excellent, good, fair, or poor) is crude in terms of being amenable to dollar quantification. However, the measure is simple, which makes it attractive, especially for contingent valuation studies. While self-rating may not be usable for obtaining a value measure, it may be usable as a shifter in a function explaining health values since the state of one's health is an influence on how much one is willing to pay to avoid various specific symptoms or diseases.

Health Risk Appraisal

Health risk appraisal (HRA) is a tool for assessing the potential impact of individual behavior on the probability of dying from selected causes. In the course of a computerized HRA, information about an individual's lifestyle and personal and family health history is elicited from a subject. This information is then compared with age, race, sex-specific mortality data, and epidemiologic statistics to determine whether a person has a greater or less-than-average risk of dying from a selected cause, usually within the next 10 years. A printout informs the subject of the outcome. Most HRAs are based on the work of Robbins and Hall and the statistical tables of Geller and Gestner (1981). The objectives of the appraisal are to estimate individual risk with some degree of accuracy and, by identifying risky behavior, help individuals modify or eliminate negative habits before the development of disease or disability (Goetz, Duff, and Bernstein 1979; Dunton 1981; Hettler 1981; Schultz 1984).

The appraisal begins with a self-administered questionnaire. Each response is assigned a numerical "risk factor," which is then multiplied with the average risk of dying from each major cause of death. In the case of multiple risk factors for a single cause of death, a "composite risk factor" is calculated and then multiplied by average risk. The resulting disease-specific risk projections are then summed to form a "total projected risk." This is then compared to average risk to yield a new term, "risk age," or "appraised age"—that is, the age of an average person with the same mortality risk as the respondent (Beery et al. 1986, p. 6).

This appraised age can be readily compared with actual age. If the total risk is greater than average (the appraised age is greater than the actual age), appropriate behavior modifications are suggested. If the suggestions are followed, the individual can hope to lower the overall risk projection, as expressed by the value of the "achievable age." For example, a 34-year-old may have the risk characteristics of a 30-year-old (appraised age) but an achievable age of 29.

It is important to recognize that HRA instruments are, despite widespread use, still in an early stage of development. Concern has been expressed about the quality of the data elicited by a self-administered questionnaire and the accuracy of the risk measurement (Beery et al. 1986; Sacks, Krushot, and Newman 1980; Fielding 1981; Schoenbach, Wagner, and Karon 1983).

10.5. Implications for Valuing Serious Illness

The approaches to the definition and measurement of health that have been reviewed in this section serve to bring out the complex nature of this subject matter. The question becomes, How are we to measure health in the present study in view of the complexities?

A first implication that stands out is that measurement in terms of ill health is appropriate in view of one concern of the present study, with values of eliminating undesirable environmental effects. As reviewed earlier, the possible diseases and symptoms caused by environmental pollutants can be described rather definitely in terms of ill health effects.

A second implication is that a broad definition of health effects is needed, extending beyond physical pain to mental well-being and beyond this to the functioning of the individual. Conceptually, one wants to value all the significant deleterious effects of the illnesses being studied.

Third, the fact that broad classes of illness are to be studied among many people in the population means that a basically simple approach must be followed. People must be able to think meaningfully about the measures, and it must be feasible to take the measurements and analyze them operationally as they pertain to large numbers of people. While the first and second implications go in the direction of detail and complexity, the third implication indicates that compromises with the first two implications will have to be struck.

If we look ahead to ensuing chapters of this book, additional implications are obtained. Thus a fourth implication is that the present state of health may affect values attached to contracting particular diseases. It is important to relate changes in health status to existing levels of health. A fifth implication is that a person's entire stream of life experiences with and without a disease affects how the disease is valued. A person's age is particularly relevant, as is his or her expectation as to the course of events in his or her life without the disease. Sixth, one must look beyond health effects encountered with certainty to situations of uncertainty. Most people will never contract the diseases being considered. Environmental improvements will reduce the probability of contracting the disease. Health measurement must give attention, not only to certainty scenarios, but also to risk reduction in the context of uncertainty scenarios.

The first, second, and third implications help in choosing between existing health measurement approaches. The third, fourth, and fifth implications indicate needs for extensions and refinements of these approaches. Finally, the fact that the present study gives particular emphasis to devising contingent valuation approaches to serious illness affects choice of health measures.

One of the clearest conclusions from these implications is that measurement in terms of ill health effects is called for in the present study. In view of the need for operational simplicity, symptom descriptions in terms of average conditions brought about by a disease are the basic approach recommended here for studying values connected with serious illness. The symptom descriptions need to be supplemented by allowance for full effects of the symptoms on mental well-being and functioning of individuals. In a contingent valuation approach, this can be done by making the respondent aware of a wide range of effects of the symptoms.

For getting at the effects of existing health levels on valuations, self-rating of health has much to offer. It is more readily available than more sophisticated measures, and the need for precision is less great for measuring the existing health level than the specific effects of the disease being valued.

The health risk appraisal approach, which takes the trouble to relate highly specific individual characteristics, including age and lifestyle factors to health prospects, is highly congenial to the framework of the present study, which stresses the importance of life experiences and alternative future life-path scenarios. It plays a prominent role in some of the approaches to health valuation developed later in this study.

The multiattribute utility function approach has much to recommend it conceptually for some purposes, but it is not used here largely because it appears operationally too complex for this study. Respondents in contingent valuation experiments can and should be encouraged to take account of the multifaceted nature of health effects in framing responses, which is consistent with multiattribute utility functions. But quantifying the utility function as such is not attempted here where we are concerned with going directly to dollar valuations of the sum of all the effects of an illness.

The later parts of this study build on the choices among existing health measures implied by the above remarks. Refinements to the health measurement approaches are developed taking account of individual circumstances in a life-cycle context with certainty and uncertainty scenarios.

11

The Quantity and Quality of Life: A Conceptual Framework

Sherwin Rosen

11.1. Introduction

Serious professional interest in benefit-cost analysis of projects involving safety, illness, and death probabilities has its origins in environmental concerns beginning in the 1960s as a practical policy matter and in the work of Schelling (1968) and Mishan (1971) as an intellectual one. These authors showed how to put the problem into the willingness to pay framework of applied welfare economics, which has been the guiding principle in economic research in this area ever since. Subsequent research has followed two distinct conceptual lines. Beginning with the important paper by Usher, one line has followed a strict life-cycle framework. Building on the paper by Yaari (1965), work by Conley (1976), Cropper (1977), Arthur (1981), and Ehrlich and Chuma (1984) has built increasingly elaborate models of life-cycle valuation criteria. Another line, and one that has tended to guide most empirical work, uses a simplified single-period model without explicit regard for life-cycle considerations (e.g., Thaler and Rosen 1975; Jones-Lee 1976; and Rosen 1981). The single-period models are conceptually simpler than life-cycle models but may miss some important considerations that arise in the fully dynamic life-cycle setting that the problem obviously requires.

This chapter is concerned with life-cycle models of safety and health evaluation. One of its goals, at least by implication, is to show the close relationship between life-cycle and single-period models. This is achieved by stripping away many of the detailed complexities of life-cycle dynamics to reveal the internal structure of the problem most clearly and in the most elementary manner. In fact, this is most easily done in a deterministic setting, in which a person has a fixed longevity and is allowed to optimize consumption and labor supply decisions over his or her fixed length of life. The solution to the optimal program naturally leads to a simple formula for putting dollar values on suitably small increments of longevity, using the principles of duality theory. Models of this type are discussed in the following two sections. First a simple consumption allocation problem is analyzed, and the valuation equation exhibited. Then the model is complicated in a number of ways. I show that most of the principles underlying the simplest model carry through for all variations on the theme. This model may be extended to include valuation of morbidity as well as of longevity.

While deterministic models are useful in their great simplicity, they suffer obvious defects in terms of realism. Therefore the remainder of this essay turns to stochastic models using actuarial calculus and the insured-consumption-loans device for dealing with intertemporal budget constraints introduced by Yaari (1965). The insurance features of these schemes allow the analysis to separate allocation decisions regarding consumption and labor supply from uncertainty regarding length of life. The exposition brings out the intimate connection between deterministic and stochastic models and shows that the same types of parameters are relevant for both. Chief among these is a parameter that is naturally interpreted as reflecting the inherent substitution between "quantity" (or longevity) and "quality" of life. It is closely related to the economic concept of intertemporal substitution. Estimates of the "values of life" from existing empirical studies allow rough imputations of this parameter, which ultimately relate to the question of how much of the economy's wealth should be spent on safety, health, and longevity concerns. Other relevant factors are shown to include the rates of interest and time preference, the level of wealth, and the person's stage in the life cycle.

An interesting implication of this analysis is that personal valuations of life expectancy inevitably vary over the life cycle. This important point is the inevitable consequence of the finiteness of life itself and the effect of discounting. Hence a person who chooses an action when young that affects subsequent mortality may live to regret it later, in the sense that, within the circumstances he finds himself later, he would have somehow "preferred" not having taken the earlier action. However, there is nothing either inconsistent or irrational in this type of behavior since, by hypothesis, the full future consequences of current actions are foreseen when they are chosen. It does mean, however, that the benefit side of any cost-benefit calculation on these matters must take account of the life-cycle structure of valuations and will be sensitive to the age and demographic composition of the population and how it changes over time.

11.2. The Value of Longevity: A Deterministic Model

I consider here a deterministic problem that sets many of the essential ideas for the valuation of life expectancy. Consider a person with time-separable preferences for consumption over a lifetime of length T:

$$U = \int_0^T u[c(t)]e^{-at}dt, \tag{11.1}$$

where the concave function $u[c]$ evaluates the utility of consumption c at time t and a is the constant rate of time preference. The person is endowed with a fixed wealth W at the beginning of life and has a fixed investment opportunity that yields a return of r. The problem to be considered is how the person would allocate his wealth over consumption at each point in the life cycle. The solution to this problem yields the valuation we seek.

Let $W(t)$ represent remaining wealth at time t, and let dW/dt be the change in wealth at time t. Then the budget constraint facing this person may be written in flow terms as

$$\frac{dW}{dt} = rW - c, \tag{11.2}$$

which has a ready interpretation. The term rW is the income from investing current wealth at rate of return r, and c is the amount that is consumed out of this income. If consumption falls short of current income, the person's wealth must be increasing, while if current consumption exceeds current income, his wealth must be decreasing.

The formulation of preferences in (11.1) is consistent with the situation of an unattached individual who has no heirs and therefore no bequest motive. I impose the condition that the person cannot die in debt, and since he does not wish to leave wealth (there are no heirs), there is a boundary condition for the differential equation in (11.2) that $W(T) = 0$. The person will obviously wish to consume all endowed wealth over the entire life cycle. Using this boundary condition and integrating (11.2) yields an equivalent budget constraint in terms of stocks:

$$W = \int_0^T c(t)e^{-rt}dt. \tag{11.3}$$

Initial wealth equals discounted lifetime consumption.

Consider the problem of maximizing U in (11.1) subject to constraint (11.3). Let $V(T, W; r, a)$ denote the maximum of U given that the sequence $c(t)$ is optimally chosen. Clearly V is a function of the parameters of the problem, which are T, W, r, and a. This *value function* allows us to calculate the value of longevity. Let v denote the value of longevity, defined as the maximum amount of wealth a person would willingly give up to extend his life by a small increment dT. In exchange for an increment dT, the person would be willing to pay as much wealth as would keep V at its initial level. This is therefore nothing more than the marginal rate of substitution between T and W implicit in V. Totally differentiating V and setting the result equal to zero, we have

$$v = -\frac{dW}{dT} = \frac{\partial V}{\partial W}. \tag{11.4}$$

To evaluate this expression, it is necessary to first solve the maximum problem.

Associating a Lagrange multiplier m with constraint (11.3), first-order conditions for maximization of (11.1) subject to (11.3) are

$$u'(c)e^{-at} = me^{-rt} \quad \text{for all } t. \tag{11.5}$$

The marginal utility of consumption is proportional to the positive multiplier m, suitably discounted by the difference between r and a. To simplify even further, let us analyze the leading case where $r = a$. Then (11.5) implies $u'(c) = m$, which in turn implies $c(t) = c$, a constant for all t on $[0, T]$. That is, life-cycle consumption is "flat" and the same at all ages, an especially pure form of the permanent income hypothesis. Using this result and substituting into (11.1) defines V as (since $r = a$)

$$V = \int_0^T u(c)e^{-rt}dt = u(c)\int_0^T e^{-rt}dt$$
$$= u(c)\left(\frac{1}{r}\right)(1 - e^{-rt}) = u(c)A(T), \tag{11.6}$$

where $A(T) = (1/r)(1 - e^{-rT})$ is simply the value of an annuity received for T periods at rate of interest r. The term $A(T)$ is the "correction factor" for finite life.

Now from the budget constraint, after substituting $c(t) = c$, we have

$$W = \left(\frac{c}{r}\right)(1 - e^{-rT}) = cA(T). \tag{11.7}$$

Therefore $c = W/A$, which is just the finite life-corrected level income that exhausts the endowment W at T exactly. Putting (11.6) and (11.7) together, we have

$$V = u\left(\frac{W}{A(T)}\right)A(T). \tag{11.8}$$

There are two immediate consequences of (11.8). First, V is strictly increasing in W:

$$V_W = \frac{\partial V}{\partial W} = u'\left(\frac{W}{A}\right) > 0; \tag{11.9}$$

that is, greater wealth makes a person better off. Second, the effect of T is confined to its influence through A. Now A is increasing in T since an annuity that lasts longer has a larger value. But A has two effects on V. It has a negative effect through its influence on the first term in $u(\cdot)$ in (11.8), but it also has a direct positive effect through the multiplicative second term in (11.8). Concavity of $u(c)$ implies that the second direct effect dominates and that V is increasing in A:

$$V_A = \frac{\partial V}{\partial A} = -\left(\frac{W}{A}\right)u'\left(\frac{W}{A}\right) + u\left(\frac{W}{A}\right) + u\left(\frac{W}{A}\right)$$

$$= u\left(\frac{W}{A}\right)(1 - \varepsilon),$$

(11.10)

where $\varepsilon = cu'(c)/u(c)$ is the elasticity of the function $u(c)$. We require $0 \le \varepsilon \le 1$ for the problem to be well conditioned and for the marginal condition (11.5) to characterize the optimum. Therefore $V_A > 0$. Though there is no direct value of length of lifetime T in preferences in this problem, its value is induced by its effect on A. From the definition of $A(T)$, we have $A'(T) = e^{-rT} > 0$.

We are now prepared to evaluate v. Totally differentiating (11.8),

$$dV = u\left(\frac{W}{A}\right)A\left[\varepsilon\frac{dW}{W} + (1 - \varepsilon)\left(\frac{A'}{A}\right)dT\right].$$

(11.11)

Setting (11.11) equal to zero, the value of longevity is

$$v = -\frac{dW}{dT} = A'(T)\left[\frac{1 - \varepsilon}{\varepsilon}\right]\left(\frac{W}{A}\right)$$

$$= e^{-rT}\left[\frac{1 - \varepsilon}{\varepsilon}\right]\left(\frac{W}{A}\right).$$

(11.12)

Equation (11.12) displays some interesting properties:

i) The term v is increasing in wealth (given ε). Longer life is more valuable to wealthier persons, and they are willing to pay more to extend it. This is one reason why life expectancy is longer in societies with greater wealth, which spend some of its own safety devices and on lifestyles that promote longevity. Notice, however, that in this formulation $-d\log W/dT$ is *independent* of W: all individuals are prepared to pay the same percentage of their wealth to extend life when preferences are of this form.

ii) An especially interesting and unusual implication of (11.12) is the role of the term in ε, which relates to the curvature properties of the function of $u(c)$. This in turn is related to the question of intertemporal substitution possibilities in consumption. To see this most clearly, let us examine some limiting cases. First, look at what happens in the limit as ε goes to unity, so that $u(c)$ goes to a linear function of c. Then, according to (11.1), U is essentially summable in $c(t)$, and all that matters to the person is total consumption over the life cycle and not at all how a given total is distributed over ages. One big consumption bash at some time is equivalent to many periods of much smaller consumption levels, for example. Here we have V_A = 0, so v goes to zero as well. A person is not willing to pay to extend life when ε = 1 because the increased horizon is completely offset by lower per-period consumption: V = W in this case, which is independent of T. This is a case of perfect substitution between the "quantity" and "quality" of life, equivalent to perfect intertemporal substitution in consumption across periods.

At the opposite extreme, consider what happens when ε goes to zero. Here the indifference curves in the $c(t)$ hyperplane exhibit "elbows" and fixed proportions (in the ε = 1 case, they are straight lines), so intertemporal substitution possibilities are nil. Now the person is willing to pay large amounts for greater life expectancy since each year of life becomes "essential." The main point is that limited substitution of consumption across years of life implies that quantity and quality of life are imperfect substitutes for each other. There is an inverse relation between the value of longevity and the degree of intertemporal substitution in consumption in life-cycle preferences.

iii) Substituting for the definition of $A(T)$ in (11.12), we have

$$v = \frac{e^{-rT}}{1 - e^{-rT}}\left[\frac{1 - \varepsilon}{\varepsilon}\right]Wr, \qquad (11.13)$$

and it follows that partial of v with respect to T is less than zero. Hence a person with a smaller horizon is prepared to pay more to extend life than a person with longer horizon. In particular, this result implies that, other things being equal, younger persons are willing to pay less to extend their life than older persons prepared to pay. That v itself changes over the life cycle may cause a person to, in some sense, regret past decisions. However, there is nothing inconsistent with this when preferences are time separable and discount rates are constant over age.

iv) The term v is not necessarily decreasing in r (given that a adjusts conformably). This experiment applies to a comparison of two societies, one in which persons are impatient and have high rates of time preferences, and one in which they have more foresight. In both, however, the interest rate adjusts to the rate of time preference. There are two effects: on the one hand, the term in the exponentials in (11.13) is decreased by an increase in r. On this account, the value of longevity tends to fall. But, on the other hand, the term in Wr is increased, and real income is larger. The second effect dominates if T is short enough, but if T is sufficiently long, then v will fall. It is surprising that the effect of a change in time preference and interest rates (together) cannot be signed.

Let us now examine the internal consistency of the solution. Suppose that the program derived above has proceeded for s periods. From that point on, the person has $T' = T - s$ years of life left and has already consumed a fraction of initial endowed wealth. Let W' denote current wealth (after s periods have passed by). Then

$$W' = \int_0^{T'} \left(\frac{W}{A}\right) e^{-rt} dt = \left(\frac{W}{A}\right) B, \qquad (11.14)$$

where $B = (1/r)(1 - e^{-rT'})$ is the value of the remaining annuity for T' periods. Now it is clear that the optimal program from time s onward remains the same as before because the budget constraint becomes, from point s onward, the integral from zero to T of $c(t)e^{-rt} dt = cB = (W/A)B$, and we have already determined c to be equal to W/A. Another way of saying this is that the new budget constraint becomes $W' = cB$, so $c = W/A$ also solves the "new problem" from s forward. The person does not change his plan. However, the value function changes as the person ages:

$$V' = \int_0^{T'} u\left(\frac{W}{A}\right) e^{-rt} dt = u\left(\frac{W}{A}\right) B, \qquad (11.15)$$

so the value V' when there are $T - s$ periods left in smaller than the value V when there are T periods remaining because $B < A$. That the value function is decreasing with age (reaching its minimum at the age of death T) is due to the fact that terms are continually lopped off from the sum of discounted utilities of further consumption as the person ages. Now in terms of remaining wealth, we have $c = W/A = W'/B$, so $V' = u(W'/B)B$ is in precisely the same form as (11.8) above, with B replacing A. Substituting from the above, we find

$$v' = ve^{rs}, \qquad (11.16)$$

so the value of life grows exponentially with age (s) in this case.

The relationship between v' and v in the expression immediately above makes clear the economic rationale for increasing value of life with age. In this deterministic problem, the experiment tacks on extra years at the end of the program, and these terms are necessarily discounted to present value. Something might have very large value at the time it occurs (as it does, for example, for a person at death's door, so to speak, in this problem). However, if the event will only occur sometime in the future, its current value is greatly reduced by discounting. Even though a young person and an old person will have the same value of longevity when they actually reach age T, at their current age, this is discounted by a different amount due to horizon differences.

This simple point has some important practical implications and even survives to stochastic models where the length of life is random rather than deterministic. It means that risks and actions that have long latency periods and that are long deferred can have small value to many people, especially young people. The young may appear "reckless" on this account, but such "recklessness" is rational. To illustrate the point further, suppose there is an opportunity to extend life by dT, which costs a fixed amount independent of age. Then, since L is increasing in age, there is a threshold age, call it s° such that people who are younger than s° do not purchase the opportunity, while those whose age exceeds s° purchase it. Similarly, if the market provides an opportunity to trade money and wealth for shortened life expectancy (as in risky jobs, for example) there is another threshold age $s^{\circ\circ}$, such that people who are younger than $s^{\circ\circ}$ voluntarily make the trade and undertake the risk, whereas those who are older than $s^{\circ\circ}$ do not do so.

11.3. Extensions of the Deterministic Model

Nonconstant Consumption

The strong result that $c(t) = c$ in the model above derives from the assumption that $r = a$. It is well known that, when these two parameters are unequal, then $c(t)$ is either decreasing or increasing. To illustrate, consider an example in which r exceeds a. Then application of (11.5) shows that $c(t)$ is increasing. To make further progress, we need to be more specific about $u(c)$, so assume the constant elasticity case where $u(c) = c^{\varepsilon}$, with $0 < \varepsilon < 1$. Detailed analysis reveals that the relevant discount factor in this case is $q = (a - \varepsilon r)/(1 - \varepsilon)$. Defining $A^{\circ} = (1/q)(1 - e^{-qT})$, we obtain the following expressions for V.

In the case where $q = 0$, V becomes

$$V = W^{\varepsilon}T^{1-\varepsilon}. \tag{11.17}$$

In this case, there is direct valuation on T itself because the effective discount rates is zero (and only sums matter, not discounted sums). Here we find

$$v = \left(\frac{1 - \varepsilon}{\varepsilon}\right)\left(\frac{W}{T}\right), \tag{11.18}$$

which is increasing in W and decreasing in ε and T, much as before. In the more probable cases where q is not equal to zero, we find

$$v = W^{\varepsilon}(A^{\circ})^{1-\varepsilon} = \left(\frac{W}{A^{\circ}}\right)^{\varepsilon}A^{\circ}$$
$$= u\left(\frac{W}{A^{\circ}}\right)A^{\circ}, \tag{11.19}$$

which has a form very similar to the simpler case where $r = m$. In all cases, therefore, the conclusions are very similar to the analysis above and need not be repeated.

Age-dependent Preferences and the Quality of Life

The model so far has assumed that the utility function $u(c)$ is constant over life and has no age-dependent factors built into it. However, it is intuitively clear how the presence of such factors would affect the analysis. Suppose, for example, that the quality of life deteriorated with age, so the utility function $u(c)$ is decreasing over time. Then the value function would be adjusted conformably and the value-of-life calculation would take this into account—for example, if life got progressively worse with age, then a person would not pay as much to extend it, obviously.

For example, introduce the exogenous age-dependent factor in a multiplicative way as follows:

$$U = \int_0^T u[D(t)c(t)]e^{-at}dt. \tag{11.20}$$

Here the term in $D(t)$ represents a consumption correction factor to make "real" consumption equivalent across ages. For example, if $D(t)$ is decreasing in age, it takes an ever-increasing amount of consumption to make up for the lower "efficiency" of consumption as a person ages. In this case, the marginal condition in (11.5) above is simply altered by multiplication of the left-hand side by $D(t)$. If we also assume that $D(t) = e^{-Dt}$, then the analysis is virtually identical to the case where the discount rate of time preference does not equal the rate of interest. Again, the refinement is a minor one.

Bequests

Suppose now that the person has heirs and that at the time of death all remaining wealth is transferred to these heirs. The standard way to incorporate a bequest motive into a life-cycle problem is to introduce a bequest function into the utility function. Thus, write

$$U = \int_0^T u[c(t)]e^{-at}dt + e^{-aT}f(W_b), \tag{11.21}$$

where the first term is similar to the one in (11.20), and the second term reflects the person's utility of bequests. The amount of bequests are W_b, which yield utility (discounted to present value) of $e^{-aT}f(W_b)$. Now the wealth constraint becomes

$$W = \int_0^T c(t)e^{-rt}dt + W_b e^{-rT}, \tag{11.22}$$

and the necessary conditions to the maximum problem are

$$
\left.\begin{array}{c}
u'(c)e^{-at} = me^{-rt}, \\[2mm]
f'(W_b)e^{-aT} = me^{-rT}.
\end{array}\right\} \tag{11.23}
$$

and

Assuming $r = a$ again for simplicity, we have

$$
u'(c) = f'(W_b) = m, \tag{11.24}
$$

and the constraint becomes

$$
W = cA + W_b A', \tag{11.25}
$$

where A and $A' = dA/dT$ were defined above.

Using these conditions and applying the envelope theorem to V, we find

$$
\frac{\partial V}{\partial W} = m,
$$

and

$$
\frac{\partial V}{\partial T} = [u(c) - m]e^{-rT} - re^{-rT}[f(W_b) - mW_b]. \tag{11.26}
$$

Using (11.24) and simplifying yields

$$
v = -\frac{dW}{dT} = e^{-rT}\left[c\frac{1 - \varepsilon}{\varepsilon} - rW_b\frac{1 - \varepsilon^\circ}{\varepsilon^\circ}\right], \tag{11.27}
$$

where $\varepsilon^\circ = f'(W_b)W_b/f(W_b)$ is the elasticity of the bequest function. Thus the presence of bequests and bequest motives reduces the value of life in and of itself because of the offsetting benefit to heirs of the person's demise. Of course, this strong conclusion is built on some special assumptions, of which two are particularly important. One is that the utility of own consumption may itself be affected by the presence of heirs and children in the household. People tend to have children because they want to and because it increases their own utility over and above any effect of bequests. Hence the presence of heirs may make life itself worth more to the person, which tends to increase the value of longer life rather than to reduce it. Second, the heirs may suffer a loss of utility from the person's death, and this utility loss should be valued by the person himself if he is altruistic (this altruism is really a form of reciprocal altruism). This factor would also tend to increase the value of longer life.

Labor Market Activities

Let us now consider a person who has endowed wealth W, as before, but who also has the opportunity to work at an hourly wage rate w. It is necessary to alter the utility function to handle this case because some valuation must be placed on leisure. Let L be leisure and normalize so that $0 \leq L \leq 1$. Then $(1 - L)$ is the amount of time devoted to work. Maintaining time separable preferences as before, write the utility function as

$$U = \int_0^T u[c(t), L(t)]e^{-at}dt, \qquad (11.28)$$

where the utility function $u[c, L]$ has conventional properties. The person has two sources of income in this problem. One is endowed wealth and the other is (endogenously chosen) earnings $w(1 - L)$. The intertemporal budget constraint equates the present discounted value of earnings plus endowed wealth to the present discounted value of consumption over the life cycle:

$$U = \int_0^T w(t)[1 - L(t)e^{-rt}]dt$$

$$= \int_0^T c(t)e^{-rt}dt. \qquad (11.29)$$

Optimality conditions for choice of $c(t)$ and $L(t)$ that maximize (11.28) subject to (11.29) are

$$U_c(c, L)e^{-at} = me^{-rt},$$
$$U_L(c, L)e^{-at} = mwe^{-rt}. \qquad (11.30)$$

Solving these two equations along with the budget constraint yields the optimal trajectories for L and c.

We can place this problem in the context above by making the simplifying assumption that $r = a$ and that $w(t) = w$. Then (11.30) implies

$$\frac{U_L(c, L)}{U_c(c, L)} = w,$$

$$U_c(c, L) = m, \qquad (11.31)$$

which imply that $c(t) = c$ and $L(t) = L$ are constants over the life cycle. Therefore, we may write

$$V = \max_{c,L}\{u(c, L)A + m[W + w(1 - L)A - cA]\}, \qquad (11.32)$$

where again A is the present value of an annuity that lasts for T periods. Using the envelope property of a maximum, we find

$$V_W = m[(1 - L)A],$$

$$V_T = \{u(c, L) + m[w(1 - L) - c]\}A'$$

$$= \left[u(c, L) - m\frac{W}{A}\right]A', \qquad (11.33)$$

where the second equality in the last expression follows from the budget constraint. Therefore

$$v = \frac{V_T}{V_W} = \left[\frac{u(c, L)}{u_c(c, L)} - \frac{W}{A}\right]A' \tag{11.34}$$

since $m = u_c$ from the marginal conditions. Defining the elasticity $E = cu_c/u$ as before, (11.34) becomes

$$v = \left[\frac{c}{\varepsilon} - \frac{W}{A}\right]A'. \tag{11.35}$$

This may be written in yet another way: solving for c from the budget, we have $c = W/A + w(1 - L)$. Substitute this into (11.34) and rearrange:

$$v = \left[\frac{W}{A}(1 - \varepsilon) + w(1 - L)\right]\frac{e^{-rt}}{\varepsilon}. \tag{11.36}$$

Look at (11.35) first. The value of longevity has both a positive and negative term (of course suitably discounted—$A' = e^{-rT}$). The positive term is the level of consumption adjusted by the inverse of ε, and since ε cannot exceed unity, the actual value of consumption is a lower bound for this term. The negative term W/A is just the level income available from an endowment of nonhuman wealth W at interest rate r from T periods. This must be subtracted from the adjusted consumption level because an increment of life T lowers the annuity value of income available from W: it must be spread over a longer interval, and consumption in earlier periods is lowered on that account.

The second form of v in (11.36) shows that the value of longevity has a relationship with observed income as well as with observed consumption. The first term in this expression is $(W/A)(1 - \varepsilon)e^{-rt}/\varepsilon$, precisely the same as when leisure is not considered in the problem. To this we need to add the extra income available from work when the person lives longer. However, it is not the extra earnings alone that must be added, but that amount divided by ε. That is, observed earnings is a lower bound to the extra adjustment and is only an unbiased estimate when ε is very close to unity. Again, this adjustment reflects imperfect substitution between quantity and quality of life when consumption and leisure are not perfect substitutes intertemporally.

Retirement

The foregoing model is assumed that the person worked over his whole life and would be relevant for a situation of "early" death. However, for most people work patterns over the life cycle follows a systematic course of full-time work up to a certain age followed by a full-time retirement. The model above may be extended to cover this case most easily by assuming that the wage w is available up to some retirement age, say T°, at which time w drops to zero and the person consumes full-time leisure. The the utility function must be written

$$U = \int_0^{T^\circ} u[c_1(t),\, L(t)]e^{-at}dt + \int_{T^\circ}^T u[c_2(t),\, 1]e^{-at}dt, \qquad (11.37)$$

where c_1 denotes consumption during the years in which a person works and c_2 denotes consumption when the person is retired and leisure is fully consumed $(L = 1)$. The budget constraint is conformably altered to

$$W + \int_0^{T^\circ} w(t)[1 - L(T)]e^{-rt}dt$$

$$= \int_0^{T^\circ} c_1(t)e^{-rt}dt + \int_{T^\circ}^T c_2(t)e^{-rt}dt, \qquad (11.38)$$

and the optimal program chooses $L(t)$, $c_1(t)$ and $c_2(t)$ to maximize U subject to the budget constraint as before. Omitting details and making the same simplifying assumptions as above yields an expression for v of the form

$$v = c_2[(1 - \eta)/\eta]A', \qquad (11.39)$$

which looks very much like the first problem considered here. There are two minor differences. First, the relevant consumption level is that applicable to retirement rather than to preretirement. The second is that the adjustment factor—the elasticity term—is calculated at the retirement utility level of leisure where $L = 1$: $\eta = c_2 u_c(c_2, 1)/u(c_2, 1)$. It is not at all obvious whether η falls short of or exceeds the corresponding elasticity calculated at the preretirement optimum utility: this would depend on the precise form of preferences. Nor is it entirely obvious, without more structure on preferences, whether c_2 exceeds or falls short of c_1. This would depend on the nature of complementarities and substitution between consumption and leisure, about which little can be said in general. However, the budget constraint does imply

$$c_2 = \frac{\dfrac{W}{A^\circ} + w(1 - L) - c_1}{\dfrac{(A - A^\circ)}{A^\circ}}, \qquad (11.40)$$

where A° is the annuity formula for T° periods, and A is the formula for T periods. It is clear that the longer the period of retirement, the smaller is c_2 and the lower the value of v, ceteris paribus. It is also clear that v is larger for people with greater nonhuman and human wealth because retirement consumption will be larger in these cases.

11.4. The Value of Morbidity

The ideas in the last two extensions provide a basis for beginning to evaluate morbidity. Imagine the following situation: the person is ill for exactly S periods, after which time he becomes "whole." During the period of illness, utility is $G(c_1, L_1)$, while during the normal (well) period utility is $u(c_2, L_2)$ as before. Here the subscript 1 refers to these variables in the well state. For the demarcation of illness to make any sense, we must have $G(c, L) < u(c, L)$ when both functions are evaluated at the same arguments. Then illness makes the person worse off. In addition, a person who is ill cannot work on the same terms as one who is well. Represent this by a drop in the wage: if the wage in state 2 is w, then the wage in state 1 is bw, where $b < 1$. In addition, medical and other expenses may be required if the person is ill. Denote these, as a flow, by Z.

The budget constraint for this problem is

$$W + \int_0^s bw[1 - L_1(t)]e^{-rt}dt + \int_s^T w[1 - L_2(t)]e^{-rt}dt$$

$$= \int_0^s [c_1(t) + Z]e^{-rt}dt + \int_s^T c_2(t)e^{-rt}dt. \quad (11.41)$$

Of course it may turn out that the person chooses not to work in state 1, in which case the first earnings expression in (11.41) is zero. Again, maintaining separability for analytical convenience, lifetime utility is

$$U = \int_0^s G[c_1(t), L_1(t)]e^{-at}dt + \int_s^T u[c_2(t), L_2(t)]e^{-at}dt. \quad (11.42)$$

If we assume that $r = a$ and that w is independent of t, we again find that the c's and L's are constant in the optimum program, so that

$$V = \max \Bigg(G(c_1, L_1)A_s + u(c_2, L_2)(A_T - A_s)$$

$$+ m\{W + [cw(1 - L_1) - c_1 - Z]A_s \quad (11.43)$$

$$+ [w(1 - L_2) - c_2]\} \Bigg),$$

where A_t is the annuity formula for t periods.

We are interested in how much wealth a person would be prepared to pay to reduce the period of illness by an increment dS. This again is a marginal rate of substitution calculation comparable to the definition of v. Hence, define M as the corresponding value of morbidity:

$$M = \frac{dW}{dS} = \frac{V_S}{V_W}. \tag{11.44}$$

From (11.43) and the envelope theorem, it follows that

$$V_S = (G - u)A_S + [y_1 - y_2 - (c_1 + Z - c_2)]A'_S,$$
$$V_w = m, \tag{11.45}$$

where $y_1 = bw(1 - L_1)$ and $y_2 = w(1 - L_2)$ are earnings in states 1 and 2, respectively. Applying the definition (11.44),

$$M = \left[\frac{u(c_2, L_2) - G(c_1, L_1)}{m} + (y_2 \right.$$

$$\left. - y_1 + Z) + (c_1 - c_2) \right] A'_S. \tag{11.46}$$

This expression shows that the value of morbidity reduction is composed of three distinct parts. One part is the difference in earnings between the two states, or "forgone earnings" commonly found in practical work. To this must be added the cost of medical care and related expenses (Z), which is also commonly incorporated in empirical measures. However, these measures usually excluded two other components that are more difficult to measure. The first of these is the dollar value of the utility loss of illness, reflected in the first term in the expression for M—division by the marginal utility of wealth converts the utility difference to an equivalent dollar magnitude. This term would be related to the concept of "pain and suffering" associated with personal injury litigation. Its magnitude obviously varies with the degree of debilitation and also with the extent to which the relative marginal utilities of consumption and leisure are affected by the illness and the extent to which "leisure" and consumption in the ill state are complements or substitutes. Little can be said about this in general, and it must be analyzed on a case-by-case basis. The third term is the difference in consumption between the two states, which is almost always ignored in empirical work. To the extent that consumption in the ill state falls short of consumption in the well state, that difference should be subtracted from a willingness to pay measure. To the extent that it is true, the "pain and suffering" term is be offset.

To understand this last adjustment a little better, write the two components combined:

$$\frac{u(c_2, L_2) - G(c_1, L_1)}{m} - c_2 + c_1$$

$$= \frac{[u(c_2, L_2) - mc_2] - [G(c_1, L_1) - mc_1]}{m}. \quad (11.47)$$

Now m equals the marginal utility of consumption in each state, by the first-order conditions of the maximum problem, and can be thought of as the shadow price of consumption in each state. Then each of the terms in square brackets above is total utility in the state minus the utility cost of consumption in that state, or a measure of "rent" in that state. It is the difference in these rents between states that must be imputed to the valuation of morbidity. It seems clear that the rent in the well state would exceed that in the ill state, so forgone earnings and medical bills would understate the true cost of morbidity. The extent to which it would understate the truth, however, would depend on the precise properties of preferences and how the illness affects $G(c, L)$.

11.5. The Value of Life Expectancy: A Stochastic Model

Preliminaries

The following examines a stochastic decision problem in which life expectancy is uncertain. While this changes some of the details of analysis, the main thrust of the deterministic model carries through with minor alternations.

Analysis of the stochastic case requires some attention to the statistical description of life chances, and a brief review of some actuarial concepts for describing probability distributions over length of life is warranted. Let $F(t)$ be the probability of surviving until age t at most. Then $1 - F(t)$ is the survivor function, the probability of surviving to at least age t, or more. Define $f(t) = dF(t)/dt = -d[1 - F(t)]/dt$ as the density function of length of life: the probability of surviving to age t exactly. The age-specific death rate, or hazard rate, is the probability of death at age t given that one has survived up to that age. It is a conditional probability. Denoting the hazard or death rate at age t by $h(t)$, it is $h(t) = f(t)/[1 - F(t)]$ or, from the relationship above,

$$\frac{d\log[1 - F(t)]}{dt} = -h(t). \quad (11.48)$$

Integrating (11.48) and using the boundary condition $F(0) = 0$ (we only look at survivors at birth), yields the fundamental relationship between the hazard rate and the survival rate

$$[1 - F(t)] = \exp\left[\int_0^t h(z)dz\right],\qquad(11.49)$$

where exp means the exponential e.

The importance of equivalence (11.49) lies in its relation to the problem at hand. The hazard $h(t)$ is naturally associated with the undertaking of risks to life and is the natural primitive for studying the valuation of life-threatening actions. However, the survivor function is the natural primitive for studying expected utility and expected wealth. Equation (11.49) shows precisely how the two are related.

At some cost of realism, great simplicity in understanding the nature of the problem is achieved by studying some special cases. In particular, assume $h(t) = h$, so the death rate is constant at all ages (the case of constant hazard). Then it follows directly from (11.49) that

$$\begin{aligned} F(t) &= 1 - e^{-ht}, \\ 1 - F(t) &= e^{-ht}, \\ f(t) &= he^{-ht}. \end{aligned}\qquad(11.50)$$

The probability density of length of life $f(t)$ is exponential in this case. Furthermore, life expectancy itself, call it $Y(t)$, is simply related to the death rate as

$$\begin{aligned} Y(t) &= \int_0^\infty tf(t)dt \\ &= \int_0^\infty hte^{-ht}dt = \frac{1}{h}. \end{aligned}\qquad(11.51)$$

Note that life expectancy is independent of current age in this case. No matter how long one has lived there are always $1/h$ years left on average. This is highly unrealistic, but the convenience of analysis more than makes up for it. The more general case is analyzed by Arthur (1981), to which the reader is referred for details.

Suppose now that the hazard rate is a step function. That is, the step function is $h(t) = h_1$ for $t < T$, but then it jumps to a higher level beyond some age T: $h(t) = h_2$ for $t \geq T$. Then application of (11.49) yields

$$\begin{aligned} 1 - F(t) &= \exp(-ht) & \text{for } t \leq T \\ &= \exp[(h_2 - h_1)T - h_2t] & \text{for } t > T. \end{aligned}\qquad(11.52)$$

Now the survival function is exponentially declining at rate h_1 for $t < T$, but its slope shows a point of discontinuity at T. It declines at a larger rate for $t > T$ than for $t < T$. Here we would find that life expectancy is decreasing with age, so long as $t < T$.

Any pattern of $h(t)$ could be approximated as a sequence of step functions in this way. Since the mechanics of this are straightforward, they will be omitted here. Instead, we turn to the choice problem.

Optimal Choices

The fundamental method follows the deterministic approach above. Let us begin by ignoring work decisions and describe tastes by an intertemporally separable utility function in the sequence of consumption $c(t)$. If a person lives exactly t years, then his utility is postulated to be

$$U(t) = \int_0^\infty u[c(z)]e^{-at}dz, \qquad (11.53)$$

which follows precisely the form of the deterministic model. However, in an uncertain world, a person lives t years only with probability $f(t)$. Therefore apply the expected utility theorem to $U(t)$. A person's expected lifetime utility is

$$\begin{aligned} EU &= \int_0^\infty U(t)f(t)dt \\[1ex] &= \int_0^\infty u[c(z)]e^{-az}f(t)dzdt \\[1ex] &= \int_0^\infty u[(c(t)]e^{-at}\int_0^\infty f(z)dzdt \\[1ex] &= \int_0^\infty [1 - F(t)]u[c(t)]e^{-at}dt, \end{aligned} \qquad (22.54)$$

where the second-to-last equality follows by a change in the order of integration. We see that the relevant utility expression incorporates the survival rate $1 - F(t)$, and that is why it is a fundamental concept for the problem. Substituting from above, preferences follow

$$EU = \int_0^\infty u[c(t)] \exp\left[-at - \int_0^T h(z)dz \right]dt, \qquad (11.55)$$

so the hazard rate works exactly like a discount rate. To make this even more transparent, suppose $h(t) = h$ is constant. Then $EU = \int_0^\infty u[c(t)]e^{-(a+h)t}dt$, and the "effective" discount rate is $a + h$. The force of mortality h makes a person act more "impatiently" and to weigh the future less heavily.

Budget constraints in problems such as this create a host of conceptual difficulties revolving around the question of how to cope with the fact that the person might die in debt. These issues have been thoroughly explored by Yaari (1965), and there is little to add to that discussion here. Hence we adopt a natural solution in which a person is not allowed to die in debt and can borrow and lend on a perfect capital market at rate of interest r. The constraint of budget balance at each possible point in the life cycle is enforced by an actuarial insurance-debt system. It amounts to the following. Whenever a person makes a loan he is compelled to at the same time take out an insurance policy of equivalent value, such that if he dies at any time during the course of the loan, the insurance indemnity is sufficient to pay off the remaining balance. As is well known, this is equivalent to an actuarial annuity system in which a cohort of identical individuals turn over their wealth to the insurance-finance company and contract for their optimal consumption bundle $c(t)$, which persists as long as and for however long they live. Those who die early effectively subsidize the fund ex post since their assets have exceeded their consumption claims. These subsidies are used to pay the consumption claims of those individuals who survive longer than average. We can represent this in a simple manner as follows.

If a person lives for exactly t periods and contracts for $c(z)$, the present discounted value of his claims is $\int_0^t c(z)e^{-rz}dz$. The probability of surviving for exactly t periods is $f(t)$, so the expected discounted value of the claim $c(z)$ is equated to the person's initial wealth W under an actuarial, no-load system. The budget constraint is

$$W = \int_0^\infty f(t)\int_0^T c(z)e^{-rz}dzdt = \int_0^T [1 - F(t)]c(t)e^{-rt}dt, \quad (11.56)$$

where the second equality follows from the same change in order of integration as above. Again, it follows that the influence of the survival term $[1 - F(t)]$ in this expression is to increase the effective discount rate. It is interesting to note that, even if r and a are zero, there is a well defined optimization problem, something that is not true in a deterministic problem with an infinite horizon (because the objective function becomes unbounded in that case).

The economic problem is to choose $c(t)$ to maximize (11.54) subject to the constraint in (11.56). Associate a multiplier m with the constraint and note that the term in $[1 - F(t)]$ is common to both the objective function and the constraint and therefore factors out of the optimality conditions. Then the first-order conditions for the stochastic problem duplicate those of the deterministic problem. We have

$$u'[c(t)]e^{-at} = me^{-rt} \quad \text{for all } t. \quad (11.57)$$

The interpretation is straightforward. The life insurance features of the annuity arrangement allow the person to do whatever he would have done in the deterministic problem and to insure the death risk over consumption streams by the law of large numbers applied to his cohort. In particular, assume $r = a$. Then (11.57) implies $c(t) = c$, a constant, and the person contracts for a constant consumption stream up to the point of his death, no matter how long he lives. From the budget constraint, we have $c = W/\int_0^\infty [1 - F(t)]e^{-rt}dt$, so the amount of consumption available under this scheme depends on the person's wealth, the rate of interest, and the precise age pattern of survival probabilities.

Valuation Formulas

Consider the case where $h(t) = h$. Then (11.56) implies $W = c/(r + h)$, just the formula for the value of a perpetuity of c at discount rate $(r + h)$. In this case, (11.54) becomes $EU = u(c)/(r + h)$, or instantaneous utility discounted at rate $r + h$ forever. Therefore

$$V = EU = \frac{u[W(r + h)]}{r + h}. \tag{11.58}$$

This looks very similar to the deterministic problem. Define v' as the value of changing the probability of death, h. Then

$$v' = \frac{\dfrac{\partial V}{\partial h}}{\dfrac{\partial V}{\partial W}} = \frac{dW}{dh}, \tag{11.59}$$

where v' is amount of money the person would have to be paid to increase the death rate confronting him by dh. From (11.58)

$$V_W = u'(c),$$

$$V_h = \frac{(r + h)Wu'(c) - u(c)}{(r + h)^2}. \tag{11.60}$$

Therefore, in the constant hazard case with $r = a$,

$$v' = \frac{\dfrac{u(c)}{u'(c)} - (r + h)W}{(r + h)^2} = \frac{W}{r + h}\frac{1 - \varepsilon}{\varepsilon}, \tag{11.61}$$

where again ε is the elasticity of $u(c)$ with respect to c, and $0 < \varepsilon < 1$. Comparing this with equation (11.12) of the deterministic model, we see that the term in h serves as the correction factor for finite life, rather than the annuity term A in (11.12). Otherwise, the expressions are identical and have identical implications. The term v is increasing in W and decreasing in ε for the same reasons as were spelled out above. In particular, the role of quantity versus quality of life substitution as reflected in ε remains exactly the same as before. It is also true that v' is decreasing in r, and is also decreasing in h.

We can find an equivalent expression in terms of the expectation of life, $\bar{t}$, since $\bar{t} = 1/h$ when the hazard is constant. Then $dh = -dt/t^2$, so

$$\frac{dW}{d\bar{t}} = \frac{W}{\bar{t}(r\bar{t} + 1)}\frac{1 - \varepsilon}{\varepsilon}. \qquad (11.62)$$

A person with a longer life expectancy is willing to pay less to extend it.

Valuations of Workers

Let us now extend the stochastic model to include choice of work and earnings as well as consumption. Then, similarly to the deterministic models, the one-period utility function must be written $u(c, L)$, where L is leisure. This function replaces $u(c)$ in the definition of expected utility in (11.54). A worker has a source of earned income as well as endowed wealth. If he can earn $w(t)$ per unit of time, earned income is $w(t)[1 - L(t)]$, which when discounted to present value and including allowances for mortality becomes $\int_0^\infty w(t)[1 - L(t)][1 - F(t)]e^{-rt}dt$. This must be added to the term in W on the left-hand side of the budget constraint in (11.56). The first-order conditions for choice of $c(t)$ and $L(t)$ duplicate equation (11.30) in the deterministic model. With $r = a$ and $w(t) = w$, the value function becomes

$$v = \max_{c,L}\left\{[u(c, L) + m[w(1 - L)\right.$$

$$\left. - c]\int_0^\infty [1 - F(t)]e^{-rt}dt + mW\right\} \qquad (11.63)$$

since $c(t) = c$ and $L(t) = L$ under these circumstances.

Assume $h(t) = h$. Then the integral term in (11.63) is merely $1/(r + h)$, and maximum expected utility is the perpetuity value of $u(c, L)$ held at its optimal values of c and L, at discount rate $r + h$. In this case we find

$$\frac{-V_h}{V_w} = \frac{\dfrac{c(1 - \varepsilon)}{\varepsilon} + w(1 - L)}{(r + h)^2} \qquad (11.64)$$

as the capital sum the person would be willing to give up to reduce the death rate by dh. This expression is similar to (11.61) with the addition of the earned income term since the opportunity to work has value.

Expression (11.64) does not closely relate to empirical work in this area. Much of the empirical work on the value of life uses labor market data and estimates the risk premium necessary to induce a worker to undertake a risky job. For the problem at hand, the relevant risk premium is nothing more than $-V_h/V_w$, which is, in this case,

$$\frac{-V_h}{V_w} = \frac{\dfrac{c(1 - \varepsilon)}{\varepsilon} + w(1 - L) - c}{(1 - L)(r + h)}. \tag{11.65}$$

From this experience, we may infer something about the intertemporal substitution parameter ε.

As an example, consider the study of Thaler and Rosen (1975). (Ippolito and Ippolito [1984] produce a similar estimate from much different data.) Thaler and Rosen estimate $-V_h/V_w$ in terms of the weekly wage as \$3,520 in 1968 dollars. In their sample, average weeks worked are approximately 50, and the average worker earned about \$6,600. Since this is a low-income population, the bulk of consumption expenditure must have come from earnings, so ignore savings and assume $c = w(1 - L) = \$6,600$. Substituting this and $(1 - L) = 50$ into (11.65) and rearranging, we have

$$\varepsilon = \frac{\dfrac{6,600}{176,000}}{r + h}. \tag{11.66}$$

Hence the estimate of ε depends on assumed values of r and h. In the Thaler and Rosen sample, h is about 2.5 per 1,000, decomposed into 1.5 per 1,000 normal life table experience plus an additional 1.0 per 1,000 excess risk from working conditions among people in hazardous jobs. Hence any realistic interest rate swamps the effect of h. For this population, $r = 10\%$ would appear to be a plausible lower bound. If so, then $\varepsilon = .39$. If $r = 15\%$, the estimate of ε drops to .26. Presumably these are upper-bound estimates among the population at large because most workers are not found in risky jobs. Their value of ε must be no greater and most probably lower than indicated if they find it advantageous to work on safer jobs at lower rates of pay. Hence, from this evidence, we get an upper bound of ε in the .25–.40 range.

Now return to equation (11.61), and convert it into logs:

$$\frac{d \log W}{d \log h} = \frac{h}{r + H} \frac{1 - \varepsilon}{\varepsilon}. \tag{11.67}$$

Substituting the values above yields as estimate for $d \log W/d \log h$ in the range .04–.05. That is, the people in this sample would have been willing to give up $\frac{1}{2}\%$ of their wealth for a 10% reduction in the death rate. Presumably the equivalent sum for the average person in the population is larger than this because of the selection effect mentioned above. Notice however, that the term in $h/(r + h)$ is even smaller for such persons (because their values of h are smaller), and this dampens any effect of a smaller value of ε. Notice also, as a rough-and-ready approximation, the term in h would be much larger for older persons, so they would be willing to pay a much larger fraction of their wealth.

Now consider an experiment related to the specification in (11.52). This is interesting because it is closely related to long-term hazards with a latency period of length T. Thus, for example, a person with a "normal" risk exposure h_1 may undertake some action now that has no effect on death probabilities until periods later, at which time the death rate jumps to h_2. Exposure to some chemicals may take this form. Again maintaining $r = a$ for simplicity, from (11.52), (11.54), and (11.56) we have

$$
V = \max\left\{ u(c) \int_0^\infty [1 - F(t)]e^{-rt}dt + m\left(w - \frac{c}{[1 - F(t)]e^{-rt}dt} \right) \right\}
$$

$$
= \max[u(c) - mc]\left(\frac{1}{r + h_1} \right)[1 - \exp[-(r \quad\quad (11.68)
$$

$$
+ h_1)T]]\left(\frac{1}{r + h_2} \right) \exp[-(r + h_2)T],
$$

from which it follows by the now familiar manipulations

$$
\frac{-V_{h_2}}{V_w} = \frac{c\dfrac{1 - \varepsilon}{\varepsilon} \exp\left(-\dfrac{r + h_1}{T} \right)}{(r + h_2)^2},
$$

$$
\frac{V_T}{V_w} = \left[c\frac{1 - \varepsilon}{\varepsilon} \exp\left(-\frac{r + h_1}{T} \right) \right]\left[\frac{h_1 - h_1}{r + h_2} \right],
$$

and

$$
\frac{V_T}{V_{h_2}} = (h_2 - h_1)(r + h_2). \quad\quad (11.69)
$$

The first expression in (11.69) shows how much the person is willing to pay to reduce the later hazard. This again depends on the intertemporal substitution parameter ε and the level of consumption, as before. It also depends on how far away the hazard is from the present—the further away it is, the smaller the willingness to pay to reduce it—and on the rate of interest. The second expression in (11.69) shows how much the person would be willing to pay to push the increased hazard a little bit further away from now. This also depends on c and ε and is decreasing in T and increasing in the difference $h_2 - h_1$. The third expression, written for completeness, is the marginal rate of substitution between the level of the new hazard and the time of its occurrence.

The most important thing to notice about these valuations is that they are time or age dependent. The willingness to accept risks of this form is largest for younger people, and the willingness to pay to avoid them is largest for older individuals (when the person is old enough to have passed beyond $t = T$, the formulas revert to the form of [11.61]). This is basically due to the force of discounting, which includes not only the interest rate but the hazard rate itself. Furthermore, these expressions make no allowance for pain and suffering and the manner of death, but including such factors would have the effect of increasing their absolute values without affecting their intertemporal patterns.

Changing valuations over the life cycle raises some tricky issues for risks that are irreversible. Thus suppose the market provides an opportunity for undertaking a risk exposure of the type above which increases wealth or utility in other ways. Then we would again find some critical age, beyond which a person would not undertake the risk but before which he would. Suppose this action affects h_2 permanently, so there is no going back on the decision once it has been undertaken at the early age, and the person is stuck in a permanently high-risk class at some time in the future. Then as the person ages, he would perhaps have ex post regret about his earlier actions. However, there appear to be no inconsistencies (in the sense of irrational choices) in this type of behavior because, by hypothesis, all these effects are foreseen in the first instance. The point applies to any type of gambling behavior. A gamble may appear to be very favorable ex ante, but ex post realizations often lead to regret, about which nothing can be done, and which is already factored into the initial decision to undertake it. The same is true in this case, where by assumption all the information is on the table.

Nonetheless, in evaluating such hazards for the purposes of social policy and cost-benefit analysis, one would certainly like to take account of different valuations by people of different ages since it is the sum of all valuations that matter. That a person might have a different valuation at different points of time and age is properly accounted for in these sums, and no allowance need be made for the fact that the person will change his valuation at some future time. This conclusion is of course conditioned on the manner in which the problem has been set up, which assumes perfect information and a perfect capital market. If capital markets were imperfect and the insurance charge did not fully reflect the increased future risk for any given person, there would be a moral hazard effect. The social value of risk would exceed the private value because individuals would have a tendency to shift risks excessively to the insurance fund. Too many risks would be undertaken. And, of course, similar statements apply if assessments of future hazards are biased (in either direction) by the persons undertaking them.

11.6. Interpretation and Applications

Major Results from the Life-Cycle Model

Chapter 11 has been motivated by the question, "How much of the economy's wealth should be spent on safety, health, and longevity concerns?" The answer depends on the way individuals (or households) appraise their own life situations and how they make decisions they judge to be optimal in light of those situations. This chapter has provided a framework that identifies the underlying decision variables and guides the valuation of policy decisions designed to improve people's life prospects.

The intimate relation between quality of life and longevity, or quantity of life, has emerged in the development of the intertemporal model. Valuations of increased life expectancy, in reductions in periods of illness, and in reductions in risk of death have been explored. Labor force participation and the value of increased longevity were also taken into account. Results derived from the model include widely recognized effects, such as forgone earnings and medical expenditures, and also more frequently overlooked effects such as the utility of consumption and leisure, differences in the utility of consumption and leisure, and differences in consumption between various states of wellness.

Several parameters play key roles throughout the development of the model, and others are important to special parts of it. Perhaps of greatest interest among the former is the elasticity of lifetime consumption. This relates to intertemporal substitution and reflects the close relationship between the quality and quantity of life. Other parameters in this category are the rates of interest and time preference, the level of wealth, and the person's stage in the life cycle. Of interest in the other category of parameters, pertaining to special parts of the model, is a "consumption correction factor," which takes into account the fact that people's utility capacities change over their life cycles. This is particularly important in empirical work because it pertains to people's endowments, which are important in explaining their valuations. Another special parameter is the hazard function parameter, which measures an individual's probability of dying at any given age. This is another aspect of endowment. It is central to the treatment of the effects of uncertainty on choice and is of particular interest in valuing threats to health that involve latency, which is represented by a discrete increase in the hazard of death after a number of years elapse.

One of the results is that younger people are willing to pay less to extend their lives than older people. The primary reason is that the return to a younger person is deferred so far into the future that its present value is reduced by discounting. It is quite possible that the person when older will regret actions taken earlier in life because extended longevity has become more important in the meantime. Nevertheless, the now-regretted actions must be regarded as rationally made, at least when preferences are time separable. A similar result is obtained in the analysis of risks to health that change the probability of death after an intervening period of latency. Once again, the farther into the future the increased risk is deferred, the less a person is willing to pay now for its reduction.

There are additional effects of age on willingness to pay for risk reduction. One must distinguish between the age of the respondent at the time the question is asked and the age at which the risk occurs. To illustrate, consider two men, one 18 and the other 45, who have identical preferences and lifetime earnings streams. The distribution of date of death conditional on reaching age t ($t = 18, . . .$) is the same for both persons. The only difference between them is that the 45-year-old has followed for 27 years the consumption path which the 18-year-old will eventually follow. There are three willingness to pay amounts to compare:

1) The amount the 18-year-old will give up today to avoid a marginal increase in his conditional probability of death at age 18.
2) The amount the 18-year-old will give up today to avoid a marginal increase in his conditional probability of death at age 45.
3) The amount the 45-year-old will give up today to avoid a marginal increase in his conditional probability of death at age 45.

With perfect annuities markets and a rate of time preference equal to the market rate of interest, amount 1 > amount 2 and amount 1 > amount 3. The fact that amount 1 > amount 2 means that a reduction in risk of death 27 years hence is less valuable than a reduction in current risk of death. This point is made in this section and has obvious relevance for valuing risks with long latency periods.

The fact that amount 1 > amount 3, that is, that the 18-year-old will pay more to reduce his *current* risk of death than the 45-year-old (at least according to the theoretical model), needs to be made clearly. One can reverse this inequality by assuming imperfect capital markets, which constrain the individual to consume no more than his income when he is young, and a hump-shaped earnings stream; however, under the assumptions of this section, amount 1 > amount 3.

The elasticity of the life-cycle consumption function, which is closely related to the intertemporal substitution of consumption, has a strong bearing on both the value of extended life and the value of reducing hazards that occur later in life. The greater a person's ability to substitute present consumption for future consumption, the less interest that person has in providing for the future. The value of the intertemporal substitution parameter is a key importance in understanding trade-offs between the quantity and quality of life in this framework.

Elasticity of consumption is estimated to have an upper bound of 0.25–0.40. This rather low elasticity implies that quantity and quality of life are poor substitutes for each other, which in turn varies the value of extra years of life.

Allowing for reduced capacity for consumption during later years of life requires a consumption correction factor. The implication of diminishing capacity is that, unless real consumption can be maintained, the value of longevity is reduced. This is an important implication because people's consumption-capacity prospects and expectations can be approximated empirically.

The fact that people value extensions of life the older they get has implications for labor market behavior. Supposing that opportunities to extend life a given amount have a constant cost independent of age, then there is a threshold age below which people are willing to accept shortened life expectancy in exchange for increased money return, whereas people above the threshold will not accept the trade.

Application of the framework to some available sample evidence yields the result that people would give up $\frac{1}{2}$% of their wealth for a 10% reduction in the death rate. The equivalent amount for an average person in the population would probably be greater.

Life Experiences and the Willingness to Pay to Avoid Serious Illness
The life-cycle approach to serious illness was applied in later parts of this study in experimental focus group sessions. It was hypothesized and found to be the case that age makes a great difference in the way a person perceives the consequences of risks to health, either with certainty or varying degrees of probability. Focus group explorations of hypothetical life-path experiences showed graphically that people in their twenties have little or no interest in their health prospects for their seventies or even their fifties. A different picture emerges from the responses of people in their fifties or sixties. The theoretical contributions of this section provide the rationale for this behavior and point the way to empirical solutions to the problems raised by these focus group encounters.

The contingent valuation questions to be considered in Chapter 13, which grew out of the framework here and knowledge gained from focus group experience, emphasize comparisons between life paths. In some cases, individuals were required to rank alternative paths that embody different trade-offs between suffering and life expectancy. Different kinds and durations of suffering were considered. Finally, uncertainty was introduced, and valuations of risks were sought within streams of experience that embody both sickness and death.

Perfect health is generally not the alternative to symptoms, diseases, or health risks that are reduced by successful public policy. The value of improved prospects must be weighed against alternatives that carry risks of their own. Thus a person is generally trading one stream of illnesses for another, less undesirable one. It is this change, rather than a transition to perfect health, that contributes the benefit of the public policy.

The life-path approach constitutes in a number of ways a departure from conventional methods of valuing health benefits. The distinguishing feature of the approach is its treatment of the whole stream of experience as the focus of analysis. Good health, illness, and death are viewed as inseparable in analysis as in life. As in other areas of life, people make choices for more or less health and longevity. To an important degree, people choose greater or lesser amounts of health and longevity depending on their values for these goods relative to their other wants and needs. The life-path approach is an appropriate means of obtaining health values because it is based on willingness to pay in view of the totality of substitutions that people make over time in response to changes in health risks. Methods that attempt to value health or longevity as one period-events, and especially methods that disregard age, run the danger of missing important determinants of health values.

12

Modeling of Choices
with Uncertain Preferences

Charles Kahn

12.1. Background

People have many occasions in their lives to take actions to avoid or reduce
risks. In order not to spend all their resources on risk avoidance, they implicitly estimate the value of risk reduction, and they try with more or less success
to carry risk avoidance only to a point justified by the costs. Risk avoidance
is often unconscious or subconscious. Its value is often imperfectly estimated, even when the events to be avoided are catastrophic, because the
probabilities are small and outside the realm of everyday experience. Thus
people tend not to know their own minds on the subject or risk.

Nonetheless, the reduction in health risks constitutes the major benefit
of many government policies and regulations. Responsible determination of
the correct standards for such policies requires knowing the values placed
by individuals on reductions in health risks. Ultimately, there are only two
ways to determine individuals' values. One is to observe market behavior
and, through the logic of revealed preference, to make inferences about
individuals' tastes. The other is to ask individuals directly about their preferences. In the case of most public goods, there are few markets in which
individual preferences can be revealed—indeed, this scarcity of markets is
the reason government must be concerned with the problem in the first
place. Thus surveys and interviews will inevitably be central to assessing the
public's demand for health risk reduction.

Researchers have, however, run into serious difficulties when they have
attempted to interpret individuals' responses to questions about their preferences in risky situations. Many economists are suspicious of survey responses about willingness to pay, feeling that they are subject to strategic
manipulation by the respondents. In the case of survey data on risk tolerance, there are much more immediate problems: answers elicited appear to
be at odds with the standard economic theories of risk aversion. Worse, they

I thank Ed Schlee for valuable suggestions.

appear to be inconsistent with the fundamental assumptions of rational decision making. Therefore, to be able to use survey data to establish the value of the benefits from risk reduction, we need a framework that will enable us to interpret that data consistently in a cost-benefit analysis. This chapter will provide the conceptual basis for such a framework, based on the concept of "uncertain preferences."[1]

The chapter shows how the concept of uncertain preferences can be used to model the problem of making choices about risky alternatives when knowledge is imperfect. It critiques the psychological literature on risk and relates the concept of uncertain preferences to the economic literature on behavior toward risk. It then provides a set of theorems indicating how individuals with uncertain preferences will process information in order to respond to survey questions. It uses these theorems to suggest techniques for reducing inconsistency and inaccuracy in respondents' answers to questions about risky events, drawing implications for the use of contingent valuation in the study of serious illness.

12.2. An Overview of This Chapter

The framework I propose is one in which it is costly for individuals to determine their own preferences and therefore unlikely that their responses to survey questions will reflect their true choices with absolute accuracy. I will demonstrate how cost-benefit analysis can be interpreted in such an environment and indicate some implications for the handling of surveys of individuals' risk tolerance.

This approach is consistent with much recent work in cognitive psychology and can in fact be understood as an economic reinterpretation of some of that field's analysis. It differs, however, from the approach taken by much recent work in economic theory. Section 12.3 outlines the recent theoretical alternatives to expected utility, the reasons why they have been advocated, and the reasons why I feel these approaches are not adequate to handle the problems inherent in the use of surveys. It also analyzes the conceptual problems with cost-benefit analysis when individuals are uncertain about their own preferences and the limitations and uses of surveys in those circumstances. Section 12.4 briefly reviews psychological models of decision making of relevance to the problem. Section 12.5 develops a model of uncertain preferences that translates the psychological models into a cost-benefit framework. Section 12.6 provides theorems that can be used to improve surveys' effectiveness in gathering information about the true un-

---

1. The strategy we propose can be reinterpreted in the state preference framework. The subject's utility function depends on an unknown state of the world; he invests in signals designed to shed light on the unknown state. See Schmalensee (1972) and Graham (1981; 1992).

derlying preferences. Section 12.7 considers extensions examining problems arising from interrelated answers, limited memory, and biased priors. The final section summarizes the implications as applied to the health survey.

12.3. Theoretical Problems

Expected Utility Theory and Its Critics

For more than 2 decades expected utility theory has been the dominant paradigm in economics for modeling individual decision making under uncertainty. The main appeal of the formulation has been theoretical; the axioms from which the expected utility theorem is derived are simple, elegant, and for the most part intuitively unobjectionable. The framework has proved to be a solid foundation on which to develop both macroeconomic and microeconomic theories and to be a handy and reliable maintained hypothesis in empirical work examining markets in which uncertainty is a consideration.

While the theory has been dominant, it has not been without objections and challenges, both on theoretical and empirical grounds. The theoretical objections have centered on the so-called independence axiom. The independence axiom, as illustrated in Figure 12.1, says that lottery A is preferred to lottery B if and only if a compound lottery, in which A is the prize with probability p and in which C is the prize with probability $(1 - p)$, is preferred to a compound lottery in which B is the prize with probability p and in which C is the prize with probability $(1 - p)$, for all A, B, C, and p. Although this assumption seems a priori reasonable, it is not as fundamental as the other axioms upon which expected utility theory is based. The main

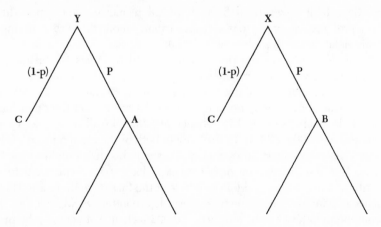

Figure 12-1   Independence Axiom

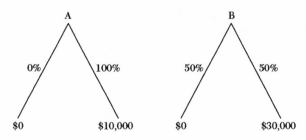

Figure 12-2   Allais Paradox (A)

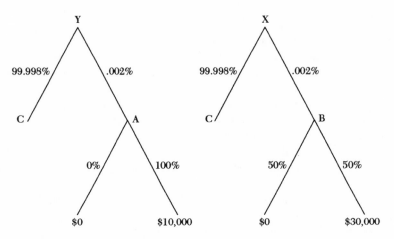

Figure 12-3   Allais Paradox (B)

objections to it have arisen from empirical results in which individuals' stated preferences appear to violate this axiom. Among the earliest examples of this violation are those by Allais (1953).

A simple version of the phenomenon noted by Allais is illustrated in Figures 12.2 and 12.3. Virtually all individuals of moderate income prefer $10,000 with certainty (call this outcome A) to a 50% chance at $30,000 and a 50% chance of receiving nothing (call this lottery B). On the other hand, many individuals prefer a 0.1% chance at $30,000 (call this X) to a 0.2% chance at $10,000 (call this Y). Holding to both of these announced preferences violates expected utility theory. To show this, it is only necessary to realize that the distribution of outcomes in lottery X is equivalent to the distribution in a compound lottery where at the first stage there is a 0.002% chance of winning, where the prize is a ticket to lottery B, while lottery Y is a compound lottery in which there is a 0.002% chance of winning the prize, which is a ticket to A.

Allais cited the independence axiom as the weak link in the chain and called for its abandonment. Striking as examples of this form were, they had little effect on the mainstream of economics because Allais built no coherent theoretical structure to set as a rival to expected utility theory. The first completely developed analysis that dropped the independence axiom is by Machina (1982), who also surveys the empirical objections to expected utility and indicates which of them can be addressed by his extended theory.

Machina analyzes an extension of expected utility theory in which the independence axiom is replaced with the less restrictive assumption that preferences are smooth in changes in gambles. He demonstrates that expected utility theory still holds as a local approximation describing individuals' tastes for relatively small changes in gambles around a (possibly random) initial wealth level. Any properties that we wished to attribute to expected utility functions—for example, declining risk aversion, or regions of relative risk loving—can now be attributed to the so-called local utility functions at various initial wealth levels. This is valuable, for it permits us to rationalize not only the Allais paradox but also the observation by Markowitz (1952) that individuals continue to buy both insurance and lottery tickets as their wealth changes. Expected utility theory can rationalize purchases of each by postulating regions of risk aversion at levels of wealth below the initial wealth and regions of risk loving at levels of wealth above the initial wealth. However, as the individual's initial wealth changes, one sort of behavior or the other should be abandoned according to the simple theory, and this does not appear to happen. Machina resolves the problem by appeal to variations in the local utility function as the individual's wealth changes.

A similar type of analysis can rationalize the Allais paradoxes: the local utility function is again not independent of the entire set of outcomes available to the individual at the time the decision is made. Thus there is nothing unexpected in the fact that the existence of a chance at C affects the preferences for A versus B.

However, as Machina (1982, pp. 307–8) himself notes, there are several observations in the experimental work on risk preferences that cannot be squared with expected utility theory even when extended in the Machina manner. Most of these are violations, not of the independence axiom, but of the assumption that preferences are dependent only on the distribution of outcomes that the lottery yields, not the form in which the lotteries are presented.[2] In the language of psychology, stated preferences appear to depend on the context in which the alternatives are "framed."

A striking example of this phenomenon appears in the work of Kahneman

2. Another objection of current interest is that agents may violate "probabilistic sophistication." See, e.g., Machina and Schmeidler (1992).

and Tversky (1979). They build examples in which preferences are altered when initial wealth is increased by a fixed amount and the outcome of the gambles offered is decreased by the same amount in all realizations. Note therefore that the assumption that is being violated is an extremely basic one, namely, that preferences depend only on the final distribution of outcomes. Another, equally basic situation of inconsistency of preferences is described in the work by Grether and Plott (1979), who trace the evidence of their particular "preference reversal phenomenon" through several experimenters' works. This phenomenon is the fact that individuals, when asked to state a certainty equivalent for a gamble, will often choose a value that is greater than the dollar value they will in fact choose in preference to that same lottery. That is, given a lottery A, an individual will claim that he is indifferent between A and some dollar payoff D, and then, in fact, if offered a choice between A and some lower payoff L, choose L. This observation apparently violates no less an assumption than that of the transitivity of preferences; no extension of "expected utility" theory can adequately handle it, and in their survey Grether and Plott conclude that the explanation must lie in some sort of information-processing problem.

However, once we have decided that it will be necessary to include the difficulties of information processing as part of our modeling of the decisions made by individuals facing risk, then these same difficulties can be used to explain the other phenomena that the dropping of the independence assumption was intended to address (see below). Nor is the dropping of the independence assumption without cost. Observers have generally agreed as to the normative desirability of the independence assumption. If we are trying to develop a framework for cost-benefit analysis, these normative arguments carry considerable weight. For if we drop the independence assumption, we will be faced with a certain time inconsistency in our subjects' preferences over lotteries. While there is nothing self-contradictory in this fact, we will then discover that we can change individuals' welfare simply by restricting their ability to change their minds about which choices they will make.[3]

For instance, suppose we use the lotteries described in Figure 12.3. Suppose we start by only allowing the individual lottery B in the event that the .002% chance arises. Then before the outcome of this chance, the individual's utility is equal to the utility associated with lottery X. Now suppose we expand the choices available to include the choice either of lottery B or lottery A in the event that the chance arises. The result is a *decrease* in the

3. This point is controversial. Machina (1989) argues that such examples assume "consequentialism," an assumption that is not necessarily appropriate for non-expected-utility maximizers. But see Hammond (1989) for a different view, as well as Border (1992) and Border and Segal (1992).

individual's current utility from X to Y. The individual's reasoning against the increase in his choice set is as follows: "Should the chance arise, I know I will pick lottery A because as of that date I will prefer it to lottery B, but in fact, from my current perspective I prefer lottery A to lottery B; thus my utility has decreased by my not being able to prevent myself from picking this currently less desirable alternative."

Another recently revived alternative to expected utility—regret theory—generates similar difficulties. This alternative theory assumes that the individual decision maker makes choices based, not on the distribution of outcomes, but on the distribution of the difference between the chosen outcome and the outcome not chosen. This approach, based in minimax strategy game theory, was a popular early rival to expected utility theory, and it has recently been advocated by Loomes and Sugden (1982). A major difficulty with the theory is that it implies an intransitivity of preferences since individual preferences are not independent of the set from which the choices are made. The authors of the article argue eloquently that there is nothing "irrational" about such a model of behavior and that there is no logical inconsistency in the structure. Although this is true, allowing this assumption does equal damage to the welfare analysis. For if we let the government expand the set of available choices, we again find that utility can decrease, as individuals choose less preferred alternatives because of the intrusion of seemingly irrelevant alternatives.

In short, it appears that the price in terms of difficulties with welfare analysis is too high to pay, especially given the less drastic modifications that can be made to rationalize the observed responses to risk surveys and still keep the fundamental welfare-economics structure intact.

Conceptual Problems with Welfare Analysis When Tastes Are Uncertain

Thus I conclude that the best way to proceed in trying to interpret surveys of individuals' attitudes toward risk is to retain the independence axiom but admit that individuals do not know their own tastes with certainty. There should be nothing counterintuitive in this position: most people do not deal regularly with issues of risk; most people therefore are not likely to be very expert in stating their preferences over risky alternatives. Under the circumstances, it is not surprising that, when presented with a complicated set of alternatives among which to choose, most people make choices that seem to imply that their preferences are intransitive. However, we would expect the same thing to happen if we presented real world consumers with multivariate bundles of goods and asked them to choose among them. As long as we kept the bundles the same in most dimensions and only varied a few at a time, we might have reasonable hope to obtain a consistent ranking. But when we ask individuals to rank among pairs of highly dissimilar bundles, we would not be surprised to find apparent inconsistencies in their preferences. Individuals are likely to make mistakes and to be subject to the utility equivalent of "optical illusions" when describing their preferences.

The crucial test is the subject's reaction if confronted with the apparent inconsistency of some set of preferences. Suppose we say to a particular individual after an interview, "You have said you prefer A to B, you prefer B to C and you prefer C to A. Do you see any inconsistency in these statements?" If the individual's answer is, "Yes, upon reflection I prefer A to C," then we are home free. If his or her answer is "Yes, I see a problem there, but I cannot tell which of my statements are incorrect," then we have a problem since the decision task is so difficult for the individual that he cannot straighten out his preferences even upon reflection. Nonetheless, our hypothesis of consistency of preferences is still intact. Only if the individual says, "No, I see no problem at all with those statements," are we in deep trouble, for then the individual must mean by the word "preferences" something quite different from what we mean by the word. In the case of Grether and Plott's (1979) preference reversal phenomenon it is extremely likely that, if confronted with the apparent contradictions in their statements the subjects would agree that their preferences would need revision. It is less clear from the evidence that this is the case in the Allais paradox cases. But at least in multiattribute problems, descriptions of individuals' decision making processes seem to indicate that transitivity of preferences are an underlying assumption in their own actions (Payne, Braunstein, and Carroll 1978).

To summarize, my position is the following: if individuals do not have consistent preferences and deny that their own preferences need to be consistent, we cannot do welfare economics. If preferences are asserted by individuals to be consistent, then there is at least the possibility that progress can be made. However, given that we can no longer assume that individuals know their preferences, the question remains, "What is the correct set of criteria for making welfare judgments?"

One approach is to argue that the correct criterion is the criterion that would be used by the politician hoping for reelection. Voters make their decisions as to whom to reelect without being forced to think carefully through their casually stated preferences. If they do not know what their preferences would be if they had thought through the situation sufficiently, it is of no concern to the politician—those "true" preferences must be irrelevant for reelection. If that means that different preferences might be elicited by stating the decision problem in different ways, then so be it; we must state the decision problem in the form that the politician in power chooses to state it and then record the answers as accurately as possible.

The drawbacks of this point of view are obvious. Presumably, if the approach were explained to any voter, he would prefer that an alternative approach be adopted by the investigator. Since the problem stems from the cost and difficulty in eliciting individual preferences, a voter might prefer that the investigator use more extended surveys, spending sufficient time and resources with each individual interviewed. Care should be exercised by going through the initially stated preferences of the individual in sufficient detail to determine if there are any inconsistencies in them, by double-checking those inconsistencies with the individual, by presenting the decision problem in several different formulations to double-check that the individual is not being swayed by illusions of the presentation, and finally by giving the individual sufficient practice at answering decision problems of the sort we are dealing with to allow him to train himself in determining his own preferences.

This approach, if explained to the average voter, would presumably draw greater support than the initial one. Even if the voter himself is not picked for the interview, as long as he regards himself as sufficiently typical in his tastes, he will prefer having a proxy go through this more extensive interview to get at what his own true preferences are likely to be. Nonetheless, the average voter is still likely to have reservations about this procedure. The extensive interviewing is largely a matter of "education." From the investigator's point of view, it is the individual educating himself about his own preferences. From the point of view of a suspicious outsider, it could easily be the interviewer educating the subject as to what his preferences *should* be. These suspicions are likely to be particularly strong if the conclusions of the investigation go against the surface preference of the outside observer. In short, the procedure must be carefully tailored to ensure that there is no presumption as to what are the "right" or "wrong" preferences in the situation—beyond the basic requirement of transitivity.

This is particularly difficult to achieve since people will be dealing with questions to which moral strictures are commonly placed. Many people believe gambling to be morally wrong and maintenance of health at all costs morally correct. In assessing the value to one individual of another individual's health, moral perceptions will play even greater a role. One way of characterizing the difficulty is to describe an individual as having two sets of preferences—the preferences of his "selfish self" and the preferences of his "socially conscious self"—and then trying to decide, not which preferences actually count in individual decision making, but which *should* count for welfare analysis. Another, probably more fruitful way of describing the situation is to say that individuals' stated preferences depend on their audience. Many of the causes of this dependence can be reduced to a desire for various sorts of approval—desire to appear to be a sophisticate, a moral individual, a member of the team. Nonetheless, we do not need to distinguish between the various reasons for stated preferences to vary. Our operational definition of "true" preferences is those that would dominate in the privacy of one's own home—or in the privacy of the voting booth. It still then is an open question as to whether the normative standard *ought* to be the sum of individuals' private preferences. As a practical matter, however, it should not be surprising to find that individuals will report different preferences to an interviewer than they will declare to friends or through their actions. The difficulties that arise when individuals ascribe moral rankings to alternative sets of preferences are outside the primary focus of this work; nonetheless, such difficulties will inevitably complicate the analysis. Ultimately, there is probably no resolution of the issue, and the only procedure open to the investigator will be an examination of the extent to which individual preferences are influenced by the groups in which they find themselves during the interview.

12.4. Psychological Studies

Cognitive psychologists have not been concerned with the ethical/public policy question of which statements of preferences *should* be taken into account in the determination of public policy. In contrast, they have studied much more carefully the question of what structures we can use to model preferences that underlie the apparently inconsistent choices individuals make.

An early version of a formulation that allows for inconsistent answers to choice questions is the random utility model (Thurstone 1972), which in effect posits the existence of a distribution over possible consistent underlying preferences and then assumes that each question is answered with respect to a draw from one of the distributions. Note that the random utility model is not easily reconciled with economic models of decision making. For instance, it is not equivalent to a model in which the consumer has Bayesian priors about his own preferences. Such an account would instead yield a more complicated, but still perfectly consistent, set of preferences over lotteries—indeed, the structure could be aggregated into a state preference model in the ordinary way.

The assumption underlying the Thurstone model is that there is a difference between the purely intellectual question, "Which do you like better?" and the economic question, "Which will you take?" (cf. Little 1956). The random utility model simply assumes that over time an individual's preferences change randomly so that the answer can vary stochastically to the question when repeated. An alternative formulation, and one much more useful from our point of view, is that the underlying preferences are constant but the structure by which these preferences are translated into decisions is stochastic (Luce 1959; Tversky 1972). There has been much concern in that literature with the equivalences or nonequivalences between various formulations of the random utility model. For our purposes, however, the issues are two: what rational calculus can underly such a model, and what implications will it have for welfare economics? Our job as economists is to delve through the stochastic portion to the underlying preferences; our task in a survey, then, is to minimize the noisiness of the response, and it therefore becomes important to understand where the noisiness comes from.

This investigation belongs to the subfield of psychology known as decision research. Its investigation involves several methodologies not normally used in economics, including such techniques as "verbal protocols" (the investigation of subjects' reports of their own behavior) and records of subjects' use of information in the decision process (Payne et al. 1978). A useful distinction made in this field is between decision making based on alternative ranking versus decision making based on attribute rankings. Alternative ranking involves the process normally treated in economics—all alternatives are measured in some common scaling, and the highest of these scalings indicates the preferred alternative. In attribute processes, the various attributes attached to the alternatives are ranked, and then these rankings in various dimensions are compared to determine an overall ranking. The latter is useful when the trade-offs between the different attributes are difficult for the individual to determine, but the cost is that such systems of decision making easily result in intransitive rankings. Various authors in this literature have focused on various procedures by which attribute rankings are accomplished (a brief survey is included in Aschenbrenner [1981]). Kahneman and Tversky (1979) focus on the various considerations that arise in the process of decision making in complicated situations. Among them are the "isolation" phenomenon and the "anchoring" phenomenon. By "isolation" is meant the focusing on the aspects that are perceived as the main contrasts between the two available alternatives, treating as precisely equal the aspects perceived as of smaller difference. Thus the Allais paradox can be explained as an approximation error due to the decision maker's initial estimate that there is relatively little difference between probabilities of .002% and .001% as opposed to differences between outcomes of $10,000 and $30,000. The phenomenon of "anchoring" is a perceptual dependence on initial conditions, a tendency to estimate values as closer to values already examined. Grether and Plott's (1979) preference reversal can then be rationalized as a tendency for certainty equivalents to be anchored to the winning payoff in a gamble.

Thus it would appear that the phenomena most likely to pose problems in interpreting surveys of risk preferences can be understood without abandoning the independence assumption. My job is then to provide an economic basis that can rationalize the use of such structures.

12.5. An Economic Model

Components

The basic component of this model is a set of prior preferences that describe the individual's beliefs about his own tastes in the event that he makes no expenditures to examine those tastes. The individual can also expend an amount of psychic costs to improve the sample of his tastes. The expenditure gives him a draw as to his own tastes, which in conjunction with his priors can be used to derive new tastes. Each new draw can be added to the set.

We now need memory to store the draws. The simplest story is that memory is infinite, so that each draw is stored and we can at any point find the set of consistent preferences representing an individual's beliefs at that point. The more difficult, but possibly more interesting model, has finite memory, so that after some point more draws can only be added by dropping the information in earlier draws.

The next step is to allow degrees of investment in reducing the uncertainty over the prior preferences. Greater investment entails a greater psychic cost but allows a sharper prediction as to preferences. Given previously learned information, we can imagine the individual as choosing to think more or less carefully in attempting to answer the latest question. This is a useful distinction for understanding the problems of "anchoring" since individuals' initial response will make it worthwhile not to spend as much energy in attempting to answer subsequent questions, relying instead on the initial answers to provide clues. It also has testible implications in the case where memory is limited since the anchoring should diminish as the length of time between related questions on the survey increases.

So far we have not discussed the role of the closeness of one outcome to another. To do so requires the addition of a metric to the problem, which describes the "similarity" between outcomes, and therefore the degree to which the guess on one outcome affects the likelihood of responses on other outcomes. Once this metric is established, it becomes useful to describe the situation where different questions elicit different sorts of investments in introspection, some being more useful to answering one question, and some to answering another.

Finally, we will drop the assumption of unbiased estimating by the decision maker and consider the effects of limited forms of bias on the outcomes. This last modification will be necessary to understand preference reversals due to "framing."

Formal Model Statement

Suppose that there are I alternatives being considered, each with an unknown utility U_i. Let U be the vector of these utilities, and let $F(U)$ be the joint probability distribution over U. To begin with, we will take the U_i to be independently and identically distributed (i.i.d). Throughout this essay, our examples will assume that the U_i's vary normally and independently, with prior means m_i and precisions h_i (i.e., 1/variance).

The individual can, by spending a psychic cost of k, receive extra information about his true preferences. We assume that the extra information gained by this "introspection" is a draw of two random variables that are estimates of U_i and U_j, which we call V_i and V_j, respectively. We assume

$$V_i = U_i + e_i,$$

where e_i is a measurement error that in our examples we will assume to be distributed as a normal with mean zero and precision g_i, independent of all other errors e and of all U_i's (and similarly for the distribution V_j).

Given any string of information $\{V_1, V_2, \ldots\} = S$, we can derive posterior distributions of the utilities of the alternatives $F(U|S)$. In the case of normal distributions, a simple application of Bayes's rule shows that, given a draw of V_i, the posterior distribution of U_i is normal with mean

$$m_i^*(V_i) = (m_i h_i + v_i g_i) / (h_i + g_i)$$

and precision

$$h_i + g_i.$$

If no draw is made, the individual's expected utility if given a choice between U_1 and U_2 is

$$\max \{m_1, m_2\}.$$

If the draw is made, utility is

$$\max (\{m_1^*(V_1), m_2^*(V_2)\} - k).$$

The first model we will consider is to solve the following Bayesian decision problem: the individual is presented with a series of alternatives, where each alternative is a pair of outcomes, one of which he will receive. He is asked to make his choice. For simplicity, we will assume that at each instant he treats the question being asked him as the last problem he will face. (In fact, the problem is more complicated since an individual might be expected to anticipate that a series of questions will occur and modify his introspection accordingly. We will ignore this refinement. If the reader wishes, he or she can assume that the survey is structured so that at each stage there is an extremely low probability of any one participant's receiving an additional question. This makes it possible to ignore the likelihood of extra questions at every stage.)

The decision problem for the individual—namely, how many draws to invest in—can be formulated either sequentially or nonsequentially. These formulations mirror the strategies analyzed in the research literature. The nonsequential formulation (Stigler 1961) has the individual precommit to a fixed number of introspections. The sequential formulation (Kohn and Shavell 1974) allows the individual at every step to consider further expenditure on introspection based on the results he has learned so far. Although the specific optimal strategies differ between these two formulations, the general outlines are similar. Since our problem is a specific version of the search problem, we will consider ourselves free to switch back and forth between the two formulations in the examples that follow, depending on which yields the more tractable analysis in any specific application.

In this structure it will not generally be optimal for the individual to eliminate all uncertainty about his own tastes—indeed, it will not generally be possible. It can be shown that

THEOREM 12.1.   Less information is acquired (1) the greater the difference between prior estimates of the m_i's, (2) the lower the variance of the prior estimate of either U_i, (3) the greater the variance of the noise in any estimate, and (4) the greater the cost of information acquisition.

On the other hand, the posterior announced preferences are more accurate (1) the greater the difference between prior estimates of the m_i's, (2) the lower the variance of the prior estimate of either U_i, (3) the lower the variance of the noise of any estimate, and (4) the lower the cost of the acquisition of information.

In actual experiments, it is often the case that, instead of receiving the payoff with certainty, the subject only receives it with some probability less than one. For this modification we have

THEOREM 12.2.   When the probability of actually receiving the payoff decreases, subjects (1) expend less effort in determining their own tastes, and (2) give less accurate ex post predictions of those tastes.

These conclusions are immediate from the model, but they do lead to some natural considerations for survey design: difficult questions will simply not be given much consideration. Questions that yield potentially great payoffs in that it is costly to answer incorrectly will be given more consideration, but ex post they are still likely to lead to inaccurate answers. Questions that the individual considers easy to answer ex ante will not be given much additional consideration by the individual.

Next we consider the effects of the answer to one question on the answer to subsequent questions. Note that, in this model, repeating the same question several times in succession yields no new information since the individual has already optimized and thus has no reason to make further introspections. However, it turns out that expending information on answers to one question will, in general, yield information useful to answers to other questions.

Suppose we ask the individual about a completely new pair of alternatives. In the model in which all alternatives have independent distributions, previous introspection has thrown no light on his preferences with regard to these new alternatives. Thus his behavior is the same as if the questions had never been asked. However, consider the case where the second question gives us as an alternative one of the options already considered in the first question. Now previously gathered information becomes useful, and the subjects' responses will be affected.

There are two considerations. First, having answered one question already means that the answer to the second question will start from a more accurate assessment of the beliefs than would otherwise be obtained. This decreases the likelihood of extra investment but increases the expected accuracy of the ex post announced choice.

The second consideration depends on the realizations actually obtained in response to the first question. If the realization causes expected values of the two alternatives in the second question to move further apart, then the likelihood is that there will be less investment in examining the second question. However, if the realization brings the values of the two alternatives closer together, then investment in answering the second question will tend to increase. On average, these two possibilities balance, and we have the first consideration dominating. Therefore although the presence of preceding related questions on a survey may in any instance increase or decrease the amount of investment used in determining the answer to subsequent questions, we can nevertheless conclude that

THEOREM 12.3. Expenditure on introspection on average decreases through the survey, while accuracy increases.

Among other things, this result predicts a decline over time in the attention paid by respondents to questions within a survey—a tendency often observed—without needing to postulate a fatigue factor.

More generally, this interrelationship will be observed in any model in which answers to one question help answer another. We will consider in more detail below the case where priors for various alternatives are no longer independent. But the phenomenon can occur when priors are independent as long as there is some dependency in the sampling. The example of this discussed above is the simplest one. Another case occurs when introspection reveals information, not about the two alternatives independently, but only about the difference between their values:

$$U_j - U_i + e.$$

(We will call this the case of "sampling of differences."). In this case, whenever we find that an individual indicates that i is preferred to j, it means that we can expect that i has a higher value than initially anticipated and, therefore, is more likely to be preferred to other alternatives as well, and conversely for j. Thus, even in the case of independent valuations, a primitive form of anchoring emerges.

12.6. Valuation Questions

Answering a Series of Questions

Given this structure, there will be nothing paradoxical about a sequence of answers to questions leading to apparent intransitivities; it will simply be the case that between answers additional information has been derived. It will also be perfectly possible for individuals to reverse their answers on subsequent repetitions of a question, provided that other questions have intervened that have led the individual to seek more information.

Suppose we now consider asking a third question and that there are only the three alternatives, U_1, U_2, and U_3, under consideration. If preferences are perfectly known, then the entirety of the information can always be revealed with three questions, and often with two. If preferences can only be determined with a cost, there may be a gain from asking an apparently redundant question. In our model we have

THEOREM 12.4.   Suppose the first question determines that U_1 is preferred to U_2, and the second question determines that U_2 is preferred to U_3. Then (1) in response to the third question, "Do you prefer U_3 to U_1?" there is a finite possibility of the answer exhibiting an apparent intransitivity. (2) In response to the third question, "Do you prefer U_2 to U_1?" there is a finite probability of the answer exhibiting a reversal of preferences.

In any case, later answers are more likely to reflect true preferences than are early answers in the list.

THEOREM 12.5.   Suppose furthermore, that we continue to cycle through the questions in the same order indefinitely. Then the probability is zero that there is no number n such that for all questions beyond the nth no further investment in introspection is made. In order words, responses eventually settle down, and preference reversal ceases. Moreover, at the point where further investment has ceased, there will be no intransitivities in the response.

In short, this model with infinite capacity for recall allows preference reversal and intransitivity, but only as transient phenomena. Once further investment in introspection ceases, preferences are stable and transitive. This result, although useful as an insight, is not as strong as it might appear, for it is not possible based solely on the responses to determine whether investment in introspection has ceased. In our normal distribution model, we have the following result as well.

THEOREM 12.6.   For any number n there is a finite probability of obtaining unchanged results through n cycles with no intransitivities and a preference reversal in the $(n + 1)$st cycle.

The proof of this theorem depends on the fact that normal distributions are unbounded. We conjecture that, if the model is modified to deal with bounded distributions, this last theorem will no longer hold and more positive results can be obtained.

So far, none of our conclusions are altered if we use the "comparison" formulation for introspection (recall that this is the formulation in which draws give, not two values V_i and V_j, but merely the difference between them). The following result depends specifically on using the comparison formulation.

THEOREM 12.7. Suppose that the initial question determines that U_1 is preferred to U_2. Then, if investment yields only an estimate of the difference between the valuations of alternatives, it cannot be the case that a third question reverses the answer to the first question.

Proof. There is no incentive for further investment in response to the third question since the second question only reduces the estimate of U_2.

If introspection gives estimates of both U_i and U_j, the conclusion of the theorem is weakened:

THEOREM 12.8. Suppose the initial question determines that U_1 is preferred to U_2. Then preference reversal in question 3 is more likely if question 2 determines that U_2 is preferred to U_3 than if it determines the reverse.

In the case where two questions have already been asked, we are now in a position to compare the relative usefulness of various possible third questions. Here are the two relevant cases to consider.

CASE 1. Suppose the first question reveals that U_1 is preferred to U_2 and the second question reveals that U_2 is preferred to U_3. Then the most useful third question is to compare U_1 with U_2 again, rather than to compare U_1 with U_3. In both cases, it is optimal for the investigator to base his predictions of true underlying preferences on the last two of the three responses; however, these optimal predictions are more accurate when question 1 is repeated than when the new comparison is made.

CASE 2. Suppose the first question reveals that U_1 is preferred to U_2 and the second question reveals U_3 is preferred to U_2. Then the most useful third question is obviously to compare U_1 with U_3.

The resultant principles can be summarized quite neatly: redundancy in questions can be useful. If redundant questions are used, it is more useful to double-check the earliest questions and the ones that full ranking indicates represent the closest calls. When redundant questions are used, rely on later rather than earlier answers.

Comparison versus Scaling Questions

For the purpose of this section, we will assume that introspection yields an estimate of the value of only *one* alternative. We now wish to consider the difference between the effects of the following two questions: comparison questions ("Which alternative do you prefer?") and scaling questions ("How much do you value alternative X?") Both are commonly used in risk analysis and risk surveys, and some of the difficulties with the results stem from the noncomparabilities of the two sorts of questions.

We need to establish some payoff associated with the answer to the latter question. In actual surveys this is typically accomplished by announcing to the individual that he will participate in what is equivalent to a second-price auction (Vickrey 1961) with his announced valuation as his bid. Since truth telling is a dominant strategy in such circumstances, in the case where introspection is costless, this gives the individual an incentive to answer correctly.

Giving the individual whichever alternative he says he prefers is also an incentive to answer accurately. The issue then is which format leads to greater introspection and therefore greater accuracy in answering. In fact, comparison questions are special cases of scaling questions since the second-price auction framework in effect chooses the value of the alternative randomly and then presents the individual with the realization, if the individual's bid indicated he would prefer it, and the initial alternative otherwise. A comparison question is thus a special auction in which the bid that will win is known with certainty beforehand.

Therefore the relative merits of the two forms of question can be determined by resolving the following: which random distribution of alternative valuations induces the individual to invest most in determining his valuation of a specific alternative? The answer is the following:

THEOREM 12.9.   Investment in introspection in evaluating a proposed offer is greatest when the value of the alternative to the proposed offer has a distribution with mass concentrated at the expected prior utility of the proposed offer.

Proof (Outline).   By the results of the initial section, we know that, among offers with identical variance, the one giving the closest mean utility to the proposed offer elicits the greatest investment. Thus concentrating all mass at the mean is of greater value than dissipating it across alternative possibilities.

If we know the individual's prior mean, then the best way to elicit accurate preferences is to have the individual choose between the alternative and the certain offer of the prior mean utility. In any application, of course, we will not know the decision maker's priors. Thus, making a fixed alternative offer will yield variable amounts of investment across individuals depending on how close it matched each individual's prior mean. One approach then is to ask casually what the mean valuation of the individual is ("how much is this offer worth to you?") and then to give the offer or the estimated value to the individual, whichever he prefers. The paradox of the difference between estimates made in some of the preference reversal literature is partially resolved then by the fact that greater investment is made when the actual offers are in prospect. This framework does, however, yield refutable propositions since the initially stated preferences should be reversed about half of the time. If reversal occurs more than half the time, we must assume biases in the individual's initial estimates. Analysis of this situation must wait until the final section.

In any event, this analysis also gives a useful rule of thumb for scaling the distribution of offers in the alternative used in a scaling question: they should mirror the investigator's estimate of prior means in a population sample.

12.7. Extensions

More General Distributions of Priors

Thus far we have assumed a great degree of homogeneity: all alternatives and all estimations have been assumed to have independent distributions. In fact, much of the richness of a real decision problem comes from the nonindependence of these distributions.

The structure we have developed allows for outcomes to be "similar" in several senses. First, two outcomes may have the same expected utility. Second, two outcomes may be considered similar if it is relatively easy to tell which one is preferred to the other. Finally, outcomes may be similar because there is a correlation between information about one of them and information about the other—so that one becomes a useful predictor of the other. Each of these notions is important in describing the effects of learning about preferences and the relationship between learning about one alternative and learning about the next. In this section we begin to establish a framework that will enable us to explore this relationship.

To consider the effects of nonindependence, we will assume that all alternatives have a factor representation, so that the utility associated with any alternative is

$$U_i = \sum_i b_i X_i,$$

where the b's are weights and the X's are i.i.d. underlying factors. If we make this assumption, then we will describe one alternative U_i as a good predictor of another U_j if the two are closely correlated. In this framework, correlation is simply

$$\sum_{ij} b_i b_j \left(\sum_i b_i^2 \sum_j b_j^2 \right)^{1/2}.$$

In this framework, the answers to a question about an alternative are affected similarly by having asked previous questions about it or by having asked previous questions about a good predictor of it. In either case, the variance of estimate of the alternative is reduced, answers become more accurate, and the likelihood of further investment in introspection declines. In particular, any conclusion from preceding sections about the behavior of multiple questions applies approximately when all the alternatives in one of the questions in the sequence is replaced by a good predictor of those questions with mean utilities scaled up or down proportionately.

A second form of interdependence is attributable to interrelations in the error structure in the sampling. Suppose again that all the U_i's are independent but that the e's in the various draws have a factor representation:

$$e_i = \sum a_i x_i.$$

The closer the correlation for any two alternatives i and j, the more can be learned from a given attempt to compare them. If we identify the x_i's with various measurement errors associated with the forms in which alternatives are presented, it is apparent that we desire a presentation that is as consistent as possible across alternatives. Moreover, if questions are designed to give the individual aid in learning about the forms of measurement error, then we can hope that associated errors may disappear in subsequent questions, as values of particular x_i's are learned.

So far, we have assumed that the individual is passive in his choice of alternatives upon which to make introspections, only choosing the number of examinations to make of any given alternative. As long as homogeneity assumptions are maintained, there was little cost associated with this additional simplification; in answering a question about preferences between U_i and U_j, it was always more useful to introspect on those two alternatives than upon any other set. Once homogeneity is dropped, however, this need no longer be the case, as the following example demonstrates.

EXAMPLE.   Suppose there are three alternatives, U_1, U_2, and U_3, and that U_1 is a good predictor of U_2, while U_3 is independent of either. Suppose furthermore that the error structures for U_2 and U_3 are highly correlated, while the error structure for U_1 is uncorrelated with the other two. Then, if the correlation between U_1 and U_2 is sufficiently high, it is optimal for the individual to decide between U_1 and U_3 by introspecting on U_2 and U_3.

In other words, the structure is now sufficiently rich to rationalize the use of proxies and heuristics. If a decision is to be made where the measurement problems are sufficiently difficult, then the decision maker finds it advantageous in his work to substitute for the initial decision a set of alternatives that are good predictors but for which the measurement problems are less acute—for instance, to simplify a complex lottery by substituting certainty equivalents for certain branches.

Note that, although this structure can explain the use of heuristics, it cannot explain any biases observed in the heuristics used. For example, suppose we structured a problem so as to make one set of heuristics most natural in one instance and a second set in a second instance. The model as it stands would not predict that every individual's answer be identical in the two instances, but it would predict that, on average, stated preferences would be the same in either realization.

The Effect of Limited Memory

It is important to realize that the framework as it has been described so far still has a significant limitation. An important simplifying assumption we have used is that of "perfect recall." No experiment, once made, is ever forgotten. Information becomes more and more precise as more and more questions are asked. This simplifying assumption leads to testable implications. As noted before, preference reversals and intransitivities occur in the model, but as transient phenomena. As more and more questions are asked, the number of reversals becomes rarer and rarer, and the effects of anchoring to the previous questions dies out.

If these predictions are not upheld by the data, a natural way to keep preference reversals occurring is to allow for imperfect memory. We simply need to assume a limited memory capacity, so that records can only be kept for a fixed number of experiments. If the number of examinations made exceeds this fixed limit, then each new examination replaces an earlier result. Beyond that point, we simply condition priors only by the last N observations (where N is the capacity of memory), rather than by the entire history.

Note in particular that this model is an extension of the basic random utility model. In our new framework, we would interpret the random utility model as a special case in which memory can only contain one experiment at a time. A limitation of the simple random utility model is that responses cannot be autocorrelated, as they can when memory is allowed. In contrast, in a finite memory model there is no tendency for preference reversals to die away or expenditure on introspection to cease. The following results are immediate.

THEOREM 12.10.   The smaller N is, the more are preference reversals, and the more likely are observed intransitivities.

THEOREM 12.11.   For a given question let $R(n)$ be the fraction of the times that the answer is reversed between instances of posing the question, when the number of intervening questions is n. Assume that for some n, say n°, there is no memory—that is, none of the introspection that entered into answering any question is left n° questions later. Then any period n less than n°, $R(n)/R(n^\circ)$ measures the extent to which memory endures n periods.

Again, these results, although useful conceptually, are of less use in empirical implementations if the actual capacity of memory is large. For if it is, the interview session would have to continue for a sufficiently long time to gather a large amount of data relative to the memory capacity. Some investigators have attempted to overcome this limitation by posing some questions in several sessions with large amounts of time intervening. The theorems may serve as a basis of determining the success of this technique.

Biases

In the previous sections we considered several cases where inconsistencies resulted; however, the Bayesian structure left the implication that the inconsistencies could not systematically be weighted in one direction or another. In this final section, I develop models that will allow for systematic biases in individuals' estimates.

It is extremely difficult to develop a Bayesian account in which individuals are subject to bias. For example, consider a problem in which an individual is paid a reward for correctly estimating the length of a line. Suppose he has a measuring stick that is biased, and suppose he has had previous experiences with the biases of this measuring stick. Then his estimates will be made so as to undo any such biases. The only way that there will be a biased estimate is if the individual has not yet learned the biases of his instruments; once learned, rationality requires that they be compensated for.

In the case of estimating the utility of prospects, it is easy to believe that individuals have not yet learned all of the biases in their measurements. It is also easy to believe that, unless they experience the gambles they are estimating their preferences over, they will not learn these biases during a questioning session, except inasmuch as these biases lead them into a logical contradiction.

In contrast, we will wish to be extremely careful in incorporating biases into the model. The difficulty with assuming them is that they are too powerful. By assuming sufficiently complicated forms of bias, it is possible to rationalize any sequence of preference announcements. Therefore, in this section we will content ourselves with modeling the biases as occurring only in the priors and not anywhere else in the description. At one point we will demonstrate that, for a certain class of examples, this is informationally equivalent to assuming that the biases occur elsewhere.

The introduction of biases imposes a conceptual problem: in what sense can we obtain evidence of biases? I propose the following interpretation: biases can be evident from a systematic set of information that influences tastes. For instance, if the data show a systematic tendency for alternative 2 to be valued more highly than alternative 1 at the beginning of an interview than at the end, then this is evidence of some bias; individuals in initial periods might be expected to take advantage of this statistical regularity as a source of exploitable information about true preferences.

These biases can be incorporated by assuming bias in the individual's priors. Let us suppose that individual preferences are drawn from a population with some given distribution. If individuals' priors are unbiased, then their priors as to their own tastes equal this population distribution. More generally, in cases where not all individuals are identical a priori, prior beliefs are defined as unbiased if, for any particular prior, the sample distribution of true beliefs of individuals holding that prior is identical with the prior.

We consider only the case of infinite memory. In this case, "true" preferences are simply the asymptotic distribution after infinite numbers of samplings. Moreover, in this case, since the influence of priors dies out with time, biases disappear. The existence of such biases can easily be tested, by comparing distributions of preferences implicit in initial questions on a survey with those implicit in final questions on a survey. The result of such an investigation will be of use in adjusting the results of short surveys to correct for prior biases.

A second way of formulating the account is to assume that the biases are not in the priors but in the process of introspection. For instance, imagine that, in introspections about one outcome U_1, the mean of measurement error e_1 is not zero, while in the corresponding outcome U_2, the mean is zero. However, suppose that both e_1 and e_2 are treated by the decision maker as being zero-mean variables. Then the greater the amount of introspection that has occurred, the more likely alternative 1 is to be preferred to alternative 2. Of course, identical results would be obtained if priors were biased against alternative 1 and introspection were unbiased. Thus, we will continue to use the formulation in which we ascribe all bias to the priors.

Similar, but more subtle, forms of bias can be demonstrated through overdependence on initial introspections, overvaluation of current information, and so forth. In all cases, the test of bias boils down into a claim that, statistically, the answer to a question conditioned on any information set or on a set of previous questions should equal the answer to the question conditioned on any additional information. If not, then the earlier estimates were not making use of the available information. To have anchoring in this sense will require bias.

For our purposes, the most interesting example of bias is the case where the conditioning event is the form in which an alternative is presented. If there is no bias in the preference priors, then statistically about as many people should prefer an alternative independent of the form of its presentation. In what follows, I will generate an account within which biased priors can account for the inconsistencies and therefore can generate preference reversals of the form described in Grether and Plott (1979).

Example of Biased Priors Generating Preference Reversals

Suppose U_1 is a complicated alternative that has a factor structure

$$X_1 + X_2 + X_3.$$

Suppose U_2 has the structure $X_1 + X_2$, and suppose U_3 has the structure $X_1 + X_3$. Also, suppose we wish to compare U_1 with U_4, which has the structure X_4. All X's are normally i.i.d.

Suppose that the measurement error structure for the U's is

$$V_1 = U_1 + e_1,$$
$$V_2 = U_2,$$
$$V_3 = U_3,$$

and

$$V_4 = U_4 + e_4.$$

Suppose that e_1 is large compared to X_2 or X_3 so that it makes sense to compare U_4 with one of the predictors U_2 or U_3 rather than directly with U_1.

Now suppose that U_2 and U_3 are ex ante identical so that it does not matter which the comparison is made with, and finally suppose that the costs k are sufficiently great that a single draw is optimal.

Under these circumstances, without bias we would predict that statistical results would pick U_1 or U_4 with frequencies independent of whether V_2 or V_3 were used as the predictor. In contrast, suppose the true distribution for U_2 is

$$X_1 + X_2 + h,$$

where h is positive. Then although the individual treats the predicting alternatives as equivalent to alternative U_1, alternative 2 is likely to be preferred to alternative 1. The result is that U_1 is announced as preferred to U_4 more often if the comparison is carried out by means of U_2 than if it is carried out by means of U_3.

If the biases in individuals' estimations enter through the priors as I have described them here, then we have a testable implication. Questions asking the individual to compare U_1 with U_2 or U_3 will cause the individual to invest in introspection along those dimensions, reducing the influence of the priors and making it more likely that h is included in the measurement. Thus we have

THEOREM 12.12.   If biases occur in the priors, then they will be reduced by questions that focus on the comparisons in which the biases occur.

In this example, if two presentations of the data apparently lead to different preferences, then the biases might be reduced by asking directly for comparisons either of the two presentations or of each with the predictor that we expect has been derived from it.

12.8. Summary and Implications for Contingent Valuation

The model of uncertain preferences in this chapter provides a framework to guide the application of contingent market methods to estimate the value of health risk reduction. Following a critique of expected utility theory and a discussion of the theory of individual values and behavior toward risk, I have developed a series of theorems that resolve difficulties with survey responses in terms of the behavior of a rational respondent making a costly examination of his or her own preferences when faced with questions that call them into play perhaps for the first time.

The key to the problem of obtaining consistent, valid measures of risk values, according to the theory that has been developed here, is dealing with the fact that people are often highly uncertain about what their risk preferences and values actually are. This is to be expected because people infrequently have occasion to think carefully about risky events. They seldom have occasion to examine their own reactions to the influences of opinion-molding surface events. Careful, systematic reflection is required, just as is required before deciding on an operation, a risky investment, or other difficult decisions that arise from time to time in everyone's life. While bias may enter into the valuation process, the economic approach of this chapter postulates that people learn to correct for the influence of their own biases when they become aware of them. I have developed a model and derived a series of theorems that have implications applicable to the task of eliciting consistent, valid risk reduction values.

The propositions of this section, which come from a model of rational behavior, replace assertions from the psychology literature that apparent preference reversals and sensitivity to framing show that people are irrational. Here, these phenomena are viewed as being due to the costliness of information.

Theorem 12.1 concerns reducing an individual's uncertainty about his own preferences. The question posed is how an individual can make the best choice when faced with a pair of alternatives. The theorem says that less new information is required the greater the difference in the value received from each available choice. It also says that, the more certain the individual is about the values of the alternatives, the less new information is required to make the right choice. Finally, less new information will be acquired the greater the cost of acquisition.

The remainder of Theorem 12.1 contains several propositions about the accuracy of preferences that are stated after an individual has acquired additional information. The theorem holds that announced preferences are more accurate the greater the difference in value received from each available choice. Preferences are stated more accurately when individuals are more certain about the value of the alternatives they face. Finally, announced preferences are more accurate the lower the cost of acquiring new information.

An application of Theorem 12.1 is found in the use of the floating starting point in sequence of iterative bids. Consider the seven-symptom health questionnaire described in Chapter 7. The sequence proceeds from an arbitrary starting bid of $100 to get rid of the least bothersome symptom. The starting point for the next bid, concerning the most bothersome symptom, is set at twice the first bid, based on the guess that such a value might be a fairly close approximation to the respondent's value. The theorem says that the respondent will think more carefully about his preferences at the outset the closer the guess is to his value for the contingent market product.

Theorem 12.2 concerns outcomes of risky situations in which the values associated with alternatives may not actually be received but are received only with a probability less than one. The theorem states that people expend less effort in getting to know their own preferences the smaller the probability of actually receiving the stated values of alternative choices available to them. It also states that actual expressions of their preferences are less accurate the more uncertain it is that they will receive the payoff.

The fact that no actual transactions occur in the contingent market surveys is a disincentive to careful thought on the part of respondents. This has been recognized by researchers for a long time. The disincentive is partially overcame in public policy applications by appealing to respondents' willingness to cooperate in accomplishing an important endeavor.

Theorem 12.3 pertains to the way people allocate their efforts to know what their risk preferences are. If people reflect on a series of alternatives, they will devote less and less effort and attention to later alternatives to the extent that they are related to alternatives previously considered. A similar result occurs when there is dependence in the sampling and people discover the values they place on differences.

One of the most difficult decisions in the construction of the health surveys is to decide on the number of contingent valuation questions to ask. Experience reveals that there is a trade-off between the quality of responses and the volume of information sought. Theorem 12.3 explains this experience. When long question sets are asked about similar contingent products, people tend not to think independently about each of them. It tends to be their reliance on previous introspections rather than often-postutated fatigue that produces this result, according to the theorem.

The theorem implies that a series of related questions can lead people to think about the differences between contingent goods rather than considering them as independent alternatives. This behavior can be exploited by encouraging people to think about differences as they express their values for programs. For example in the seven-symptom health questionnaire of Chapter 7, people were asked to carefully consider each symptom in turn and rank them from least to most bothersome. Bids were then obtained for the two extreme symptoms; iteration was used to encourage as much thought as possible. Bids for the five intermediate symptoms were then written down directly on the assumption that the comparison exercise had made their values apparent.

Theorem 12.2 addresses the problems of preference reversal and intransitivity that are frequently observed in expressed valuations of risky outcomes. If preferences are uncertain and information is costly to obtain, inconsistencies or outright reversals may occur as individuals reflect upon their preferences. True preferences are more likely to be stated during later stages of reflection. A related theorem states that, if reflection on the same list of risky alternatives continues, a point is reached where further reflection will not be attempted, and expressed inconsistencies are eliminated. This result depends on several assumptions, among which is the one that the individual does not forget any of the earlier steps in the reasoning process. If the reflection process produces only estimates of the differences in outcomes, then further probing of preferences cannot produce preferences reversals, simply because there is no incentive for such further probing of these outcomes.

In constructing the health questionnaires described in Chapter 7, an effort was made to utilize apparent preference reversals as part of the process of respondent introspection about preferences. For example, in thinking about how much they would be willing to pay to relieve symptoms, respondents sometimes change their minds about their beliefs when they were working out their rankings. Accordingly, they were encouraged to change their responses, several times if necessary, until they arrived at a set of rankings and values that satisfied them.

The following theorems suggest additional approaches to stimulating introspection about preferences where preference reversals and intransitivities are present in survey responses. These hold considerable promise for further work.

The practical content of Theorems 12.5–12.8 is that repeated questions concerning preferences are often useful. If repeated questions are used in the reflection process, it is most useful to double-check the earliest questions and the ones in which the earlier rankings suggest the closest calls.

Reflection about preferences frequently takes one of two forms: comparison—which alternative do I prefer? and scaling—how much do I value alternative X? The question that induces the greater amount of investment in additional information is the superior question to use in any given circumstances. Theorem 12.9 states a condition on the most effective way to stimulate effort to get new information. Suppose one constructs an offer of alternatives: one whose value is sought, and another whose value is fixed as some given stated value. The best given stated value is that closest to the prior value of the alternative of interest, that is, the value before new information has been acquired.

Theorem 12.9 has a very important lesson for the construction of contingent market goods. It received careful application in the seven-symptom questionnaires. This was accomplished by framing willingness to pay questions in terms of the respondents' endowments, with which they were familiar and presumably had clear ideas about in utility terms. Additional amounts of symptoms were then added to those they already experienced. Thus respondents were presented with two alternatives: alternative X— their current situation, and alternative Y—the situation with added symptoms. They were then in effect asked a scaling question—how much do you prefer situation X? Theorem 12.9 says that, by relating the policy alternative $(Y - X)$ to the respondent's own endowment, rather than some less familiar reference point X', the respondent invests more effort in thinking about his own real preferences.

Further work needs to be done along these lines on the life-path scenarios on heavy symptoms reported in Chapter 13. For example, certainty scenarios begin with a person of age 50 and present life-path alternatives with later ages. Application of theorem 12.9 suggests that people who are younger or older than 50 do not have strong prior beliefs about their health values at age 50 and will not invest much effort in making accurate willingness to pay statements about the alternatives. Investment in introspection would be increased if these scenarios were tailored to each respondent's actual situation.

The foregoing theorems assume that there are no memory limitations that reduce the effects of information gathering about preferences. Relaxing this assumption yields a theorem that says that, the more limited is memory capacity, the more numerous will be instances of preference reversals and intransitivities.

Theorems 12.10 and 12.11, of limited empirical usefulness when memory capacity is large, provide a method of measuring the extent to which memory endures during a period of reflecting about preferences.

A problem of importance in discovering the values of uncertain preferences is the presence of bias. The problem is for the individual to learn the size and direction of his biases and correct them in discovering his underlying preferences. Questions arise during reflection in which biases occur. Theorem 12.12 states that biases will be reduced by questions that focus on comparisons of alternatives in which the biases occur.

In conclusion, the framework I have built, although rudimentary, allows us to address several of the most vexing problems that arise in researchers' attempts to make use of data from risk surveys. It has been constructed as a series of nested generalizations starting from expected utility theory and gradually dropping or modifying assumptions that have been refuted in one or another examination of responses to survey questions.

Although the outlines of the model at every level are clear, there remains much to be done. In particular, when the homogeneity assumptions are dropped, there remain a great variety of unexplored possibilities. It will be most useful to tailor specifications of assumed structural relationships between the priors on various alternatives or the measurement errors of various acts of introspection to the specific description of the alternatives in any particular experiment. Once this is done, we can begin to make useful inferences from watching individuals' behavior in the face of specific complicated offers and learn which sorts of simplifications individuals actually make in estimating preferences.

Similarly, there is much work to be done in specifying particular biases to which we would wish to attach the priors. Here previous psychology studies will be most useful for providing insight as to the most reasonable specifications. Tendencies to overestimate small probabilities and to underestimate large quantities can be among those considerations we capture in the biased priors. In short, although the structure is now available, much work remains to be done in terms of specific applications.

13

Design of Contingent Valuation Approaches to Serious Illness

Robert Fabian, Lyndon Babcock, Anthony Bilotti, and George Tolley

13.1. Special Problems of Contingent Valuation Encountered with Serious Illness

The valuation of serious illness entails a number of analytic problems that are fundamentally different from the valuation of minor illness and light symptoms experienced occasionally by everyone in relatively unpatterned ways throughout their lives. Thus the analysis of serious illness requires different analytic techniques from those employed in the study reported in Part 2, even though it builds on the survey research knowledge obtained there.

Two facets of behavior, relatively unimportant to the study of light symptoms, are introduced when valuing serious illness. The first of these is risk. Serious illness, dreaded by people at some stage of their lives, is a prospect they face with varying degrees of probability. Because people have some control over the probability of serious illness, their behavior in the face of serious health risks is an important measure of the value they attach to good health prospects. Hence it is important to understand people's attitudes toward health risks.

The second facet of health behavior is the way prospects vary over a person's lifetime. In younger persons, choice and consequence are often separated by many years. Over time, one's health prospects change, and behavior tends to be modified accordingly. At the same time, life expectancy becomes a matter of conscious concern. How one responds to these inter-related matters depends in large measure on the social and economic circumstances of one's life and on how one has cared for his health in the past. Thus the focus of research on the valuation of serious illness turns to an integrated view of serious illness and death in the context of a person's overall life-cycle experience.

Accordingly, Chapter 10 explicitly introduced the concept of health as a behavior-dependent condition of overall well-being. Operationally, a narrower version is adopted—health is measured in terms of its absence or in terms of the amount and types of the person's ill health. This narrower operational definition preserves the perspective of the broader, more satisfactory definition by being embedded in a life-cycle model of quantity and quality of life, developed in Chapter 11.

Chapter 12 addressed the problem of eliciting expressions of people's behavior toward risks to health. Respondents will have thought about these matters to a greater or lesser extent and adjusted their behavior accordingly. The research challenge is to obtain quantitative equivalents to the sometimes nebulous attitudes that govern health behavior in the face of risks. The current state of utility theory leaves unanswered the question how best to obtain these quantitative equivalents in a form suitable for use in welfare analysis. Chapter 12 provides the inquiry required to guide the investigation along sound theoretical lines.

The goal of this chapter is to present the empirical framework that resulted from the conceptual investigation described in the earlier chapters of Part 3. This empirical framework takes the form of a four-module approach to the valuation of health-risk reduction. The first module, health experience, quantifies the respondent's health endowment according to the operational definition of health established in the conceptual work of Chapter 10. Health costs and defensive measures, the second module, quantifies certain important money outlays and nonmarket behavioral costs incurred on behalf of health. The module on risk perception and risk behavior prepares respondents to think carefully about the kinds of probabilities involved in behavioral decisions about serious illness and longevity. This involves a preparatory session to impart an intuitive grasp of the elementary principles of probability. It also obtains information about respondents' behavioral responses to a variety of risky situations. The fourth module presents the contingent valuation questions used to obtain values related to longevity and reduction of risk of serious illness. The goal of these questions was to integrate prospects for serious illness and death into an integrated life-cycle approach. The questions progress from simple life-experience situations to more complicated life-path situations involving various probabilities of serious illness and death.

The four-module approach requires about 3 hours to complete, including breaks for relaxation. Designing a survey of this complexity and duration is a novel research enterprise. Past economic survey experience suggests it to be too taxing of respondents' patience and stamina. In view of this experience, the necessity of taking steps to avoid fatigue was apparent. Taking several breaks at intervals defined by the modules is the simplest of these. Use of the health risk appraisal program also serves this purpose by providing an interactive computer program approach to obtaining information about the respondents' health endowments. Respondents are aware that the program output gives them information about their own health status, which is expected to sustain their interest and energy while at the same time providing information that will enable the contingent valuation questions to be tailored to their own life situations. Considerable thought has also been given to devising entertaining probability-teaching devices that can accomplish their task with a minimum of effort. The contingent valuation questions themselves are designed to capture the interest of respondents. Life-path situations are presented with the assistance of such devices as a type of roulette wheel that respondents manipulate and with various card game analogies with which many are familiar. Last, the incorporation of in-depth marketing-research interview techniques is recommended, in order to make the exercise as effective as possible.

Much work on morbidity has pertained to non-life-threatening diseases, including Part 2. At the other extreme, there have been many studies of mortality, as reflected in an extensive value of life literature. Serious illness has been relatively neglected. Only the cost of illness approach has given much attention to serious illness. As was brought out in Part 1, which concerned comparative analysis of approaches to valuing health, the cost of illness approach suffers from crucial conceptual problems, and at best it gives lower-bound estimates.

Serious illness involves valuation problems that combine pure morbidity effects and value of life and mortality effects. It might be thought that serious illness could involve only morbidity and not mortality. However, there are two important reasons why the valuation of serious illness must be concerned with both morbidity and mortality. First, most serious illness is life threatening. Increased risk of death becomes a cost of the illness along with more usually recognized morbidity effects such as medical expenditures, lost work, and discomfort. Second, serious illness affects the quality of life in an extreme way. The value of life is affected by the quality of life as well as its quantity. That is, the value of life depends on well-being during life as well as the number of years lived. The traditional value-of-life literature may be interpreted as pertaining to duration, or number of years of life, assuming cause of death does not affect the quality of life.

In this regard, the usual value-of-life approach to death from a disease like cancer, coming at the end of a lingering illness, understates the costs of cancer. Cancer reduces the number of years of life—which is taken account of by the traditional value-of-life approach—and it also reduces the quality of life while living—which is ignored in the traditional value-of-life approach.

Recognizing that serious illness involves both the quality and quantity of life leads to a reformulation where morbidity and mortality are considered in a common framework. One of the most important results of using this framework is to view values of serious illness in terms of trade-offs between the quantity and quality of life. Here we develop and apply this framework.

In addition to raising questions about the relationships between the quantity and quality of life, serious illness is more complicated than nonserious illness because risk is an important consideration. Perception of risk is a prerequisite to intelligent valuation of serious illness. Just as with death, the value attached to serious illness with certainty is different from the value attached to small changes in the probability of the illness, which in the aggregate mount up to the same number of deaths.

People's knowledge of risks and their abilities to verbalize their attitudes toward risks are notoriously difficult areas, which must be dealt with if the contingent valuation approach is to have hope of yielding reliable results. In addition to perception and knowledge about risks, issues arise concerning behavior in the face of risk. The degree of risk aversion will influence how greatly people value a reduction of the probability of the problem of a serious illness.

The present section draws on the three previous sections in devising a contingent valuation approach to serious illness. It first states why in-depth interview techniques are needed in the valuation of serious illness. Then the basic structure of a four-module interview approach is described. The four modules pertain to (1) health experience, (2) health costs, including defensive measures, (3) risk, and (4) contingent value questions. Next, it describes the four modules in detail. Finally the chapter draws implications from preliminary experimentation with the modules and makes recommendations for further work.

13.2. Rationale and Overview of the Four-Module Approach

Early focus group efforts indicated that respondents have great difficulty in a short interview in forming quantitative opinions on small-probability risks and heavy health damages outside their everyday experience. An in-depth four-module approach was therefore developed. The four-module approach establishes the basis for intensive interviewing for the study of life-threatening illness.

Health Experience

The first module, health experience, establishes the respondents' health endowment and health habits as part of the explanation of willingness to pay survey responses. It also helps respondents focus their attention on the subject of the survey and prepares them to give carefully thought-out answers.

Health Costs and Defensive Measures

The second module deals with the costs of maintaining health and treating illness. It considers defensive measures taken to promote health and avoid illness as well as expenditures to treat illness. Respondents are asked to recall the number of days of work and recreation that were lost because of illness and also the number of such days that were partially impaired by illness. Defensive measures include all behavior intended to avert risks to health and life. They comprise actions identifiable by market expenditures and also behavior that is costly to the individual in a nonmarket sense. Nonmarket preventive measures include both abstinence and health-producing activities that in part, at least, do not yield utility directly.

Measurement of these activities is part of the empirical framework for studying behavior toward risk. They are an important part of the behavior by which people reveal the values they place on improved life and health prospects.

Risk Perception and Risk Behavior

The third module, risk perception and risk behavior, gives the respondent an intuitive grasp of probability and discusses the importance of the concept in everyday life. Fundamentals of probability are discussed using everyday language supplemented by physical devices such as urns from which drawings illustrating randomness and chance are made. Following this grounding in probability, the respondents' attitudes toward risk and perceptions of the danger of various activities are explored. Respondents are asked how they attempt to keep risks down in their life at present. They are asked what they would do if exposed to greater or less risks than at present.

Contingent Valuation Questions

The fourth module pertains to the construction of the contingent market. The contingent valuation (CV) exercise provides the basic valuation data that permit estimation of the benefits of health risk reduction. The CV module has been designed in segments.

The first segment concerns mortality, for which alternative approaches to presentation have been developed. The first is the excess deaths approach, which pertains to the increases in death rates in various age groups because of some particular cause of death, such as cancer. The second is the life expectancy approach, which states the average age of death in the U.S. population and establishes contingent market programs that would increase life expectancy. Bar charts that illustrate the probability of living beyond age 50 with and without the program are introduced. The third method is the life shortening approach. This is similar to life expectancy, except that it can be presented without mention of probabilities. A bar chart illustrates the average remaining number of years at 5-year age intervals beginning at age 50. Program effects can be shown by changing the height of the bars. The last two methods devised to present mortality are a lottery wheel and a card game. The lottery wheel has a spinning arm with a pointer that comes to rest in a zone of the board that corresponds to a given life experience. Probabilities are clearly illustrated by the relative sizes of the zones or segments. The relative sizes of death/illness zones increases as age increases. The wheel is useful in conveying the probabilities of occurrence of many life-health situations. The card game involves the chance occurrence of drawing a card indicating that a sickness such as a heart attack will occur. The respondent is asked about willingness to pay to reduce the number of sickness cards in the deck.

In the second segment of the CV module, questions about several kinds of illness of varying degrees of seriousness are asked. Two types of contingent markets are utilized. In the first, a disease-specific approach is used in which disease is mentioned by name. In the second, a health attribute approach is used in which only the symptoms are mentioned.

In the next section of the CV module, several specific and explicitly depicted comparative life paths are presented, with symptoms and illnesses of varying severities and different life expectancies. Respondents are asked first to rank alternative life paths according to their preferences. A hypothetical life-path endowment is postulated, and willingness to pay and accept questions are asked, based on respondent rankings. The questions are constructed so as to reveal the strengths of preferences in choices involving severity of symptoms and length of life. These trade-offs are offered in terms of certainty prospects.

The following section explores how health valuations are affected by the existence of risk. The respondent is offered one life path with certainty and pairs of alternative life paths—one better and one worse—with various probabilities. Respondents are asked about their willingness to pay for the scenarios.

Willingness to pay questions are asked based on the life-path preferences. A base life-path endowment is established, and programs that would improve or prevent deterioration of the environment are offered. The program effects are linked to the life paths. Linkages are not established between dollar bids and probability statements. It would be possible in future work, however, to apply the contingent valuation structure to obtain statements of willingness to pay for risk reduction.

Based on the four-module formulation and focus group experience, refinement and development of alternative approaches for each of the modules was undertaken. The approaches are illustrated in the next four subsections. They provide the basis for possible future field work.

13.3. First Module: Health Experience

The first module, health experience, develops the information and preference context of the questionnaire. It serves two research purposes. The first is to focus the respondents' attention and research their references on the subject of the survey and prepare them to give carefully thought-out answers. The second purpose is to establish the respondents' health endowments and health habits as part of the explanation of willingness to pay responses to survey questions. The questions encourage the respondents to link health status to the behavior and activities of daily living. Their perceptions about psychological well-being and degree of control over personal health reinforce the connection between health and behavior, which will be important later in reflecting on the value of health preservation or improvement.

Obtaining detailed knowledge of respondents' experiences with specific kinds of life-threatening illness is an important part of the health appraisal framework. Detailed information about specific health problems of interest in the survey supplement the more general health status information obtained earlier. The empirical framework integrates mortality into the study of behavior toward risks to health and life. Some recent theoretical contributions have recognized that death has important endogenous elements in life-cycle choices, but the present study goes farther than others in empirically integrating mortality into the investigation of the value of risk reduction in a life-cycle context. It accomplishes this by making the prospective life path of the respondent the basis for the contingent market good. The following abridged set of health status questions was developed to meet these ends.

Self-assessment of health status:

1. In your own opinion, which one of the following best describes your current health status:
    1. Excellent
    2. Good
    3. Fair
    4. Poor

Belief concerning control over health:

2. Which one of the following best describes the control you have over your health?
    1. There is little I can do because it is beyond my control.
    2. I can do some things, but they have little effect.
    3. My actions have a moderate effect.
    4. My actions have a great effect.

Detailed questions on health status:

3. Are you unable to do certain kinds of amounts of work, housework, or schoolwork because of health?
    Yes___ No___
    If "yes" then go to 4.

4. Have you been unable to do this work for more than 3 months?
   Yes___ No___

5. Does health limit the kind of vigorous activities you can do, such as running, lifting heavy objects, or participating in strenuous sports?
   Yes___ No___
   If "yes" then go to 6.

6. Has health limited the kinds of vigorous activities you can do for more than 3 months?
   Yes___ No___

Questions about sick days:

7. What conditions (such as specific illness and injuries) caused you to stay in bed?

8. How many of the days that you lost from market work did you stay in bed all or most of the day?
   ___days

9. During the last year, how many days did you cut down for as much as a day?
   ___days
   What condition caused you to cut down?

General questions about health perceptions:

10.	Definitely true	Mostly true	Don't know	Mostly false	Definitely false
According to the health professionals, my health is now excellent	5	4	3	2	1
I try to avoid letting illness interfere with my life	5	4	3	2	1

Focus group experience indicated that respondents are willing to answer these questions. They served their intended purpose well but consumed too much time in a conventional interview context. For use in a half-day, in-depth interview, however, their use is feasible and deserves further consideration.

13.4. Second Module: Health Costs and Defensive Measures

Much of the material in this module is very similar to the modules on health costs and defensive measures already presented in Part 2. The earlier material will not be repeated here. In addition to the earlier material, defensive measures toward serious illness that have low probability risk are explored.

An illustration will be presented here of questions about willingness to undertake changes in lifestyle to reduce risk of serious illness. The illustration centers on diet.

> Referring again to cancer probabilities, imagine you were told by your physician that the cancer life path is what you had to look forward to—because of some condition he had just discovered. He offers you a program, however, which will give you a 50% chance of avoiding the cancer scenario and getting the health scenario instead. His terms are this: stop smoking, stop drinking, and immediately adopt a special diet (not shown here). Would you accept the doctor's program?
>
> Yes___ No___
>
> If yes: Are you confident that you would be able to adhere to these terms for the rest of your life?
>
> Very confident___
> Somewhat confident___
> Doubtful___
> Virtually no chance___
>
> If no: Suppose the doctor told you that you could be *certain* of improving your prospects to the health scenario. Would you accept the doctor's program?
>
> Yes___ No___
>
> If no: What is the most difficult part of the doctor's program for you? Rank them 1, 2, 3.
>
> Diet___
> Drinking___
> Smoking___
>
> If Diet: Would you accept the doctor's program if it only required the special diet?
>
> Yes___ No___
>
> If no: Would you accept the doctor's program if there were no dietary restrictions at all?
>
> If yes: Repeat above.
> If no: [Eliminate second most difficult part of doctor's program and repeat.]

Building on this illustration, iteration on defensive measures could be used as part of the contingent valuation modules considered below. Hypothetical future life experiences would be ranked from worst to most desirable. The respondent would then be endowed with the worst path and asked to bid for more desirable alternatives. Bidding would be in terms of defensive measures involving smoking, drinking, diet, and exercise. Iteration would be used to determine how much averting behavior would be tolerated in order to improve life prospects by various amounts. Some experimentation with uncertainty could be introduced by setting the probability of payoff equal to 50%. Respondents would be asked how confident they are of being able to stay on the various programs and which parts of the programs are the most difficult. The later responses would be used in further iterations by eliminating the most difficult parts of a rejected program and asking if it would then be an acceptable price to pay for a preferred life path.

The rest of this iterate-on-defensive-measures approach entails eliciting willingness to pay (WTP) in dollars for the programs, based on their careful thought about sacrifices made for measures they are already taking.

13.5. Third Module: Risk Perception and Risk Behavior

A major result of work with focus groups is recognition of the need to carefully educate respondents in the basic concepts of probability and risks. The procedures, whose principles are discussed in detail in Chapter 12, are necessary if respondents are to be able to respond intelligently about low-probability threats to life and health.

It is furthermore important to delve into people's general risk perceptions because they underlie judgments and choices in particular risky situations. The risk perceptions help to explain choices in contingent markets for health risk. Asking respondents to reflect on these attitudes brings them more clearly to mind, improving the quality of contingent valuation responses.

Examination of people's actions in various risky situations reveals attitudes toward risks, just as do their prior perceptions of risk. These risk attitudes, formed over long periods under innumerable influences, are important determinants of behavior toward health risks and are therefore likely to be important to analysis. Responding to risk behavior questions also helps prepare the respondent give well-considered contingent valuation answers.

It is thus apparent from the focus group experience that a major experimental effort is required to develop teaching devices that will permit the effective use of probabilistic contingent markets in health. Basic drills for teaching probability are not presented here. The defensive measures module contains some information on risk behavior that could be extended. Building on the present module, games have been devised using a lottery wheel and cards directly in contingent valuation questions, as will be reported.

The presentation in the present section is limited to questions on risk perception, which are as follows.

Risk perception, relative to past:

1. Relative to your parents' experience, the risks to health and safety you are faced with are:
    1. Much less
    2. Somewhat less

3. About the same
4. Somewhat greater
5. Much greater

General awareness and concern:

2. Risks to health and safety come from a variety of activities, substances, and technologies. Which causes the greatest, second greatest, and third greatest concern to you? (Put appropriate number in each box.)

1. Crime	9. Smoking
2. Swimming pools	10. Motor vehicles
3. Nuclear power	11. Food preservatives
4. Alcoholic beverages	12. Asbestos
5. Pesticides and herbicides	13. Water pollution
6. Home gas furnaces	14. Job risks
7. Air pollution	15. Other (specify) _____
8. Power lawn mowers	

[   ] Greatest concern
[   ] Second greatest concern
[   ] Third greatest concern

Ranking questions about causes of concern about risks and also about household production of health and safety:

3. Much has been said about various risks to health and safety. Using a scale of 1 to 10 going from least risky to most risky, enter the number you feel best describes the risk.

Crime	Swimming Pools	Nuclear Power	Alcholic Beverages	Pesticides and Herbicides	Home Gas Furnace	Air Pollution
[ ]	[ ]	[ ]	[ ]	[ ]	[ ]	[ ]

Power Lawn Mowers	Smoking	Motor Vehicles	Food Preservatives	Asbestos	Water Pollution	Job Risks
[ ]	[ ]	[ ]	[ ]	[ ]	[ ]	[ ]

4. To what extent are the risks known by people exposed to the risk? Use the following scale.

   risk level known precisely   1 2 3 4 5   risk level not known at all
   Knowledge   [   ]   (Enter the number 1, 2, 3, 4 or 5)

5. To what extent through your own actions can you control exposure to the risk? Use the following scale.

   exposure can't be controlled   exposure can be completely
   at all by individuals   1 2 3 4 5   controlled by individual
   Exposure control   [   ]   (Enter the number 1, 2, 3, 4 or 5)

6. To what extent can you by personal efforts and use of available resources control the outcome if you are exposed to risk? Use the following scale.

outcome can't be controlled   outcome can be completely
at all by individuals   1 2 3 4 5   controlled by individual
Consequence Control   [   ]   (Enter the number 1, 2, 3, 4 or 5)

This set of questions, while effective when used in a focus group session, would be too long for a door-to-door survey. Use of these questions in a half-day, in-depth interview setting would be effective, however.

13.6. Fourth Module: Contingent Valuation Questions

Mortality

Several methods of presenting mortality risks were developed and tested in focus groups. Five methods are reported here: excess deaths, life expectancy, life shortening, use of a lottery wheel, and use of a card game.

The willingness to pay questions used in this module would in practice be replaced by the iterative-bid approach developed in Chapter 7.

EXCESS DEATHS. The following sample illustrates the excess deaths approach—possibly the most easily understood idea of mortality risk:

We have all used the term "epidemic" to describe the outbreak of a disease. An epidemic is said to exist when more people develop an illness—measles, flu, for example—than is expected under normal conditions. Similarly, the term "excess deaths" can be used when more people die from a certain illness or condition than is normally the case. For example, suppose that on average, 1,000 people die every year in fires in the United States. If 5,000 people were to die this year in fires, those additional 4,000 deaths could be thought of as "excess," that is, more than could normally be expected to occur. Some scientists warn that pollution of the air and water cause excess deaths in the population today.

Q. How much would you be willing to pay to eliminate one excess death due to air pollution?

LIFE EXPECTANCY. Various approaches were tested to present the idea of life expectancy, changes in life expectancy, and people's willingness to pay to get improvement or avoid decline. One type of life expectancy question offered a rather elaborate contingent market to the respondent. The following example contains explanatory narrative that relates life expectancy to cancer and illustrates a life path for a person of age 50 by means of the bar charts.

Of all the possible consequences to human health arising from pollution problems, the threat of cancer may be the greatest source of concern. It is the only major cause of death which has continued to rise since 1900. It is difficult to determine how great a role pollution plays in causing cancer. People differ in age, place of residence, occupation, health status, diet, and lifestyle, and all of these factors together influence the probability of developing cancer.

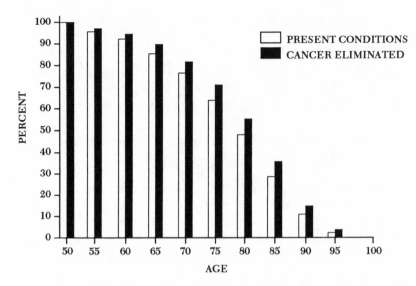

Figure 13.1. Probability of Survival with and without Threat of Cancer (for Life-Expectancy Question)

Please look at the first set of bars. [See Figure 13.1.] These bars illustrate the overall probability of a person surviving from the age of 50 to the ages shown. For example, the likelihood of living to age 80 is about 48%, to age 85, about 30%, and so on. (Of course, it is impossible to predict how and when a person will die; many factors will influence that event. The probabilities shown here are national averages.)

Now look at the second set of bars. They show the probabilities of surviving to advanced age but also the changes in the percentages if cancer were eliminated as a cause of death. Without cancer, the chances of living to be 80 or 85 would increase to 55% and 37%, respectively.

Suppose that it were possible to devise programs that would eliminate all cancer.

Q. How much would you be willing to pay for the programs?

Cropper stated in conversation that asking a person to value changes in life expectancy is somewhat ambiguous and does not necessarily measure what one wants to measure. Suppose D_j represents conditional probability of death at age j and $q_{j,t}$ represents the probability of surviving to the beginning of the jth year given that one is alive at age t. It follows that

$$q_{j,t} = (1 - D_{t+1}) \ldots (1 - D_{j-1}), \quad j \geq t. \tag{13.1}$$

Furthermore, life expectancy (LE) at age t can be show to be

$$LE_t = \sum^{T} q_{jt}. \tag{13.2}$$

Equation (13.2) indicates that a change in life expectancy is ambiguous in the sense that there are many sets of changes in the $q_{j,t}$'s consistent with a given change in life expectancy. Furthermore, it seems that what one wants to value is the D_j's. Cropper suggests that it might be better to ask people to value a change in the conditional probability of death at various ages.

LIFE SHORTENING. The life-shortening method of presenting mortality risks to respondents is similar to life expectancy except that it does not require a discussion of probabilities.

The absence of probability from the discussion makes this approach easier to understand than the life expectancy approach. Also it is possible to use one chart to illustrate remaining life for people in every age group. This makes it easy to tailor the question to the endowment of each individual respondent. The remoteness of the contingent market product for many respondents remains a problem, however. An example of the life shortening approach is as follows.

Consider how many more years you can expect to live once you reach the age of 50. Of course, you would hope to live as healthy and as long a life as is possible. Please look now at [Figure 13.2], which depicts in graphic form the national averages for remaining lifetime, expressed in years. Note for example that a 65-year-old can look forward to 16 more years, etc.

Q. How much would you be willing to pay for a program that would extend your life by 2 years?

LOTTERY WHEEL. The lottery wheel is the most graphic portrait of mortality experience developed so far. It is a device that involves the respondent

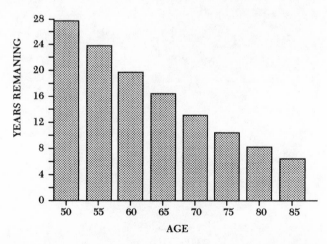

Figure 13.2. Remaining Years of Life at Various Ages (for Life-Shortening Question)

in an activity that builds up an idea of a person's risk of death under varying conditions.

The prototype wheel is 2 feet in diameter and consists of a wooden arm spinning on a skate board wheel bearing affixed to a sheet of plywood. Nails, equally spaced at the periphery, divide the circle into 90 segments. A piece of flexible plastic at the end of the arm hits the nails and provides Las Vegas–type noise and forces the arm to stop within a single segment (between two nails). Paper overlays depict a wide variety of pie charts that show age of death and health-disease distributions for different ages. The pie charts depict different size segments that correspond to different likelihoods of being in good health, having heart disease, and so on, at various ages. The pie charts are constructed to reflect the probability distribution for populations at 5-year intervals beginning at each decade of life. A sample is shown in Figure 13.3.

Contingent market goods were constructed for testing in focus groups by depicting the mortality expectation of a 50-year-old person with and without cancer risk. This is done by showing the actual expectations of the person in one ring of a pie chart and the calculated expectations of death with

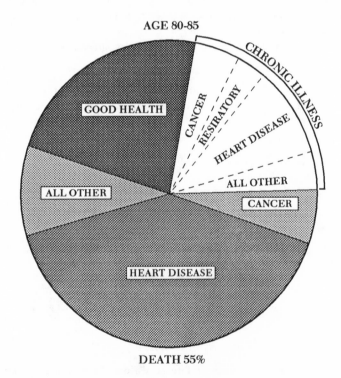

Figure 13.3.   Pie Chart for Mortality Lottery Wheel

cancer removed in another ring. Repeated spinning of the "wheel of death" gives the participant a sense of improved prospects in the absence of cancer. When the participant is adequately prepared, willingness to pay questions to get the without-cancer lottery are asked.

Testing of the lottery wheel in focus groups indicated that it has a great deal of promise for future use in both mortality and morbidity contingent-valuation work.

CARD GAME. As probabilities become smaller, the probabilities generally become more difficult for respondents to interpret. Some people, however, have acquired a sense of small probabilities in connection with work or leisure activities. People who play cards are examples of such people.

An example making a link between card games and probabilities encountered in health risks follows. Unexpected painless mortality from heart malfunction is a health risk that carries quantifiable probabilities for persons of given age, general health, and personal characteristics. A contingent market can be established by proposing a card game to persons in various risk categories, with hands dealt from a deck in which the probability of heart malfunction corresponds to the probability for people of their category. Respondents are then asked how much they would pay to reduce the number of heart malfunction cards in the deck.

Morbidity

Several different approaches were developed for posing contingent valuation questions on serious morbidity. The approaches are discussed in this section.

SPECIFIC DISEASE APPROACH. In the specific disease approach, diseases are named, allowing for the possibility for semantic effects in the valuation of risk reduction. A bronchitis question is illustrated in the following question.

Chronic bronchitis is an illness affecting about 3% of all adults in the United States. Bronchitis is an upper respiratory disease which causes coughing and chest pain. In addition to physical discomfort, many people with chronic bronchitis become discouraged and depressed about this illness. In addition to cigarette smoking, air pollution is a cause of chronic bronchitis, and it also aggravates the condition. Treatment of chronic bronchitis with medicine is helpful but tends to create side effects.

Q. How much would you be willing to pay per month to eliminate the risk of bronchitis?

Aside from the semantic effect of mentioning a specific disease, a problem in this question is the precise amount of risk that is being eliminated in the contingent market.

The following question, concerning cancer, combined illness with substantial risk of death. The death risk was presented implicitly to the respondent by revealing the overall experience in the U.S. population:

Chemicals in the environment, in the air, in water, and in some foods are believed to be significant causes of cancer in the United States. These cancers include cancers of the lung, kidney, and liver. Today about half of all cancer patients die of the disease, and about half survive. A great many cancer patients, both those who die and those who survive, have to undergo radiation, chemotherapy, or surgery, often in combination, which for many is a highly uncomfortable and emotionally trying experience.

Q. How much per month would you be willing to pay to eliminate the risk of getting cancer of the lung, kidney, liver, or some other organ?

General references to the experiences of the entire U.S. population are limited by the fact that they do not give respondents the kind of graphic description of illness that assists them in judging the value of removing or lowering the risks they face. The health attribute and life-path approaches, which follow, add the desired element of realism to the contingent market product.

HEALTH ATTRIBUTE APPROACH. The health attribute approach focuses entirely on the effects of diseases and avoids naming the underlying causes. Semantic effects can be tested by listing the symptoms caused by a disease in one survey and actually naming the disease in another, comparable survey. An example of the health attribute approach follows. In practice, the ranking and iterative bidding approach described in Chapter 7 would be used.

Physical discomfort effects of illnesses include coughing, pain with each breath, and other effects. I will ask about each effect separately. Each of these effects would continue for many years, unless the question says that is it for several months.

a. Frequent, persistent coughing $_____per month
b. Chronic throat irritation $_____per month
c. Gripping pain with each breath $_____per month
d. Itching and smarting of eyes $_____per month
e. Frequent nausea, feeling of need to vomit for $_____per month
   several days each week for several months
f. Whole body discomfort, feeling rotten all over for $_____per month
   several days each week for several months

It was discovered in focus group experiments that numerous questions in quick succession are not conducive to carefully considered answers. Instead, answers may become rather mechanical unless broken up with intervening discussion and preparatory thinking on the part of the respondent. This consideration limits the number of bids that can accurately be obtained.

Life-Path Approaches Combining Morbidity and Mortality

Life-path approaches represent a progression toward the creation of a realistic setting in which respondents can relate to health problems that are either current, possible in the next few years, or in the distant future. The approach is to construct several parallel life paths with a number of common elements and ask contingent valuation questions on each. Respondents who might not be able to value an isolated event such as dying 2 years earlier in 40 years may well be able to express a preference for one life path over another and assign dollar values to the preference.

Both morbidity and mortality considerations are embodied in the life-path scenarios. Consideration was given to measuring interactions between them and valuing trade-offs. Scenarios were developed in terms of certain alternatives and in terms of uncertainty, as will be described in this section.

CERTAINTY SCENARIOS. Table 13.1 shows three alternative life paths, characterized by either cancer, emphysema, or heart attack. They differ substantially in the overall quality and length of life that is offered. The example illustrates the certainty approach to life-path analysis.

Respondents are asked to rank the life paths in order of desirability and express a willingness to pay to avoid the less preferred life paths. Focus group experience indicates that this is a promising method of obtaining values. It imparts reality to the contingent market alternatives that are offered.

Possibilities exist to tailor the scenarios for special purposes. Distinct symptom modules form the life-path building blocks. A set of life paths can be built from the symptom sets and combined with different ages at death. The life paths can be ranked, and values expressed, relative to a base case path. The results could be used in policy analyses that detail the disease effects of illness by symptom and age of death more completely than at present, but they would also be usable in the present state-of-the-art policy evaluations.

UNCERTAINTY SCENARIOS. The following survey segment substituted probabilities of obtaining the life paths for the certain alternatives of the previous questionnaire. A simple probability display device was used to convey the idea of risks and help the respondent make probabilistic choices. This example illustrates the questionnaire approach:

Each of us faces an uncertain future concerning our health and length of life. Knowledge about health is increasing, however, and we are learning more about how we can influence our own prospects. Public health officials are learning more about how government policies can improve the health and life expectancy of the general population.

We are very interested in your views about the value of health improvements. I

TABLE 13.1.   Life-Path Scenarios

Age	Cancer Scenario	Emphysema Scenario	Heart Attack Scenario
50	Good health.	Good health.	Good health.
55		Symptoms (which probably began earlier) become apparent: loss of energy (e.g., climbing stairs tires you out; shortness of breath, difficulty in breathing). Breathing difficulties result in increasing work absences.	
60	Relative good health, but health becomes noticeably reduced from that at 50.	Symptoms become increasingly severe. Health deteriorates to the extent that early retirement is necessary.	Relative good health, but noticeably reduced from that at age 50.
65	Health reductions continue but with no serious illnesses. You continue to be able to do a full day's work, but you retire at age 65.	Lung deterioration reaches point where you intermittently must use a portable bottled oxygen supply to reduce breathing difficulties while walking.	Health reductions continue but with no serious illnesses. You continue able to do a full day's work, but retire at age 65.
70	Cancer symptoms become apparent, and chemotherapy is initiated. Side effects include nausea. You feel the need to vomit several days each week. There are periods of improved well being, but on other occasions you feel rotten for days at a time.	You become bedridden and require continuous bottled oxygen to reduce breathing difficulties.	Still no serious illnesses.

TABLE 13.1. (*continued*)

Age	Cancer Scenario	Emphysema Scenario	Heart Attack Scenario
74	Chemotherapy and side effects continue, but otherwise you lead a normal life.	Death due to heart failure.	
76	Cancer spreads throughout your body, and death occurs.		
78			Sudden and painless death occurs due to heart failure.

would like to ask you some questions about a matter of importance to people—how you feel about the uncertainties and risks to your future health.

The life-path scenarios presented above in Table 13.1 would then be combined with a probability analysis to see how much people would be willing to pay to reduce the risk of the more undesirable scenarios.

13.7. Implications and Further Work

The proposal for the in-depth four-module approach that has been developed in this chapter grew out of findings from focus group experiments. For example, early focus group work indicated that respondents had difficulty grappling with life-threatening illness in a short interview. It became apparent that a major experimental effort would be required to devise effective probabilistic contingent markets in health. Several experimental games were tested that may develop into useful approaches in future work.

Equally difficult was the task of getting respondents to think seriously about contingent payoffs defined far into the future. Younger respondents in particular found it was difficult to place any value on an extra year of life or health at age 70 or 75. Because some policy benefits are likely to be of this type, it will be particularly important to address the problem of deferred benefits in future work.

The role of the participant's own health endowment became the subject of thought during this early period. Two objectives became apparent. One was to have a standard, well-defined contingent product for which all respondents would bid. The second was to make the contingent market as realistic as possible by relating it to the respondent's own experience. This eliminates the need for the respondents to try to imagine having a hypothetical endowment and then imagine hypothetical departures from that endowment.

The first module of the four-module approach, health status, developed the methods required to establish the respondent's endowment, to tailor contingent market goods to the individual's own circumstances, and to start the respondent to think about health preferences that have usually not received much attention. The second module, defensive measures, investigates and records the activities that people take to avert illness or threats to life and health. These activities include health practices, changes in lifestyle, and also expenditures on market goods that contribute to health. Risk perception and risk behavior is the third module. Its purpose is to convey an understanding of probability that is adequate to understand and respond to questions that elicit the value of health improvements that are plausible results of environmental policy. The work of the first three modules is brought together in the fourth module, contingent valuation. Contingent market health products, realistically tailored to each respondent's health endowment, are formulated. Respondents are assisted in thinking carefully about the value that these health products would have in their lives and in expressing their willingness to pay for them. Program effects are presented in terms of alternatives that can be obtained with certainty and also as alternatives that will occur only with various stated probabilities.

Risk age, life-shortening, life expectancy, and lottery-of-life approaches are used in constructing life-path scenarios. Further research is necessary before the most effective approaches can be identified.

Life-path scenarios are promising. Methods and information for relating them to policy effects need to be developed. Even apart from the latency problem, a person faces a stream of altered life-path prospects from different points in the future depending on when the disease is contracted. The problem exists when the probability of contraction of disease is independent between time periods. It also exists when there is a latency period, which merely complicates slightly the estimation of probabilities of when the disease will be contracted. Future research needs to address two closely related concepts, as follows.

Level of Discrimination

Intuitively, one would expect that individuals could value some risk reductions more meaningfully than others. For example, the probability or risk of death could increase from almost zero to 1/6 (if one should choose to play Russian roulette), or it could increase from 1.1/1,000,000 to 1.8/1,000,000 (odds perhaps associated with an increase in an environmental trace concentration of some toxic substance). Somewhere between these extremes, an average respondent likely would lose the ability to discriminate between one risk and another. Future research would attempt to approximate this discrimination threshold.

Level of Complexity

There are other complexities in addition to discrimination that make it difficult to distinguish between and ultimately value one risk versus another. Pertinent information is helpful in this regard. Increased information beyond some point, however, has less value and eventually is counterproductive. Pertinent variables include (1) age specificity (present age and age of death), (2) disease specificity, (3) cause of death, (4) cause of the cause of death (risk factors such as alcohol, obesity, and air pollution), and (5) level of health or morbidity (physical status, level of disability).

Thus, at one extreme, a respondent might be given virtually no information prior to being asked to value a change in health or death risk. At the other end, very explicit life paths, tailored to the individual, could be provided. Future research should identify minimum information levels needed to obtain meaningful contingent valuations.

14

Future Directions for Health Value Research

George Tolley and Robert Fabian

Our inquiry into the value of human health and its place in people's larger system of preferences has encompassed diverse theoretical and empirical domains. Throughout, it has been an economic inquiry, and yet it has incorporated much from the medical and public health literatures. Our attempt has been to evaluate, integrate and develop the necessary concepts into a functioning body of knowledge. In this chapter we note several areas where further research would contribute to the measurement of health values. Chapter 13, on valuing serious illness, contains many suggestions for future contingent valuation work. These issues are not raised again here, but they are extended by several of the more general topics discussed in this chapter.

14.1. Defining the Units to Be Valued

Far from being mundane or obvious, the choice of units in which to express morbidity values raises important questions as to what form estimates of illness effects to be valued will take, and how these interact with information available to estimate values. Among the problems is how to arrive at averages in view of a number of underlying reasons for differences in values.

Context for Use of Morbidity Values

The need for morbidity values arises in conjunction with use of other kinds of information having largely to do with effects in physical terms. Ideally, the units in which the physical effects of illness are expressed would be straightforward and known beforehand. The approximate range of physical effects of various kinds would be known beforehand. Actually, the state of knowledge about physical morbidity effects is fragmentary to the point of being seriously incomplete in many cases. It cannot be foreseen unambiguously at the time morbidity values are prepared since new research continues to throw light on these effects. A major challenge in developing morbidity values is to make them usable in conjunction with highly imperfect and disparate physical health estimates that are subject to change and not prepared with valuation problems in mind.

Health Valuation and Clinical Outcomes

An expanding body of information is accumulating based on how health status is affected by clinical treatment, often using large samples. Critical analyses of clinical databases and their prospects are given by Rosati et al. (1982), Laszlo (1985), and Pryor et al. (1985). Information is obtained from physician's descriptions in technical terms of medical status of patients before and after treatment. Sometimes the information is obtained from questionnaires filled out by patients responding more generally in terms of pain and physical and social dysfunction. Some of this research is called *medical outcomes research*. Ellwood (1988) develops the idea of a comprehensive national database containing health-outcomes information understandable to patients. This database would contain patient-based information of the kind described in Stewart, Hays, and Ware (1988).

Health values research needs to be linked much more closely to the expanding information base described in the preceding paragraph. The problem is especially great for the physician-based information, which is technical and as a practical matter is likely to be too detailed for direct practical use in valuation. A virtually infinite number of conditions would have to be valued. Cooperation between physicians, economists, and health professionals is needed to categorize and simplify the technical physical descriptions into classifications that would then be used in willingness to pay and qualy studies attempting to value the outcomes.

The problem is in some ways simpler for the information on clinical outcomes obtained from patients since questionnaires on clinical outcomes use the same general approach to health status as has been used in willingness to pay and qualy research. Hence the challenge is to link up much more explicitly the questions asked in the two types of research, requiring cooperation between health outcomes researchers and health value researchers.

An important lesson from outcomes research for health value measurement is the possibility of standardizing questionnaires for various kinds of symptoms, diseases, and functional disabilities, using both willingness to pay and qualy formats. This would make it possible to quickly and efficiently adapt a format to obtain health values for specific health conditions as needed. Health values so obtained could become part of a widely available database. Replication of research results, modification of questionnaire strategies for obtaining information, cross-checking of suggestive patterns or anomalies, and reconceptualization of health valuation itself would be promoted by an administrative framework that encouraged the interchange of survey techniques, instruments, and results. Interpretability of results for comparative purposes would be an especially important benefit of institutionalized research sharing because researchers would come to be familiar with each others' work. Much of the painstaking labor necessary to formulate a health value research project could be reduced, and the body of reliable and interpretable health values would grow rapidly.

Health Valuation and the Environment

Still greater challenges are raised by environmental health research, where the physical outcomes cannot be measured so directly. Estimates of physical illness effects of environmental changes are obtained from relationships specifying physical health responses to doses of environmental change. A health valuation task is to develop morbidity values that will be usable in conjunction with results obtained from these dose-response relationships.

Environmental dose-response work sometimes relates death rates in general to environmental pollution levels, often without identifying specific diseases causing the increased death rates. Environmental pollution is an example of an area where health values play an important role in policy formulation. Examples of dose-response relationships that estimate incidence of symptoms are those where the responses are expressed as rough measures of functioning, commonly used in mass health surveys, such as work-loss days or restricted activity days. These measures share with other more refined symptom measures the need to value, not only work loss or restriction of activity, but also medical costs and pain and suffering. The valuation problems encountered in use of work-loss days and restricted activity days will be discussed later.

A feature of these incidence dose-response relationships is that they do not specify the severity of the disease or symptom. Morbidity valuation must grapple with what the average degree of severity is. The answer to this question is not available directly from an incidence dose-response relationship and requires bringing in additional information in order to specify the morbidity values to be used.

Severity measures are sometimes often only judgmental. Classifications such as light, average, or heavy degree of symptom may be used, in contrast to objective measurement in physiological terms. A challenge in morbidity valuation is to place values on imprecise, often subjective, measures of severity.

SYMPTOM DAYS. Usable dose-response relations divide into those that deal directly with symptoms and those that deal with named diseases. Correspondingly, morbidity valuation divides into a concern with valuing symptoms on the one hand or valuing cases of a named disease on the other hand.

Symptoms are sometimes expressed in terms of symptom days. Examples are coughs, tearing of eyes, and stuffed-up sinuses. A framework for valuing symptoms should, first, provide an estimate for an average day of the symptom. Second, the framework should allow for more refined estimation than may be available in those rarer cases where severity and other reasons for differences in value of a given type of symptom can be taken account of in a policy analysis.

In meeting either of the two needs noted in the preceding paragraph, attention must be given to reasons for differences in values. Estimation of differences in value attached to a symptom can be carried out reliably only if attention is actually given to differences in severity. The need is made all the greater by the fact that information about severity will remain far from ideal. The need for attention to reasons for differences in values extends to estimation of the value of an average symptom day since how dispersion is treated will affect the average.

We now turn to how the development of a usable set of morbidity values is affected by dispersion in symptom day values.

DIFFERENCES IN SEVERITY. Differences in the severity of symptoms constitute a first source of dispersion in values. Severity may be affected by degree of environmental change. For example, a small increase in ozone levels will cause mild headaches, while a large increase will cause severe headaches. Assumptions about severity of symptoms underlie any evaluation of morbidity.

Subjects of continuing investigation are the extent to which severity distinctions can be dealt with at all and, if severity is in fact considered, the extent to which degree of severity can be measured objectively as opposed to being treated largely on the basis of rough subjective measures. As already suggested, in many practical cases, judgmentally defined distinctions between light, average, and heavy severity of symptom may be the best that can be hoped for. An aim for many illnesses will be to estimate symptom values for this threefold judgmental classification, without going further into severity since dose-response work will not permit more greatly refined distinction.

SENSITIVE GROUPS WITHIN THE GENERAL POPULATION. One reason to be concerned with severity of symptoms is that health damages are increasingly recognized to be particularly important for sensitive groups. Sensitive groups include the old, the young, those already ill, and those prone to allergic reactions. In the future, dose-response relations for these groups, rather than just for a population as a whole, may become available. A hypothesis is that attention to sensitive populations will concentrate on estimating incidence and not severity of symptoms or diseases, but, in light of the probably greater severity with which sensitive populations are affected, some attention to severity may eventually be possible. Still, judgmental distinctions about severity rather than exact measures are likely to be the rule.

DURATION OF SYMPTOMS. Another issue, which like severity is of particular importance for sensitive groups, pertains to duration of symptoms. For symptoms of a given severity, duration affects value of a symptom day. An occasional day in which coughing is experienced among mostly cough-free days may have a different value from a day of exactly the same type that is added to an existing long string of coughing days. Differences in values estimated for those with and without preexisting conditions may provide some basis for taking account of effects of duration.

For most of the general population, changes in environmental quality due to a policy are likely to lead to only marginal changes in which preexisting symptoms at a zero or very low level are changed by a very small amount. One needs to value a small change and not be concerned further with duration. Sensitive groups, however, include those with preexisting conditions. They will value an extra day of symptoms more highly if there is increasing marginal disutility of days in a string of symptom days. Sensitive groups also include persons for whom a deterioration of environmental quality will trigger an allergic reaction, so that they go from zero or a low level of symptoms to a high level of symptoms even though the rest of the population is affected little.

PEOPLE DIFFERENCES MORE GENERALLY. Values may differ even for symptoms of a given severity and duration because of differences among people other than their susceptibility. Socioeconomic characteristics have been found to explain some variation in values people attach to symptoms. An even more important consideration is that values differ for reasons that cannot be easily observed. Values will be affected by specialized occupational considerations for which data are not readily available, such as being a singer, for whom respiratory symptoms pose severe problems, or engaging in a particular kind of physical activity greatly affected by a disease.

Finally, people differ in their attitudes and constitutional resilience toward pain and suffering. These differences will lead to dispersion in values even after every other reason for differences has been allowed for. One person will place an extremely high value on a symptom, while the same symptom makes relatively little difference to another person who otherwise appears identical.

The lower bound to a symptom value is zero for a person who does not care about the symptom, while the upper bound for a person who greatly minds pain can approach the entire amount of resources at his disposal. For this reason, the typical or modal value of a symptom may understate value when applied to population as a whole. The average value will be higher than the typical or modal value because of the existence of some very high values for people for whom pain and suffering is particularly important. Failure to take account of the asymmetry in the dispersion of morbidity values is a source of systematic underestimation of values when typical or modal values are used as average values.

Values per Case of Disease

Having discussed the morbidity valuation needed for results from dose-response relationships that are given in symptom terms, we turn now to results given in terms of number of cases of named disease, which will most often be used in connection with chronic rather than acute or short-term illness. Continuing the environmental policy example, a threefold classification of effects of pollutants on chronic disease is needed. First, pollutants may be responsible for the onset of a chronic disease, without resulting in death. Second, pollutants may aggravate existing chronic conditions, again without resulting in death. Third, pollutants may be responsible for the onset or aggravation of a chronic disease, with resultant death.

The first two effects are pure morbidity effects. The third effect combines morbidity and mortality. It involves morbidity associated with terminal illness, which has been neglected in valuation procedures. There has been a tendency to value pure morbidity on the one hand and to value pure mortality on the other hand, neglecting the fact that the illness preceding death is a component of the value attached to fatal illness. For example, death rates due to cancer may be calculated, to which are assigned dollar amounts from the value-of-life literature, which have been estimated without distinction as to cause of death. This procedure neglects morbidity leading up to death.

Because of high medical costs and large amounts of suffering associated with lingering painful diseases, morbidity leading up to death may be extremely large for some diseases, outweighing morbidity values for diseases that do not result in death. The various issues surrounding duration, severity, and averaging that were discussed in connection with symptom measurement apply as well to the three types of chronic morbidity effects.

Implications

These methodological issues connected with the units in which morbidity values are expressed need to be viewed in conjunction with the discussion of the varied symptom and disease effects discussed above in the section on choice of case studies. They bring home the importance of attention to the units problem in developing a morbidity value framework and carrying out research to estimate values. Symptom measures may be in terms of dichotomous distinctions—such as absence or presence of a symptom—and they may vary from subjective reporting of a symptom—such as fatigue, or pain in extremities, as from neuritis or neuralgia—to quantitatively monitored effects—such as synapse times or IQ. The symptom effect may be temporary (reversible) or permanent (irreversible). Information from dose-response relations may or may not give information about duration of temporary symptoms.

Morbidity valuation will have to supply supplemental information about average duration when it is not given. When severity of symptoms is not specified, an average severity must be estimated for purposes of morbidity valuation.

When dealing with named diseases, rather than symptoms, average values for a case of the disease must be estimated. Issues include the proportion of cases in which the disease is fatal, the duration of the disease in both fatal and nonfatal cases, and the severity of the disease. The growing literature on health outcomes research is helping to supply some of the missing information. See, for example, the conference volume edited by Lohr (1989), as well as Ellwood (1988), Stewart et al. (1988), and Greenfield (1989).

Explicit recognition of the issues surrounding the units of morbidity valuation is, in short, an important component of research design. The uncertainties surrounding the many averages that must be struck may make it imperative to develop ranges including high, low, and medium estimates. The factors underlying the ranges and how they are arrived at need to be spelled out.

14.2. Cost of Illness Estimates

Attempts to estimate morbidity values have taken account of some, but very seldom all, of the components of morbidity value that have been mentioned. The most voluminous work throwing light on morbidity values is the cost of illness literature, which has dealt mainly with observable medical outlays for treatment of illness, as well as earnings losses.

Strengths of the cost of illness approach include the existence of much data on the subject and the measurability of the costs in more objective terms than is possible for other components of morbidity value. Among the weaknesses are problems of the adequacy and comparability of the data. The major weakness is that the cost of illness approach measures at best only part of total morbidity value since the other components of morbidity value noted above are usually ignored or treated casually.

Even within its own relatively narrow framework, the cost of illness approach encounters a number of problems. The figures are not put on a per-case basis, as is required for use in connection with dose-response relations. Much of the work on cost of illness in the present volume was concerned with putting cost of illness estimates for respiratory and heart conditions on a per-case basis.

Other problems frequently pointed out include how to allocate common costs among different illness, use of prevalence versus incidence approach, nonuniform treatment of discounting to arrive at present values, allowance for unemployment, allowance for productivity growth, labor force participation assumptions, and valuation of nonmarket time, which is a particularly severe problem for the elderly and others not in the labor force.

A number of conceptual problems in the use of cost of illness estimates apparently have not yet been explored, even within the relatively narrow realm of estimating medical costs and forgone earnings. One issue pertains to the medical services and technology used in treatment. These affect the quality of treatment as well as costs of illness. The issue is complicated by the fact that the marginal cost curves are discontinuous or kinky because they are determined by availability of services.

For example, in a large urban center with a highly developed central hospital complex, a wide array of treatments and equipment may be available that are quite costly but that have substantial benefits to patients. In a rural area, however, traditional and less costly treatment may be used, partly because of lack of availability of alternatives. A result can be that the large urban center may appear to have much higher pay scales and the like for comparable medical personnel. The basic reason for this anomaly is that cost of illness measures ignore differences in the benefits of illness treatment. Morbidity value should take account of how the well-being of a patient is affected by the quality of medical treatment he or she receives while sick.

Differences over time in treatment techniques and between different areas make this problem important, particularly if use is to be made of bottom-up studies to be referred to below, which are conducted at widely different times in different places. The problem should be tractable if explicit attention is given to it, as suggested below.

Cost of illness investigations divide into top-down studies, which begin with national aggregate data and deal with allocation of costs to particular diseases, and bottom-up studies, which are case analyses of patients dealing in detail with their experiences. Top-down studies have the advantages of relying on secondary data, which can be relatively inexpensive to obtain, and of being comprehensive in their coverage. They suffer from inaccuracies associated with assumptions that must be made in using aggregate data. The forgone earnings estimates are particularly crude, either being based more on assumptions than actual estimates of effects on earnings, with only rough measures of work loss, or on number of days in which activity was not at full potential. Shifts to lower productivity work and occupational shifts are examples of earnings loss effects not captured.

Bottom-up studies have the advantage of reflecting the actual experience of people with illnesses. A very important advantage is that bottom-up studies sometimes contain information going beyond medical costs and forgone earnings to attempt to get at additional effects. The existence of a few attempts to deal with other effects denoted as psychological costs are noted by Hu and Sandifer in *Synthesis of Cost of Illness Methodology* (1981). At least in a fragmentary way, other cost of illness studies have dealt, albeit sometimes very crudely, with some of the additional components of morbidity value referred to above in discussing the conceptual foundations of benefit measurement. Bottom-up cost of illness studies and other follow-up studies of patients thus give hope of providing some information on components of value beyond medical costs and forgone earnings.

The bottom-up studies are more fragmentary and disparate in their methodology. Pertaining usually to small samples, they pose problems of generalizing of results. Nonetheless, they are one source of evidence that could be important to the study of health values.

14.3. Conceptual Foundations of Benefit Analysis

Basic theoretical models for morbidity and mortality valuation, incorporating previous conceptual results and extending them, were developed in the work reported in this volume. These models, with some further extensions, are needed.

The literature of the past few years has led toward professional agreement on a general approach to viewing benefits of morbidity reduction. The approach to benefits is derived from utility theory. It recognizes that a conceptual willingness to pay, leaving a person as well off without morbidity as with it, is the value which empirical research should try to estimate.

For some purposes, it is useful to follow this approach further and conceive of a demand for health, the marginal value of which depends on the amount of health. A change in environmental quality, for example, shifts the marginal cost of health and affects the difference between the sum of the marginal benefits and marginal costs of health. The change in this sum provides a measure of morbidity value associated with a change in environmental quality. Constancy of the marginal utility of income and possible shifts in the demand for health when costs change are issues that need to be recognized either as small enough in most cases to be considered second-order effects or as big enough in other cases to be allowed for in estimation. For example, for minor illnesses they may well be safely neglected, but for major illnesses ways to deal with the effects may need to be developed.

In any case, the benefit or morbidity value derived from the demand for health has a number of components. In addition to measurable medical costs and loss of earnings, the components include other effects on the individual that may be more difficult to measure—such as side effects and aftereffects extending to pain and stress—and consequences more remote in time—such as later disease due to lowered resistance, and psychological stress caused by divorce or bankruptcy.

In addition to all the effects mentioned in the preceding paragraph that ensue as a result of experiencing an illness, morbidity values include costs connected with the threat of illness even if it is not actually contracted. For example, a policy improvement that lowers the incidence of a disease or symptom will have benefits in addition to the reduction in effects when the illness is contracted, due to the reduced threat of the disease.

The morbidity values connected with the threat of illness are of at least two kinds. First, if people are risk averse, the reduced threat of the disease may be worth something to them even if they do not contract the disease. For example, benefits from Alzheimer's research discussed in Chapter 16 extend to people who have not contracted the disease because their dread of this possibility is reduced. This benefit accrues to all age groups and is probably large. Second, if the threat is reduced, actions people take to protect themselves from contracting the illness will be reduced. So-called averting behavior or avoidance costs become part of morbidity value.

Finally, as they are beginning to be recognized as needing much more emphasis, all of the above components of morbidity value pertain not only to the individual contracting the illness but also to others. Family members are affected by a person's illness for a variety of reasons, not the least of which is that they care about the well-being of the person. Also, the psychological toll on family caregivers to persons afflicted with Alzheimer's disease or other forms of mental illness can be very great. Value to others extends beyond the family to society at large. Charitable giving and other altruistic behavior are examples of the existence of values extending beyond the family.

There is no presumption that any of the several components of morbidity value that have been noted are more or less important than others or that some should be neglected because they are less tractable. Adequate comprehensive measures of morbidity value should attempt to include all the components.

14.4. Life-Cycle Considerations

Morbidity values for all symptoms and diseases can be expected to vary to some extent by age. Ideally, average morbidity values would take account the age composition of the population. Whether these refinements are warranted for nonserious short-term or acute morbidity should be considered, but age refinements may not be among the most important refinements for this type of morbidity.

For serious and chronic illness, in contrast, age may be such a crucial factor that it should receive much explicit attention. For example, for chronic irreversible conditions, such as nerve damage, the morbidity will affect the person for the rest of life. As a special case, the values attached to low birth weights and birth deformities require evaluation of an entire life stream of experiences with and without the effects with age at death being affected as well. Generally, morbidity values require estimating the difference in value attached to quality of life with and without a symptom for the remaining years of life.

A conceptual approach is required where utility is seen to be the sum of satisfactions over an entire remaining life span in an intertemporal setting. The morbidity value so calculated will depend heavily on age at which the health damage occurs.

The foundations for evaluating morbidity in this setting are provided by Sherwin Rosen, as exemplified in Chapter 11. Rosen's work provides a model of how value of life (mortality) varies with age. It is important to extend this framework to the valuation of morbidity. Questions are whether the value of a given type of irreversible illness rises or falls with age and by how much depending on various characteristics of the individual. A basis is provided for empirical estimation, as will be discussed in connection with proposed empirical approaches.

14.5. The Discount Rate

Research on the problem of discounting future benefits is another life-cycle consideration. It must take account the fact that health choices at both the individual and social levels involve commitments over long time horizons. Everyone makes personal decisions that affect their entire lifetime of health and, occasionally, the health of the following generation not yet born. Social choices—public health policy—must focus on the acute, immediate health problems of society, particularly its most needy members, and also on re-source commitments that will bear fruit only after some or all of society's present members are dead. What view individuals and society adopt—the long view or the short, or rather the balance that is struck between them—is one of the most important health decisions.

An adequate framework for analyzing the rate of time discount that underlies health decisions must incorporate these within- and between-generation conditions, and it involves questions of concern in economics not yet fully resolved. We turn now to a brief discussion of needs. We distin-guish three cases differing in weights given to people's preferences within a cohort, and within each case we consider four methods of intercohort weighting.

Lipscomb (1989) also utilizes a within-cohort/across-cohort frame ork.

However, he views the across-cohort problem largely as an equity problem and is concerned with using multiattribute utility functions to elicit time preferences for within-cohort analysis. The most important antecedent appears to be Cropper and Portney (1990), who also consider the distinction between within- and across-cohort discounting, and do so using a rigorous economic framework. Their discussion is in terms of intergenerational compensation, whereas our discussion goes into details of intergenerational welfare without assuming compensation. Neither Lipscomb nor Cropper and Portney make the distinctions between the three cases and four methods that we do.

Our case 1 weights the discount rates of all persons born at the same time equally. Each person carries equal weight when values are added up to the cohort level of health demand. Individual health preferences are an expression of each person's internal rate of time discount. Case 1 accepts these internal discount rates with equal weights for all members of society.

In the case of symptom or dysfunction avoidance over a number of years, the willingness to pay approach accepts people's internal discount rates. Strictly speaking, when estimates of willingness to pay for symptom reduction for a single year are aggregated to find values attached to a chronic condition that lasts for a number of years, the respondents' internal discount rate should also be used for consistency.

Case 1 distinguishes four methods of treating people who belong to different cohorts. It recognizes that people strike a balance between time periods in all their decisions and that health decisions would be distorted if they do not also reflect this balance. While maintaining this balance within cohorts, the first method is egalitarian between cohorts. Expressions of willingness to pay for health improvements from different cohorts of the population would count equally. Unborn cohorts receive the same benefits as those currently living, as they move through their life cycles. Their internal rates of discount would apply, but the benefits for any one cohort would not be discounted back to the present. Future cohorts are not discriminated against by applying a universal discount rate that gives them less weight than the most current cohort.

The second method allows for a less-than-certain probability that society will survive to future generations and discounts their benefits accordingly, at a rate that is lower than people use in their personal decisions.

The third method recognizes that knowledge spillovers from present to future generations make people born later wealthier. If everyone has the same utility function (perhaps a constant rate of risk aversion) and knowledge increases per-person income at a known rate (e.g., 2% per year), then it ought to be possible to calculate a discount rate that maximizes social welfare, which might either be above or below zero.

Method 4 makes the assumption of dynastic utility. In one variant of method 4, parents weight the utility of their descendents equally with their own. This is like case 1, in which all future generations in effect are treated as if they lived today. As another variant, an extremely altruistic current generation might consider their descendents' utility to be more important than their own. The most realistic variant is probably that the present generation gives future generations somewhat lower weight than their own. However, social policy might want to explicitly override the private valuations.

Case 2 accepts people's internal discount rate and assumes that everybody has the same utility function (probably constant relative risk aversion). Case 2 drops the assumption that people's valuations within a cohort are to be weighted equally, however, and weights the values according to the marginal utility of income to them, giving greater relative weights to the valuations of the poor than the rich, as in the optimal taxation literature. Concerning people belonging to different cohorts, the same four methods as described for Case 1 are applicable.

Case 3 drops the assumption that everyone's internal discount rate is to be accepted as revealed in their behavior. Poor people, for example, might discount the future excessively in making intertemporal decisions, when their behavior is compared to norms that are judged to better represent their interests. Downward adjustments in their discount rates would be called for. Another possibility is that the aggregate internal discount rate, as determined by cases 1 and 2, might be so low as to work against the interests of the poor, whose needs are for programs with near-term payoffs, in which event, case 3 would entail raising the within-cohort discount rate. The four methods for people belonging to different cohorts as in cases 1 and 2 are applicable in case 3.

Quantification of discount rates implied by the 12 situations (three cases × four methods) is needed, along with reasoned debate and compromise leading to a more coherent choice of discounting procedures to be used in health valuation.

14.6. The Statistical Value of Life

Currently available empirical estimations of the statistical value of life have played an important role in the health value estimates reported in this book. Because decisions regarding health are made in a life-cycle context, however, it is important to have value-of-life information that is age specific. In Chapters 14 and 15, for example, we rely on a study (Miller 1986) reported in Miller, Calhoun, and Arthur (1990) that derives an estimate from published research for persons whose average age is 38 years, with 39 years' average life expectancy. From this the authors derive the statistical value of a life year, which we use in a number of our estimates. The medical literature, however, reports illness profiles that begin at widely differing ages. In our work we have adjusted for normal life expectancy for these different ages, but we do not have the necessary information to adjust for likely variations in the statistical value of a life year. Estimation of value of life by age remains a challenging area of future economic research.

14.7. Reconciling Cost per Qualy and Willingness to Pay Criteria

Kaplan and Bush (1982) suggested the widely cited guideline for evaluating health-care programs reported in Table 6-1. Their criterion is reasonable cost per qualy, as judged by extensive experience in evaluating health care programs. In this book, we have applied a competing concept in the valuation of health programs—the value of a life year. This concept is equivalent in meaning to the value of a qualy measured in dollar terms. It is derived in turn from the value of a life, as discussed in Chapter 14. Based on the work of Moore and Viscusi (1988) and Miller, Calhoun, and Arthur (1990), we adopted a range of life-year values of $70,000, $120,000, and $175,000. Thus, if a medical program costs $120,000 per qualy, we would conclude, subject to some important caveats, that people are willing to pay enough for this program to justify it. The cost per qualy guideline, by contrast, would tend toward rejection of the program. Policies guided by the cost per qualy criterion tend to result in inadequate resources being devoted to the health sector, according to the value-of-life criterion. The problem is not an easy one to resolve. Raising the acceptable cost-per-qualy ranges would offend the experienced judgments of people in the public health community. Lowering the value of a life year would do some violence to a large body of careful economic research. Chances are there is a large amount of resources that fall within the zone of inconsistency. Hence, there is likely to be a large payoff to additional research in the area.

This work could take several directions. A first step might be to identify projects that fall within the disputed zone. Select, say, three fairly diverse projects within the zone that present varying analytical problems. Carefully conduct independent studies of qualy gains from the programs, on the one hand, and willingness to pay for program benefits, on the other hand. Carefully measure program costs in a manner that is compatible with the way the benefit accounts have been constructed. We now have three criteria for judging the project: cost per qualy, net present value based on willingness to pay, and the value-of-life-year evaluation based on the qualy measure and the exogenous value of life that is used. Comparative studies of this type would have important methodological value in addition to yielding useful health value information.

14.8. Risk

The more serious the illness, the more likely it is that risk will be a consideration in determining morbidity value.

Along lines suggested by Edna Loehman, who contributed to this passage, consider the state-dependent utility function $U(A;s)$, where A is full consumption defined as the composite of market and nonmarket goods affecting satisfaction, and where s is the state of wellness. Let c be morbidity cost, again defined in terms of the composite good and, hence, as noted earlier including pain and suffering. Wellness s is not known with certainty but instead has a probability distribution, which is shifted by exogenous factors such as environmental quality q. Morbidity cost c is not known with certainty either since it depends on the state of wellness and on other factors not completely foreseen even given the state of wellness.

Let the joint probability of c and s be denoted $f(c,s;q)$. Then expected utility is

$$EU = \iint U(A' - c; s)\, f(c,s;\, q)\, dc\, ds,$$

where A' is full income expressed in terms of the composite commodity available before payment of morbidity costs. Since we are free to choose the numeraire, let the units in which the composite good is measured be dollars. The value in terms of dollars of an increase in environmental quality from q to q' is the amount of money that would be given up so as to leave the person at the same level of well-being in the new state of environmental quality as the old. Denote this value as P, defined by

$$\iint U(A' - c; s)\, f(c,s;\, q)\, dc\, ds = \iint U(A' - c - P; s)\, f(c,s;\, q')\, dc\, ds.$$

In view of nonlinearity of the utility function, with diminishing marginal utility of the composite good leading to risk-averse behavior, P will be greater than the expected difference in morbidity costs c, where, as we have noted, c measures full costs in terms of the composite of market and nonmarket goods. The difference between P and the expected difference in morbidity costs is the extra risk cost of threat of illness due to risk aversion.

If there were actuarially fair insurance against all morbidity costs, then a person could pay for insurance that would leave him or her as well off in one state of health as another. The extra risk cost for threat of illness would not have to be paid. One would make an insurance premium payment when well that would decrease utility somewhat in the well state but, because of insurance coverage of morbidity costs, would leave him as well off when sick as when well. Besides eliminating risk cost, insurance premiums would provide a perfect measure of morbidity value.

Several implications related to risk and insurance need to be taken account of in estimating morbidity values. A first implication is that health insurance reduces morbidity costs by reducing the risk component of cost. A second implication is that, since normally at best only part of the market good component of morbidity costs (medical costs and possibly part of forgone earnings) are insurable, significant components of morbidity value remain uninsurable. As a result, for serious illness, large risk costs may still exist.

Principal-agent problems and other features of insurance in practice raise further implications. For example, a person who is insured has less incentive to economize on medical expenditures when sick since someone else is paying at that point. Thus, insurance may raise costs as measured in traditional cost of illness studies. The raising of costs is in part a genuine social cost, but looking at the costs alone neglects the benefits from the extra treatment. Risk and insurance have been grossly neglected in the estimation of morbidity values. They should receive careful attention in the conceptual formulations and empirical approaches of future research.

14.9. Averting Behavior

Increasing attention has been given to averting behavior, which involves the bearing of costs to avoid getting a disease or symptom. Taking account of averting behavior in an adequate way has remained elusive. The existence of averting behavior implies, for example, that damages measured from dose-response relationships may understate benefits of environmental improvement. In the extreme, if a disease is so terrible that it will be completely avoided, then a reduction in threat of the disease will have no effect whatsoever on incidence of the disease. The benefits of reducing the threat will take the form entirely of reduction in costs of averting behavior that no longer needs to be engaged in. More generally, the benefits of reduced probability of contracting a disease or symptom consist of reductions in the various components of morbidity value when sick, plus the reduction in costs of averting behavior.

Research efforts to measure costs of averting behavior have been hampered by need for more refined conceptual formulations and by lack of adequate data. Models of averting behavior frequently assume that people succeed in equating the marginal benefits and marginal costs of averting behavior. In econometric formulations of health production functions, where health is estimated to depend on environmental quality and measures of averting behavior, comparison of the marginal productivities of environmental quality are sometimes used to arrive at the averting behavior component of environmental benefits. In some studies, the assumed algebraic form of the health production governs the estimated relation between observed illness and averting costs.

Measures of averting behavior activities have included doctor visits, use of bottled water, and refraining from smoking, among others. These measures do not capture all or even the most important parts of averting behavior. Furthermore, the reasons that people engage in the measured activities may often have little or nothing to do with averting behavior motives.

One form of averting behavior is obtaining early diagnosis. The averting behavior takes the form not so much of routine checkups as it does visiting a doctor promptly in response to a symptom. The fact that most doctor visits are made for purposes of being treated for sickness rather than for getting checkups calls into question how to measure costs of early diagnosis. It is doubtful that people succeed in equating marginal costs and marginal benefits of an activity such as obtaining early diagnosis. People's responses to changes in marginal costs and marginal benefits of averting behavior—even if observable—are probably not very useful as benefit measures.

The early attempts that have been made to measure averting behavior are valiant and suggest efforts that indicate the formidable challenges posed by this area. Ground rules for further productive work on averting behavior may be suggested. Crude measures available in mass surveys are unlikely to provide usable measures of averting behavior. Models should not assume that people succeed exactly in attempts to equate marginal costs and benefits of averting behavior. Models that explicitly allow for lack of perfect knowledge may have more promise. Differences among people in the efficiency of obtaining knowledge and the bearing of costs to obtain knowledge about the costs and benefits of averting behavior should be recognized.

Averting behavior may need to be analyzed in conjunction with medical costs during sickness, which should be treated as an endogenous variable. For example, one hypothesis is that people who make low investments in averting behavior also tend to have lower medical costs when sick because they are less active in seeking effective treatment. Hypotheses of this type have implications for averaging of per-case morbidity values and relating them to various socioeconomic characteristics. They might also be of some help in estimating averting costs.

A frontal attack on averting behavior at the micro level, perhaps based on a case-study approach, may be needed to establish the order of magnitude of averting costs. Back-of-the-envelope calculations might then be possible, with attention to major differences in averting behavior between different types of illnesses. These could be used for order-of-magnitude adjustments to morbidity values.

14.10. Value to Others

Reductions in morbidity damages lead to values that extend beyond the individual physically affected to other persons. How far those values extend and their importance have hardly been explored at all. When a person is made better off physically, other family members will experience increased satisfaction due to love and dependence within the family. Friends and loved ones outside the family may experience similar benefits, but to a lesser degree. Further removed from the individual is the rest of society, consisting of people who do not know the individual personally. The existence of altruism as a general phenomenon suggests that these people too derive some benefits from a person is made better off.

Values within the Family

Theoretical efforts to understand interdependent utilities provide a basis for examining the benefits to others derived from health improvements experienced by an individual. In "A Theory of Social Interactions" (1974), Becker develops the idea of what he terms *social income,* defined as "the sum of a person's own income (his earnings, etc.) and the monetary value to him of the relevant characteristics of others, which I will call his social environment" (p. 1063). This idea is developed to explain behavior of family members or members of other social units in which interdependency is important. Becker's *A Treatise on the Family* (1980) extends the analysis and further provides a theoretical basis for examining value to others of an increase in the well-being of one individual.

A theoretical contribution by Cropper and Sussman, "Families and the Economics of Risks to Life" (1988) more specifically relates to a health effect, namely mortality. The paper examines the influence of dependents on willingness to pay for reduced risk of death. It extends the value-of-life literature, which recognizes that the distribution of consumption over time is important and that the dollar value of utility derived from life generally exceeds lifetime earnings. The value of life is assumed to depend on whether the family's consumption over time is important and that the dollar value of utility derived from life generally exceeds lifetime earnings. The value of life is assumed to depend on whether the family's consumption is higher when the person is alive or dead. This in turn depends on the availability of actuarially fair insurance and the extent of accumulated assets to finance postretirement consumption. The presence of fair insurance and accumulated assets are found to reduce the value attached to the person's life.

The Cropper and Sussman analysis deals only with effects on family consumption. To take account of love and altruism toward others in the family, the analysis would need to be extended to allow the utility of one individual to enter another person's utility function. This effect would allow the existence of family members to unambiguously raise the value of life, as seems intuitively plausible.

Values for Society at Large

Going beyond the family, the elimination of polio exemplifies values to society at large of a reduction in a health threat. Charitable giving for Easter Seals, the March of Dimes, the Kidney Foundation, and the numerous other health-oriented nonprofit organizations are concrete evidence that people at large care about the health of others.

In an empirical attempt to estimate value of health to others, our contingent valuation study of light symptoms included one question on this subject. People were, in fact, found on average to bid more for an improvement for everyone in the United States than for just themselves. The value attached to well-being of another need not be very large on a per-person basis for the total of value summing over people at large to give a very high addition to value, above the value a person himself experiences from his increase in health.

This discussion underscores the need to further develop the concepts required to analyze value to others and to devise different ways to get some idea of quantitative importance of value to others of an increase in health.

14.11. Conclusion

Health care has come to be increasingly recognized as a major economic problem. Most of the discussion, particularly what comes before the general public, has focused on cost, financing, and the delivery of services. Much less discussed, but essential to sound policy analysis, are the preferences and priorities among consumers of health services. The purpose of this book has been to advance our understanding of the demand side of the health policy problem. We have attempted to advance the theory of health demand measurement, assess existing methods of measuring health values, and provide a synthesis of health values from a variety of different sources, including our own research. While the analysis of health demand has been reasonably comprehensive, a number of areas needing further development have become evident along the way and have been discussed as research needs in this chapter. We hope that we have demonstrated that enough is known now to apply health values widely in policy and that much is to be gained by further efforts to improve estimates of health values.

PART FOUR

Policy

Overview of Part Four

Two concluding chapters provide the policy focus of the book. Chapter 15 presents state of the art health values. These values are a synthesis of our own research and other studies, including qualy values from the public health literature expressed in monetary terms. Chapter 16 discusses the use of health values in several important areas of public health policy.

Health values can pertain to mild transitory conditions, at one extreme, and to long-lasting, complex disabilities ending in premature death, at the other extreme. The Chapter 15 health value tables are organized according to increasing degree of complexity. The tables begin with morbidity symptom values, both mild and severe. They then take up morbidity dysfunction values that are described behaviorally. The tables then evaluate, in present value terms, conditions that last over periods of years. Finally, an application to a representative case of Alzheimer's disease is built up, which combines qualy values with disease descriptions from the medical literature. Health values are presented in a versatile framework that applies to many kinds of policy outcomes. The framework is flexible enough to accommodate new values as they become available.

Chapter 16 demonstrates that health values are important to a highly diverse set of health policy problems. Regulations affecting health and safety are a first policy area. For example, knowledge of health benefits of the Clean Air Act are of importance in view of the costs of compliance. Occupational Safety and Health Administration regulations and workers' compensation are responses to the problem of job safety to which a knowledge of health values can contribute.

Cost containment is the second policy area. Health values have an important role to play regardless of what national policy decisions are made concerning cost containment. Cost containment strategies for the pap smear test, mammography, coronary care units, bypass surgery, and cholesterol reduction are evaluated, where health values are used to augment knowledge about the cost effectiveness of these programs. Health maintenance organization cost containment experience is also evaluated using health values.

Medical research expenditures, the third policy area, are considered by

321

an application of health values to an illustrative evaluation to Alzheimer's research expenditures, drawing on the Alzheimer's analysis of the previous chapter.

Health values are used to estimate the benefits of programs directed at smoking and drinking as examples of the fourth policy area—public health policies that encourage better lifestyles.

Much economic analysis has been focused on the treatment of health problems by the legal system, the fifth policy area. Empirical knowledge of health values is essential in grappling with the problem of pain and suffering as a basis for legal claims. Efficient penalties for workplace hazards depend on this knowledge, as does the distinct but related question of equity.

Clinical practice is the sixth and last policy area we consider. Whether doctors should play an active role in the allocation of health care resources is a much-debated question. We argue that doctors do have an allocative responsibility, and health values provide doctors with useful background information that can help them in carrying out their responsibilities.

15

State-of-the-Art Health Values

George Tolley, Donald Kenkel, and Robert Fabian

15.1. Introduction

The strengths, weaknesses, and major results of the various approaches to solving the problem of valuing health effects are discussed in the earlier chapters of Part 1. A synthesis of these results, from studies that value different aspects of health and use different methodologies, is the goal of this chapter. As a result of the different methodologies used, the results will vary in terms of accuracy and in how complete a value estimate can be reached.

To organize the issues involved, a framework for value estimates is developed in Section 15.2. The framework describes what health effects it would be desirable to value, and what a complete value estimate would include. The goal is to develop a framework that can be augmented with data already available or likely to be available in the future. In practice, estimates of the health effects of a policy and the values of those effects must be made together. Value estimates will be meaningless unless they correspond to the range of health effects likely to result from plausible policy scenarios, and this problem is considered.

The capstone of this chapter is provided in remaining sections, which present a set of state-of-art health values suitable for use in policy analysis. Section 15.3 outlines the scope of health values presented in the chapter and describes the structure and progression of the tables.

Section 15.4 discusses estimates of the value placed on morbidity, specifically the value placed on relief from various symptoms, diseases, and conditions. Acute, short-term symptoms and diseases are included, as well as chronic, long-term health problems. Symptoms range from mild to severe and, in some cases, life threatening. A wide variety of theoretical and empirical approaches underlie the values reported in these tables.

Section 15.5 extends the estimates to consider the value of relief from health problems as they interfere with a person's ability to function mentally, physically, or socially. By placing the value of health in a broader context, the dysfunction value estimates in this section complement the morbidity value estimates of Section 15.4.

Section 15.6 is a discussion of mortality values. The concept itself requires a careful operational definition to make it useful and understandable.

This definition, supplied by existing economic theory, is applied in this part of the chapter to devise value estimates for various fatal illnesses and conditions. The difference between the symptoms of a serious illness and that illness, or a similar one, accompanied by death, is explored in this section.

Section 15.7 shows how the basic value estimates can be combined to extend the valuation approach to an even wider range of health conditions. This section places serious illness symptoms and conditions in a setting that spans a considerable portion of a person's life. The preceding estimates, by contrast, were daily or yearly values. The life-cycle conditions described in this section in part are constructed from symptoms and functional conditions already valued on a daily or yearly basis. This section is therefore an extension of the preceding analysis of serious illness. The concluding part of this section, pertaining to Alzheimer's disease, is the most detailed analysis of life-cycle values presented in this chapter. It provides the basis for a still more detailed treatment of that disease in a practical policy setting in Chapter 16.

Use of the state-of-art health values in the analysis of various policies is considered in Chapter 16.

15.2. A Framework for Valuing Health Effects

The empirical literature on health values for public policy, while in its early stage of development, has already addressed many policy-making requirements. Symptom-specific and disease-specific values have been estimated. Light-symptom values have been studied, as well as life-threatening health impairments. Single day, multiple day, yearly, and life-cycle values have been developed. Different levels and durations of health impairment have been studied. The importance of incorporating attitudes toward risk in measuring people's health values has been recognized and embodied in a number of studies.

The health values reported in this chapter comprise all the aspects of the empirical literature just outlined. The values we have chosen are based on the values derived earlier in this book, as well as values we have found readily adaptable from other literature, which are included because they allow a reasonably consistent picture when brought into an overall framework.

Two remaining reasons may be noted why the development of the values is justified. First, a reasonably large body of work already exists on the value of health. Since the studies often use different methodologies and do not always yield easily comparable values, this body of work is not accessible to many who are interested in policy. So one advantage of developing the set of values is that it makes the results of this body of work available for applied analysis. The second reason is that the development of values produces an initial point that can incorporate an expanding body of empirical data de-

TABLE 15.1. Framework for Health Values

Health Effects Valued	Value Reflects
Acute or short-term morbidity:	
Light symptoms	Physical and mental discomfort
Marginal change in time spent ill	Work time lost
	Other time lost
	Medical expenditures
	Costs of averting behavior
Aggravation of previously existing chronic morbidity:	
Chronic lung conditions	A larger degree of the above
Chronic heart conditions	Individual's health status is already low
Marginal and nonmarginal changes in time spent ill	
Other	
Increased incidence of nonfatal chronic morbidity:	
Chronic lung conditions	All of the above
Chronic heart conditions	Lifestyle and work changes due to
Cancer	existence of chronic illness
Other chronic morbidity	
Mortality:	
Unforeseen instant death	Mortality risks
Chronic lung conditions	Morbidity preceding mortality valued
Chronic heart conditions	as above
Cancer	Psychic costs of imminent death
Other death causes	

rived from a variety of sources and methodologies that will continue to become available.

The framework for valuing health effects discussed in this section is summarized in Table 15.1. The framework addresses two types of questions involved in forming a set of values for the health effects of any policy. First, for what types and ranges of health effects would we like to have values? Second, for the health effects we would like to value, what would constitute a complete and conceptually correct value estimate?

Other parts of this book contain a more complete discussion of the issues involved in answering these questions. What is involved in a complete value estimate was developed on a theoretical basis in Chapter 2. A preliminary investigation of valuing serious or life-threatening illness was the focus of Part 3. Table 15.1 and the discussion below is a less formal presentation of the main highlights of the theoretical analysis.

A conceptually correct estimate of the value of an improvement in health involves several steps. First, for morbidity, is an estimate of what an individual would be willing to pay for a change in his health status. Second is an estimate of what an individual would be willing to pay for a reduction in the risks of mortality. This latter estimate should reflect the value of the morbidity preceding mortality, as well as the value of the mortality risks alone.

There are several reasons why an individual would value a reduction in acute morbidity. First, there is the value of discomfort: the direct disutility of illness or symptoms, which in more severe cases might be termed pain and suffering. Second, there is the value of work time lost due to illness or symptoms. This can be measured directly as the value of the forgone earnings the individual actually incurs (allowing for the possibility of paid sick leave). Third, there is the value of other time lost, time devoted to housework, leisure time, and so on. Fourth, there are the direct costs of medical expenditures incurred because of the illness or symptoms. Finally, there are the costs of averting behavior, or preventive actions, taken to offset the impact of bad health.

For the value of chronic morbidity, all of the above components of the value of acute morbidity remain relevant. Of course, the discomfort may be more severe, and the forgone earnings, lost time, medical expenditures, and averting behavior may be more significant. In addition, there are special considerations required for chronic conditions. Since the condition may restrict activity and cause discomfort for a much longer period of time, the individual may be forced to make large changes in lifestyle and occupation. Certain strenuous leisure activities or occupations may not be possible. So even if work time or leisure time is not lost, the person with the condition may not earn as much or enjoy leisure as much. (The influence of chronic conditions on earnings has been explored by Crocker et al. [1979].)

Mortality values include the value of morbidity that precedes death as well as the amount individuals are willing to pay to avoid increased mortality risks. Valuing morbidity that precedes mortality involves the same considerations discussed in valuing chronic morbidity. Valuing mortality risks results in what has been termed the *value of a statistical life*.

To complete the framework, several further steps must be taken to estimate the value of health. First, the analysis must take into account the fact that health involves a high degree of uncertainty. Graham (1981) addresses the general problem of benefit-cost analysis under uncertainty and investigates how what an individual would pay for a change in risk may be related to what an individual would pay for a certain change. An expression for what an individual would be willing to pay for a change in health risks is derived in Chapter 2. However, in the discussion above of the value of morbidity, health is treated as a certain good, and the complete value measure developed corresponds to a standard consumer surplus measure under certainty. Most of the existing empirical work values certain changes, although some of the qualy-based value estimates reflect attitudes toward risk. In general, for small changes in the incidence of common illnesses or symptoms (e.g., coughing), treating uncertain changes as if they occur with certainty does not seem very misleading. At the other extreme, valuing mortality risks by the amount an individual would be willing to pay to avoid certain death is clearly inappropriate, and so the value of mortality risks, or the so-called value of a statistical life, is used. In between these extremes, the change involved if an individual develops a new chronic condition is probably large enough that recognition of the inherent uncertainty is necessary. The value of a change in risks of incurring a chronic condition is the subject of the contingent valuation studies by Viscusi, Magat, and Huber (1991) and Cropper and Krupnick (1992). Risk is also incorporated in some of the qualy-based estimates, namely those based on von Neuman–Morgenstern utility functions.

The framework developed above applies primarily to the values individuals place on their own health. The problem of the differences between individual and societal values is discussed in Chapter 3, and the contingent valuation results discussed in Part 2 are interpreted in light of the differences. A useful example of the differences between societal and individual perspectives on health problems is the recent study of the external costs of smoking and drinking (Manning et al. 1989). The social consumption equivalent approach developed by Arthur (1981) is a suggestive general approach. We have concentrated on individual valuations and recommend further analysis emphasizing values to close family members along the lines discussed in directions for future work in Chapter 14. Societal values may often need to be considered on a case-by-case basis according to the health intervention being considered. Individual valuations provide the starting point for societal valuation and involve fewer ambiguities.

15.3. Guide to the Health Value Tables

The health value tables giving state-of-the-art estimates are presented later in this chapter. In the present section, we give an overview of the ground to be covered and make some general comments on the sources of the values.

Table 15.2 presents values that people would be willing to pay to avoid acute short-term morbidity and nonfatal chronic morbidity from a number of symptoms. Values are for a day of symptoms or a year of symptoms as appropriate.

Table 15.3 presents a selection of value estimates of various dysfunctions. By dysfunction is meant inability to perform, as opposed to illness symptoms, such as pain, that cause disutility without interfering with function. The estimates of dysfunction values are based on qualy studies and willingness to pay values derived from them.

Table 15.4 gives mortality values by cause of death taking account of illness accompanying death. The values bring out the important conclusion that there are fates worse than death—the basis for comparison being unforeseen instant death.

Table 15.5 draws on earlier results to calculate present values at onset of disease for a prolonged period of illness, with and without shortening of life. Table 15.6 is a specialized application of present value estimates tailored to willingness to pay to avoid Alzheimer's disease. The values in Table 15.6 provide the basic building blocks from which aggregate benefits of a plausible national research policy can be estimated and compared with policy costs. The benefit analysis of Alzheimer's research policy, carried out in Chapter 16, is an application of this chapter's health values to one of the areas of policy interest described in Chapter 1.

The state-of-the-art estimates in the tables are based on the four empirical approaches to valuing health reviewed in Part 1: the cost of illness approach, the contingent valuation method, the health production approach, and the qualy approach. All values are expressed in terms of 1991 prices and have been updated from the original values reported in other chapters of this book, using the Department of Commerce deflator for personal consumption expenditures.

In judging the usefulness of the evidence presented in the tables, an important criterion is how complete the value estimates are in relation to the framework developed above. An incomplete value, no matter how precisely estimated, yields limited information on the true value of the health effect.

In general, the most complete estimates come from the contingent valuation studies because they represent direct elicitation of willingness to pay. The health production studies may yield estimates of the complete value of health, depending upon the specifics of the derivation. The cost of illness studies are always only partial measures of the value of health. Since the relationship between these partial values of health and the complete value is not systematic, the partial values provide only corroborative evidence.

As brought out in Chapter 6, the estimates based on quality-adjusted life years, or qualys, are like contingent valuation estimates in that they rely on subjective opinions voiced by respondents. While qualy-based estimates are complete, they may not be as accurate as the contingent valuation estimates because the approach does not directly elicit monetary willingness to pay values. In qualy studies, respondents are asked to evaluate the health states in utility terms rather than in terms of dollar values. Basically respondents are asked to rate the health condition on a zero-to-one scale, where one represents good health and zero represents death.

To bridge the gap between the qualy approach and the economic willingness to pay approach, we converted the qualy responses into dollar values. The dollar equivalent of a healthy year with a utility or qualy value of one is taken as the value of a life year. The dollar value of a life year, in turn, is derived from the value of a statistical life, an important and well-developed concept in applied welfare economics. As explained below, qualys are converted to willingness to pay values assuming the value of a life year is $120,000, in the medium case. With the dollar value of a life year in hand, we use qualy results by multiplying the utility or qualy loss by the value of a life year, scaled to the appropriate unit of time. For example, for a day with an earache the estimated medium willingness to pay reported in Table 15.2 is the qualy loss (.16) times the value of a life year, $120,000, divided by the number of days in a year, or $55.

The conversion of qualy estimates into willingness to pay estimates represents an important development in the valuation of health effects. Our medium value of a life year is the same as in Miller, Calhoun, and Arthur (1990), who precede us in the utilization of qualy values to obtain dollar measures of health values. Another useful study along these lines is Mauskopf and French (1989). Jones-Lee, in his study of nonfatal road injuries (1989), also provides a theoretical critique and some empirical applications of methods of converting qualys to health values very similar to what we do.

A crucial component of the conversion process is to estimate the value of a life year. Based on a value of a statistical life of approximately $2 million, Miller, Calhoun, and Arthur derive the value of a life year as $120,000, using a discount rate of 6 percent. The estimate is based on an average age of 38 with a life expectancy of 39 remaining years. The lowest value they consider used a 2% discount rate and gives a value of a life year of $70,000. Moore and Viscusi (1988), using a compensated wage differential approach, estimated the value of a life year to be $175,000. Ranges for qualy-based values in this chapter reflect ranges in the value of a life year resulting from the foregoing considerations, as well as the range on the value of a statistical life as discussed in the mortality section (Section 15.6).

15.4. Morbidity Values

This section presents details on the morbidity value table (Table 15.2). The table starts with acute or short-term morbidity and then proceeds to chronic conditions.

Acute Values

As reflected in the first part of Table 15.2, research on acute or short-term problems has produced estimates of the value of a day of a wide variety of symptoms, illnesses, and injuries. Each of the basic approaches to valuing health is represented in the list of values as well. Major sources are as follows. (1) The combination of the Paringer and Berk (1977) and Hodgson

TABLE 15.2. Acute and Chronic Symptom Values

Health Effect	Value Estimate for Acute or Short-Term Morbidity (in 1991 $/Day)		
	Low	Medium	High
Headache	25	65	145
Earache	30	55	75
Eye irritation	25	55	130
Sinus	25	45	80
Throat	10	35	55
Asthma	30	45	130
Mild food poisoning	50	80	120
Severe food poisoning	75	130	190
Severe rash	45	80	115

	Value Estimate for Chronic Morbidity (in Thousands of 1991 $/Year)		
	Low	Medium	High
Broken lower leg	2	5	15
Overweight for age and height	6	10	15
General tiredness, weakness or weight loss	9	15	22
Medium angina	8	14	20
Severe angina	20	35	50
Bronchitis	20	30	60
Blindness	25	45	65
Renal dialysis	35	60	90
Emphysema	25	50	150
Lung cancer	40	80	130
Partial paraplegia	35	60	90
Complete paraplegia	45	80	115
Quadriplegia	75	130	190
Severe brain damage	80	140	200

SOURCES.—See text.

and Kopstein (1984) studies provide a cost-of-illness value for an average respiratory illness. The value is expressed in terms of an average or restricted-activity day (RAD); see chapter 3 for details. (2) The original contingent valuation study described in Part 2 provides values for a day of a range of light symptoms. Based on the descriptions of a symptom day given as part of the contingent valuation experiment, these days are interpreted as average RADs. (3) Qualy studies, based on estimates of utilities, are an important source of values that can be converted to willingness to pay estimates. Qualy estimates by Kaplan et al. (1976) and Miller et al. (1990) are used for some of the acute and morbidity values. (4) The Loehman et al.

(1979) contingent valuation study provides values for mild and severe days of several combinations of light symptoms. (5) The Cropper (1981) health production study can be used to derive a value for a severe or work-loss day, in theory due to the actual experienced acute illness. (6) The studies by Gerking and Stanley (1986) and Dickie and Gerking (1991) give estimates based on the household production function approach. (7) Respiratory symptom values relying primarily on contingent valuation are reported by Portney and Mullahy (1986), Hall et al. (1989), Harrison and Nichols (1990), Thayer et al. (1990, 1991), and Harrison et al. (1992).

Several of the acute morbidity values in Table 15.2 place major reliance on contingent valuation studies, which have produced a range of results. The ranges reported in Table 15.2 are further influenced by studies based on other methods used as corroborative evidence. The values from the new study described in Part 2 are used as follows. The mean values based on the sample including all plausible nonprotest bids are used as medium estimates. Examination of the median values and other aspects of the distribution of values from the present study are also taken into consideration in the general process of forming the range of values. These considerations suggest that for our results the mean value is the most robust estimate of an average individual's willingness to pay.

Estimates from other contingent valuation studies mentioned in the above sources are used also. They are not exactly comparable, however, for several reasons. First, in terms of symptom severity, the average day valued in the present study may be somewhere between the mild days and the severe days valued in other studies. Second, values in several of the contingent valuation studies are for combinations of symptoms, none of which are exactly the same as what is valued here, though several are similar. Third, differences in the values stem in some cases from use of median values. In a random sample of the entire population, it is reasonable that some individuals will place very high values on their health. In standard benefit analysis, justified by the potential Pareto improvement criterion, all individuals' values should be given equal weight, even if the values are far above the average. If median values are used, however, the values of people with high values are implicitly given very little weight. So though reporting median bids avoids overstating values due to the effect of very high bids that may be inaccurate (i.e., not a true reflection of willingness to pay), legitimately high bids are also given little weight.

The median values from other studies are used principally in the development of the low range of estimates, though some weight is placed on these values in the (subjective) calculation of medium estimates. Some weight is also placed on the mean values from Loehman et al. (1981) and others that are much closer in magnitude to our estimates. The outlier prob-

lem of a few excessively high values indicates these means are overesti-
mates, so lesser weight is placed on them.

The medium values based on the above considerations for average days
of specific symptoms are as follows: sinus, $45; throat, $35; eye irritation,
$55; headache, $65; asthma, $45.

Regarding other acute morbidity values, Kaplan, Bush, and Berry (1979)
contribute several values based on their multiattribute utility function. Respondents were asked to evaluate the health states in utility terms, however,
rather than in terms of dollar values. Basically, they were asked to rate the
health condition on a zero-to-one scale, where one represented good health
and zero represented death. This is the qualy approach described in Chapter 6.

Qualys are converted to dollar values as explained earlier. For example,
for mild food poisoning the medium estimated willingness to pay per day is
the qualy loss 0.25 times the medium value of a life year, $120,000, divided
by the number of days in a year, or 0.25 times 120,000 divided by 365, which
equals about $80. The low estimate using $70,000 as the value of a life year
is about $50. The high estimate using $175,000 is $120.

Burning or itching rash on large parts of the body causes about $80 worth
of value loss per day in the medium case, applying our estimates of the value
of a life year to the qualy results of Kaplan, Bush, and Berry (1979). Using
the same procedure, the following symptom values in Table 15.2 are drawn
from Miller, Calhoun, and Arthur (1990): mild food poisoning, with medium value of about $80 per day; and severe food poisoning, about $130
per day.

Chronic Morbidity

Chronic morbidity values derived from Miller, Calhoun, and Arthur (1990)
include broken leg, with a medium loss of about $5,000 assuming 3 months
of impairment; blindness, with medium value loss of $45,000 per year;
and paraplegia, about $70,000 per year. Severe brain damage and com-
plete quadriplegia are fates worse than death, with annual losses of about
$140,000.

Kaplan, Bush, and Berry (1979) contribute several chronic morbidity values to Table 15.2, which we have derived in the same manner as described
above from their multiattribute utility function. These values include obesity, at $10,000 per year; pain, stiffness, and numbness, at $18,000 per year;
and tiredness, at $15,000 per year. Miller, Calhoun, and Arthur (1990) and
Viscusi, Magat, and Huber (1991), as well as judgmental considerations,
were used to derive the bronchitis value of $30,000 per year.

We found evidence on the value of angina in our contingent valuation
study. In this experiment, individuals who on the whole had little experience
with heart conditions were asked to value relief from additional days of

angina. For a day of mild angina, the means ranged from $90 to $130 (medium estimate $110), depending upon the endowment. For a day of severe angina, the means ranged from $160 to $370 (medium estimate $210).

These daily values appear to be generally consistent with qualy studies of angina. Torrance and Feeny (1989, table 1), in a survey of the qualy literature, report qualy losses of 0.1 for mild angina, 0.3 for moderate angina, and 0.5 for severe angina. These values are based on clinical judgement and imply value losses of $12,000–$60,000 per year, assuming a value of life year of $120,000. Miller, Calhoun, and Arthur (1990), evaluating several qualy studies of angina, select 0.12 as the qualy loss for medium angina and 0.3 as the loss for severe angina. Following Miller, Calhoun, and Arthur, we take $14,000 per year to be the value loss for medium angina and $35,000 per year for severe angina.

Regarding cancer, while it is difficult ex ante to distinguish conditions that will eventually be fatal from those that will not, it is useful analytically to first consider the value of the morbidity alone and then consider the morbidity that precedes mortality. Later, in the discussion of morbidity leading to death accompanying Table 15.4, we develop comprehensive measures of certain fatal diseases, which include consideration of the morbidity component of Table 15.2. This section focuses on valuing 1 year of a case of lung cancer.

Valuation of lung cancer in Table 15.2 is based largely on cost of illness estimates. Hartunian, Smart, and Thompson (1981) estimate that the first year of lung cancer involves almost $40,000 of medical expenditures and forgone earnings. From separate cost of illness studies (Paringer and Berk 1977; and Hodgson and Kopstein 1984) an average case of any cancer involve costs of almost $10,000. Since lung cancer is more serious and thus more costly than an average of all cancers (including a large number of relatively nonserious neoplasms of the skin), $40,000 seems reasonable.

Additional evidence that relief from cancer is highly valued is found in Jones-Lee, Hammerton, and Philips (1985). Given a choice of preventing 100 deaths from either cancer, heart disease, or motor vehicle accidents, most of Jones-Lee's survey respondents preferred to prevent the cancer deaths and were willing to pay correspondingly higher amounts do so on the average. The results also seem to imply that relief from the morbidity associated with even nonfatal cancer is valued highly. So doubling or even tripling the cost of illness estimate may be conservative. The values for a case of lung cancer are $40,000, low; $80,000, medium; and $130,000, high.

Comparing Acute and Chronic Values

The conceptual framework for valuing health effects summarized in Table 15.1 describes how the value of relief from an acute health problem will differ from the value of relief from a chronic problem. Looking at the value estimates from Table 15.2, it is now useful to compare empirically the acute and chronic values. The comparisons are relevant for valuing another class of health effects—aggravation of previously existing chronic morbidity. Air pollution is an example of a policy problem that may have its most significant impacts on those who already have certain chronic conditions. A change in air pollution could cause either a marginal change in time spent ill (e.g., 1 day) or possibly a nonmarginal change (e.g., a week or more).

By definition, a chronic health problem involves a longer time period of illness or disability than an acute problem; in Table 15.2 the chronic values are on a yearly basis while the acute values are on a daily basis. The average value of a day with a chronic condition is easily obtained from the estimates of the value of a year. The more difficult question is how the average value compares to the marginal value of relief from an acute health problem. If the average is greater than the marginal, the value of a year of chronic illness will be greater than 365 times the value of a day. If the marginal is greater than the average, the reverse will hold.

Given the differences in approaches and health conditions considered, it is probably not very useful to directly compare the value of a year to 365 times a roughly comparable daily value. However, results from several contingent valuation studies allow similar direct comparisons for chronic health conditions that last less than a year. The general pattern found is that, when respondents value a day of relief from an acute problem at, say, $30, they value 10 days of relief from a similar chronic problem at substantially below $300. This pattern, found in the original study described in Part 2 as well as in other studies reviewed in Chapter 4, suggests that the average value is less than the marginal. To reflect this observed empirical relationship, Brajer, Hall, and Rowe (1991) develop and use an adjustment factor to value multiple days of relief from air pollution symptoms based on estimates of the value of 1 day of relief. Use of the adjustment factor reduced their estimates of the total benefits of cleaner air.

However, the observed empirical relationship might be due to problems with the applications of the contingent valuation method. The exact change in health being valued in the contingent valuation studies has important implications for the relationship between average and marginal values. Suppose a person who is healthy 355 days out of the year values a day of relief at the margin at $30. Assuming diminishing marginal utility of health, when valuing a nonmarginal improvement in health, say 10 more days, the average will be less than the marginal. The average is based on the values of the 356th healthy day through the 365th healthy day, which are all below the $30 value placed on the 355th healthy day. But for a loss of health of 10 days, the average will exceed the marginal. The average in this case reflects the values of the 345th through 354th healthy day, which are all higher than $30, again based on the assumption of diminishing marginal utility of health.

When a sample of healthy individuals are asked in a contingent valuation study to value chronic illness, the change in health under consideration is often necessarily a loss. For instance, part of the study in Part 2 addressed the value of 30 days of symptoms, while the typical respondent's actual experience was only a few days of the symptoms. The typical respondent could not possibly gain an additional 30 healthy days a year. The survey instrument explicitly asked respondents to value 30 additional days of illness, beyond their own experience. For a typical respondent this is equivalent to asking them to assume their health endowment was about 330 days a year, rather than about 360. Whether the respondents could meaningfully value 30 additional healthy days given that endowment is questionable since it is outside of their actual experience.

More generally, because people are unfamiliar with chronic health problems, when responding to contingent valuation questions they may tend to underestimate the value of relief. Krupnick and Cropper (1992) directly explore this possibility. They compare the values of chronic lung disease reported by a group with no particular familiarity with the disease to the values reported by a group composed of relatives of persons with the disease. They find no evidence that willingness to trade off health risks (riskrisk trades) depends upon familiarity with the disease, but in risk-dollar trades, people who have a relative with chronic lung disease were willing to forgo more income to reduce the health risks. The contingent valuation studies that suggest the average value of a day with a chronic problem is below the marginal value of acute relief use a methodology closer to the risk-dollar approach of Krupnick and Cropper. (It is not exactly the same since these studies valued certain changes, not changes in risks.) This means it is possible that the reason the average is below the marginal is that the respondents were unfamiliar with the chronic condition.

The relationship between the average value of a day of a chronic health problem and the marginal value of day with an acute problem can not be resolved without additional research. While empirical evidence from several contingent valuation studies suggests the average is below the marginal, this may reflect healthy respondents' unfamiliarity with chronic problems. The same general effect may appear in the qualy-based studies, as well. It is probably extremely difficult for a person in good health to appreciate fully the implications of quadriplegia, for example.

An extra complication, and an extra reason additional research is needed, is that unfamiliarity with chronic conditions may lead to over-estimates instead of underestimates of the value of the health problem. It seems likely that the costs of a severe loss in health or functioning are particularly high in the short run. Over time, people learn to enjoy life despite their health loss. A person's health stock can be viewed as an important input into many household production processes that ultimately yield utility or satisfaction. Over time, people can learn to use substitute goods and services instead of health in household production. Habits, which can be analyzed using the model of rational addiction developed by Becker and Murphy (1988), play a similar role. Giving up a long-standing activity or lifestyle can involve large losses in the short run, but after the habit is broken the forgone activity will not be highly valued. So while life after a severe health loss or disability may be much different than before, in the longer run the overall loss in utility may be small. People unfamiliar with these aspects of life with a health loss or disability might tend to place an unrealistically high value on avoiding chronic health problems.

15.5. Dysfunction Values

The usefulness of health-value measurement can be extended by viewing health and health impairments in a social context. Disease and other causes of physical disability impair a person's ability to function in various ways. The health benefits of some public health programs can be evaluated most appropriately in terms of functional impairment. Alzheimer's disease research, to be considered in more detail here and in Chapter 16, is an example. Treatments that delay, ameliorate, or perhaps eventually even cure this disease are probably best viewed in terms of restored mental, physical, and social functioning. Other kinds of policies, such as air-pollution reduction, produce health effects best looked at in terms of symptom or disease reduction. Table 15.3, which follows the functional approach, thus complements the symptom- and disease-specific approach of Table 15.2.

The health values of Table 15.3 are qualy based, coming from studies by Kaplan, Bush, and Berry (1979), Drummond, Stoddart, and Torrance (1987), and others reviewed by Miller, Calhoun, and Arthur (1990). As described earlier, the first step in developing the qualy-based estimates is to measure utility on a zero to one scale, one representing health and zero death. (A fate worse than death has a utility-loss value greater than one.) In the next step, we converted utilities to yearly dollar estimates of willingness to pay to avoid dysfunction by applying the value-of-life-year estimates of $120,000 to the utility-loss estimates, as explained earlier.

The function framework is taken from Kaplan, Bush, and Berry (1979), with some additions. The Kaplan et al. results are in two additive parts— function level and symptom-problem complex. Three functions are described—mobility, physical activity, and social activity. In describing a utility or qualy level, a person is evaluated on each of these functional categories, which range from no dysfunction to severe dysfunction. Also in-

TABLE 15.3. Dysfunction Values

Function	Value Estimate (in Thousands of 1991 $/Year)		
	Low	Medium	High
Mobility:			
Can't drive; need help to use bus or train	10	17	25
Physical activity:			
Walk with physical limitations	5	8	12
Social activity:			
Do work, school, or housework but other activities are limited	4	7	10
Do limited work, school, or housework	5	9	13
Cognitive functioning:			
Trouble learning, remembering, or thinking clearly	24	41	60
Retardation:			
Needs special education	14	24	35
Severe work limitation	35	60	88
Need help in self-care	42	72	105
Very severe retardation	56	96	140
Physical, emotional, social limitations:			
Physical limitations (needs help getting around house, community; can do personal care; some limitations on work, play, and going to school); socially and emotionally okay	42	73	106
Severe physical limitations (same as above but unable to work, play, go to school); socially and emotionally okay	53	90	131
Severe physical limitations, emotionally okay, but socially has few friends and contacts	70	120	176
No physical limitations, but emotionally anxious and depressed; socially has few friends and contacts	23	40	58
Severe physical limitations, emotionally anxious and depressed; socially has few friends and contacts	76	130	190

SOURCE.—See the text.

cluded in the person's qualy rating is a score on the symptom-problem complex scale. This ranges from no symptoms through a variety of more or less severe symptoms.

Several additional functional categories are included in Table 15.3. These are mobility, activity, cognitive functioning and physical, emotional, and social state. These categories overlap those of Kaplan et al. and were created to accommodate other health states derived from Drummond et al. and Miller et al.

The Kaplan et al. results permit evaluating a variety of health states by combining their components in various ways. We have chosen to evaluate individual functional components from Kaplan et al. by holding other component values constant. For example, by examining two different mobility values while holding the other components constant, we get a utility or qualy value for a change in the mobility state. Further, by starting with the highest mobility state, no mobility dysfunction, and equalizing the other function levels, we can interpret the mobility change in terms of the lower mobility function value. For example, the first Table 15.3 entry, "can't drive; need help to use bus or train," entails a utility loss of 0.14 compared to unrestricted mobility. The dollar value loss corresponding to this utility state is $17,000 per year.

Table 15.3 values are selective in representing the values that can be derived from the utility functions. Nevertheless, a number of patterns can be observed. Relatively modest degrees of mobility and activity limitation in the top of the table produce value losses in the range of $7,000–$17,000 annually. As physical functioning becomes more restricted, however, and ability to function in the community declines, we get a valuable glimpse of the extent to which disvalues mount. Important physical limitations with some social limitations cause disvalues to mount to $73,000 per year. Adding still more severe physical limitations raises disvalues to $90,000 per year. Inability to perform self-care is a major additional impediment, reducing utility to zero. The annual disvalue is $120,000.

Anxiety and depression accompanied by few friends and contacts is estimated to have an annual disvalue of $40,000. Combined with severest physical limitations, it results in annual disvalues of $130,000, a fate slightly worse than death.

Cognitive losses produce relatively large disvalues in Table 15.3. From Kaplan, Bush, and Berry (1979), trouble learning, remembering, or thinking clearly produces annual losses of $40,000, about the same as the depression disvalue from Drummond, Stoddard, and Torrance (1987). Retardation disvalues from Miller, Calhoun, and Arthur (1990) progress very steeply, from $24,000 per year for relatively mild retardation to $96,000 per year for very severe retardation. The Miller et al. retardation variable "severe work limitation" causes annual losses estimated at $60,000, while "need help with self care" raises the annual disvalue to $72,000. This compares with a category from the Drummond et al. with utility loss of 0.5, or $60,000, conservatively assuming no other dysfunction losses.

Table 15.3, while highly selective, deals with a wide variety of functional disabilities of interest in policy. The correspondingly wide range of losses in value is to be expected. The quantitative estimates provided here may serve to reduce the uncertainty about the size of that range. Equally important, these estimates contribute to a foundation for lifetime values, taken up in Table 15.6 and discussed in Chapter 16.

15.6. Mortality

Table 15.5 presents estimates of the value of mortality risks. Valuing mortality risks involves two steps. First, the value of pure mortality risks is estimated. This corresponds to the value of an unforeseen instant death often estimated in the value-of-life literature, with no significant morbidity preceding the death. The second step is to value different causes of death differently, to reflect the differences in the morbidity preceding mortality.

A number of revealed-preference studies, based on hedonic analysis of labor markets or analysis of consumption activities, and contingent valuation studies estimate the value of more or less pure mortality risks (Viscusi 1986) or the value of an unforeseen instant death (in a statistical sense). These estimates are reviewed by Blomquist (1982), Violette and Chestnut (1983), Jones-Lee (1989), Fisher, Chestnut, and Violette (1989) and Miller, Calhoun, and Arthur (1990). In terms of 1991 values, these reviews suggest a range from several hundred thousand dollars per statistical life to estimates of over five million dollars. Jones-Lee (1989) finds an overall mean of the

TABLE 15.4.   Ratings of Serious Conditions

A. By Cause of Death		
Cause of Death	% Ranking Disutility Highest	Mean Willingness to Pay for Reduction (in Millions of £)*
Motor accidents	11	7.53
Heart disease	13	13.23
Cancer	76	23.12

B. By Type of Injury (Rating by %)			
Type of Injury	Not as Bad as Death	As Bad as Death	Worse than Death
Lose an eye	92.1	5.0	2.8
Badly scarred for life, and in a hospital for a year	87.5	7.7	4.7
Confined to a wheelchair for the rest of your life	48.6	27.7	23.8
Permanently bedridden	36.7	33.4	30.0

SOURCE.—See the text.

*The value is a single payment to reduce the number of deaths from these causes by 100 next year; it is not a value of statistical life.

revealed preference studies of $2.06 million and an overall mean of the contingent valuation studies of $2.35 million. Support for a value of around $2 million also is found in the Gegax et al. (1987) study that incorporates both wage-hedonic analysis and contingent valuation and is also close to the value used by Miller, Calhoun, and Arthur (1990). Weighing these considerations, the medium value (1991$) for an unforeseen instant death reported in Table 15.5 is $2 million. The low and high values are $1 million and $5 million.

An approach to placing a value on mortality from specific illnesses is to make calculations similar to the prevalence-based approach to estimating costs of illness. The calculations are based on the fact that every current death due to a condition is associated with a much larger prevalence of cases that eventually will be fatal. Suppose, for instance, that the average life expectancy with a certain condition is 10 years. If the mortality rate in the population has not changed in recent years, then a steady-state relationship will have been reached, and for every death from the condition there will be 10 person years of morbidity preceding mortality. If a policy intervention reduces the number of new cases by, say, 100 per year, then for the first few years morbidity will fall without a corresponding fall in mortality. Eventually, however, a steady state will be reached in which 100 lives per year will be saved by the interventions as well as 1,000 person years of morbidity.

To develop a low value for avoiding a death preceded by morbidity, the values of the years of morbidity are added to the low value for an unforeseen instant death. The yearly morbidity values used are the medium estimates developed for valuing nonfatal chronic conditions. These are conservative values for the value of morbidity preceding mortality since eventually fatal conditions are more serious and thus more costly than nonfatal conditions. In addition, no allowance is made for the psychic costs of death from dread diseases.

In developing the medium and high values, the low values are used as a starting point. However, we include estimates of the dread aspects of morbidity preceding mortality. Results reported by Jones-Lee, Hammerton, and Philips (1985) provide evidence on the values of deaths from cancer, heart disease, and unforeseen instant death (specifically, from motor vehicle accidents, which are assumed to be instant). See Table 15.4. Given a choice of preventing 100 deaths from either cancer, heart disease, or motor vehicle accidents, most respondents preferred to prevent the cancer deaths. The different values can be quantified to some extent by examining the amounts people were willing to pay to prevent the 100 deaths from the different causes. While the question is not worded so as to elicit the value of a statistical life, the amounts should indicate the relative values for the three causes. The means of the responses indicate that preventing 100 deaths from heart disease may be worth almost twice as much as preventing

100 instant deaths. Preventing 100 cancer deaths is valued at about three times the value of 100 instant deaths. Taken literally, this suggests that doubling or even tripling the value of an instant death may approximate the value of a death from cancer or heart disease. In contrast, the duration of healthy years of life is generally greater than the duration of sickness preceding death. In any case, as Jones-Lee et al. conclude, the results suggest that people "would be willing to pay very substantial sums to avoid the protracted period of physical and psychological pain prior to cancer death" (p. 68).

The qualy-based estimates and additional findings from Jones-Lee, Hammerton, and Philips (1985) also imply that many people see some forms of disability as fates worse than death. One question related to the seriousness of different types of injury, from losing an eye to being confined to a wheelchair for life or being permanently bedridden. Since the study focused on motor vehicle safety, the injuries described are not specifically relevant for some policies. However, as many chronic conditions get progressively worse (ending in death), they generally involve periods of severe limitations of activity, possibly to the point of confinement to bed. How people rate being confined to a wheelchair for life or being permanently bedridden in the Jones-Lee et al. survey is therefore relevant to the morbidity preceding mortality associated with, for example, lung cancer, emphysema, and heart disease. Jones-Lee et al. found that about one-half of the sample of about 1,000 individuals felt that being confined to a wheelchair was as bad or worse than death. Over one-half felt that being permanently bedridden was as bad or worse than death, with almost one-third (30%) ranking it worse than death.

For outcomes viewed as at least as bad as death, it seems reasonable that an individual would be willing to pay the value that would be paid to avoid unforeseen instant death plus the number of years of illness preceding death times the value of a life year. This approach may be applicable to a death from cancer. The value of a death from heart disease, possibly involving a smaller but still significant degree of restriction of activity, should also be valued a great deal higher than an instant death. A death from bronchitis may involve less restriction of activity, but the duration of illness may be prolonged. Due to less dread associated with bronchitis, its medium and high values are not raised as much as for heart disease and cancer.

The medium and high values for a death from bronchitis, heart disease, and cancer are based on the value of a similar nonfatal condition and the evidence from Jones-Lee, Hammerton, and Philips (1985) suggesting how the value of an instant death may relate to the value of a death preceded by a prolonged period of morbidity. The low values are prepared as described above, using a prevalence-based approach. The low, medium, and high values are, respectively, a death from bronchitis, at $1.3 million, $2.5 million, and $5.5 million; a death from heart disease, at $1.25 million, $2.75 million, and $6 million; and a death from cancer, at $1.5 million, $4 million, and $9.5 million.

15.7. How to Combine Values

Some policy applications require estimates of the lifetime values of health states rather than daily or yearly values of specific conditions. Table 15.5 fills some of this need by presenting values of pure mortality and mortality preceded by various severe health conditions. In other applications, it is useful to explicitly separate severe conditions that involve no shortening of life from those that contain life shortening as part of their utility loss. We now present examples of some of the ways the value estimates from earlier tables can be combined. Unless otherwise noted, values in this table are derived from Miller, Calhoun, and Arthur (1990) and pertain to a 38-year-old person with 39 years of life expectancy.

The lifetime cost of a severe condition with no life shortening can be calculated as the discounted present value of the stream of annual costs. The correct rate at which future benefits and costs should be discounted remains a difficult issue to resolve, particularly in the context of health risks (Gramlich 1990; Cropper, Aydede, and Portney 1992). Using a fairly standard discount rate of 6%, taking the yearly value loss from blindness to be $45,000 from Table 15.2, the lifetime value loss is $650,000 for a 38-year-old with 39 years of life expectancy. Partial paraplegia, with an annual utility loss of 0.65, causes a lifetime value of about $900,000. For angina with an onset at age 55, the lifetime value is $180,000 for a mild case and $450,000 for a severe case. These are developed using the annual values of $14,000 (medium case) and $35,000 (severe case), reported in Table 15.2. Utility losses and the associated willingness to pay for relief from a given health problem are likely to vary depending on age at which they occur. Documen-

TABLE 15.5. Mortality Values by Cause of Death

Category (per Statistical Life)	Value Estimates (in Million $)		
	Low	Medium	High
Unforeseen instant death	1	2	5
Asthma/bronchitis	1.3	2.5	5.5
Heart disease	1.25	2.75	6
Emphysema	1.4	3.5	9
Lung cancer	1.5	4	9.5

SOURCES.—See the text.

tation of this dependency is not common, and more attention should be devoted to the problem.

Instead of building up the lifetime value from annual values, two studies use the contingent valuation method to directly place a value on a lifetime of chronic bronchitis (Viscusi, Magat, and Huber 1991; Krupnick and Cropper 1992). These studies are discussed in more detail in Chapter 4. The studies determine people's willingness to pay to reduce the risks of chronic bronchitis, and the results can be summarized as the value of a statistical case of chronic bronchitis. The estimates are generally comparable to the lifetime values built up from annual values, whose range is from $400,000 to $1,000,000.

The lifetime value of life-shortening maladies can be calculated as the present value of lost life years plus the present value of qualys lost during life. Calculations imply that complete paraplegia accompanied by a 15-year reduction of life has a value-loss estimate of $1,300,000. Complete quadriplegia that shortens life by 22 years causes an estimated value loss of $1.9 million. The underlying utility loss is 1.09 each year, and the value loss would be higher without premature death. In the case of severe brain damage, a yearly utility loss of 1.16 accompanied by a 5-year reduction of life leads to a value loss of $2 million. Severe burns occurring to a 60-year-old causes an estimated utility loss of 1.35 each year and a 5-year shortening of expected life span. The medium estimated value loss is $1,800,000. Life-cycle retardation values, based on yearly values in Table 15.3, progress steeply from $400,000 (needs special education) to $1,400,000 (very severely retarded).

Table 15.6 combines lifetime value estimates for health states associated with Alzheimer's disease. This presents a more extended example of combining values and is organized to be the starting point of a specific research task—a benefit analysis of returns to research on Alzheimer's disease. This work is reported in Chapter 16.

The framework is based on the analysis of the temporal course of the disease described in DeJong, Osterlund, and Roy (1989) and Reisberg et al. (1989). Reisberg et al. describe the disease's progression in terms of a global deterioration scale (GDS) that has seven clinically differentiable stages, ranging from no subjective complaints of memory deficit to severe cognitive and functional decline (pp. 24–25). Following DeJong et al. (p. 549), we have combined the GDS stages into three levels—early, middle, and late. The durations of these levels are taken from figure 1 of Reisberg et al. (p. 34). In Table 15.6, the early level has a duration of 7 years; the middle stage lasts for 3.5 years, and the late stage in Table 15.5 ends where death commonly occurs, according to Reisberg et al. (p. 35). This stage lasts 6.5 years.

Three estimates of willingness to pay are given for each level in Table

TABLE 15.6. Alzheimer's Values Estimated
by Stage of Disease

Stage of Disease	Present Value (in Thousands of $)
Level 1—early (7 years):	
High (Kaplan et al.)	275
Medium (Miller et al.)	134
Low (Drummond et al.)	121
Level 2—middle (3.5 years):	
High (Drummond et al.)	177
Medium (Miller et al.)	123
Low (Kaplan et al.)	113
Level 3—late (6.5 years):	
High (Drummond et al.)	383
Medium (Miller et al.)	274
Low (Kaplan et al.)	209
Lifetime loss (7 years):	
High (Drummond et al.)	680
Medium (Kaplan et al.)	596
Low (Miller et al.)	530

Sources.—See the text.

15.6. The basic sources are Kaplan, Bush, and Berry (1979), Drummond, Stoddart, and Torrance (1987), and Miller, Calhoun, and Arthur (1990). We obtain utility-loss estimates by making judgments about what coordinates of the multiattribute utility functions estimated by these authors best represent the respective levels of Alzheimer's disease. For example, using the Drummond et al. loss estimates, we arrive at a utility loss of 0.18 qualys for each of 7 years of early Alzheimer's stage; 0.72 qualy loss for the 3 years of the middle stage; and a 1.12 worse-than-death qualy loss for the 6.5 years of the late stage. The lifetime loss as shown in Table 15.6 is $680,000, $600,000, or $530,000, depending on which authors' estimates are used. These numbers are interpretable as amounts that a 62-year-old would be willing to pay to avoid the disease at its onset, knowing that otherwise he would suffer its consequences.

15.8. Conclusion

We have developed state-of-the-art health values that can be applied to the analysis of a variety of policies. Extensive applications will be presented in the next chapter. The set of values presented here is not complete but points the way toward the development of a fuller set of values in future research. We look forward to continual improvements in methodology.

16

The Use of Health Values in Policy

George Tolley, Donald Kenkel, Robert Fabian,
and David Webster

This book has been about how to value human health when making public policy decisions. Chapter 15 developed a set of state of the art health values. Up to this point, however, the use of the estimates has mainly been implicit in the discussion. This chapter is explicitly concerned with the use of the health value estimates in policy. We begin by reviewing a general framework.

Our discussion then turns to examples of the contribution health value estimates can make in the policy areas discussed in Chapter 1: (1) health and safety regulation, (2) medical cost containment, (3) medical research priorities, (4) encouraging better lifestyles, (5) health and the courts, and (6) the use of health values in clinical practice. We show how the economic approach contributes to answering the following questions: What is the value of the health improvements that resulted from the air quality improvements over the 1970s? Which health care interventions are desirable? Is the trade-off between health and cost containment implicit in health maintenance organizations acceptable? Should we allocate more resources into research on Alzheimer's disease? Should we spend more money on school-based health education programs to discourage smoking? Should we increase the tax on alcoholic beverages to reduce drunk driving? Are the health values developed in this book useful for assessing damages in legal cases involving wrongful injury or death? Should health values be used in a clinical setting?

16.1. The Role of Health Values in an Evaluative Framework

Consider a problem of valuing health for policy of the following general form. A change in government policy is being considered, and while the new policy may have many objectives and effects, some of the effects are changes in human health. To judge whether the policy is desirable requires comparing the health gains or losses caused by the policy to other results of the policy. The value of the change in health can be expressed as a product of two terms:

$$\text{value of change in health} = \text{value per unit of health} \\ \times \text{change in health due to policy.}$$

As an example, part of the benefits of an antismoking campaign would be calculated as the value of a case of lung cancer times the predicted reduction in the prevalence of lung cancer. Choice of units in which to express changes in health will depend upon the context of the policy and on the state of knowledge about physical health effects. Possible units include a case of illness or a day spent with a particular symptom or set of symptoms. For serious illnesses and mortality, the units chosen would correspond to probabilities of the event.

The main concern of this book has been estimating the first term in the expression above, the value per unit of health. The problem of reliably estimating the second term, the change in health due to a policy, is also quite formidable. In fact, this step may be more difficult and problematic than the more controversial step of placing a value on health. Part of the problem is the often limited state of knowledge in the physical and life sciences; for instance, as explained in the first example below, the scientific evidence on the health effects of air pollution is quite mixed. Another part of the problem is the complexity of tracing through the effects of a policy. Answers to the seemingly simple question, "What are the health effects of this policy?" often must come from many disciplines, making collaborative projects crucial.

Fortunately, estimates of the health effects of policies are becoming increasingly available, so that it is at least sometimes possible to take such estimates "off the shelf" of completed research results. In still more cases, it is possible to distill estimates fairly easily from the research literature, although a substantial commitment on the part of the analyst may be required. In the examples below, finding an estimate of the health effects of smoking was fairly simple, but more work was needed to trace through the effects of an antismoking policy. Evaluating Alzheimer's research was an even more involved project.

It is important to reemphasize that the *changes* in health are to be measured and valued, not the total costs or damages of a disease. In contrast, many previous studies have focused on totals; it is common to see estimates of the total costs of an illness or even of all illnesses. For instance, Bloom and Carliner (1988) estimate that for the United States the total costs of AIDS in 1986 was $8.5 billion, and they predict costs of $48.8 billion for 1991. But it is hard to see how knowing the total costs of AIDS in the United States provides guidance for the rational formation of health policies. In this, as in most cases, no practical set of policy changes could eliminate AIDS. Estimates of the total costs of an illness, or the total benefits of eliminating an illness, do not contribute to the difficult problems of allocating scarce resources among competing ends.

The implicit use of estimates of the total value of health problems seems to be to set priorities. However, one of the first lessons in economics is that totals should not be used to set priorities when decisions are made at the margin. For example, estimates that the total economic costs of cancer far exceed the total economic costs of AIDS do not prove that cancer should be given a higher priority in policy. As AIDS is a relatively new condition, a great deal remains to be learned about it, so possibly programs aimed at AIDS could be more valuable. That is, the estimated value of the change in policy may be larger for anti-AIDS policies because, at the margin, anti-AIDS policies have larger impacts on health. Estimates of the value of health are only useful if they relate to realistic changes in policy.

In many examples, such as an anti-AIDS program, estimates of the value of health provide essential information needed to calculate the benefits of the policy. A complete analysis of the policy would include estimates of the costs of the program, as well as consideration of other aspects of the policy including equity or fairness issues. In other situations—for example, a decision to limit medical spending—the policy might result in health losses, so health value estimates help determine the costs of the program. To complete the policy analysis again requires more information, particularly on the benefits of the policy that must be weighed against the value of the health losses.

The use of the health values in the analysis of specific policies is demonstrated in the series of examples below. Two general types of analysis are carried out. The first type tries to determine the ideal or optimal use of a policy tool. In this type of analysis, the health values are used to determine whether the marginal benefits of using the policy tool to a greater or lesser extent exceed the marginal costs. Examples considered below are occupational disease policies and medical research spending. The second type of analysis focuses on whether a particular program, or change in policy, is desirable. In this type of analysis the health value estimates are used in estimating the benefits and costs of the policy change. Examples of this type of analysis are changing policies toward health maintenance organizations or implementing new school health education programs. The examples below develop specialized versions of these two general approaches.

The examples were chosen to illustrate the wide range of important policies for which the health values are needed. However, the health value estimates are only one part of the analysis. The choice of examples was also constrained by the availability of evidence on policy effectiveness and costs, the remaining parts. At times, the examples draw heavily from existing studies, such as Freeman's (1982) study of air pollution and Phelps's (1988) study of drunk driving. At other times, we undertake original analyses of Alzheimer's research or antismoking campaigns to help make the point that applying health values is feasible for a range of policies.

16.2. Health and Safety Regulation

The Environment

The Clean Air Act as amended in 1970 established a substantial federal role in regulating industries and vehicles to improve air quality. Although the act was amended again in 1977, and a new Clean Air Act was passed in 1990, the 1970 amendments are usually seen as the beginning of the current approach to air pollution policy. As Portney (1990a) notes, at about the same time there was a burst of federal regulation in many areas: new agencies created included the Environmental Protection Agency, the National Highway Traffic Safety Administration, the Consumer Product Safety Commission, and the Nuclear Regulatory Commission. A common goal of this regulation was to improve the safety and health of the U.S. public. As an important example of this type of regulation, we discuss the value of the health benefits created by air pollution control, using the new value estimates in this book.

An excellent study by Freeman (1982) provides the starting point for the analysis. Freeman estimates the national benefits associated with observed changes in air quality between 1970 and 1978. Summarizing available evidence, he assumes that the urban population of the United States experienced about a 20% reduction in suspended particulates and sulfur dioxide over these years. He then predicts the effects of this reduction as a first step in estimating national benefits. Freeman notes that, ideally, to evaluate the Clean Air Act amendments we should compare the actual air quality in 1978 with the quality that would have been experienced in 1978 if the act had not been amended. Data limitations and limited resources force him to make the simpler but possibly misleading comparison of actual levels in 1978 with actual levels in 1970.

Freeman (1982) reviews a number of studies in order to predict the health effects of the 20% reduction in air pollutants. The lack of agreement between these studies is striking, and to take this into account Freeman states his synthesis estimates in terms of a range with lower and upper bounds. He also provides his subjective judgment about the most reasonable point estimate, namely, that there were 13,900 deaths avoided due to the air quality improvement, with the range of estimates being from 2,780 to 27,800. In terms of a comprehensive measure of morbidity, his point estimate is that there were 29 million fewer restricted activity days.

Freeman reviews additional studies to arrive at synthesis estimates of the dollar values to attach to the mortality and morbidity effects. For mortality, he uses a value of a statistical life of $1 million. His most reasonable point estimate of the value of mortality benefits is therefore $13.9 billion. For morbidity, he values a restricted activity day at $40. Part of the morbidity benefits are therefore $1.16 billion. To this he adds $1.9 billion to reflect a 2% reduction in direct medical costs. His most reasonable point estimate of the total health benefits is about $17 billion.

Given the detailed and careful nature of Freeman's (1982) analysis, it is a simple matter to revise his calculations using this book's new health value estimates. Chapter 15 provides exactly comparable estimates of the value of a statistical life and the value of a restricted-activity day, with one slight difference. Freeman added a 2% reduction in medical costs to his estimates of the value of reduced mortality and morbidity. As he notes, in principle an estimate of willingness to pay to avoid an illness that might lead to death should include the willingness to pay to avoid medical costs. The estimates of willingness to pay he uses mainly relate to the value of an instant accidental death and so do not reflect large medical costs. He adds the medical cost reduction to take this into account. Chapter 15 contains estimates of the value of mortality depending upon the cause of death. By design, these estimates already include medical costs and other factors that are estimated to make preventing a lung cancer death much more valuable than preventing an instant accidental death. The upshot is that our mortality and morbidity estimates are more comprehensive, and so we do not need to add medical costs. The only intentional omission is that our estimates relate to individual willingness to pay and do not reflect the value of health to others.

We now calculate the value of the air quality improvement from 1970 to 1978 using Freeman's and our most reasonable estimates. For morbidity, we estimate that the 29 million fewer days of restricted activity are worth $30 each, for a total of $870 million. For air-pollution-related mortality, if we estimate that a statistical life is worth between $2 million and $3 million depending on cause of death and we use $2.5 million as an average, avoiding 13,900 deaths is worth $34.75 billion. So the total benefits of the air quality improvement are estimated to be $36.65 billion, over twice Freeman's original estimate. Part of the difference is accounted for by inflation since Freeman's estimates are in 1978 dollars while ours are in 1991 dollars. Expressed in 1991 dollars, Freeman's estimate is almost $30 billion. Our new estimate is still more than 20% larger than Freeman's after adjusting for inflation.

Our revision of Freeman's (1982) estimates demonstrates the recent methodological advances in valuing health. If we went further and calculated lower and upper bounds, however, a very wide range would result. Partly this is because of the still imperfect state of knowledge about the value of health. The state of scientific knowledge about the health effects of air pollution is even more uncertain; Freeman's upper-bound estimate of

the number of deaths avoided is 10 times larger than his lower-bound estimate. Portney (1990a) observes that the lower bound should be even lower
because "credible studies conclude that the criteria air pollutants have *no*
adverse effects on health *at present levels in most places*" (p. 56, emphasis
in original). Continued efforts are clearly needed to further refine the estimates of the value of health and the scientific estimates of the health effects
of air pollution.

Beyond this example pertaining to the aggregate benefits of air pollution
abatement, environmental regulatory impact analysis at the federal level and
in the design of policy in some studies now almost routinely use health
values of the type recommended in this book as an important consideration
in evaluating individual evaluation policies, representing one of the areas of
greatest advance in the use of health values.

Job Safety

Health values are an essential part of an economic policy analysis of job-
related problems of health and safety, inasmuch as disease and injury are
costs that need to be managed efficiently and equitably. Workers' compensation, product liability suits, and Occupational Safety and Health Administration regulations have evolved to address the problems of occupational
health and safety. As Viscusi contends, however, these approaches "have
failed to provide a comprehensive strategy for achieving efficient levels of
health risk and fair compensation for all disease victims" (1984b, p. 60).
Viscusi develops an occupational disease policy that addresses equity and
efficiency issues. The health values reported in this volume are useful in
implementing the policy.

Central to Viscusi's proposal is the requirement that policy components
impinging on health be coordinated so that their overall impact has the
desired equity and efficiency effects. Viscusi's first policy prescription is to
impose upon employers the optimum inducement to reduce health hazards.
This is accomplished by a tax linked to current exposure levels. A firm that
produces a hazardous work environment has the choice of paying a tax commensurate with the hazards or reducing the hazards. The firm will choose
to incur the cost of reducing the hazard so long as the reduction in tax
liability is greater. Beyond that point it will pay the tax. Such a tax satisfies
Viscusi's efficiency criterion.

The second policy guideline pertains to fairness, or equal treatment of
equals. Achieving equity requires that different diseases be comparable and
that diseases and accidents be measurable on the same scale. It also requires
that occupational and nonoccupational hazards be treated similarly. With
these considerations in mind, social policy should include a standard of
minimally acceptable compensation for hazard victims.

From these two policy principles, Viscusi derives a third policy guide-line—the distinction between past and future health hazards. The tax on workplace hazards should be set solely with a view to inducing optimal reductions in future illness or injury. The adequacy of funds to compensate past victims is a separate issue. If penalty tax receipts are inadequate, they should be augmented by a broad-based payroll tax, which will not affect hazard-reduction decisions of the firm. Product liability suits retain a role in Viscusi's framework, but judgments should be reduced by the amount of compensation already paid.

Enough has been said about Viscusi's program to indicate the role of the Chapter 15 health values in occupational health policy. To achieve efficient hazard abatement, the penalty tax should be related to the ex ante or expected value lost by hazard victims. In addition, the firm must know the incremental cost of abating the hazard. Figure 16.1 illustrates a solution to the efficiency problem. The variable V represents the marginal value of a disease case, for example, respiratory symptoms caused by emissions from an industrial process in a manufacturing plant. A symptom day might be the unit of measurement, as in Table 15.2, where values in a range around $40 per day are reported. MC is the marginal cost of abatement to the firm with no abatement. The origin, I, represents the number of symptom days per day in the plant with no abatement. The optimum level of abatement, D_o, gives a net welfare gain to the workers of the area Ie $40. The firm is required to pay a tax of D_oOV_oe, equal to the remaining respiratory damage

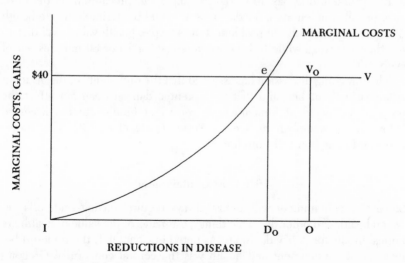

Figure 16.1   Tax for Optimal Disease Abatement

suffered by the workers. As the firm moves along its abatement schedule, MC, its output supply curve shifts downward. The resulting reduction in output and employment is part of the adjustment to a social optimum brought about by the pollution tax.

The respiratory-symptom example is a relatively simple application of the Chapter 15 health values within the Viscusi framework. Current measurements of disease or symptom rates or accident rates give the value of point I in Figure 16.1. The dollar value of curve V can be treated as known. Many other applications are more complicated, however. Table 15.1 reflects this complexity. Exposure to many kinds of health hazards produce diseases with small probabilities; many hazards produce disease symptoms only after latency periods. Emphysema, heart disease, and lung cancer are examples. Many health states require consideration of their effects over the entire life cycle. Paraplegia (Table 15.2) and Alzheimer's disease (Table 15.6 and this chapter) are examples. Time preference and risk aversion accordingly must enter into estimation of the V curve in Figure 16.1, as they do to varying degrees in Table 15.6.

One need not of course know the exact values along the abatement schedule to implement the policy. The major point is that, if the firm knows it will have to pay for death or injury caused willingness to pay values of the type estimated in this book, it will have incentives to take abatement actions to the point where the extra health benefits of the actions justify the extra costs.

This analysis assumes that workers' avoidance efforts are not affected by inducements imposed on the firm. If accident or disease avoidance behavior were a problem due, say, to workers taking fewer precautions in the presence of full compensation for damages, it would be desirable to use health values in dealing with the problem. For example, health values will dictate whether it is worthwhile to have workers rest for 10 or 30 minutes out of every hour.

The foregoing discussion has assumed that the probability of the accident is known without bias and that the potential damages can not affect the probability of accident. Similar caveats regarding these matters as discussed below on courts apply here. See also Posner (1992, chap. 13), "The Choice between Regulation and Common Law."

16.3. Cost Containment

Since cost containment will almost always require making trade-offs between health and other desirable things, estimates of the value of health are critical inputs for policy decisions. As noted in Chapter 1, the trade-off between cost containment and health was the central concern of Oregon's project to set medical priorities for Medicaid patients and the LORAN

Commission's related project for the Harvard Community Health Plan. In this section we consider these two projects in more detail. Then we contrast our approach with cost effectiveness analysis. Finally, we give an example evaluating the effectiveness of health maintenance organizations (HMOs) in containing costs.

The Oregon Project

Priority-setting for allocating Medicaid funds was first considered by the Oregon legislature in 1989 (Golenski et al. 1989). A later version was rejected in 1992 by the White House in a well publicized and controversial decision. Oregon faced the necessity of confronting resource limitations in establishing eligibility requirements for Medicaid assistance. As an example of the stark choices they faced, "Medicaid could either extend its funding for basic health care to include about 1500 persons not covered previously, or continue to fund a program of organ-transplantation (bone marrow, heart, liver and pancreas) for a projected 34 patients" (Welch and Larson 1988, p. 171). The expected $2.2 million cost for the 34 transplant patients was projected to double within 2 years in view of federal Medicaid statutes. Furthermore, "there was no way the state could limit its funding to a prescribed number of transplants" (ibid.).

The task of establishing priorities was given to a panel of experts, composed of physicians, nurses, social workers, and health and social program administrators. They developed lists of care categories and ranked them. An executive group consolidated the work, defined broad areas of health services to be offered through Medicaid, and developed management guidelines. The community at large was involved through a random telephone survey, community meetings, and public hearings.

The Oregon program commendably recognizes the scarcity of medical resources and the necessity to make choices among treatments. It is beyond the scope of this chapter to fully evaluate the Oregon experience, which ran into difficulty at the federal level because of conflict with the Americans With Disabilities Act. The Oregon plan comes close to a rational approach to health care resource allocation, and we hope the difficulties can be overcome without scrapping it. Our major point is that further efforts along the lines of the Oregon approach could be improved by using an explicit health value approach. In place of prioritized lists that beg the question of how much treatments are worth, health values give scientific estimates based on objective evidence expressed in a common metric.

The excess of the value of a treatment above its costs, per dollar of government cost, would be calculated for each treatment and given to the panel as an aid in its recommendations. Ideally, one would rank the treatments according to this criterion and go down this list until program funds are exhausted. We do not advocate a mechanistic approach but, rather, argue that better decisions would be made if the calculations for the treatments were made available as an aid, as follows.

In deciding on how to get the most for a limited amount of government funds available to support health treatments, the benefits per treatment need first to be estimated using results of the type developed in this book. The benefits are the willingness to pay for the increase in well-being brought about by a treatment. Second, the benefits per treatment need to be multiplied by incidence, or number of people who will receive the treatment, to arrive at the total benefits if the condition is eligible for inclusion in the program. Third, the program funds that will be used up by treating the condition need to be subtracted from the total benefits to arrive at the net program benefit from this treatment. The criterion is

$$\text{net program benefit} = bN - C,$$

where b is the value of increase in well-being from one treatment, N is number of people who will receive the treatment, and C is cost of including the treatment in the program. Cost C might be further broken down into program cost per treatment, c, times number of treatments N.

The treatments need to be ranked according to this criterion, ideally going down the list until program funds are exhausted. A common nonserious condition (low b) affecting large numbers of people (large N) treatable at low cost (low c) would rank high. So would a serious condition whose treatment gives dramatic symptom reduction (high b) even though it affected fewer people (lower N) and even if costs per treatment were greater (greater c). The criterion provides a way of balancing magnitude of symptom relief, incidence, and program costs. While we advocate preparing lists using the $bN - C$ criterion recommended above, we do not recommend overly mechanistic application. Distributional considerations, institutional constraints such as the Americans for Disabilities Act, and unavoidable political override may keep the list from being followed exactly. We still strongly believe that having the criterion lists explicitly calculated as an aid to decision makers, even if the lists are not followed exactly in final policy actions, would have an exceedingly salutary effect in leading to better use of program funds.

Our suggested procedure is different from that in the Oregon project, which ranked treatments by creating 17 categories of condition-treatment pairs (Menzel 1992, p. 22). The categories were ranked by experts according to importance to society (40% weight), the individual (20% weight), and their necessity to basic care (40% weight). Each of 709 condition-treatment pairs was assigned to a category. Rankings within categories were derived from a telephone survey of Oregon citizens in conjunction with Kaplan and Anderson (1988).

The Oregon procedure abandons serious measurement of preferences. To us, the importance to society and to the individual of basic health care will vary from one health condition to another. We would start with value to the individual in each case, elicited by careful willingness to pay or qualy questionnaires, placing reliance in the first instance on preferences of the public at large as the people whose well-being will be affected. We would modify these values carefully and judiciously on a case-by-case basis to allow for greater knowledge of some effects by experts. The questionnaires administered to the sample of the public would try to the maximum extent to encourage expressions of value for basic care and importance to society. In place of arbitrary 40-20-40 weights and additivity defining 17 categories into which to put treatment pairs, which gives an aura of precision but in our view only results in obfuscation, we stress case-by-case evaluation using citizen preference as the starting point and, in many cases, the ending point of evaluations of treatment benefit.

After deriving the rankings described above, the Oregon procedure goes into a reasonableness checklist used to modify the rankings. The checklist includes (1) "public health impact," (2) "social costs," (3) "effectiveness of treatment," (4) "cost of nontreatment," (5) "incidence" and (6) "cost of medical treatment" (Menzel 1992, p. 21). We would not have such a checklist. To us, all these considerations are already included and given proper balancing in our suggested $bN - C$ criterion. The first four items in the checklist enter into the estimation of treatment benefit b. With regard to "public health impact," an infectious disease whose treatment will reduce disease among others would be taken account of by explicitly estimating the increase in well-being of others who would not get the disease as a result of the treatment of one particular individual. "Effectiveness of treatment" multiplies b. For example, if a treatment is 100% effective, b is not affected. If the treatment is on average 50% effective, b is multiplied by .5. The same types of considerations apply to "social costs" and "costs of nontreatment." They should be explicitly estimated and included in b.

Finally "incidence" is our N, and "cost of medical treatment" is our C. They are already in our formula. All the reasonableness considerations go into one coherent framework for comparing treatments.

Hadorn (1991b) observes that the original Oregon prioritization, based on quality of well-being rankings, often placed minor ailments ahead of life-threatening problems for which highly effective treatments exist. The reason is that many people suffer from the minor ailments, yielding greater additive benefits than saving the lives of the few. This anomaly caused public and expert reaction against the original list. Hadorn regards this as a fatal utilitarian flaw in the prioritization process: "People cannot stand idly by when an identified person's life is visibly threatened if effective rescue measures are available" (1991b, p. 2219).

Hadorn's observation uncovers a shortcoming in the Oregon elicitation process, not in the health value approach, as he claims. This should be obvious from the public's reaction that the list did not reflect their preferences. It should have become evident that value to others—altruism—is an important part of health values and that it is of great importance to health value measurement in a prioritization context. People should have been asked if they would be willing to forgo minor reduction in discomfort or pain and suffering to accommodate a more severely stricken, anonymous fellow citizen. Value to others, whether in the health context or other valuation settings, has been recognized for some time as important.

In addition to these major reservations about the evaluation framework used in the Oregon project, we are very concerned about the apparent abandonment of systematic value measurement. In our view, to reach reasoned judgments about what it is worth to give up to get health benefits, some attempt to obtain monetary equivalence is necessary, either through direct willingness to pay measures or assigning values to qualy ratings.

The previous chapters have important implications about how to obtain these values that we would like to see followed in the Oregon and similar projects. An example discussed by Hadorn, bleeding into the brain treatable by surgery, drawn from the Oregon priority list, is useful to illustrate some of the problems, particularly when probabilities are involved (1991a, pp. 14–15). Without treatment, the probability of death within 5 years is 0.95. (Hadorn's example is stated in terms of percent of patients, which we interpret here as probabilities facing a representative patient.) Survivors face serious physical, social, and cognitive disabilities, about equal to death in utility terms. The probability of dying with surgery is 0.2. The probability of dying or surviving with disabilities approximately equal to death in utility terms is 0.6. Twenty-five percent of survivors will suffer qualy loss of about 0.15. Twenty-five percent of survivors will live symptom-free lives. These outcomes can be framed in many different ways. It could be stated, for example, that without treatment patients face certain death or its equivalent in utility terms, but with treatment they have a 40% probability of normal life or life with serious but bearable symptoms (utility loss of about 0.15). Different descriptions would yield different evaluations, so much effort would need to be given to achieving a formulation that yielded relatively unbiased responses. The framing problem is a very difficult one, which our Chapter 13 focus group experience instructs us requires experimentation and pretesting to get right. It should be emphasized that the probabilities involved in the problem are of the utmost importance because risk aversion, indeed dread, become important factors in people's reactions. Care must be exercised if the framing problem is approached in a modular fashion, as in the Oregon project, by combining utilities or values associated with death and functional disabilities, multiplied by appropriate probabilities. We are skeptical that the modular approach will give accurate results in this case. Two considerations are paramount. First, do the combined components of the problem, evaluated separately, closely approximate the given problem in the mind of the respondent? Second, does the probability calculation carry the correct implications for risk aversion present in the mind of the respondent? Part of the answer, but only part, is found by carefully examining the assumptions underlying the expressions of willingness to pay or the utility function employed.

Elicitation of values, in our experience, requires rather extensive preparation of respondents in the case of life-threatening conditions. This is especially true when probabilities are involved. Focusing respondents' attention on the essential aspects of the problem, elicitation devices such as ranking and iterative bidding, conveying probabilities, and other matters relevant to the Oregon problem are discussed at length in Chapter 13.

The LORAN Commission

A second attempt at prioritization was made by the Harvard Community Health Plan (HCHP), where directors came to recognize the impossibility of providing its 360,000 members with the benefits of the virtually boundless expansion of medical technology that is occurring. In 1985 they established the LORAN Commission "to develop guidelines for evaluating and approving new medical technologies that might benefit HCHP's membership" (LORAN Commission 1988, p. 10). The work of the commission was conducted with nationwide objectives in mind "in response to a call to confront issues of national significance" (p. 10). The commission was composed of distinguished citizens from a wide cross section of society.

The case of Baby L led the commission to the consensus that choices must be made that preclude the universal provision of available technologies and interventions. Baby L was oxygen deprived at birth and suffered profound brain damage. She was blind and deaf, had no control of her arms and legs, and could breathe only occasionally by herself. There was no prospect for recovery. Baby L received care that in two years had "cost well over $1 million, her home nursing care cost $7000 a month" (p. 17). Some commission members had believed in the adage, "Everything medically possible must always be provided" (p. 15). The case of Baby L convinced them to abandon that belief.

One witness suggested a solution: "Assign a value to the intervention and compare it with values assigned other interventions. . . . The Commission's members embraced his concept, but could not accede to a mathematical formula, concluding that simple formulas for comparing the values cannot be found" (p. 20). The solution the commission recommended was to establish a number of years' worth of earnings that should be devoted to extending a member's life for 1 year (p. 39). Recalling the Baby L tragedy, they said, "As more and more years of earnings of others are devoted to extending a life for a short time, it becomes clear that choices must be made between competing goods. A rational analysis of this kind can offer guidance" (p. 39).

While the LORAN Commission recognized the inevitability of choices and is highly commendable in this regard, to us the use of the number of years worth of earnings to be devoted to extending a life for 1 year as a criterion is a non sequitur. It has nothing to say about the quality of the life extended, much less the vast number of medical procedures that do not affect longevity. We again recommend using scientifically measured health values based on willingness to pay concepts, either state-of-the-art values for the population at large or values from carefully constructed surveys of the organization's membership, emphasizing willingness to pay and quality-of-life approaches. Based on these results, the ranking criterion suggested above for the Oregon program would be used as an aid to decisions.

A Critique of Cost-Effectiveness Analysis, or Which Health Care Interventions Are Desirable?

As the Oregon and LORAN Commission examples show, the use of explicit health values in setting medical care priorities has not yet gained wide acceptance. However, the closely related technique of cost-effectiveness analysis is increasingly accepted and can provide a starting point for the more complete analysis. Table 16.1 partially reproduces a list of cost-effectiveness ratios for a series of medical interventions prepared by Russell (1989). For each intervention, the cost-effectiveness ratio shows the cost per year of life saved. From Chapter 15, the medium estimate of the value per year of life saved is $120,000. Thus it is a simple matter to estimate the per-unit net benefits for each intervention; these are presented in the last column of Table 16.1. As long as there are no additional constraints on policy decisions, all interventions with positive net benefits should be undertaken. The total net benefits from each intervention will depend on the size of each program, but as long as the per-unit costs and health values are roughly constant for the range under consideration the same set of interventions will meet the benefit-cost criterion for adoption.

The data in Table 16.1 on frequency of Pap smears provide an example of the potential of this type of analysis for cost containment strategies. The Pap smear is a test for cervical cancer and its precursors and is a standard part of preventive medicine for women. However, a study cited by Russell (1989) estimates that, while the cost per year of life saved by testing every 3 years is fairly low, costs dramatically increase if testing is done every 2 years and are even higher on for annual tests (Eddy 1989). As Russell explains, the high costs of the testing programs results because millions of women must be tested, but the vast majority will never develop cervical

TABLE 16.1. Net Benefits of Selected Health Care
Interventions

Medical Intervention	Cost per Year of Life Saved [*] (1986 $)	Net Benefits [†]
Pap smear:		
Every 3 years	14,300	105,700
Every 2 years	451,200	-331,200
Every year	1,144,000	-1,024,000
Mammography:		
40–50:		
Physical exam only	35,500	84,500
Mammography added	144,100	-24,100
55–65:		
Physical exam only	16,700	103,300
Mammography added	90,100	29,900
Coronary care units:		
4% risk	226,400	-106,400
10% risk	107,500	12,500
20% risk	53,800	66,200
Bypass surgery:		
Left main disease	5,600	114,400
Three-vessel disease	10,600	109,400
Two-vessel disease	25,800	94,200
One-vessel disease	44,100	75,900
Cholesterol reduction: [‡]		
40, 240, low risk	180,000	-60,000
40, 240, high risk	21,000	99,000
40, 300, low risk	94,000	26,000
40, 300, high risk	11,000	99,000
60, 240, low risk	280,000	-160,000
60, 240, high risk	23,000	97,000
60, 300, low risk	160,000	-40,000
60, 300, high risk	13,000	107,000

[*] SOURCE.—Russell (1989), and references therein.
[†] Net benefits are calculated valuing a year of life at $120,000.
[‡] The first number is age, the second is total serum cholesterol level, and "low risk" and "high risk" summarizes other risk factors for heart disease.

cancer and so receive no benefits from the testing. The costs of screening such a large number must be compared with the years of life gained by a much smaller number. Valuing a year of life at $120,000, testing more frequently than every 3 years does not yield positive net benefits, implying that the resources required for more frequent testing are more valuable in other uses.

This type of analysis of medical interventions has already made some impact on health policy and has the potential for a far greater impact. In making recommendations concerning preventive care, the American Cancer Society, the Blue Cross/Blue Shield National Association, and the American College of Physicians cite Eddy's studies of the screening for cervical and breast cancer. The question of coverage of preventive care is also a concern in the design of Medicare and Medicaid policies. If the calculations in Table 16.1 are confirmed in more detailed analyses, both public and private insurers should design coverage so that the frequency of Pap smears is every third year. Since about half of adult women in the United States report having a Pap smear within the past year, this would mean a substantial reduction in average frequency. Policy must be designed carefully, however, because currently annual use is much more likely among well-educated, younger women (Kenkel 1990). The challenge for policy is to decrease the frequency of use in those groups, while maintaining and even increasing use in other population subgroups.

In reviewing Table 16.1, it stands out that the majority of the interventions pass the test of having positive net benefits. Moreover, this result is not particularly sensitive to the value placed on a year of life; most interventions continue to yield positive net benefits even using much lower values per life year saved. It also seems unlikely that the studies reviewed by Russell share a systematic bias in estimating costs. Another interpretation of the results may explain resistance to cost containment efforts: Americans on average place a high value on health, so that many medical interventions will be judged as a desirable use of scarce resources.

The conclusion that many of the interventions are in fact desirable highlights a fundamental weakness of cost-effectiveness analysis. Russell's (1989) cost-effectiveness estimates reveal that providing bypass surgery for men with heart disease is more cost-effective than many of the cholesterol reduction interventions considered. (As an aside, this contradicts the conventional wisdom that prevention is cheaper than cure.) But given the high values placed on saving a year of life, both bypass surgery and cholesterol reduction for high risk groups are justified. If the health care budget is limited so that all interventions cannot be undertaken, cost-effectiveness analysis yields the correct implication that bypass surgery should receive priority. The calculation that the cholesterol reduction interventions yield positive net benefits means, however, that, if this is the case, the health care budget is too small: additional resources spent on health care are more valuable here than in their next best alternative use. This type of conclusion cannot be drawn from pure cost-effectiveness studies but is required to make rational cost containment policies.

Cost Containment in Health Maintenance Organizations

In addition to questioning the desirability of specific medical interventions, other cost containment proposals involve much wider ranging reforms of the U.S. health care system. Empirical research on the costs of HMOs provides a good example of the trade-offs involved in such cost containment strategies and illustrates the usefulness of the estimates of the value of health in making the policy decisions.

The prevailing fee for service (FFS) system is often criticized because with third-party payments neither the physician nor the patient have the correct incentives to keep costs down. For both, it makes sense for the physician to provide medical care until the marginal benefits approach zero or practice what has been called "flat of the curve medicine." The patient receives more care, the physician receives more income, and the insurance company is left paying the bill. By combining the roles of health care provider and insurer in one organization, proponents claim that HMOs can provide physicians with the correct incentives to contain costs. In contrast, even though at the margin the benefits of the medical care are low, there still will be some health losses due to the lower utilization of care. That is, there is still a trade-off between cost containment and health, and policy makers should encourage HMOs only to the extent they are willing to accept this trade-off.

As an extreme case, consider the following question: if there were no HMOs in the United States, would the health benefits be worth the additional health care costs? Answering this question involves the counterfactual experiment of predicting the levels of health and health care costs that would have occurred if HMOs had never established a foothold in the health care sector. Analysis of counterfactual situations is a tool from economic history that provides an interesting perspective on the impact of policies and historical events. For many years, state medical societies through their own actions and state legislation were able to prevent the growth of HMOs. However, beginning in the 1970s federal legislation encouraged their growth, in part by requiring employers to offer an HMO as a health insurance option whenever a federally qualified HMO was available. (For brief history of the growth of HMOs, see Feldstein (1983, pp. 346–47.) The counterfactual experiment sheds light on whether this reversal on policy towards HMOs produced more benefits or costs.

Without HMOs, total health care costs would be higher. To estimate the change in total health care costs, we begin with evidence on the effect of HMOs on costs at the level of the individual enrollee. After a comprehensive review of empirical studies, Luft (1978) reports that total costs for HMO enrollees are 10%–40% lower than those for comparable persons with conventional health insurance, mostly due to lower hospitalization rates. The Rand Health Insurance Experiment provides additional evidence that the cost savings are real and not a result of favorable selection into HMOs. An experimental group was randomly selected into an HMO and compared to other groups in FFS insurance plans. The pure effect of membership in the HMO is estimated to be about a 30% reduction in medical expenses, again mainly due to lower hospital admission rates (Manning et al. 1987). Based on existing research, a conservative estimate is that health care costs are 10% lower for HMO enrollees than for people outside of HMOs.

An estimate is that in 1987 there were 30 million HMO enrollees in the United States, out of a total population of 239.2 million people. Personal health care expenditures in the same year totaled $442.6 billion (Health Insurance Association of America 1989). Using the assumption that expenditures are 10% lower in HMOs, per capita expenditures for an HMO enrollee are therefore estimated to be $1,686, and per capita expenditures for people outside HMOs are estimated to be $1,874. For the counterfactual of no HMO enrollees, the simplest assumption is that all 239.2 million people would spend at the higher rate of $1,874 each. So total personal health care expenditures are estimated as $448.3 billion, an increase of $5.7 billion compared to the actual level.

At the same time, without HMOs, health status would improve, due to the health losses that occur when HMOs reduce the amount of medical care provided. In general, the Rand study indicates that these losses are small. The Rand researchers report that "the mean person in the fee-for-service plan appeared to derive few or no benefits from the additional hospital services" (Manning et al. 1987, p. 266). However, they also found some evidence of poorer health outcomes among HMO enrollees, particularly among persons who were both in poor health at the start of the experiment and of low income. Specifically, the low-income initially sick group assigned to the HMO experienced an average of almost 4 more bed days per year than those assigned to the most generous traditional insurance plan; the HMO enrollees also experienced significantly more serious symptoms (Manning et al. 1984). This increase in days confined to bed combined with a serious symptom will be assumed to be the most important change in health status associated with HMOs. Using the Rand criterion, approximately 10% of the 30 million HMO enrollees, or 3 million people, would fall into the initially sick/low income category. Under the counterfactual of no HMOs, each of these 3 million people will experience 4 fewer bed days, or 12 million fewer bed days totally.

The question posed earlier now becomes, Is reducing the amount of suffering by 12 million bed days worth spending an extra $5.7 billion? Rather than shy away from such a question, the health values developed in this book allow us to confront it head on. Chapter 15 contains estimates of the values of a day of morbidity from various causes. The highest value placed on avoiding acute morbidity is for severe food poisoning, at $130 a day (medium estimate). Using this value, the 12 million extra bed days are valued at $1.56 billion. Compared to the actual situation with 30 million HMO enrollees, the counterfactual of no HMOs is judged to be a less desirable situation. The benefits of HMOs, in the form of cost containment, are much greater than the value of the health losses.

An additional concern may be with the distributional consequences of HMO policies since the health losses due to HMOs were estimated to be concentrated on low-income HMO enrollees. This type of problem is not unique to health policies, however, and standard methods could be used to calculate both the efficiency and equity effects of policies (Gramlich 1990). The crucial point is that such calculations should be part of cost containment decisions, so that the important trade-offs can be explicitly recognized. This is in contrast to the way health policy has often been made. As Fuchs and Zeckhauser (1987, p. 267) put it, the myth that we will spare no expense to save a life or cure a disease has meant that many mechanisms of cost containment must work in the shadows.

To bring cost containment into the daylight requires confronting the value of health directly. Each medical intervention should be judged on the basis of whether the health improvements are worth the extra costs, instead of on the basis of whether there exist measurable health improvements. Similarly, a cost containment strategy should not be rejected simply because health outcomes deteriorate. The relevant question is whether the lost health is valued more or less highly than the cost savings. Although giving up our myths may be difficult, we believe that research on the evaluation of medical technologies and practices, combined with value estimates of the type this book contains, are adequate for the task if policy analysts have the will.

16.4. Medical Research Expenditures

Introduction

One of the goals of medical research clearly is improved health status for the victims of disease. Since the resources available for medical research are increasingly scarce, policy makers need to consider the benefits of medical research relative to its costs when deciding both the level of investment in medical research and its distribution among competing research interests. Value of health estimates provide the critical link between medical advances and their benefit to society. By combining the health advances with the value that individuals place on those advances, estimates of medical research benefits can be obtained. Estimates of medical research benefits and costs can then be used by policy makers to select research projects that deliver the greatest expected benefit per dollar invested.

Framework

Investment in medical research produces uncertain health status benefits. A given level of investment in medical research does not guarantee a discovery that can be converted to a treatment that will ameliorate the symptoms of a disease. A more realistic representation of the return to a given level of medical research investment would be an expected benefits function:

$$\text{expected benefits} = (Pr) \cdot (\Delta s) \cdot (\Delta H)/\Delta s) \cdot (\$/H), \quad (16.1)$$

where Pr = probability of discovery, ΔH = change in health status due to discovery, and $\$/H$ = value of change per unit of health. The probability of discovery is a function of the current level of investment in the research area, as well as past investment and exogenous influences.

The path from discovery in the laboratory to the development of an efficacious treatment administered by health professionals is a long one. Uncertainly looms at every step in the process. For example, there is no certainty that a discovery made at a basic level can be applied to a given disease; even if it can, development of a concrete treatment from the theoretical context of the discovery is not guaranteed.

Benefits are not the only component of medical research investment subject to uncertainty. The cost of medical research that delivers a given benefit is also uncertain. It is costly to make a medical discovery, costly to convert the discovery to a clinical application, and costly to diffuse the treatment developed from the discovery. Ex ante, these costs are not known with any degree of certainty.

Finally, our estimates of the value of medical research are imprecise in many respects. For example, to the extent that the individual's utility function does not include the utility of family members, our estimates are biased downward due to the exclusion of external benefits to the therapy, both familial and societal. Family members, especially caregivers, could place a high value on any improvement in health status achieved by medical research. Our assumptions about the manifestation of Alzheimer's disease in the general population could be more sophisticated. Our estimates nevertheless lay the foundation for a general methodology for the allocation of medical research funding among various projects.

Equation (16.1) is for a single discovery that will either be made or not with a given probability. Building on this idea, we wish now to consider a more general framework. Assume for simplicity that the goal of the medical research enterprise is to "alleviate suffering, improve the quality of life, and enhance survival." One of the inputs in the production of this goal, or benefit function, is medical research. Making a distinction between basic research and applied research as different inputs in the medical research benefit function, a "discovery," x_i, or an increase in the stock of basic research knowledge, is produced in field i as follows:

$$x_i = g_i(k_i, u_i),$$ (16.2)

where g_i is the production function that converts k_i into basic research knowledge. The inputs include skilled and unskilled labor, capital, laboratory equipment, and so on. To allow for the uncertainty in the research process, the production of a discovery is also a function of a random variable, u_i. In this specification, there is some chance that an ambitious project using large amounts of labor, capital, and other inputs will not produce a research discovery, depending upon the realization of the random variable u_i. Similarly, while a discovery is more likely when more inputs are used, there is some chance that a very small project will result in an important discovery.

Basic research knowledge in fields $i = 1, \ldots, n$ become inputs in the production of an applied research discovery in field j, yielding expected benefits B_j as follows:

$$B_j = g_j(k'_j, x_1, \ldots, x_n, v_j) \cdot h_j(s_j, d_j, q_j, e_j) \cdot w_j(z_j).$$ (16.3)

Equation 16.3 is an extended version of equation (16.1) that makes the distinction between basic and applied research. In (16.3), the g_j function is an applied research discovery, or increase in the stock of applied research knowledge. It is the counterpart to Δs in (16.1). It depends on direct inputs into applied research, $k'_1, \ldots, x_n$, and a random variable v_j. For example, a basic research discovery might be applied to Alzheimer's disease and produce the discovery of an effective therapy. A distinction can be made in terms of the labor component in each level of production. The inputs k_i include scientists involved in basic biomedical research, while the inputs k'_j include scientists who bridge the gap between basic research and clinical applications of this research. Many feel that increasing the numbers of physician-scientists is essential for the success of the research enterprise. Finally, making the probability of a discovery a function of a random variable v_j again allows for the inherent uncertainty in the research process.

The change in health resulting from an applied research discovery is given by the h_j function. It is the change in health status due to the discovery and is the counterpart to $(\Delta H/\Delta s)$ in equation (16.1). The change in health status is a function of the exogenous parameters s_j, d_j, g_j, and e_j. It is a positive function of s, the size of the population that is affected by the disease; d, the duration (over the life cycle) of the disease in the individual; q_j, the quality of life reduction the disease imposes on the individual; and e_j, the negative externalities produced by the disease. The effects of all of these factors can and should be estimated quantitatively. Notice also that many of these are the same factors represented in the criterion we recommended to aid decisions in the Oregon program.

Finally, w_j (z_j) is the willingness to pay for a unit increase in health and is ($/H$) in (16.1). It is the variable of primary concern in this book. The random variable z_j is due to residual variation in assigning dollar values.

Substituting equation (16.2) into (16.3) and taking expectations yields an expression for the expected benefits of medical research:

$$EB_j = \int \ldots \int g_j[k'_j, f_1(k_1, u_1), \ldots, f_n(k_n, u_n), v_j] \cdot h_j(s_j, d_j, q_j, e_j)$$
$$\cdot w_j(z_j) \times F(u_1, \ldots, u_n, v_j, e_j, z_j) \, du_1 \ldots du_n dv_j de_j dz_j.$$
(16.4)

The cost side is brought in by cost functions for producing x_i and B_j:

$$C_i(k_i) \text{ and } C_j(k'_j).$$
(16.5)

Allocation of medical research funds faces the constraint

$$F - \sum_j C_j(\cdot) - \sum_i C_i(\cdot) = 0,$$
(16.6)

where F is the total budget that can be distributed among various research endeavors.

Rational allocation attempts to solve the following problem:

$$\max_{\{k_i k'_j\}} EB_j + u \cdot \left[F - \sum_j C_j(\cdot) - \sum_i C_i(\cdot) \right] \text{ for } i$$
$$= 1, \ldots, n \text{ and } j = 1, \ldots, m. \quad (16.7)$$

Setting the partial derivatives with respect to labor inputs equal to zero gives first-order conditions:

$$k_i: \sum_j \frac{\partial EB_j(\cdot)}{\partial x_i} \frac{\partial x_i(\cdot)}{\partial k_i} - \mu \cdot \frac{\partial C_i(\cdot)}{\partial k_i} = 0,$$

$$k'_j: \frac{\partial EB_j(\cdot)}{\partial k'_j} - \mu \cdot \frac{\partial C_j(\cdot)}{\partial k'_j} = 0,$$
(16.8)

indicating that the contribution of basic research input k_i to basic research knowledge times the contribution of basic research to actual patient benefit B_j should equal its marginal cost, and the contribution of applied research labor input k'_j to patient benefit should equal its contribution to patient benefit. The first-order conditions implicitly define a set of demand functions for labor, capital, and all other inputs. Maximum benefits will be obtained when the ratio of marginal benefits to marginal costs is equalized for all inputs i and j. While this is a standard result, and a far more elaborate and complicated set of assumptions could be considered, we can bring these conditions to bear on the question of the appropriate level of funding for various research projects.

Even at this level of generality, considerations stand out that call for explicit measurement. For example, more funds should be invested in applied research that is focused on diseases that affect large segments of the population (s effect), on diseases with long durations (d effect), on diseases that severely reduce the quality of life (q effect), and on diseases with large negative externalities (e effect). In deciding whether to invest in basic versus applied medical research, more should be invested in basic research the more the basic research can increase benefits in several areas of applied research (x_i enters several B_j functions).

Those concerned with allocation of the medical research dollar should be urged to use a framework of this type to evaluate expected benefits relative to costs and to aid in distributing funds among different medical research projects. The framework provides a way to organize scientific information and opinion about projects.

The Institute of Medicine's "Funding Health Sciences Research" (1990) is one of a surprisingly few studies that attempts to deal seriously with the overall allocation of medical research funding. The committee concludes that resources should be steered away from specific research projects toward the labor and capital components of the research enterprise. The committee argues that "support for research project grants has been heavily favored at the expense of training facilities" (ibid., p. 7). Overemphasis on investment in "nondurable" inputs in the research enterprise (individual research projects) at the expense of the most "durable" inputs (labor and capital) for extended periods of time will "threaten the long term integrity of the entire system" (ibid., p. 6). In addition, the committee recommends "that Congress, administrators and scientists employ a priority setting framework for allocating funds to meet long and short term research needs in order to correct and maintain the appropriate overall balance among the individual components of the research establishment (people, projects, and facilities)" (ibid., p. 17).

While many solutions have been proposed for problems presented by the present allocation of medical research funds, most of them argue for a general increase in the level of medical research funding. The Institute of Medicine should be applauded for proposing a solution that involves the reallocation of existing research funds. However, the report does not go far enough in several respects. First of all, exactly how much of the medical research budget should policy makers divert to the labor and capital components of the research enterprise? Second, since labor and capital are components of individual research grants, which research grants should receive increased funding? The point here is that unbundling individual research grants into their labor and capital components is virtually impossible. Therefore, increases in funding for labor and capital are tied to increases in funding for specific medical research projects, and this implies emphasis on certain research projects at the expense of others. For example, in its recommendation 4.6, the committee recommends "that the universities and research institutions disburse Biomedical Research Support Grant funds through faculty peer review groups to support new research initiatives, especially those of young investigators" (Institute of Medicine 1990, p. 17). While this approach will increase the stock of talented scientists, it will increase the number of talented scientists doing biomedical research. If increasing labor and capital investment involves increasing funding in certain areas of research at the expense of others, how do policy makers decide which areas of research are deserving of increased funding? Finally, while the report acknowledges the need for a "priority setting framework," what form should this framework take?

According to the Institute of Medicine's (1979) *DHEW's Research Planning Principles: A Review*, two of the foremost goals of the research enterprise are to "advance the fundamental knowledge base of the health sciences, and to translate fundamental knowledge into improved diagnostic, treatment and preventive interventions, and thereby help to alleviate suffering, improve the quality of life, and enhance survival" (Institute of Medicine 1979, p. 11). The means by which to achieve these goals are the various disciplines of medical research, which include the biomedical sciences, the clinical sciences, and the population-based sciences (ibid., p. 14). It is important to note that each of these disciplines contains both fundamental and applied components, the line between which is often fuzzy.

Alzheimer's Example

Alzheimer's disease, particularly debilitating due to the dehumanization of the victim, is of increasing concern due to the rapidly growing ranks of the nation's elderly and the increasing prevalence of Alzheimer's disease among them. In an era of scarce research dollars and fierce competition for those dollars, policy makers must decide how much to invest in Alzheimer's research. In the example below, health values are used to estimate the benefits of Alzheimer's research. We have imagined the following scenario: a discovery is made in 1995 that significantly improves the health status of individuals suffering from Alzheimer's disease. We then ask all the individuals suffering from Alzheimer's disease in a 35-year period how much they would be willing to pay to have their health status changed from prediscovery health status to postdiscovery health status. This bid by the group of Alzheimer's patients is our estimate of the value of Alzheimer's research. Since willingness to pay surveys have never been done for individuals with Alzheimer's disease, our bids are constructed using both the quality-adjusted life year (qualy) estimates and the value-of-life estimates presented in Chapter 15. Our Alzheimer's example can be summarized as follows:

i) application of estimates of the incidence of Alzheimer's disease to actual and projected U.S. population figures to obtain the number of people in the U.S. with Alzheimer's disease for a 40-year period;
ii) adjustment of the Alzheimer's population, taking into account the average mortality of the U.S. population;
iii) subdivision of the surviving Alzheimer's population into three degrees of severity, depending on their stage in the progression of the disease;
iv) derivation of the annual willingness to pay for the Alzheimer's population for 5-year intervals; and
v) calculation of the U.S. Alzheimer population's discounted willingness to pay for the improvement in health status achieved as a result of medical research.

Our example begins with the actual and projected U.S. population distribution for ages 65 and over in Table 16.2. Derivation of the number of individuals with Alzheimer's disease requires combining either incidence or prevalence estimates with U.S. population figures. We decided to use estimates of the *incidence* of Alzheimer's disease in order to incorporate the temporal dimension of Alzheimer's disease in our analysis. Our incidence estimates come from a study by Sayetta (1986, table 5). Sayetta's estimates are based on the Baltimore Longitudinal Study and were used in our example for three reasons. First, Sayetta's incidence estimates are the most recent incidence estimates in the U.S. medical literature. Second, Sayetta's incidence estimates refer to senile dementia, Alzheimer's type, as opposed to general senile dementia (of which there are many types). Finally, Sayetta's estimates are derived from a U.S. sample. The average age-specific incidence

TABLE 16.2. U.S. Population Distribution (in Millions), 1980–2030

	Age 65–69	Age 70–74	Age 75–79	Age 80–84	Age 85+
1980	8.8	6.8	4.8	3.0	2.3
1985	9.4	7.6	5.5	3.3	2.7
1990	10.3	8.1	6.1	3.8	3.3
1995	10.0	8.5	6.8	4.5	4.0
2000	9.6	8.9	7.4	5.1	4.6
2005	10.9	9.0	7.3	5.4	5.3
2010	12.2	9.1	7.1	5.6	6.0
2015	14.9	11.5	8.2	5.7	6.3
2020	17.6	13.8	9.2	5.8	6.5
2025	18.3	15.6	11.3	7.4	7.2
2030	19.0	17.3	13.3	9.0	7.9

TABLE 16.3.   The Incidence of Alzheimer's Disease in the United States,
1980–2030

	Age 65–69	Age 70–74	Age 75–79	Age 80–84	Age 85+
Average age-specific incidence of Alzheimer's disease (in %):	.002234	.004478	.008978	.017996	.059061
Average incidence applied to the U.S. population (in thousands):					
1980	19.66	30.45	43.09	53.99	135.84
1985	21.00	34.03	49.38	59.39	159.46
1990	23.01	36.27	54.77	68.38	194.90
1995	22.34	38.06	60.90	80.08	236.24
2000	21.45	39.85	66.44	91.78	271.68
2005	24.35	40.30	65.09	96.28	313.02
2010	27.25	40.75	63.74	100.78	354.36
2015	33.29	51.27	73.17	102.58	369.13
2020	39.32	61.80	82.60	104.38	383.89
2025	40.88	69.63	101.00	133.17	425.23
2030	42.45	77.47	119.41	161.96	466.57

estimate of Alzheimer's disease in Table 16.3 were then applied to the population figures in Table 16.2. The rest of Table 16.3 shows how many people are expected to contract Alzheimer's disease in a given year.

In an important study, Philipson and Posner (1993) consider the fact that medical improvements for AIDS, by lowering the costs of the disease, will reduce people's efforts to avoid it. The benefits will not be as great as estimated if the effects of the medical improvement on the epidemiology of the disease are ignored. Their analysis brings out often neglected considerations for infectious diseases. These considerations do not enter our analysis because of our assumption that there is no known way to avoid Alzheimer's disease.

Our next step is to convert the number of people *contracting* Alzheimer's disease (incidence) each year into the number of people who *have* Alzheimer's disease (prevalence) each year. As one might realize, the number of people contracting Alzheimer's disease is a small fraction of the number of people who have Alzheimer's disease. Since people with Alzheimer's disease go through various stages in the disease, perhaps it is unfair to count those in the very early stages of Alzheimer's disease in the same way as we count those in the very late stages of the disease. Drawing on the temporal course of Alzheimer's disease outlined in Reisberg et al. (1989), we characterize individuals contracting Alzheimer's as being in one of three stages. In our "mild" stage, lasting for approximately 7 years, individuals exhibit decreased performance in demanding employment and social settings. In our "intermediate" stage, lasting 3 1/2 years, individuals exhibit knowledge deficits, concentration deficits, and decreased ability in performance of complex tasks such as managing finances or preparing dinner for guests. In addition, individuals exhibit deficits sufficient to interfere with independent community survival with inability to recall a major relevant aspect of current and past life. In our "severe" stage, lasting 6 1/2 years, patients exhibit a deficit sufficient to require assistance with basic activities of daily life such as dressing and bathing with general lack of awareness regarding recent events and life experiences and sketchy knowledge of personal history. In addition, individuals exhibit a deficit sufficient to require assistance with toileting and feeding, with severely impaired verbal abilities, and loss of ambulatory skills.

The construction of Table 16.5 requires two steps. In the first step we assumed people contract Alzheimer's disease, go through the three stages of the disease, and then die. In the second step we adjust the Alzheimer's population based on national mortality figures listed in Table 16.4. Table 16.5 shows the number of individuals with Alzheimer's disease, by severity, at 5-year intervals in the years 1995–2030.

TABLE 16.4. Deaths Expected from
Alzheimer's Disease per 1,000 Alive

Age	Expected Deaths per 1,000 Alive	5-Year Survival Percentage
65–69	19.10	.98090
70–74	29.01	.97099
75–79	43.45	.95655
80–84	66.00	.93400
85–89	100.00	.90000
90–94	150.00	.85000
95–99	225.00	.77500

TABLE 16.5. Alzheimer's Population, by Severity,
Decay Adjusted (in Thousands)

	Mild	Intermediate	Severe
1995	787	268	198
2000	896	311	225
2005	993	359	261
2010	1084	402	300
2015	1170	439	334
2020	1252	477	364
2025	1390	513	394
2030	1579	550	426

Now that the Alzheimer population for a 35-year interval has been estimated, we want to quantify the benefits of a potential discovery that improves the health status of individuals with Alzheimer's disease. Two components are required to estimate the benefits of a potential discovery resulting from medical research: the improvement in health status resulting from the discovery, and the value the Alzheimer's population places on those improvements. The first component requires speculation on both the nature of the therapy that medical research would deliver and the specific areas of health status the therapy would improve.

In considering possible innovations that would lead to an improvement in health status of victims of Alzheimer's disease, two avenues are explored. In the first case, a hypothetical drug therapy is examined. In the second case, a hypothetical behavioral therapy is examined. However, both hypothetical research discoveries are similar in the following respects: first, life is not extended as a result of either therapy. Second, the degenerative process of the disease is not reversed, although a discovery of this magnitude may not be far off. That is, cognitive and activities of daily living functions are never restored to their "pre-Alzheimer" status.

The possibility of drugs to treat Alzheimer's disease is frequently mentioned in the medical research community. While progress is occurring rapidly in the field, as of this writing, no widely effective drug is available. Behavioral approaches have also been considered to treat the symptoms of Alzheimer's disease. This class of treatments is based on the premise that manipulation of the environment as well as interaction between caregiver and patient can provide substantial benefits for the Alzheimer's patient. Initial interviews with the patient and the patient's family can give caregivers the information they need to customize a care plan to a patient's needs. A major tenet of the behavioral approach is to not do "for" the patient but do "with" the patient. This seems to slow the rapid decline of self-care capabilities and promote the patient's independence and self-esteem. Manipulation of the environment to reduce the likelihood of stressful or disorienting situations can reduce the frequency of agitative behavior. Establishment of a routine can increase self-care capabilities as habit replaces functions previously executed by memory. Verbal and nonverbal cues can help with a patient's lost communication skills, and meaningful and reminiscent activities can substantially improve a patient's mood.

Based on the present state of medical research, we thought it not implausible to speculate that a hypothetical drug therapy brought about by medical research could slow the deterioration of cognitive function and social-emotional function. A hypothetical improvement in behavioral therapy could slow the patient's loss of ability to perform everyday tasks, as well as reduce agitative behavior and social isolation. We now link our analysis of the health states resulting from untreated Alzheimer's disease, as well as Alzheimer's disease treated by our two therapies, to a framework that can convert health states into utility values.

Using the four components of the health state classification system developed by Drummond, Stoddart, and Torrance (1987), we first tried to match the symptoms of various stages of untreated Alzheimer's disease (Table 15.6) with one of the 960 possible health states. We then established health status improvements for each of our hypothetical discoveries. In summary, we predicted that a drug therapy could result in improvements in the "health problem" category (m_4) and the "social-emotional function" category (m_3), while a behavioral therapy could result in improvements in the "social-emotional function" category (m_3) and the "role function" category (m_2). We now have the first component required to estimate the health benefits from a potential Alzheimer's treatment brought about by medical research.

The second component required for the estimation of health benefits is the value Alzheimer's patients place on the improved health status. A widely used metric for individual's valuation (in utility terms) of health status is the qualy. To obtain qualy values for health states in our base (untreated) case, drug therapy case, and behavioral therapy case, we used the multiattribute utility function method developed by Drummond, Stoddart, and Torrance (1987). The resulting qualy values are shown in Table 16.6. To convert individual's valuation of health status changes (brought about by the new therapy) to dollar terms requires multiplication of the qualy gain by the value of life estimates from Chapter 15 ($120,000 per year). This gives us individuals' bids to change their health status from prediscovery status to postdiscovery status and, hence, gives us their valuation of the medical re-

TABLE 16.6. Qualy Values, by Case Type

	m_1	m_2	m_3	m_4	Qualy Value
Base case:					
Mild	1.00	.94	1.00	.93	.82
Intermediate	.89	.75	.86	.86	.28
Severe	.80	.50	.77	.69	− .12
Drug therapy case:					
Mild	1.00	.94	1.00	1.00	.91
Intermediate	.89	.75	1.00	.93	.46
Severe	.80	.50	.96	.86	.05
Behavioral therapy case:					
Mild	1.00	.97	1.00	.93	.86
Intermediate	.89	.85	1.00	.86	.50
Severe	.80	.75	.91	.69	.11

TABLE 16.7.   Individual Willingness to Pay, by Case
Type (in Thousands of Dollars)

	Base Case	Drug Therapy Case	Behavioral Therapy Case
Mild	21.6	10.8	16.8
Intermediate	86.4	64.8	60.0
Severe	134.4	118.0	106.8

TABLE 16.8.   Discounted Population Willingness to Pay,
by Case Type (in Billions of Dollars)

	Base Case	Drug Therapy Case	Behavioral Therapy Case
Discounted population willingness to pay	1,185	864	895
Value of therapy		321	290

search (broadly defined) that led to the discovery. These bids are given in
Table 16.7.

To arrive at the total discounted value of the medical research requires
the following: conversion of the individual Alzheimer's patient's valuation
of the medical research to the Alzheimer's population valuation of the
medical research, then discounting the dollar value by the real rate of interest. Table 16.8 contains the total discounted values. According to our estimates, the Alzheimer's population of years 1995–2030 would be willing to
pay 321 billion and 290 billion dollars for improvements in health status
achieved by the hypothetical drug and behavioral therapies, respectively.
While these benefits seem large, their expected value would be considerably
smaller if one considered the likelihood of a discovery. Comparison of the
benefits with the costs of the Alzheimer's research, and the larger benefits
associated with other forms of research, would be needed to make an informed judgment about whether the research would be justified. Assuming
that we define medical research rather broadly, our willingness to pay estimates are good proxies for the value of the medical research that led to the
development of the hypothetical therapies.

Policy makers could conceivably divide our benefit estimate by a cost
estimate to form a "benefit per dollar invested" measure of medical research directed at Alzheimer's disease. Benefits could be estimated for
various medical research projects, and the "benefit per dollar invested"
estimates could serve as a ranking mechanism. Policy makers would then
have a method by which investment levels in competing research endeavors

could be determined. Before we proceed to lay out this methodology, however, we need to qualify our "value of medical research" estimates.

The average 300 billion dollar estimate of benefits resulting from medical research aimed at ameliorating the symptoms of Alzheimer's disease, while impressive, does not take account of the probability of success of or the cost of other research and, most important, does not consider the benefits relating to benefits that might be achieved in other types of medical research.

A theme that emerges is that health values are large, as found for Alzheimer's symptoms, even though Alzheimer's research may be funded overly handsomely relative to much other medical research for which less publicity has been generated. A basic reason for large benefits is that the benefits of health research extend to future generations. We hypothesize that the benefits of more health research would exceed the costs, but that paying more attention to health values would lead to large reshuffling of medical research priorities, especially toward basic research.

Much, if not most, discussion of medical research priorities consists of advocacy for research into individual diseases, particularly those that catch the public eye because of interest group activity, for example, Alzheimers and AIDS. We are not asserting that Alzheimer's, AIDS, or any particular disease is overfunded or underfunded. To reach conclusions of this kind would require combining health values with estimates of costs of medical research and probabilities of success, which we heartily recommend but which to our knowledge no one has yet done.

There is also advocacy of increased medical research expenditure on the part of those representing the medical research establishment as a whole with relatively few attempts to recommend hard, rational choices among types of medical research. The issues of rational allocation are clearly extremely complex, especially in view of spillover effects, where research in one area benefits research in other areas. The need to de-emphasize development of expensive high-tech machine treatments that become overused once developed and crowd out more mundane but more valuable treatment should be investigated dispassionately.

16.5. Encouraging Better Lifestyles

A major challenge in the area of public health is to encourage people to choose healthier lifestyles. In a report that includes the oft-cited conclusion that as much as 50% of mortality in 1976 was due to unhealthy lifestyles, the U.S. Surgeon General made health promotion and disease prevention a high priority (U.S. Department of Health, Education and Welfare 1979). This section illustrates the use of the health values in making decisions about health promotion by analyzing two policies. The first is an extension of one of the mainstays in the antismoking campaign: the public provision of information about the health consequences of smoking. The second is a less traditional policy tool in public health: taxation of alcoholic beverages to reduce traffic fatalities by reducing alcohol consumption.

Smoking and Health Education

In most experts' opinions, smoking is the single most important health lifestyle issue; the Public Health Service estimates that smoking is responsible for approximately 320,000 deaths annually in the United States. Smoking will remain a major cause of death for years into the future. This would be true even if all smokers were to cease immediately, because of the periods of latency that precede the onset of disease. And smoking will not stop immediately; in 1985 approximately 56 million Americans between ages 15 and 84 were smokers.

A rationale for public health education policies exists if all or some smokers are unaware of the health consequences of smoking. It should be stressed that, if a perfectly informed consumer decided to smoke only after weighing the internal health costs of smoking with the pleasure it yields, most antismoking policies would be presumed to decrease welfare. With substantial external costs associated with smoking, in terms of health effects on other persons, the individual's calculation would not be socially optimal, but Manning et al. (1989) estimate that on average the external costs of smoking are approximately internalized by federal, state, and local taxes. However, this is all assuming smokers know the consequences to their health. Imperfect consumer information, however, provides a rationale for public-sector involvement that few would argue with. It remains a question of research whether the benefits of this involvement outweigh the costs.

The specific public-sector involvement to be considered is a school-based health education program for students in grades 4–7. The analysis will calculate the benefits and costs of running the program for 1 year. Information on several school health programs comes from the School Health Education Evaluation, a massive project that involved more than 30,000 children in grades 4–7 from 20 states (Connell, Turner, and Mason 1985). In terms of general effectiveness, the programs evaluated met their objectives of improving health knowledge, attitudes, and practices. For smoking, the evaluation found that "less than 8 percent of the seventh grade health program classroom students reported that they were smoking, compared to more than 12 percent of the comparison classroom seventh graders" (ibid., p. 316). Although the long-term reduction in smoking is not known, it will be assumed that the adult smoking participation rate will be 5% lower among children in the school health program. This is chosen as a reasonably conservative estimate, and several additional pieces of evidence corroborate it. Fielding (1985) reports that students exposed to newer curricula in health education have started smoking at rates 15%–50% lower than those of con-

TABLE 16.9.   Benefits of Reduced Smoking Prevalence
due to School Health Education

Cause of Death	Lives Saved	Value of Life (in $ Millions)	Undiscounted Benefits (in $ Billions)	Discounted Benefits (in $ Billions)°
Heart disease	84,555	3	254	7.7
Cancer	56,370	4	225	6.8
Chronic obstructive pulmonary disease	28,185	3.5	99	3.0
Total	169,110		578	17.5

° Assumes benefits occur 60 years in the future and a discount rate of 6%.

trol groups, which imply a 5%–10% reduction in smoking participation. Kenkel (1991) also estimates that improving health knowledge could lead to a reduction in smoking participation in this range. Using 1985 as a base year, with over 11 million students enrolled in public schools in grades 4–7, a reduction of 5 percentage points in smoking participation translates into 563,700 fewer smokers.

The next step is to calculate the improvement in health that follows the reduction in smoking. Fielding (1985) provides estimates of the annual number of heart disease deaths, cancer deaths, and chronic obstructive pulmonary deaths (COPD) due to smoking. Dividing these estimates by the number of smokers yields a smoker's annual risk of dying of each condition. Assuming a smoking lifetime of 45 years yields rough estimate of the lifetime excess risks a smoker faces: an extra 15% chance of dying of heart disease, an extra 10% chance of dying of lung cancer, and an extra 5% of dying of COPD. The second column of Table 16.9 contains the predicted number of lives saved due to the school health education program. The predictions are simply the product of the excess risks of smoking and the reduction in the number of smokers (563,700). Totally, school health education is predicted to save 169,110 lives.

The value of the life-saving effects of the school health education program can now be calculated as the product of the number of lives saved and the dollar value of a statistical life. Chapter 15 contains state-of-the art estimates of the value of a statistical life, dependent upon cause of death; the medium estimates are reproduced in the third column of Table 16.9. As can be seen in the fourth column, the calculations yield a huge estimate of the undiscounted health benefits of the education program, $578 billion. However, it makes sense to assume that the deaths averted for these fourth to seventh graders would have occurred about 60 years in the future. The present value of $578 billion 60 years from is much smaller. The last column of Table 16.9 contains the present value of the health benefits, using a discount rate of 0.06. The present value of the total benefits is $17.5 billion. The last step is to estimate the costs of the school health education program and to calculate the net benefits. Connell, Turner, and Mason (1985) report that the most expensive program involved an average cost per student of $84. Still assuming the program involves 563,700 students, this implies a total cost of $47,350,800. The bottom line is that the school health program is estimated to yield positive net benefits of over $17 billion: the value of the lives saved is far in excess of the costs of the program. Although the analysis is admittedly incomplete, in many cases correcting omissions would reinforce this conclusion. For instance, the cost estimates are based on school health education programs that emphasize more health problems than smoking. This means that the programs would yield health benefits due to other reasons than smoking reduction. Including these would increase the estimate of net benefits, probably by a substantial margin.

Death, Taxes, and Alcohol

Several empirical studies show that higher taxes on alcoholic beverages can reduce drunk driving. As Phelps (1988) puts it, this creates an opportunity for substitution between the two inevitable facts of life—death and taxes. In recent years states and the federal government have enacted policies to combat drunk driving, but Phelps notes that alcohol taxation was neglected as a possible policy tool. In fact, real alcohol taxes declined for many years, as inflation eroded the real value of federal excise taxes fixed in nominal terms. To address the question of whether alcohol taxes are too high, too low, or about right, Phelps compares the costs of increasing taxes to the benefits of reducing fatalities due to drunk driving. Phelps's study is an excellent example of the guidance for public policy provided by the type of analysis advocated in this book.

Phelps's study focuses on young drinkers and drivers, due to data availability as well as the tragic consequences of drunk driving in this group. He estimates the effects of taxation on fatalities caused by young drunk drivers by combining the results of a microdata study by Grossman, Coate, and Arluck (1987) with autopsy data on blood alcohol contents of fatally injured drivers. For instance, he estimates that a tax of approximately 35% of the retail price of beer would eliminate about half of the alcohol-related fatalities arising from youthful drivers, while a 50% tax could eliminate about three-quarters of the fatalities.

A study by Saffer and Grossman (1987) using different methods and data confirms Phelps's conclusion that increasing alcohol taxes could save lives. This does not by itself imply that increasing taxes is a good idea, however. The tax hurts everyone who consumes alcohol, in the form of lost consumers' surplus. By comparing the losses in consumers' surplus to the lives saved, Phelps calculates the optimal tax under a variety of assumptions. As one example, if youths who drink and drive have fully internalized the risk of death to themselves, the benefits of the tax are the saved lives of nondrivers. Using a value of $3 million per life, Phelps's calculations suggest that the optimal tax is about 35%.

Overall, since Phelps's study is very carefully done, his conclusion that the optimal alcohol taxes appear to lie in the range of 25%–49% or more warrants serious consideration. At least as important as his quantitative conclusions is the contribution Phelps makes to incorporate rational decision-making tools, including estimates of the value of life, into the emotional topic of drunk-driving-related deaths.

16.6. Health and the Courts

The tort liability system is often claimed to be in a state of crisis. Excessive awards for pain and suffering are a popular explanation for the problem. Setting upper limits to awards for pain and suffering, or even eliminating them entirely from tort awards, have been suggested legislative remedies. But these are arbitrary solutions that will produce anomalous effects on behavior. We argue here for measures that include utility losses from pain and suffering, resulting in values higher than traditional forgone earnings measures but lower than the sometimes capricious large amounts awarded more on misguided equity grounds than on grounds of encouraging appropriate risk-reduction behavior.

The courts make damage awards to discourage injury and to compensate those injured. If the courts are to choose levels of liability that lead to optimal deterrence, then loss of life, disease, and injury must be correctly valued and fully accounted for. The law and economics literature is clear on these matters. See, for example, Posner (1992, pp. 196–201).

This literature, however, appears to be centered for the most part on application of the value of life concept to valuation of death. Less progress has been made in the injury area. Nonpecuniary losses loom large in many of these cases. ("Because nonpecuniary losses are not clearly defined in dollar terms, it is difficult to specify the damages payment likely to be used by the courts. Formal analyses of liability rules are nearly silent on this question." [Calfee and Rubin 1992, p. 379]). Pain and suffering have long been a vexing problem for tort law. While they are a real part of cases that come to court, nevertheless they have seemed to be nebulous and undefinable. The temptation has been to dismiss pain and suffering altogether and base judgments on cost of illness and forgone earnings, which are traditional and appear to be more objective measures of loss (Posner 1992, p. 197).

Economic analysis has established that these measures are not satisfactory. Health values are more comprehensive measures that incorporate utility losses as well as costs and earnings losses that are derived from traditional market measures. The potential contribution of health values to the economic analysis of law lies in providing comprehensive measures of damage that can help determine efficient levels of liability in injury cases, as well as death preceded by pain and suffering.

While court applications of health values await future developments, "there is a slight movement, mainly in federal civil rights cases, toward the award of damages for lost utility of living ('hedonic damages')" (Posner 1992, p. 197). In a landmark death case later affirmed by the U.S. Court of Appeals in 1987, the decedent's estate was awarded $850,000 for so-called hedonic damages, based on the testimony of an expert witness (*Sherrod vs. Berry*, 629 F. Supp. s159). The expert witness, Stanley Smith, testified that appropriate damages should exceed the traditional measures of lost earnings capacity, using essentially the same arguments advanced in favor of the willingness to pay approach for public policy decisions. These measures of damage have been challenged in court however.

It is important to view the tort system, like regulation, in terms of both efficiency and equity. Then health values once again play a key, but distinct, role in the treatment of problems, once again within Viscusi's framework (1984*b*, pp. 65–70). An important example is appropriate compensation in the event of death. Dead people, it is pointed out, cannot be compensated. Therefore, goes the argument, the dead person's prior valuation of life is not relevant to any compensation that is actually paid. Furthermore, attempts to compensate heirs on the basis of the decedent's value of life sends inappropriate signals to potential plaintiffs, resulting in nonoptimal efforts at risk reduction. A corollary to this argument must be the idea that the applicability of health values derived from value-of-life literature should be restricted to cases of nonfatal disease or injury.

The key point is that the amount of compensation actually paid to (or on behalf of) a victim is a matter of equity and should be independent of the penalty tax imposed upon the perpetrator of ex ante risks, which should be designed to encourage reasonable behavior by the injurer. The amount of tax or penalty should be based on the expected loss of life from these risks to encourage optimal safety measures; whereas the amount paid to heirs may be determined by entirely different principles related to equity. This is true both in the case of regulation and tort law compensation. But having established the expected loss of life, the value curve V of Figure 16.1 is determined by applying to it an ex ante value of life. Recognizing the ex ante nature of the problem, on the one hand, establishes the relevance of health values to encouraging efficiency with regard to avoiding mortality as well as nonfatal disease or injury. The ex post matter of compensating those injured and their relatives, on the other hand, is a matter of equity, though here, too, some efficiency considerations enter. For example, the prospect of handsome awards for damages may encourage potential victims to be lax in their avoidance behavior.

Health values can form part of an approach to tort law problems in a framework that preserves proper incentives to efficient behavior as well as conferring just compensation on victims. The reason is that, if firms are to provide the optimum amount of risk reduction, they should not be liable for payments to victims that exceed the marginal damages caused by workplace hazards. Less than certain probability of detection is an economically valid reason for assessing penalties that exceed damages. It is important that potential injurers *expect* to pay for the full value of damages that they cause. We do not argue that punitive damages have absolutely no place in tort law. We do argue that excessively high deep-pocket awards encourage unreasonably great efforts to reduce risks, going beyond the point where the measures are worth the extra safety achieved and being unbalanced as compared to safety efforts in other areas.

Deep-pocket awards are as offensive to principles of equity as to efficiency just discussed. A person injured in the workplace may receive an award making him or her a millionaire, while a next-door neighbor receiving the same type of injury as a result of an act of God unrelated to work receives nothing. As a minimum, Viscusi (1989b) stresses, the amount of tort awards received by victims should be "reduced by the amount of disability compensation already received" (p. 78). This approach would maintain the priority that "victims be compensated from a social insurance fund financed by a general payroll tax" (p. 77). Taking prior compensation into account at least goes part way toward satisfying the equity principle of equal treatment of equals—specifically victims, who cannot bring a tort law suit.

We do not pretend in this discussion to offer full solutions to the problems of arranging appropriate risk-reduction incentives through the legal system, which involve problems when damagee as well as producer behavior affects probability that damages will be incurred, and other complications. The best and most comprehensive treatment of these problems we know of are in Landes and Posner (1987) and Posner (1992). Our major point, consistent with their work, is that the courts need to apply measures of damages based on sound economic principles.

16.7. Health Values and Clinical Practice

Health-care policy decisions, which have been the focus of the previous sections of this chapter, involve resource allocation at the societal level.

Concomitantly, the economic allocation of resources at the clinical level, by the individual physician, is becoming more and more widely recognized as an unavoidable necessity.

Physicians and policymakers play strongly complementary roles in the production of health—the latter being importantly concerned with the size and composition of the flow of resources into health production, the former with the use of those resources in close cooperation with the patient. Choice in the use of resources among competing uses is inevitably a concern. To the clientele of the policy maker, health is an activity competing for scarce resources at the societal level. For the patient, in contrast, health is often a dominant and immediate concern; there is resistance to viewing health as being subject to the laws that govern economic choice, especially when insurance is involved, but though it may sometimes be embarrassing to discuss, every patient knows that costs are in fact a limiting factor that often precludes measures that would be taken if they were completely free. Patients of course come from society, and every member of society is destined to be a patient at one time or another. Hence, at times the complementary roles of physician and policy maker can become disguised, just as do the interests of society and patient.

The problem goes beyond the moral hazard problem of the patient having an incentive to get all the treatment possible if third parties are paying. For example, all the other policy applications in this book concerning the value of life pertain to value in a statistical sense—that is, willingness to pay for a change in a small risk of death—as opposed to considering situations applied to a single individual where an action will have a certain or near-certain effect on whether the person lives. In his original, seminal work on the value of life, Mishan (1971) pointed out this essential distinction, noting that a person is willing to pay much more to avoid death with certainty, in which he loses his entire surplus from living, than he or she is willing to pay for adjustments in small risks of death inevitably faced in everyday life, as is assured in most of the health-policy issues considered in this book. In clinical decisions, the problem is encountered when decisions that affect whether life is prolonged with certainty or near certainty must often be made. The problem does not affect all clinical decisions since willingness to pay for much symptom relief, particularly minor symptoms, is not a matter of probability. Nonetheless, the problem is sufficiently encountered in clinical situations to raise special problems of applying willingness to pay.

LaPuma and Lawlor (1990) argue that there is a "new financial ethos" at work in medical decision making and that it is encroaching on the domain of the caregiver. To them, medical care threatens to become just another commodity as physician decisions are increasingly governed by social-science constructs that represent an anonymous average patient. Society, with its interest in making the most of scarce resources, is coming into conflict with the interests of the patient.

In dealing with the problem of health values at the clinical level, LaPuma and Lawlor focus their concern on the adequacy and applicability of the qualy, but willingness to pay and the economic demand for health are equally implicated by their comments. Diagnosis-related groups illustrate the problem. Though initially designed to guide resource allocation decisions for large groups of people, they have "been employed directly in clinical decision making about individual cases. . . . While there is nothing wrong with encouraging physicians to be efficient, the point is that both QALYs and diagnosis related groups try to combine efficiency with equity to yield a blunt, economically driven tool" (p. 2920). The authors fear that the physician's role will become redefined to include being advocate and negotiator at the policy level, as well as caregiver to the individual patient (p. 2920). Another of their fears is that quantification of outcomes for policy purposes will lead to a neglect of the physician's many intangible contributions to patients and their families (p. 2918).

The elements of a solution to these problems are stated by LaPuma and Lawlor, though they remain skeptical that they are likely to be properly implemented. "Using . . . [a qualy-based] policy to allocate resources at a high level could be tenable, . . . [and] a sound public policy statement on health care resources could be made. . . . The physician should not be in the position of defending public policy: patient advocate or public agent should be an easy choice" (p. 2919).

That the physician's role as allocative agent does not involve easy choices is becoming more and more widely recognized, however. "Physicians can no longer ignore the effect of financial constraints of clinical decision making, as some ethicists have suggested they do. . . . The end of good medical practice is best served by acknowledging rather than by denying the influence of economic realities on clinical practice" (Schiedermayer, LaPuma, and Miles 1989, p. 1305). Developing an "ethically sound framework for clinical decision making" (LaPuma, Cassel, and Humphrey 1988, p. 1809) is the challenge that faces the medical community in meeting this problem. The employment of ethics consultants and ethics committees is one part of the proposed framework. But the physician is an essential part of that framework. "Those with clinical judgment and a primary commitment to patient care are best equipped to undertake those responsibilities and to articulate the ethical values relevant to resource allocation" (ibid., p. 1811).

Morreim (1989) says that "until recently, generous third-party reimbursements enabled physicians to pursue each patient's interests with little regard for costs" (p. 1012). In recent years, the attempt to gain more effective control over the size of the health care bill, either at the national or lower levels, has pitted the interests of the individual patient against competing interests, both medical and nonmedical, of other parties. The physician's participation in cost containment raises ethical questions in the medical community.

Some are clearly skeptical about the usefulness of trying to apply health values in a clinical setting. "Many physicians and bioethicists insist that physicians can and should avoid directly compromising their patient's care to save third parties' money" (Morreim 1989, p. 1012). LaPuma and Lawlor express the same view. They say, "Medical treatments are not like other commodities that can be proffered and purchased. . . . Excluding needy patients must be an anathema to both policy-makers and physicians" (1990, pp. 2920–21).

There is an ethical dilemma to cost containment according to one notion of justice. The ethical principle, according to Morreim, is closure, which means that medical resources denied to a patient must become available to a needier patient, rather than to third parties outside the medical-care system (Morreim 1989, p. 1012). This principle might have stood unchallenged at the physician level in the era before cost containment pressure. Limits to health care took the form of inadequate access to the system and shortages of specific commodities, such as intensive-care beds or hemodialysis units. Difficult allocation decisions must be made in response to these resource limitations, and they involve clear gainers of medical benefit, as well as losers (ibid., pp. 1012–13).

As long as cost containment exerts a strong influence on medical choices, physicians will need to make clinical resource-allocation decisions or else yield an important part of the practice of medicine to others (Morreim 1989, p. 1014). A challenge to the health profession is to devise a framework that takes a prudent amount of this burden away from physicians while providing them with assistance in making the allocative choices that remain.

Fuchs (1980, p. 938) has useful advice: "It will be important to insulate the individual practitioner from explicit involvement on a day-to-day basis because of potential conflict with the commitment to do what is best for each patient. Thus, the best time for evaluations and trade-offs will usually be when decisions are made about construction of facilities, authorization of new technologies, training of personnel, and setting of standards and procedures. Practicing physicians have a great deal to contribute to those decisions."

Closer to the clinical decision level, "fiscal efficiency guidelines are now emerging throughout medicine" (Morreim 1989, p. 1013). The American College of Physicians has issued diagnostic testing guidelines for a variety of tests in collaboration with Blue Cross and Blue Shield. Health maintenance organizations have developed hospitalization- and technology-utilization guidelines. Third-party payers have developed guidelines to determine reimbursement criteria for various medical interventions (ibid.).

Measures of health values based on willingness to pay and qualy analysis provide a useful input into decision making at all levels—from the most general policy-making level to the clinical level where the welfare of particular patients is at stake. This is not to say that willingness to pay analysis is a substitute for knowledgeable judgment at any of these levels. It is rather a useful ingredient that can help to clarify those judgments regarding the important and difficult area of individual health preferences. The analysis gives policy makers a better understanding of the preferences of the community they are serving. At the clinical level, it helps practitioners reduce to some degree the subjectivity of judgments about quality of life (LaPuma and Lawlor 1990, p. 2920). Weinstein (1980) points out the complementarity of policy-level research with clinical decision making in his article on estrogen therapy. "The decision to use estrogens will, no doubt, remain an intensely personal one among the patient, perhaps her family, and her physician. Nevertheless, in a world of limited resources, it is incumbent on those of us in the research community to elucidate the impact of such decisions at the societal level. The insights thus gained should lead to even more informed and wise decisions at the individual level" (p. 315).

In their study of coronary artery bypass surgery, Weinstein, Pliskin, and Stason (1977) examined the question of surgery versus medical management from both a societal and a clinical point of view. The authors tentatively conclude that surgery is the optimal decision in several of the situations they examined. Nevertheless they judge this surgery to be questionable when viewed from the societal perspective. The analysis underscores the nature of the dilemma that can arise because allocative decisions arise at the clinical level.

One of the limitations of most existing qualy or willingness to pay analyses is that they pertain to existing or prospective conditions—end states—rather than the clinical process itself. Mooney (1989) states that qualy analysis implicitly holds that all utility is outcome based and that no utility originates in the clinical process itself (p. 150). LaPuma and Lawlor (1990) point out that physicians often give patients and family help of many kinds that does not result in an intervention with a measurable outcome. Too much attention to the qualy risks favoring the measurable outcome over the clinical process itself, to the detriment of the patient (LaPuma and Lawlor, 1990, pp. 2918, 2919).

Berwick and Weinstein (1985) argue, however, that the values created by the clinical process are just as amenable to measurement as the outcomes produced by medical interventions. The authors demonstrate, in a carefully designed study of willingness to pay for ultrasound in normal pregnancy, that the benefits of the clinical process, whether or not related to the making of medical decisions, can be quantified and valued. Benefits of the clinical process are seen to be both decisional and nondecisional and to benefit both patient and doctor. Nondecisional benefits pertain to the intrinsic value of information, such as satisfaction to the doctor or reassurance to the patient. Decisional benefits lead to medical decisions, such as choice of medication, and nonmedical decisions, such as modified behavior on the part of the patient. Almost half of expressed willingness to pay "for the test information was for uses in the nonmedical and/or nondecisional realms of their own utility" (p. 889).

Berwick and Weinstein have demonstrated that the clinical process itself is capable of being analyzed systematically for the intrinsic values that others have claimed elude analysis and that these values can be large. While some of the public health literature dismisses utility or demand analysis on the grounds that it misses the intangible aspects of important problems, the Berwick and Weinstein article in our view helps support the idea that the intangibility argument is obsolete.

Though in our view health values as part of the general background of clinical decision making have an important contribution to make, this is not to claim that distributional problems that are ethical in nature can be resolved by choice of analytic technique. Smith (1987) states, "A choice of whom to treat based on any form of cost-effectiveness assessment will always favor patients whose age or disease confers the prospect of longer and better-quality survival." He suggests that perhaps resources should be allocated to those most in need, "with the general objective of reducing health variance" (p. 1135). The egalitarian assumption of qualy analysis does not make this demand. Under that principle, a year of healthy life is to be valued equally no matter who receives it—rich or poor, young or old, and so on. Smith's suggested criterion holds that the egalitarian assumption leads to unfair allocations.

Rawles (1989, p. 146) makes the same argument, explaining that 1 year of healthy life to ten people may be less fair than 10 such years to one individual, which is certainly true as at least a possibility depending on the other circumstances of the people affected. Rawles also argues much more questionably in our view, that the precedence of life-saving interventions over life-enhancing ones is a matter of justice (pp. 145–46), seeming to argue that 1 extra year of life under miserable conditions is always to be chosen over keeping longevity the same and raising quality from misery to normal health.

Ethical principles may never be fully resolved in medical decision making, whether at the policy level or the clinical level. A contribution that economic analysis can make is to assist in revealing the preferences of the people who are involved: the general population at the policy level, individual patients at the clinical level. At the policy level, where unidentified patients are involved, preferences in the population will indeed favor those who stand to gain more because of age, extent of recovery from disease, or prospects for longer or better-quality survival. Similarly, one can approach the valuation of life saving versus life enhancing from the point of view of first principles of justice. But health value analysis makes it clear that the problem can be viewed as a problem of personal preference and choice, and it has produced a large amount of evidence that people choose to make these trade-offs in their lives. The problem involving healthy time for one person versus ten persons works the same way. Framing this example differently would reveal it more clearly to be a problem of choice. Consider ten people who each have 20 years of life expectancy. Condition A might entail 40 days of pain per year for each of them, for the rest of their lives. A time trade-off analysis might reveal that these people would be willing to sacrifice 1 year of life with condition A to have 19 years of normal health. An intervention that rid the people of this condition would be worth one qualy to each of them. Condition B might be a more severe problem pertaining to one person. This person might be able to gain approximately 12.5 years of life expectancy from an operation. After listening to a description of life after the operation, the patient might rate the quality of additional life at 0.80. This information implies a lifetime qualy gain of 12.5 years times 0.80, or 10 years for that person.

In terms of utility analysis, conditions A and B are identical. They turn out that way because of the preferences people reveal after thinking carefully about a problem. There is no other reason for regarding them as equivalent. Real-life examples would be far more complicated and the relationships among them accordingly more obscure. Analyzing them in terms of an individual person's preferences is a way of comparing them and making policy or clinical decisions in a way that makes sense.

Rawles, who was mentioned above, prefers to ignore the dimension of preferences and analyze the problem from ethical first principles. He prefers to concentrate the extra years of life in one person because "it helps to redress the inequitable distribution of misfortune in an unfair world" (1989, p. 146). Rawles thus solves the efficiency-equity problem by entirely ignoring efficiency and, in this sense, begs the question. More reasonable in our view is to recognize both efficiency and equity, and the large domain of issues where efficiency properly interpreted can contribute to solutions.

The growing pressures of cost containment have caused resource allocation decisions to penetrate down to the level of clinical practice in ways that did not exist in earlier days. This has created a need to develop principles and methods of resource allocation appropriate to clinical practice. More fundamentally, it has raised ethical problems concerning the role of the physician in the practice of medicine and the practice of cost containment.

Some authors stress the importance of unmasking the economic aspect of clinical problems that appear to be purely ethical and to minimize the influence of the economic aspect, even though it can't be eliminated (Schiedermayer, LaPuma, and Miles 1989; LaPuma, Cassel, and Humphrey 1988; LaPuma and Lawlor 1990). Other authors see the physician accepting a more active role in allocating resources at the clinical level (Morreim 1989). In this literature, the borderline between ethics and economics is drawn by considering the problem of resource scarcity and the problem of the distribution of resources.

Economic analysis has another contribution to make to this discussion. It can show that apparently ethical problems often mask questions of individual choice. Trade-offs between length and quality of life are an example of choice that recurs in the lives of everyone, and that often involve a person's own resources alone without raising distributional problems. Economic analysis can help to indicate that problems sometimes viewed as ethical are really problems of individual preference in which individuals will be better off if decisions are made according to their own choices. The principle underlying this line of reasoning is that individual preferences count as a basis for making policy and clinical decisions in medicine and should not be sacrificed to arbitrary dictums from others that are offered as ethical principles but seem questionable, as, for example, telling patients that contrary to their own wishes the quantity of life should be viewed as more important than its quality.

16.8. Conclusions

In this chapter we have discussed several areas of policy to which knowledge of health values can make contributions.

1) On health and safety regulation, as in other areas, we have emphasized the need to estimate *extra* benefits and costs applicable to a policy issue, not totals. We showed that it is quite feasible to estimate increased health values due to environmental policies and that these values are increased by adopting the broad willingness to pay approach to health values used in this book.

We have argued that health values are needed to set occupational safety standards in order to encourage employers neither to underprotect nor irrationally overprotect workers from workplace hazards relative to other hazards faced in life. We discussed the need for noncapricious compensation procedures accompanying this approach.

2) On cost containment, the benefits of 20 levels of treatments and diagnostic procedures were compared pertaining to pap smears, mammography, coronary care, bypass surgery, and cholesterol reduction. Using health values, optional levels for each category were estimated.

Health maintenance organizations as a cost containment approach were evaluated by comparing their $5.7 billion cost saving with the reduction in health values using our estimates of $1.56 billion, giving a favorable outcome since costs savings far exceed the loss in health values.

3) On medical research expenditures, we provided a framework for deciding on the allocation of funds to medical research and pointed to neglected, readily quantifiable benefit attributes that we believe should be used explicitly in the evaluation of medical research projects. These include size of population affected, disease duration, quantified effect of quality-of-life improvement to be attained, externalities, and, for basic research, the extent to which the research will contribute to areas of applied research.

We demonstrated the feasibility of quantifying medical research benefits by presenting an example estimating the benefits of a discovery that would improve the health status of individuals suffering from Alzheimer's disease. The estimate of benefits on the order of 300 billion dollars would be used in conjunction with estimates of costs of the research and probability of success, along with comparison to net benefits in other lines of medical research, in deciding on funding. It could still be true that Alzheimer's disease with its high visibility is a relatively overfunded focus of research.

4) On policies toward health lifestyle, we presented two detailed examples of quantitative estimation comparing values of health improvements with program costs, showing the central role that health values can and should play in public health policy. The first example found net benefits, or excess over costs, of $17 billion from an antismoking school education program. The second example reviewed a study by Phelps (1988), emerging with the estimate that a tax on alcohol of 25%–50% is justified in terms of lives that would be saved from reduced drunk driving.

5) On use of health values in court, we argue that sufficient objective evidence on broad-based willingness to pay estimates now exists that the courts should drop their opposition to health values that include pain and suffering and rely on accumulating research evidence and not victims' subjective claims.

We argue for using health value estimates in making damage awards, in place of deep-pocket awards that give highly distorted incentives to undertake preventive measures and bestow capricious windfalls as between those who can make a claim against someone and those suffering because of acts of God.

6) Regarding clinical use of health values, we argue that the inevitable decisions on benefits of treatments versus costs that take place in clinical settings will be undertaken better if more explicitly recognized. The gains can be particularly great in the era of third-party payment.

The discussion of the six areas as reviewed here indicates specific uses of health values. Presently, they are being followed at best to a limited extent.

An overriding idea is that gross misallocations of the medical dollar exist that could be reduced through systematic use of health values in decision making. We conclude that health values need to be used more widely and forcefully in all six policy areas.

We wish to close with two additional suggestions. The first is that benefits of more health research would exceed the costs and that paying more attention to health values would lead to large reshuffling of medical research priorities, especially toward basic research. This theme is apparent in the example of the benefits of ameliorating Alzheimer's symptoms, which were found to be large not withstanding relatively handsome funding of Alzheimer's research. A basic reason for large benefits is that the benefits of health research extend to future generations.

This said, we find remarkably little serious discussion of more specific medical research priorities. There is much advocacy for research into individual diseases, particularly those that catch the public eye because of interest-group activity, and there is much advocacy of increased medical research expenditure on the part of those representing the medical research establishment as a whole. While we have cited some scattered attempts to deal with the question of rational emphasis among types of medical research, there appears to be no constituency for rational allocation except the unorganized public at large.

The tapering off of growth in medical research expenditures, and the lack of attention to health values, with apparently undue influence of interest groups on medical research funding, suggest that more attention to rational allocation of the medical research dollar is a matter of great importance. The issues are clearly extremely complex, especially in view of spillover effects where research in one area benefits research in other areas. Consequences of research breakthroughs need to be considered, suggesting the need to de-emphasize the development of expensive high-tech machine treatments that become overused once developed and crowd out more mundane but more valuable treatment.

To further the use of health values, a National Academy of Sciences effort or a presidential commission, composed of representatives of the medical research community, practitioner doctors, health administrators, health professionals, federal and state government health policy representatives, and economists, could provide a vehicle for continuing investigation and raising of consciousness of the need for rationality in approaching medical research priorities and other health problems.

Our second suggestion is that health values have a great contribution to make in deciding on the amount of the national income to be devoted to health care. Overuse of medical services along with uneconomic cost inflation connected with third-party payment arrangements, both private and public, and commendable redistribution motives leading to subsidizing medical care for lower-income people are among major reasons for rises in health care expenditures. The search for reformed incentives, institutional arrangements, and political compromises on who will pay how much will undoubtedly continue. We would emphasize the constructive role that health values can play in deciding on overall levels of health care. While the redistribution question is always vexing, we do not find that expressed health values vary all that much among people of different incomes. One could compare the health values summarized in Chapter 15, which are representative of average health values, with estimates of the costs of achieving health improvements through provision of care to arrive at societal targets for the amount of health care that should be provided. Use of this type of objective evidence on values and costs could help greatly in attempting to reach a consensus on appropriate levels of health care.

References

Acton, J. J. P. 1973. *Evaluating Public Programs to Save Lives: The Case of Heart Attacks*. Santa Monica, CA: Rand Corp., January.

——. 1975. *Measuring the Social Impact of Heart and Circulatory Disease Programs: Preliminary Framework and Estimates*. Santa Monica, CA: Rand Corp., April.

Aday, L. A., and Eichhorn, R. L. 1972. *The Utilization of Health Services: Indices and Correlates*. Washington, DC: U.S. Government Printing Office.

Adelman, I., and Griliches, Z. 1961. On an Index of Quality Change. *Journal of the American Statistical Association* 56 (September): 535–48.

Allais, M. 1953. Le comportement de l'homme rationnel devant le risque, critiques des postulats et axiomes de l'ecole americaine. *Econometrica* 21 (October): 503–46.

American Cancer Society. 1974. *Cancer Facts and Figures*. New York: American Cancer Society.

Anderson, R., and Crocker, T. 1971. Air Pollution and Residential Property Values. *Urban Studies* 8:171–80.

Ardell, D. 1977. *High-Level Wellness*. Emmaus, PA: Rodale Press.

Arrow, K. J. 1974. Optimal Insurance and Generalized Deductibles. *Scandinavian Actuarial Journal*, pp. 1–42. Reprinted in *The Collected Papers of Kenneth J. Arrow*. Vol. 3, *Individual Choice under Certainty and Uncertainty*, pp. 212–60. Cambridge, MA: Harvard University Press, 1984.

Arthur, W. B. 1981. The Economics of Risks to Life. *American Economic Review* 71 (March): 54–64.

Aschenbrenner, L. M. 1981. Efficient Sets, Decision Heuristics, and Single-peaked Preferences. *Journal of Mathematical Psychology* 23 (June): 227–56.

Atkinson, S. E., and Crocker, T. D. 1992. Econometric Health Production Functions: Relative Bias from Omitted Variables and Measurement Error. *Journal of Environmental Economics and Management* 22:12–24.

Babcock, L. R., and Allen, R. J. 1983. Methodologies for Environmental Assessment. Final report for EPA Grant R-805476 (March).

Babcock, L. R., and Nagda, N. L. 1973. Cost Effectiveness of Emission Control. *Journal of the Air Pollution Control Association* 23 (March): 173–79.

——. 1976. POPEX-ranking Air Pollution Sources by Population Exposure. 600/2-76-063 (NTIS-PB 261 458/AS). Research Triangle Park, NC: U.S. Environmental Protection Agency.

Bailey, M. J. 1980. *Reducing Risks to Life: Measurement of the Benefits.* Washington, DC: American Enterprise Institute.

Banta, D. 1981. What Is Health Care? In *Health Care Delivery in the United States.* 2d ed., ed. S. Jones. New York: Springer Publishing Co.

Bartik, T. 1987. The Estimation of Demand Parameters in Hedonic Price Models. *Journal of Political Economy* 95 (February): 81–88.

Bayless, M. 1982. Measuring the Benefits of Air Quality Improvements: A Hedonic Salary Approach. *Journal of Environmental Economics and Management* 9 (March): 81–99.

Becker, G. S. 1964. *Human Capital.* New York: Columbia University Press.

———. 1974. A Theory of Social Interactions. *Journal of Political Economy* 82 (November/December): 1063–93.

———. 1981. *A Treatise on the Family.* Cambridge, MA: Harvard University Press.

Becker, G. S., and Murphy, K. M. 1988. A Theory of Rational Addiction. *Journal of Political Economy* 96 (August): 675–700.

Beery, W.; Schoenback, V.; Wagner, E.; and Associates. 1986. *Health Risk Appraisal: Methods and Programs with Annotated Bibliography.* National Center for Health Services Research and Health Care Technology Assessment. (June).

Bender, B.; Gronberg, T.; and Hwang, H. S. 1980. Choice of Functional Form and the Demand for Air Quality. *Review of Economics and Statistics* 62 (November): 638–43.

Bergstrom, T. C. 1982. When Is a Man's Life Worth More than His Human Capital? In *The Value of Life and Safety,* ed. M. Jones-Lee. Geneva Association Conference Proceedings. Amsterdam: North-Holland.

Berk, A.; Paringer, L.; and Mushkin, S. J. 1978. The Economic Cost of Illness, Fiscal 1975. *Medical Care* 16 (September): 785–90.

Berkman, L. F., and Breslow, L. 1983. *Health and Ways of Living.* London: Oxford University Press.

Berwick, D. M., and Weinstein, M. C. 1985. What Do Patients Value? Willingness to Pay for Ultrasound in Normal Pregnancy. *Medical Care* 23 (July): 881–93.

Bishop, R. C., and Heberlein, T. A. 1986. Does Contingent Valuation Work? In *Valuing Environmental Goods: An Assessment of the Contingent Valuation Method,* ed. R. G. Cummings, D. S. Brookshire, and W. D. Schulze, pp. 123–47. Totowa, NJ: Rowman & Allanheld.

Blomquist, G. 1981. The Value of Human Life: An Empirical Perspective. *Economic Inquiry* 19 (January): 157–64.

———. 1982. Estimating the Value of Life and Safety: Recent Developments. In *The Value of Life and Safety,* ed. M. Jones-Lee. Amsterdam: North-Holland.

Bloom, D., and Carliner, G. 1988. The Economic Impact of AIDS in the United States. *Science* 239 (February 5): 604–10.

Blum, H. L. 1980. Social Perspective on Risk Reduction. *Family and Community Health* 3 (May): 41–61.

Bockstael, N. E., and McConnell, K. E. 1983. Welfare Measurement in the Household Production Framework. *American Economic Review* 73 (September): 806–14.

Border, K. C. 1992. Revealed Preference, Stochastic Dominance, and the Expected Utility Hypothesis. *Journal of Economic Theory* 56:20–42.

Border, K. C., and Segal, U. 1992. Dynamic Consistency Implies Expected Utility (Almost). California Institute of Technology, Pasadena.

Boyle, M. H.; Torrance, G. W.; Sinclair, J. C.; and Horwood, S. P. 1983. Economic Evaluation of Neonatal Intensive Care of Very-Low-Birth-Weight Infants. *New England Journal of Medicine* 308 (June 2): 1330–37.

Brajer, V.; Hall, J. V.; and Rowe, R. 1991. The Value of Cleaner Air: An Integrated Approach. *Contemporary Policy Issues* 9 (April): 81–91.

Breslow, L. 1978. Prospects for Improving Health through Reducing Risk Factors. *Preventive Medicine* 7 (December): 449–58.

Breslow, L., and Enstrom, J. E. 1980. Persistence of Health Habits and Their Relationship to Mortality. *Preventive Medicine* 9 (July): 469–83.

Brook, R. H.; Ware, J. E.; and Davies-Avery, A. 1979. Overview of Adult Health Status Measures Fielded in Rand's Health Insurance Study. *Medical Care* 17, suppl. (July): 1–131.

Brookshire, D. S., and Coursey, D. L. 1987. Measuring the Value of a Public Good: An Empirical Comparison of Elicitation Procedures. *American Economic Review* 77 (September): 554–66.

Brookshire, D. S.; d'Arge, R. C.; Schulze, W. D.; and Thayer, M. A. 1979. *Methods Development for Assessing Air Pollution Control Benefits*. Vol. 2, *Experiments in Valuing Non-market Goods: A Case Study of Alternative Benefit Measures of Air Pollution Control in the South Coast Air Basin of Southern California*. Washington, DC: U.S. Environmental Protection Agency.

Brown, J. N., and Rosen, H. 1982. On the Estimation of Structural Hedonic Price Models. *Econometrica* 50:765–68.

Brubaker, B. H. 1983. Health Promotion: A Linguistic Analysis. *Advances in Nursing Science* 5 (April): 1–14.

Burgener, S., and Barton, D. 1991. Nursing Care of Cognitively Impaired, Institutionalized Elderly. *Journal of Gerontological Nursing* 17, no. 4:37–43.

Calfee, J. E., and Rubin, P. H. 1992. Some Implications of Damage Payments for Nonpecuniary Losses. *Journal of Legal Studies* 21 (June): 371–411.

Carlyon, W. H. 1984. Reflections: Disease Prevention/Health Promotion—Bridging the Gap to Wellness. *Health Values* 8 (May–June): 23–30.

Carroll, C.; Miller, D.; and Nash, J. C. 1976. *Health, the Science of Human Adaptation*. Dubuque, IA: Wm. C. Brown Co.

Chen, M. M., and Bush, J. W. 1976. Maximizing Health System Output with Political and Administrative Constraints Using Mathematical Programming. *Inquiry* 13 (September): 215–27.

Chestnut, L. G., and Violette, D. M. 1984. *Estimates of Willingness to Pay for Pollution-induced Changes in Morbidity: Critique for Benefit-Cost Analysis of Pollution Regulation*. U.S. Environmental Protection Agency. Boulder, CO: Energy and Resource Consultants, September.

Conley, B. C. 1976. The Value of Human Life in the Demand for Safety. *American Economic Review* 66 (March): 45–55.

Connell, D. B.; Turner, R. R.; and Mason, E. F. 1985. Summary of Findings of the School Health Education Evaluation: Health Promotion Effectiveness, Implementation, and Costs. *Journal of School Health* 55 (October): 316–21.

Cook, P. J., and Graham, D. A. 1977. The Demand for Insurance and Protection:

The Case of Irreplaceable Commodities. *Quarterly Journal of Economics* 91 (February): 143–56.

Cooper, B. S., and Rice, D. P. 1976. The Economic Cost of Illness Revisited. *Social Security Bulletin* 39 (February): 21–36.

Courant, P. N., and Proter, R. C. 1981. Averting Expenditure and the Cost of Pollution. *Journal of Environmental Economics and Management* 8 (December): 321–29.

Crocker, T. D.; Schulze, W.; Ben-David, S.; and Kneese, A. V. 1979. *Methods Development for Assessing Air Pollution Control Benefits: Experiments in the Economics of Air Pollution Epidemiology.* Vol. 1. Washington, DC: U.S. Environmental Protection Agency.

Cropper, M. L. 1977. Health, Investment in Health, and Occupational Choice. *Journal of Political Economy* 85 (December): 1273–94.

————. 1981. Measuring the Benefits from Reduced Morbidity. *American Economic Review* 71 (May): 235–40.

Cropper, M. L., and Arriage-Salinas, A. S. 1980. Intercity Wage Differentials and the Value of Air Quality. *Journal of Urban Economics* 8 (September): 236–54.

Cropper, M. L.; Aydede, S. K.; and Portney, P. R. 1992. Rates of Time Preference for Saving Lives. *American Economic Review: Papers and Proceedings* 82 (May): 469–72.

Cropper, M. L., and Freeman, A. M. 1991. Environmental Health Effects. In *Measuring the Demand for Environmental Quality*, ed. J. B. Braden and C. D. Kolstad. Amsterdam: Elsevier Science Publishers (North-Holland).

Cropper, M. L., and Oates, W. E. 1992. Environmental Economics: A Survey. *Journal of Economic Literature* 30 (June): 675–740.

Cropper, M. L., and Portney, P. R. 1990. Discounting and the Evaluation of Life Saving Programs. *Journal of Risk and Uncertainty* 3:369–79.

Cropper, M. L., and Sussman, F. G. 1988. Families and the Economics of Risks to Life. *American Economic Review* 78 (March): 255–60.

Cummings, R. G.; Brookshire, D. S.; and Schulze, W. D., eds. 1986. *Valuing Environmental Goods: A State of the Arts Assessment of the Contingent Valuation Method.* Totowa, NJ: Rowman & Allanheld.

Davis, K., and Mohs, R. 1982. Enhancement of Memory Processes in Alzheimer's Disease with Multiple-Dose Intravenous Physostigmine. *American Journal of Psychiatry* 139:1421–24.

DeJong, R.; Osterlund, O. W.; and Roy, G. W. 1989. Measurement of Quality-of-Life Changes in Patients with Alzheimer's Disease. *Clinical Therapeutics* 11 (July/August): 545–54.

Diamond, D. B. 1980. The Relationship between Amenities and Urban Land Prices. *Land Economics* 56 (February): 21–32.

Diamond, D., and Smith, B. 1985. Simultaneity in the Market for Housing Characteristics. *Journal of Urban Economics* 17 (May): 280–92.

Dickie, M., and Gerking, S. 1991. Valuing Reduced Morbidity: A Household Production Approach. *Southern Economic Journal* 57 (January): 690–702.

Dickie, M.; Gerking, S.; McClelland, G.; and Schulze, W. 1987. *Improving Accuracy and Reducing Costs of Environmental Benefit Assessments.* Report to the

Environmental Protection Agency. Washington, DC: Environmental Protection Agency, December.

Dillman, D. A. 1978. *Mail and Telephone Surveys: The Total Design Method.* New York: Wiley-Interscience.

Doll, R., and Peto, R. *The Causes of Cancer.* 1981. New York: Oxford University Press.

Drummond, M. F.; Stoddart, G. L.; and Torrance, G. W. 1987. *Methods for the Economic Evaluation of Health Care Programs.* Oxford: Oxford University Press.

Dunton, S. 1981. A Basic Introduction to the Health Hazard Appraisal. *Promoting Health.* Evanston, IL: American Hospital Association, July–August.

Eberts, R. W., and Granbert, T. 1982. Wage Gradients, Rent Gradients, and the Demand for Housing: An Empirical Investigation. *Journal of Urban Economics* 12 (September): 168–76.

Eddy, D. 1989. *Screening for Cancer: Theory, Analysis, and Design.* Englewood Cliffs, NJ: Prentice-Hall.

Ehrlich, I., and Chuma, H. *The Demand for Life: An Economic Analysis.* Buffalo: University of Buffalo.

Ellwood, P. M. 1988. Shattuck Lecture—Outcomes Management: A Technology of Patient Experience. *New England Journal of Medicine* 318 (June 9): 1549–56.

Epple, D. 1987. Hedonic Prices and Implicit Markets: Estimating Demand and Supply Functions for Differentiated Products. *Journal of Political Economy* 95 (February): 59080.

Feldstein, P. 1983. *Health Care Economics.* 2d ed. New York: Wiley.

Fielding, J. 1981. Reducing the Risk of Risk Appraisals. *Promoting Health.* Evanston, IL: American Hospital Association, July–August.

———. 1985. Smoking: Health Effects and Control. *New England Journal of Medicine* 313, pts. 1 and 2 (August 22, August 29): 491–98, 555–61.

Fisher, A. 1984. Environmental Protection Agency. In *Environmental Policy under Reagan's Executive Order, the Role of Benefit-Cost Analysis,* ed. V. K. Smith. Chapel Hill: University of North Carolina Press.

Fisher, A.; Chestnut, L. G.; and Violette, D. M. 1989. The Value of Reducing Risks of Death: A Note on New Evidence. *Journal of Policy Analysis and Management* 8 (Winter): 88–100.

Freeman, A. M. 1982. *Air and Water Pollution Control: A Benefit Cost Assessment.* New York: Wiley.

Freeman, R. A., et al. 1976. Economic Cost of Pulmonary Emphysema: Implications for Policy on Smoking and Health. *Inquiry* 13 (March): 15–22.

Fuchs, V. R. 1980. What Is CBA/CEA, and Why Are They Doing This to Us? *New England Journal of Medicine* 303 (October 16): 937–38.

———. 1982. *Economic Aspects of Health.* Chicago: University of Chicago Press, for the National Bureau of Economic Research.

———. *Who Shall Live? Health, Economics, and Social Choice.* New York: Basic Books.

Fuchs, V. R., and Zeckhauser, R. 1987. Valuing Health—a "Priceless" Commodity. *American Economic Review,* papers and proceedings, 77 (May): 263–68.

Gegax, D.; Gerking, S.; and Schultze, W. 1987. Perceived Risk and the Marginal Value of Safety. Unpublished manuscript. Laramie: University of Wyoming.

Geller, H. 1971. Mortality Tables from the National Office of Health Statistics in Prospective Medicine and Health Hazard Appraisal. In *Proceedings of the 7th Annual Meeting of the Society of Prospective Medicine.* Indianapolis: Society of Prospective Medicine, Methodist Hospital of Indiana.

Geller, H., and Gestner, N. B. 1981. Health Hazard Appraisal Calculation of Methodology. In *Prospective Medicine and Health Hazard Appraisal, State of the Art: Proceedings of the 16th Annual Meeting of the Society of Prospective Medicine.* Bethesda, MD: Society of Prospective Medicine.

Geller, H., and Steele, G. 1977. Updating of Tables of Probability of Dying within the Next Ten Years. In *Let's All Join the Lively People: Proceedings of the 13th Annual Meeting of the Society of Prospective Medicine.* Bethesda, MD: Society of Prospective Medicine.

General Accounting Office. 1988. AIDS Prevention: Views on the Administration's Budget Proposals: Briefing Report to the Chairman, Subcommittee on Labor, Health and Human Services, Education and Related Agencies, pp. 3–23. Committee of Appropriations, U.S. Senate. Washington, DC: General Accounting Office.

Gerking, S.; Coulson, A.; Schulze, W.; Tashkin, D.; Anderson, D.; Dickle, M.; and Brookshire, D. 1984. Estimating Benefits of Reducing Community Low-Level Ozone Exposure: A Feasibility Study. University of Wyoming, Laramie.

Gerking, S., and Stanley, L. 1986. An Economic Analysis of Air Pollution and Health: The Case of St. Louis. *Review of Economics and Statistics* 68 (February): 115–21.

Goetz, A. A.; Duff, J. F.; and Bernstein, J. E. 1978. Health Risk Appraisal: The Estimation of Risk. Washington, DC: The Health Corporation.

Golenski, J. D., and Blum, S. R. 1989. *The Oregon Medicaid Priority-Setting Project.* Bioethics Consultation Group for the Medical Research Foundation of Oregon. Portland, March.

Graham, D. A. 1981. Cost-Benefit Analysis under Uncertainty. *American Economic Review* 71 (September): 715–37.

———. 1992. Public Expenditure under Uncertainty: The Net Benefit Criteria. *American Economic Review* 82 (September): 822–45.

Gramlich, E. 1990. *A Guide to Benefit-Cost Analysis,* 2d ed. Englewood Cliffs, NJ: Prentice-Hall.

Great Britain Royal Commission on the National Health Service. 1979. Sir Alec Merrison, Chairman. Report to Parliament. London. July.

Greenfield, S. 1989. The State of Outcome Research: Are We On Target? *New England Journal of Medicine* 320 (April 27): 1142–43.

Grossman, M. 1972. On the Concept of Health Capital and the Demand for Health. *Journal of Political Economy* 80 (March/April): 223–55.

Grossman, M.; Coate, D.; and Arluck, G. 1987. Price Sensitivity of Alcoholic Beverages in the United States. In *Control Issues in Alcohol Abuse Prevention: Strategies for Communities,* ed. H. Holden. Greenwich, CT: JAI Press.

Grether, D. M., and Plott, C. R. 1979. Economic Theory of Choice and the Preference Reversal Phenomenon. *American Economic Review* 69 (September): 623–38.

Hadorn, D. C. 1991*a*. The Oregon Priority—Setting Exercise: Quality of Life and Public Policy. *Hastings Center Report* 21 (May–June): 11–16.

————. 1991*b*. Setting Health Care Priorities in Oregon. *Journal of the American Medical Association* 265 (May 1): 2218–25.

Hall, J., et al. 1989. *Economic Assessment of the Health Benefits from Improvements in Air Quality in the South Coast Air Basin*. Fullerton: California State University.

Hammond, P. J. 1989. Consistent Plans, Consequentialism, and Expected Utility. *Econometrica* 57:1445–50.

Hanlon, J., and Pickett, G. E., eds. 1984. *Public Health Administration and Practice*. 8th ed. St. Louis: College Publishing.

Harberger, A. C. 1972. Survey of Literature on Cost-Benefit Analysis for Industrial Project Evaluation. In *Project Evaluation*. Chicago: University of Chicago Press.

————. 1974. Three Basic Postulates for Applied Welfare Economics: An Interpretive Essay. In *Taxation and Welfare*. Chicago: University of Chicago Press.

Harrell, L.; Callaway, R.; Morere, D.; and Falgout, J. 1990. The Effect of Long-Term Physostigmine Administration in Alzheimer's Disease. *Neurology* 40: 1350–54.

Harrington, W., and Portney, P. 1987. Valuing the Benefits of Health and Safety Regulation. *Journal of Urban Economics* 22 (July): 101–12.

Harrison, D., and Nichols, A. L. 1990. *Benefits of the 1989 Air Quality Management Plan for the South Coast Air Basin: A Reassessment*. National Economic Research Associates, Cambridge, MA, March.

Harrison, D.; Nichols, A. L.; Evans, J. S.; and Zona, J. D. 1992. *Valuation of Air Pollution Damages*. National Economic Research Associates, Cambridge, MA, March.

Harrison, D., and Rubinfeld, D. L. 1978. Hedonic Housing Prices and the Demand for Clean Air. *Journal of Environmental Economics and Management* 5 (March): 81–102.

Hartunian, N. S.; Smart, C. N.; and Thompson, M. S. 1980. The Incidence and Economic Costs of Cancer, Motor Vehicle Injuries, Coronary Heart Disease and Stroke: A Comparative Analysis. *American Journal of Public Health* 70 (December): 1249–60.

————. 1981. *The Incidence and Economic Costs of Major Health Impairments*. Lexington, MA: Lexington Books.

Heacock, P.; Walton, C.; Beck, C.; and Mercer, S. 1991. Caring for the Cognitively Impaired: Reconceptualizing Disability and Rehabilitation. *Journal of Gerontological Nursing* 17, no. 3:22–26.

Health Insurance Association of America. 1989. *Source Book of Health Insurance Data 1989*. Washington, DC: Health Insurance Association of America.

Hettler, B. 1980. Description, Analysis, and Assessment of Health Hazard/Health Risk Appraisal Programs. Executive Summary, Final Report. University of North Carolina, Chapel Hill. Health Services Research Center.

Hicks, J. R. 1979. *Value and Capital: An Inquiry into Some Fundamental Principles of Economic Theory*. 2d ed. Oxford: Oxford University Press.

Hodgson, T., and Kopstein, A. 1984. Health Care Expenditures for Major Diseases in 1980. *Health Care Financing Review* 5 (Summer): 1–12.

Hodgson, T., and Meiners, M. 1982. Cost-of-Illness Methodology: A Guide to Current Practices and Procedures. *Milbank Memorial Fund Quarterly/Health and Society* 60 (Summer): 429–62.

Hoehn, J., and Randall, A. 1987. A Satisfactory Benefit Cost Indicator from Contingent Valuation. *Journal of Environmental Economics and Management* (September): 226–47.

Hoel, P. G. 1971. *Introduction to Mathematical Statistics.* 4th ed. New York: Wiley.

Horowitz, J. K., and Carson, R. T. 1990. Discounting Statistical Lives. *Journal of Risk and Uncertainty* 3:403–13.

Howard, R. A., and Matheson, J. E. 1984. *The Principles and Applications of Decision Analysis.* Vol. 2. Menlo Park, CA: Strategic Decisions Group, Professional Collection.

Hu, T., and Sandifer, F. H. 1981. *Synthesis of Cost of Illness Methodology.* Report to the National Center for Health Services Research. Washington, DC: Department of Health and Human Services.

Institute of Medicine. 1977. Reliability of Hospital Discharge Abstracts, Reliability of Medicare Hospital Discharge Records, Reliability of National Hospital Discharge Survey Data. National Academy of Sciences, Washington, DC.

———. 1979. *DHEW's Research Planning Principles: A Review.* Washington, DC: National Academy Press.

———. 1981. Costs of Environment-related Health Effects: A Plan for Continuing Study. Washington, DC: National Academy Press.

———. 1990. *Funding Health Sciences Research: A Strategy to Restore Balance.* Washington, DC: National Academy Press.

Ippolito, P. M., and Ippolito, R. A. 1984. Measuring the Value of Life Saving from Consumer Reactions to New Information. *Journal of Public Economics* 25 (November): 53–81.

Jones-Lee, M. W. 1976. *The Value of Life: An Economic Analysis.* London: Martin Robinson.

———, ed. 1982. *The Value of Life and Safety.* Geneva Association Conference Proceedings. Amsterdam: North-Holland.

———. 1989a. *The Economics of Safety and Physical Risk.* Oxford: Basil Blackwell.

———. 1989b. The Value of Avoidance of Non-fatal Road Injuries: An Exploratory Study. Newcastle: University of Newcastle upon Tyne.

Jones-Lee, M. W.; Hammerton, M.; and Philips, P. R. 1985. The Value of Safety: Results of a National Sample Survey. *Economic Journal* 95 (March): 49–72.

Kahneman, D., and Tversky, A. 1979. Prospect Theory: An Analysis of Decision under Risk. *Econometrica* 47 (March): 263–92.

Kain, J. F., and Quigley, J. M. 1975. *Housing Markets and Racial Discrimination: A Microeconomic Analysis.* New York: National Bureau of Economic Research.

Kane, R. L., and Kane, R. A., eds. 1982. *Values and Long-Term Care.* Lexington, MA: Lexington Books; D. C. Health & Co.

Kaplan, R. M. 1982. Human Preference Measurement for Health Decisions and the Evaluation of Long-Term Care. In *Values and Long-Term Care,* ed. R. L. Kane and R. A. Kane. Lexington, MA: Lexington Books; D. C. Heath & Co.

Kaplan, R. M., and Anderson, J. P. 1988. A General Health Policy Model: Update and Applications. *HSR: Health Services Research* 23 (June): 203–35.

Kaplan, R. M.; Anderson, J. P.; Wu, A.; Mathews, W. C.; Kozin, F.; and Orenstein, D. 1989. The Quality of Well-being Scale: Applications in AIDS, Cystic Fibrosis, and Arthritis. *Medical Care* 27, suppl. (March): 27–43.

Kaplan, R. M., and Bush, J. W. 1982. Health-related Quality of Life Measurement for Evaluation Research and Policy Analysis. *Health Psychology* 1 (Winter): 61–80.

Kaplan, R. M.; Bush, J. W.; and Berry, C. C. 1976. Health Status: Types of Validity and the Index of Well-being. *Health Services Research* 11 (Winter): 478–507.

————. 1979. Health Status Index: Category Rating versus Magnitude Estimation for Measuring Levels of Well-being. *Medical Care* 17 (May): 501–25.

Katz, S.; Branch, L.; Branson, M.; Papsidero, J.; Beck, J.; and Green, D. 1983. Active Life Expectancy. *New England Journal of Medicine* 309 (November 17): 1218–24.

Keeney, R. L., and Raiffa, H. 1976. *Decisions with Multiple Objectives: Preferences and Value Tradeoffs.* New York: Wiley.

Kenkel, D. S. 1990. The Demand for Preventive Medical Care. Working paper. Pennsylvania State University, Department of Economics, University Park.

————. 1991. Health Behavior, Health Knowledge, and Schooling. *Journal of Political Economy* 99 (April): 287–305.

King, T. A. 1976. The Demand for Housing: A Lancasterian Approach. *Southern Economic Journal* 43 (October): 1077–87.

Klein, S. D. 1980. Class, Culture and Health. In *Maxcy-Rosenau Public Health and Preventive Medicine.* 1st ed., ed. J. M. Lasat. New York: Appleton-Century-Crofts.

Kohn, M., and Shavell, S. 1974. The Theory of Search. *Journal of Economic Theory* 9 (October): 93–123.

Krupnick, A. J., and Cropper, M. L. 1992. The Effect of Information on Health Risk Valuations. *Journal of Risk and Uncertainty* 5:29–48.

Krupnick, A. J., and Portney, P. R. 1991. Controlling Urban Air Pollution: A Benefit-Cost Assessment. *Science* 252 (April 26): 522–28.

Lancaster, K. 1966. A New Approach to Consumer Theory. *Journal of Political Economy* 74 (April): 133–57.

Landefeld, J. S., and Seskin, E. P. 1982. The Economic Value of Life: Linking Theory to Practice. *American Journal of Public Health* 72 (June): 555–66.

Landes, W. M., and Posner, R. A. 1987. *The Economic Structure of Tort Law.* Cambridge, MA, and London: Harvard University Press.

LaPuma, J.; Cassel, C. K.; and Humphrey, H. 1988. Ethics, Economics, and Endocarditis: The Physician's Role in Resource Allocation. *Archives of Internal Medicine* 148 (August): 1809–11.

LaPuma, J., and Lawlor, E. F. 1980. Quality-adjusted Life-Years: Ethical Implications for Physicians and Policymakers. *Journal of the American Medical Association* 263 (June 6): 2917–21.

Laszlo, J. 1985. Health Registry and Clinical Data Base Technology: With Special Emphasis on Cancer Registries. *Journal of Chronic Disease* 38:67–78.

Lave, L. B., and Seskin, E. P. 1977. *Air Pollution, and Human Health.* Baltimore: Johns Hopkins University Press.

Levy, R. 1990. Are Drugs Targeted at Alzheimer's Disease Useful?: Useful for What? *British Medical Journal* 300 (April 28):1131–32.

Li, M. M., and Brown, H. 1980. Micro-neighborhood Externalities and Hedonic Housing Prices. *Land Economics* 56 (May): 125–41.

Linnerooth, J. 1979. The Value of Human Life: A Review of the Models. *Economic Inquiry* 17 (January): 52–74.

Lipscomb, J. 1989. Time Preference for Health in Cost-Effectiveness Analysis. *Medical Care* 27 (March): S232–S253.

Little, I. M. D. 1956. *A Critique of Welfare Economics.* London: Oxford University Press.

Loehman, E. T.; Berg, S. V.; Arroyo, A. A.; Hedinger, R. A.; Schwartz, J. M.; Shaw, M. E.; Fahien, R. W.; De, V. H.; Fishe, R. P.; Rio, D. E.; Rossley, W. F.; and Green, A. E. S. 1979. Distributional Analysis of Regional Benefits and Cost of Air Quality Control. *Journal of Environmental Economics and Management* 6 (September): 222–43.

Loehman, E. T.; Boldt, D.; and Chaikin, K. 1981. Measuring the Benefits of Air Quality Improvements in the San Francisco Bay Area. Draft Final Report. Washington: U.S. Environmental Protection Agency.

Lohr, K. N., ed. 1989. Advances in Health Status Assessment: Conference Proceedings. *Medical Care* 27 (March): 1–294.

Loomes, G., and Sugden, R. 1982. Regret Theory: An Alternative Theory of Rational Choice under Uncertainty. *Economic Journal* 92 (December): 805–24.

LORAN Commission. 1988. *Report of the LORAN Commission to the Harvard Community Health Plan.* New York: LORAN Commission, June.

Lucas, R. E. B. 1977. Hedonic Wage Equations and Psychic Wages in the Return to Schooling. *American Economic Review* 67 (September): 549–58.

Luce, R. D. 1959. *Individual Choice Behavior.* New York: Wiley.

Luft, H. 1978. How Do Health-Maintenance Organizations Achieve Their "Savings"? *New England Journal of Medicine* 298 (June 15): 1336–43.

Lutter, R., and Morrall, J. F. 1993. Health–Health Analysis: A New Way to Evaluate Health and Safety Regulation. *Journal of Risk and Uncertainty.*

Machina, M. 1982. "Expected Utility" Analysis without the Independence Axiom. *Econometrica* 50 (March): 277–323.

———. 1989. Dynamic Consistency and Non-expected Utility Models of Choice under Uncertainty. *Journal of Economic Literature* 27:1622–68.

Machina, M., and Schmeidler, D. 1992. A More Robust Definition of Subjective Probability. *Econometrica* 60:745–80.

Manning, W. G.; Keeler, E. B.; Newhouse, J. P.; Sloss, E. M.; and Wasserman, J. 1989. The Taxes of Sin: Do Smokers and Drinkers Pay Their Way? *Journal of the American Medical Association* 261 (March 17): 1604–9.

Manning, W. G.; Liebowitz, A.; Goldbert, G.; Roges, W. H.; and Newhouse, J. P. 1984. A Controlled Trial of the Effect of a Prepaid Group Practice on Use of Services. *New England Journal of Medicine* 310 (June 7): 1505–10.

Manning, W. G.; Newhouse, J. P.; Duan, N.; Keeler, E. B.; Leibowitz, A.; and Marquis, M. S. 1987. Health Insurance and the Demand for Medical Care. *American Economic Review* 77 (June): 251–77.

Markowitz, H. 1952. The Utility of Wealth. *Journal of Political Economy* 60 (April): 151–58.

Mauskopf, J., and French, M. T. 1989. Estimating the Value of Avoiding Morbidity and Mortality from Foodborne Illnesses. Research Triangle Park, NC: Research Triangle Institute, Center for Economics Research, May.

Mausner, J. K., and Kramer, S. 1985. *Epidemiology—An Introductory Text*. Philadelphia: W. B. Saunders.

Mayeux, R. 1990. Therapeutic Strategies in Alzheimer's Disease. *Neurology* 40: 175–80.

Mechanic, D., and Cleary, P. D. 1980. Factors Associated with the Maintenance of Positive Health Behavior. *Preventive Medicine* 9 (November): 805–14.

Menzel, Paul T. 1992. Oregon's Denial: Disabilities and Quality of Life. *Hastings Center Report* 22 (November–December): 21–25.

Miller, T. R. 1986. Benefit-Cost Analysis of Health and Safety: Conceptual and Empirical Issues. Working-Paper no. 3525–02. Washington, DC: Urban Institute, December.

———. 1989. Willingness to Pay Comes of Age: Will the System Survive? *Northwestern University Law Review* 83:876–907.

Miller, T. R.; Calhoun, C.; and Arthur, W. B. 1990. Utility-adjusted Impairment Years: A Low-Cost Approach to Morbidity Valuation. Federal Highway Administration, March.

Mishan, E. J. 1971. Evaluation of Life and Limb: A Theoretical Approach. *Journal of Political Economy* 79 (July/August): 687–705.

Mitchell, R. C., and Carson, R. T. 1986. Some Comments on the State of the Arts Assessment of the Contingent Valuation Method Draft Report. In *Valuing Environmental Goods: An Assessment of the Contingent Valuation Method*, ed. R. G. Cummings, D. S. Brookshire, and W. D. Schulze, pp. 237–45. Totowa, NJ: Rowman & Allanheld.

———. 1989. *Using Surveys to Value Public Goods: An Assessment of the Contingent Valuation Method*. Washington, DC: Resources for the Future.

Mooney, G. 1989. QALY's: Are They Enough? A Health Economist's Perspective. *Journal of Medical Ethics* 15 (September): 148–52.

Moore, M. J., and Viscusi, W. K. 1988. The Quantity-adjusted Value of Life. *Economic Inquiry* 26:369–88.

Morreim, E. H. 1989. Fiscal Scarcity and the Inevitability of Bedside Budget Balancing. *Archives of Internal Medicine* 149 (May): 1012–15.

Mullahy, J., and Portney, P. 1990. Air Pollution, Cigarette Smoking, and the Production of Respiratory Health. *Journal of Health Economics* 9:193–205.

Mushkin, S. J. 1962. Health as an Investment. *Journal of Political Economy* 70, suppl. (October): 129–57.

———. 1979. *Biomedical Research: Costs and Benefits*. Cambridge, MA: Ballinger.

Muth, R. F. 1969. *Cities and Housing*. Chicago: University of Chicago Press.

National Center for Health Statistics. 1976. *Vital Statistics of the United States, 1976*. Hyattsville, MD: U.S. Department of Health and Human Services.

National Center for Health Statistics, various dates. Current Estimates from the National Health Interview Survey, United States. *Vital and Health Statistics*.

Series 10, number varies. Public Health Service. Washington, DC: U.S. Government Printing Office.

———. 1979a. *General Mortality Statistics, 1979*. Vol. 2, pt. A. Hyattsville, MD: U.S. Department of Health and Human Services.

———. 1979b. *Vital Statistics of the United States, 1979*. Vol. 2, pt. B, sec. 6. Hyattsville, MD: U.S. Department of Health and Human Services.

———. 1990. *Health, United States, 1989*. Hyattsville, MD: Public Health Service.

Needleman, H., and Grossman, M. 1983. Health Econometric Methods for Multimedia Pollutants. Workplan for U.S. EPA Cooperative Agreement. Washington, DC: U.S. Environmental Protection Agency. September.

Nelson, J. P. 1978. Residential Choice, Hedonic Prices and the Demand for Urban Air Quality. *Journal of Urban Economics* 5 (July): 357–69.

Newsweek. 1988. Putting a Price Tag on Life. January 11, p. 40.

NHLI. *See* U.S. National Heart and Lung Institute.

New York Heart Association, Inc. 1964. *Diseases of the Heart and Blood Vessels—Nomenclature and Criteria for Diagnosis.* 6th ed. Boston: Little, Brown & Co.

Ohsfeldt, R. L. 1983. Implicit Markets and the Demand for Housing Characteristics. Ph.D. diss., University of Houston.

Ohsfeldt, R. L., and Smith, B. 1985. Estimating the Demand for Heterogeneous Goods. *Review of Economics and Statistics* 67 (February): 165–71.

Olshanski, S. J.; Carnes, B. A.; and Cassel, C. 1990. In Search of Methuselah: Estimating the Upper Limits to Human Longevity. *Science* 250 (November 2): 634–40.

Palmquist, R. B. 1983. Estimating the Demand for Air Quality from Property Value Studies. Unpublished manuscript. Raleigh: North Carolina State University.

———. 1984. Estimating the Demand for the Characteristics of Housing. *Review of Economics and Statistics* 66 (August): 394–404.

Paringer, L., and Berk, A. 1977. *Costs of Illness and Disease, Fiscal Year 1975.* Washington, DC: Georgetown University, Public Services Laboratory, January.

Parsons, P. E.; Lichenstein, R.; Berki, S. E.; et al. 1986. Costs of Illness, United States, 1980. *National Medical Care Utilization and Expenditure Survey.* Ser. C, Analytical Report no. 3, Department of Health and Human Services Publication no. 86–20403. National Center for Health Statistics, Public Health Service. Washington, DC: U.S. Government Printing Office, April.

Payne, J. W.; Braunstein, M. L.; and Carroll, J. S. 1978. Exploring Predecisional Behavior: An Alternative Approach to Decision Research. *Organizational Behavior and Human Performance* 22 (August): 17–44.

Pearce, D. W., and Markandya, A. 1989. *Environmental Policy Benefits: Monetary Valuation.* Paris: Organization for Economic Cooperation and Development.

Phelps, C. 1988. Death and Taxes: An Opportunity for Substitution. *Journal of Health Economics* 7:1–24.

Philipson, T., and Posner, R. A. 1993. *Private Choices and Public Health: An Economic Interpretation of the AIDS Epidemic.* Cambridge, MA: Harvard University Press.

Pierce, J. P.; Fiore, M. C.; Novotny, T. E.; Hatziandreu, E. J.; and Davis, R. M. 1989. Trends in Cigarette Smoking in the United States: Educational Differences

Are Increasing. *Journal of the American Medical Association* 261 (January 6): 56–60.

Pliskin, J. S.; Shepard, D. S.; and Weinstein, M. C. 1980. Utility Functions for Life Years and Health Status. *Operations Research* 28 (January–February).

Portney, P. 1981. Housing Prices, Health Effects, and Valuing Reductions in Risk of Death. *Journal of Environmental Economics and Management* 8 (March): 72–78.

———. 1990a. Air Pollution Policy. In *Public Policies for Environmental Protection,* ed. Paul Portney. Washington, DC: Resources for the Future.

———. 1990b. The Evolution of Federal Regulation. In *Public Policies for Environmental Protection,* ed. Paul Portney. Washington, DC: Resources for the Future.

Portney, P. R., and Mullahy, J. 1986. Urban Air Quality and Acute Respiratory Illness. *Journal of Urban Economics* 20 (July): 21–38.

Posner, R. A. 1992. *Economic Analysis of Law.* 4th ed. Boston: Little, Brown & Co.

Pryor, D. B.; Califf, R. M.; Harrell, F. E.; Hlatky, M. A.; Lee, K. L.; Mark, D. B.; and Rosati, R. A. 1985. Clinical Data Bases: Accomplishments and Unrealized Potential. *Medical Care* 23 (May): 623–47.

Randall, A. 1986. The Possibility of Satisfactory Benefit Estimation with Contingent Markets. In *Valuing Environmental Goods: An Assessment of the Contingent Valuation Method,* ed. R. G. Cummings, D. S. Brookshire, and W. D. Schulze, pp. 114–22. Totowa, NJ: Rowman & Allanheld.

Randall, A.; Ives, B.; and Eastman, C. 1974. Bidding Games for Valuation of Aesthetic Environmental Improvements. *Journal of Environmental Economics and Management* 2 (August): 132–49.

Rawles, J. 1989. Castigating QALYs. *Journal of Medical Ethics* 15 (September): 143–47.

Reisberg, B.; Ferris, S. H.; deLeon, M. J.; Kluger, A.; Franssen, E.; Borenstein, J.; and Alba, R. C. 1989. The Stage Specific Temporal Course of Alzheimer's Disease: Functional and Behavioral Concomitants Based upon Cross-sectional and Longitudinal Observation. In *Alzheimer's Disease and Related Disorders,* vol. 317 of *Progress in Clinical and Biological Research,* pp. 23–41. Edited by K. Iqbal, H. M. Wisniewski, and B. Winblad. Alan R. Liss, Inc.

Report of the Presidential Commission on the Human Immunodeficiency Virus Epidemic. 1988. Washington, DC: U.S. Government Printing Office.

Rice, D. P. 1966. Estimating the Cost of Illness. Health Economics ser. no. 6. Washington, DC: U.S. Department of Health, Education, and Welfare, Public Health Service.

Rice, D. P., and Hodgson, T. A. 1978. *Social and Economic Implications of Cancer in the United States.* Washington, DC: Department of Health, Education, and Welfare, National Center for Health Statistics.

Ridker, R. G., and Henning, J. 1967. The Determinants of Residential Property Values with Special Reference to Air Pollution. *Review of Economics and Statistics* 49 (May): 246–57.

Roback, J. 1982. Wages, Rents, and the Quality of Life. *Journal of Political Economy* 90 (December): 1257–78.

Robbins, L., and Hall, J. 1970. *How to Practice Prospective Medicine.* Indianapolis: Methodist Hospital of Indiana.

Robinson, J. C. 1986. Philosophical Origins of the Economic Valuation of Life. *Milbank Quarterly* 64, no. 1:133–55.

Rosati, R. A.; Lee, K. L.; Califf, R. M.; Pryor, D. B.; and Harrell, F. E. 1982. Problems and Advantages of an Observational Data Base Approach to Evaluating the Effect of Therapy on Outcome. *Circulation* 65, suppl. 2:II-27–II-32.

Rosen, S. 1974. Hedonic Prices and Implicit Markets: Product Differentiation in Pure Competition. *Journal of Political Economy* 82 (January/February): 34–55.

———. 1981. Valuing Health Risks. *American Economic Review*, papers and proceedings, 71 (May): 241–45.

Rowe, R. D., and Chestnut, L. G. 1984. Valuing Changes in Morbidity: Willingness to Pay versus Cost of Illness Measures. Report to Energy and Resources Consultants. Boulder, CO, December.

Russell, L. B. 1989. Some of the Tough Decisions Required by a National Health Plan. *Science* 246 (November 17): 892–96.

Sacks, J. J.; Krushot, W. M.; and Newman, J. 1980. Reliability of the Health Hazard Appraisal. *American Journal of Public Health* 70 (July): 730–32.

Saffer, H., and Grossman, M. 1987. Beer Taxes, the Legal Drinking Age, and Youth Motor Vehicle Fatalities. *Journal of Legal Studies* 26:351–74.

Salkever, D. S. 1985. *Morbidity Costs: National Estimates and Economic Determinants*. NCHSR Research Summary ser. Washington, DC: National Center for Health Services Research, October.

Sandman, P. 1990. Is Good Care the Best Treatment for the Alzheimer Patient? *Acta Neurologica Scandinavica* 82:37–39.

Sayetta, R. 1986. Rates of Senile Dementia–Alzheimer's Type in the Baltimore Longitudinal Study. *Journal of Chronic Diseases* 49:271–86.

Schelling, T. C. 1984. The Life You Save May Be Your Own. In *Choice and Consequence*. Cambridge, MA, and London: Harvard University Press.

Schiedermayer, D. L.; LaPuma, J.; and Miles, S. H. 1989. Ethics Consultations Masking Economic Dilemmas in Patient Care. *Archives of Internal Medicine* 149 (June): 1303–5.

Schmalensee, R. 1972. Option Demand and Consumer's Surplus: Valuing Price Changes under Uncertainty. *American Economic Review* 62:813–24.

Schoenbach, V. J.; Wagner, E. H.; and Karon, J. M. 1983. The Use of Epidemiological Data for Personal Risk Assessment in Health Hazard/Health Risk Appraisal Programs. *Journal of Chronic Diseases* 36:625–38.

Schultz, D. M. S. 1984. Lifestyle Assessment: A Tool for Practice. *Nursing Clinics of North America* 66 (June): 271–81.

Schulze, W. D.; Brookshire, D.; Coursey, D.; and McClelland, G. 1985. *Experimental Approaches for Measuring the Value of Environmental Goods*. Vol. 5. Report to U.S. Environmental Protection Agency. Washington, DC: U.S. Environmental Protection Agency. September.

Schulze, W. D.; Cummings, R. G.; Brookshire, D. S.; Thayer, M. H.; Whitworth, R. L.; and Rahmatian, M. 1983. Experimental Approaches to Valuing Environmental Commodities. Vol. 2. Draft final report for *Methods Development in Measuring Benefits of Environmental Improvements*, USEPA Grant no. CR 808-893-01, July.

Scitovsky, A. 1967. Changes in the Costs of Treatment of Selected Illnesses, 1951–65. *American Economic Review* 57 (December): 1182–95.

———. 1968. Costs of Medical Treatment, Reply. *American Economic Review* 58 (September): 939–40.

———. 1982. Estimating the Direct Costs of Illness. *Milbank Memorial Fund Quarterly/Health and Society* 60:463–89.

Scitovsky, A., and McCall, N. 1976. Changes in the Costs of Treatment of Selected Illness, 1954–1964–1971. National Center for Health Services Research, Research Digest Series, Department of Health, Education, and Welfare Publication no. (HRH) 77-3161. Washington, DC: U.S. Public Health Service. July.

Shechter, M.; Cohen, A.; Epstein, L.; Kim, M.; Lave, L.; Mills, E.; Shafer, D.; and Zeider, M. 1988. *The Benefits of Morbidity Reduction from Air Pollution Control.* Final Science Report to U.S.-Israel Binational Science Foundation. Haifa: University of Haifa, Natural Resource and Environmental Research Center, November.

Shechter, M., and Kim, M. 1991. Valuation of Pollution Abatement Benefits: Direct and Indirect Measurement. *Journal of Urban Economics* 30:133–51.

Shechter, M., and Zeidner, M. 1990. Anxiety: Towards a Decision-theoretic Perspective. *British Journal of Mathematical and Statistical Psychology* 43:15–28.

Shepard, D. A., and Zeckhauser, R. J. 1982. The Choice of Health Policies with Heterogeneous Population. In *Economic Aspects of Health,* ed. V. R. Fuchs, pp. 255–97. Chicago: University of Chicago Press, for National Bureau of Economic Research.

Sjaastad, L. A., and Wisecarver, D. L. 1977. The Social Cost of Public Finance. *Journal of Political Economy* 85 (June): 513–47.

Smith, A. 1987. Qualms about QALYs. *Lancet* 1 (May 16): 1134–36.

Smith, B. A. 1978. Measuring the Value of Urban Amenities. *Journal of Urban Economics* 5 (July): 370–87.

Smith, B. A., and Ohsfeldt, R. 1979. Housing Prices Inflation in Houston: 1970–1976. *Policy Studies Journal* 8 (December): 257–76.

Smith, R. S. 1979. Compensating Wage Differentials and Public Policy: A Review. *Industrial and Labor Relations Review* 32 (April): 339–52.

Smith, V. K. 1983. Option Value: A Conceptual Overview. *Southern Economic Journal* 49 (January): 654–68.

———. ed. 1984. *Environmental Policy under Reagan's Executive Order, the Role of Benefit-Cost Analysis.* Chapel Hill: University of North Carolina Press.

———. 1991. Household Production Functions and Environmental Benefit Estimation. In *Measuring the Demand for Environmental Quality,* ed. J. Braden and C. Kolstad. Amsterdam: Elsevier Science Publishers (North-Holland).

Smith, V. K., and Desvousges, W. H. 1985. Averting Behavior: Does It Exist? Working paper. Nashville: Vanderbilt University, Department of Economics, September.

Somers, A. R. 1980. Life-Style and Health. In *Maxcy-Rosenau Public Health and Preventive Medicine.* 1st ed., ed. J. M. Last. New York: Appleton-Century-Crofts.

Stason, W. B., and Weinstein, M. C. 1977. Allocation of Resources to Manage Hypertension. *New England Journal of Medicine* 296 (March 31): 732–39.

Stewart, A. L.; Hays, R. D.; and Ware, J. E., Jr. 1988. The MOS Short-Form General Health Survey. *Medical Care* 26 (July): 724–35.

Stewart, A. L.; Ware, J. E.; and Brooks, R. H. 1981. Advances in the Measurement of Functional Status: Construction of Aggregate Indexes. *Medical Care* 19 (May): 473–88.

Stigler, G. J. 1961. The Economics of Information. *Journal of Political Economy* 69 (June): 213–25.

Straszheim, M. 1974. Hedonic Estimation of Housing Market Prices: A Further Comment. *Review of Economics and Statistics* 56 (August): 404–5.

Sutherland, H. J.; Dunn, V.; and Boyd, N. F. 1983. Measurement of Values for States of Health with Linear Analog Scales. *Medical Decision Making* 3 (Winter): 477–87.

Thaler, R., and Rosen, S. 1975. The Value of Saving a Life: Evidence from the Labor Market. In *Household Production and Consumption*, ed. N. E. Terleckyj. New York: National Bureau of Economic Research.

Thayer, M., et al. 1990. *Estimating the Air Quality Impacts of Alternative Energy Sources: Phase II Report.* Report to the California Energy Commission. Sacramento, CA: Regional Economic Research. July.

———. 1991. *Estimating the Air Quality Impacts of Alternative Energy Resources: Phase IV Report.* Report to the California Energy Commission. Sacramento, CA: Regional Economic Research. December.

Thurstone, L. L. 1927. A Law of Comparative Judgment. *Psychological Review* 34 (July): 273–86.

Toevs, C. D.; Kaplan, R. M.; and Atkins, C. J. 1984. The Costs and Effects of Behavioral Programs in Chronic Obstructive Pulmonary Disease. *Medical Care* 22 (December): 1088–1100.

Tolley, G., and Fabian, R., eds. 1988. *The Economic Value of Visibility.* Mount Pleasant, MO: Blackstone.

Tolley, G. S.; Randall, A.; et al. 1984. Establishing and Valuing the Effects of Improved Visibility in the Eastern United States. Washington, DC: U.S. Environmental Protection Agency.

Torrance, G. W. 1986. Measurement of Health State Utilities for Economic Appraisal: A Review. *Journal of Health Economics* 5:1–30.

Torrance, G. W.; Boyle, M. H.; and Horwood, S. P. 1982. Application of Multiattribute Utility Theory to Measure Social Preferences for Health Status. *Operations Research* 30 (November–December): 1043–69.

Torrance, G. W., and Feeny, D. 1989. Utilities and Quality-adjusted Life Years. *International Journal of Technology Assessment in Health Care* 5:559–75.

Toxic Substances Strategy Committee. 1980. *Toxic Chemicals and Public Protection: A Report to the President.* Washington, DC: Toxic Substance Strategy Committee, May.

Travis, J. 1977. *Wellness Workbook for Health Professionals.* Mill Valley, CA: Wellness Resource Center.

Tversky, A. 1972. Choice by Elimination. *Journal of Mathematical Psychology* 9 (November): 341–67.

U.S. Department of Health and Human Services. 1980. *First Report on Carcinogens.* Washington, DC: U.S. Government Printing Office, July.

U.S. Department of Health, Education, and Welfare. 1969. Air Quality Criteria for Particulate Matter. Washington, DC: U.S. Government Printing Office.

U.S. Environmental Protection Agency. 1982. *Environmental Cancer and Heart and Lung Disease*. Task Force on Environmental Cancer and Heart and Lung Disease. Fifth annual report to Congress. Washington, DC: U.S. Environmental Protection Agency, August.

U.S. National Heart and Lung Institute Respiratory Disease Task Force. 1972. *Economic Costs of Respiratory Diseases*, Respiratory Disease Task Force Report on Problems, Research Approaches, Needs, pp. 205–43. DHEW Publication No. (NIH) 76-432. Washington, DC: U.S. National Institute of Health.

U.S. National Heart and Lung Institute Task Force on Arteriosclerosis. 1971. *Economic Impact of Arteriosclerosis*. Appendix D. Report by the National Heart and Lung Institute. Vol. 2. Washington, DC: U.S. Government Printing Office, June.

U.S. Public Health Service. Surgeon General's Report on Health Promotion and Disease Prevention. 1979. *Healthy People*. Washington, DC: U.S. Public Health Service, 1979.

Usher, D. 1971. An Imputation to the Measure of Economic Growth for Changes in Life Expectancy. In *The Measurement of Economic and Social Performance*, ed. M. Moss. New York: National Bureau of Economic Research.

Vickrey, W. 1961. Counterspeculation and Competitive Sealed Tender. *Journal of Finance* 16 (March): 8–37.

Violette, D. M., and Chestnut, L. G. 1983. *Valuing Reductions in Risks: A Review of the Empirical Estimates*. Boulder, CO: Energy and Resource Consultants, Inc.

Viscusi, W. K. 1979. *Employment Hazards: An Investigation of Market Performance*. Cambridge, MA: Harvard University Press.

———. 1984a. The Lulling Effect: The Impact of Child-resistant Packaging on Aspirin and Analgesic Ingestions. *American Economic Review* 74 (May): 324–27.

———. 1984b. Structuring an Effective Occupational Disease Policy: Victim Compensation and Risk Regulation. *Yale Journal on Regulation* 55:53–81.

———. 1986. The Valuation of Risks to Life and Health: Guidelines for Policy Analysis. In *Benefits Assessment: The State of the Art*, ed. J. Bentkover, V. Covello, and J. Mumpower.

———. 1992. *Fatal Tradeoffs: Public and Private Responsibilities for Risk*. New York: Oxford University Press.

Viscusi, W. K., and Evans, W. N. 1990. Utility Functions That Depend on Health Status: Estimates and Economic Implications. *American Economic Review* 80 (June): 353–74.

Viscusi, W. K.; Magat, W. A.; and Huber, J. 1991. Pricing Environmental Health Risks: Survey Assessments of Risk-Risk and Risk-Dollar Trade-offs for Chronic Bronchitis. *Journal of Environmental Economics and Management* 21 (July): 32–51.

Waldo, D.; Sonnefeld, S.; McKusick, D.; and Arnett, R. 1989. Health Expenditures by Age Group, 1977 and 1987. *Health Care Financing Review* 10, no. 4:111–20.

Ware, J. E. 1976. Scales for Measuring General Health Perceptions. *Health Services Research* 11 (Winter): 396–415.

Ware, J. E.; Davies-Avery, A.; and Brook, R. H. 1980. Conceptualization and Measurement of Health Status for Adults in the Health Insurance Study. Vol. 6,

Analyses of Relationships among Health Status Measures. Santa Monica, CA: Rand Corp.

Ware, J. E.; Johnson, S. A.; and Davies-Avery, A. 1978. Conceptualization and Measurement of Health Status for Adults in the Health Insurance Study. Vol. 5, *General Health Perceptions.* Santa Monica, CA: Rand Corp.

Weinstein, M. C. 1980. Estrogen Use in Postmenopausal Women—Costs, Risks and Benefits. *New England Journal of Medicine* 303 (August 7): 308–16.

Weinstein, M. C.; Pliskin, J. S.; and Stason, W. B. 1977. Coronary Artery Bypass Surgery: Decision and Policy Analysis. *Costs, Risks and Benefits of Surgery,* ed. J. P. Bunker, B. A. Barnes, and F. Mosteller. New York: Oxford University Press.

Weinstein, M. C., and Stason, W. B. 1977. Foundations of Cost-Effectiveness Analysis for Health and Medical Practices. *New England Journal of Medicine* 296 (March 31): 716–21.

Weisbrod, B. A. 1971. Costs and Benefits of Medical Research: A Case Study of Poliomyelitis. *Journal of Political Economy* 79 (May/June): 527–44.

Welch, H. W., and Larson, E. B. 1988. The Oregon Decision to Curtail Funding for Organ Transplants. *New England Journal of Medicine* 319 (July 21): 171–73.

Wieand, K. F. 1973. Air Pollution and Property Values: A Study of the St. Louis Area. *Journal of Regional Science* 13 (April): 91–95.

Winkenwerder, W.; Kessler, A.; and Stolec, R. 1989. Federal Spending for Illness Caused by Human Immunodeficiency Virus. *New England Journal of Medicine* 310 (June 15): 1598–1603.

Wolinsky, F. D.; Coe, R. M.; Miller, D. K.; and Prendergast, J. M. 1984. Measurement of the Global and Functional Dimensions of Health Status in the Elderly. *Journal of Gerontology* 39 (January): 89–92.

Yaari, M. E. 1965. Uncertain Lifetime, Life Insurance and the Theory of the Consumer. *Review of Economic Studies* 32 (April): 137–50.

Zeckhauser, R. J. 1970. Medical Insurance: A Case Study of the Tradeoff between Risk Spreading and Appropriate Incentives. *Journal of Economic Theory* 2, no. 1 (March) 10–26.

———. 1975. Procedures for Valuing Lives. *Public Policy* 23 (Fall): 419–64.

Zeckhauser, R. J., and Shepard, D. 1976. Where Now for Saving Lives? *Law and Contemporary Problems* 40 (Autumn): 5–45.

Zeidner, M., and Shechter, M. 1988. Psychological Responses to Air Pollution: Some Personality and Demographic Correlates. *Journal of Environmental Psychology* 8:191–208.

Contributors

Lyndon Babcock
School of Public Health
University of Illinois at Chicago

Mark Berger
Department of Economics
University of Kentucky

Anthony Bilotti
School of Public Health
University of Illinois at Chicago

Glenn Blomquist
Department of Economics
University of Kentucky

Michael Brien
Department of Economics
University of Virginia

Richard Clemmer
Department of Economics
Central Michigan University

Robert Fabian
School of Public Health
University of Illinois at Chicago

Charles Kahn
Department of Economics
University of Illinois at Urbana

Austin Kelly
U.S. General Accounting Office

Donald Kenkel
Department of Economics
Pennsylvania State University

Robert Ohsfeldt
School of Public Health
University of Alabama

Sherwin Rosen
Department of Economics
University of Chicago

George Tolley
Department of Economics
University of Chicago

William Webb
45 Hay Road
Belmont, Mass.

David Webster
Department of Economics
University of Chicago

Wallace Wilson
School of Public Health
University of Illinois at Chicago

Index

413